Machine Learning and Deep Learning in Real–Time Applications

Mehul Mahrishi
Swami Keshvanand Institute of Technology, India

Kamal Kant Hiran
Aalborg University, Denmark

Gaurav Meena
Central University of Rajasthan, India

Paawan Sharma
Pandit Deendayal Petroleum University, India

A volume in the Advances in Computer and
Electrical Engineering (ACEE) Book Series

Published in the United States of America by
IGI Global
Engineering Science Reference (an imprint of IGI Global)
701 E. Chocolate Avenue
Hershey PA, USA 17033
Tel: 717-533-8845
Fax: 717-533-8661
E-mail: cust@igi-global.com
Web site: http://www.igi-global.com

Library of Congress Cataloging-in-Publication Data

Names: Mahrishi, Mehul, 1986- editor. | Hiran, Kamal Kant, 1982- editor. |
    Meena, Gaurav, 1987- editor. | Sharma, Paawan, 1983- editor.
Title: Machine learning and deep learning in real-time applications / Mehul
    Mahrishi, Kamal Kant Hiran, Gaurav Meena, and Paawan Sharma, editors.
Description: Hershey, PA : Engineering Science Reference, an imprint of IGI
    Global, [2020] | Includes bibliographical references and index. |
    Summary: "This book examines recent advancements in deep learning
    libraries, frameworks and algorithms. It also explores the
    multidisciplinary applications of machine learning and deep learning in
    real world"-- Provided by publisher.
Identifiers: LCCN 2019048558 (print) | LCCN 2019048559 (ebook) | ISBN
    9781799830955 (hardcover) | ISBN 9781799830962 (paperback) | ISBN
    9781799830979 (ebook)
Subjects: LCSH: Machine learning. | Real-time data processing.
Classification: LCC Q325.5 .M3216 2020 (print) | LCC Q325.5 (ebook) | DDC
    006.3/1--dc23
LC record available at https://lccn.loc.gov/2019048558
LC ebook record available at https://lccn.loc.gov/2019048559

This book is published in the IGI Global book series Advances in Computer and Electrical Engineering (ACEE) (ISSN: 2327-039X; eISSN: 2327-0403)

British Cataloguing in Publication Data
A Cataloguing in Publication record for this book is available from the British Library.

All work contributed to this book is new, previously-unpublished material. The views expressed in this book are those of the authors, but not necessarily of the publisher.

For electronic access to this publication, please contact: eresources@igi-global.com.

Advances in Computer and Electrical Engineering (ACEE) Book Series

Srikanta Patnaik
SOA University, India

ISSN:2327-039X
EISSN:2327-0403

MISSION

The fields of computer engineering and electrical engineering encompass a broad range of interdisciplinary topics allowing for expansive research developments across multiple fields. Research in these areas continues to develop and become increasingly important as computer and electrical systems have become an integral part of everyday life.

The **Advances in Computer and Electrical Engineering (ACEE) Book Series** aims to publish research on diverse topics pertaining to computer engineering and electrical engineering. **ACEE** encourages scholarly discourse on the latest applications, tools, and methodologies being implemented in the field for the design and development of computer and electrical systems.

COVERAGE

- Applied Electromagnetics
- Algorithms
- Microprocessor Design
- Analog Electronics
- Computer Hardware
- Electrical Power Conversion
- Circuit Analysis
- VLSI Design
- Computer Architecture
- Chip Design

IGI Global is currently accepting manuscripts for publication within this series. To submit a proposal for a volume in this series, please contact our Acquisition Editors at Acquisitions@igi-global.com or visit: http://www.igi-global.com/publish/.

Titles in this Series

For a list of additional titles in this series, please visit:
https://www.igi-global.com/book-series/advances-computer-electrical-engineering/73675

Open Source Software for Statistical Analysis of Big Data Emerging Research and Opportunities
Richard S. Segall (Arkansas State University, USA) and Gao Niu (Bryant University, USA)
Engineering Science Reference • © 2020 • 237pp • H/C (ISBN: 9781799827689) • US $225.00

Software Engineering for Agile Application Development
Chung-Yeung Pang (Seveco AG, Switzerland)
Engineering Science Reference • © 2020 • 330pp • H/C (ISBN: 9781799825319) • US $235.00

Applied Social Network Analysis With R Emerging Research and Opportunities
Mehmet Gençer (Izmir University of Economics, Turkey)
Engineering Science Reference • © 2020 • 284pp • H/C (ISBN: 9781799819127) • US $165.00

Novel Approaches to Information Systems Design
Naveen Prakash (Indraprastha Institute of Information Technology, Delhi, India) and Deepika Prakash (NIIT University, India)
Engineering Science Reference • © 2020 • 299pp • H/C (ISBN: 9781799829751) • US $215.00

IoT Architectures, Models, and Platforms for Smart City Applications
Bhawani Shankar Chowdhry (Mehran University of Engineering and Technology, Pakistan) Faisal Karim Shaikh (Mehran University of Engineering and Technology, Pakistan) and Naeem Ahmed Mahoto (Mehran University of Engineering and Technology, Pakistan)
Engineering Science Reference • © 2020 • 291pp • H/C (ISBN: 9781799812531) • US $245.00

Nature-Inspired Computing Applications in Advanced Communication Networks
Govind P. Gupta (National Institute of Technology, Raipur, India)
Engineering Science Reference • © 2020 • 319pp • H/C (ISBN: 9781799816263) • US $225.00

Pattern Recognition Applications in Engineering
Diego Alexander Tibaduiza Burgos (Universidad Nacional de Colombia, Colombia) Maribel Anaya Vejar (Universidad Sergio Arboleda, Colombia) and Francesc Pozo (Universitat Politècnica de Catalunya, Spain)
Engineering Science Reference • © 2020 • 357pp • H/C (ISBN: 9781799818397) • US $215.00

Tools and Technologies for the Development of Cyber-Physical Systems
Sergey Balandin (FRUCT Oy, Finland) and Ekaterina Balandina (Tampere University, Finland)
Engineering Science Reference • © 2020 • 344pp • H/C (ISBN: 9781799819745) • US $235.00

701 East Chocolate Avenue, Hershey, PA 17033, USA
Tel: 717-533-8845 x100 • Fax: 717-533-8661
E-Mail: cust@igi-global.com • www.igi-global.com

Editorial Advisory Board

Table of Contents

Detailed Table of Contents

Chapter 1

  Pedro João Rodrigues, CeDRI, Research Centre in Digitalization and Intelligent Robotics,
    Instituto Politécnico de Bragança, Portugal
  Getúlio Peixoto Igrejas, CeDRI, Research Centre in Digitalization and Intelligent Robotics,
    Instituto Politécnico de Bragança, Portugal
  Romeu Ferreira Beato, Instituto Politécnico de Bragança, Portugal

In this work, the authors classify leukocyte images using the neural network architectures that won the annual ILSVRC competition. The classification of leukocytes is made using pretrained networks and the same networks trained from scratch in order to select the ones that achieve the best performance for the intended task. The categories used are eosinophils, lymphocytes, monocytes, and neutrophils. The analysis of the results takes into account the amount of training required, the regularization techniques used, the training time, and the accuracy in image classification. The best classification results, on the order of 98%, suggest that it is possible, considering a competent preprocessing, to train a network like the DenseNet with 169 or 201 layers, in about 100 epochs, to classify leukocytes in microscopy images.

Chapter 2

  Deepa Joshi, Department of Systemics, School of Computer Science, University of Petroleum
    and Energy Studies (UPES), India
  Shahina Anwarul, Department of Systemics, School of Computer Science, University of
    Petroleum and Energy Studies (UPES), India
  Vidyanand Mishra, Department of Systemics, School of Computer Science, University of
    Petroleum and Energy Studies (UPES), India

A branch of artificial intelligence (AI) known as deep learning consists of statistical analysis algorithms known as artificial neural networks (ANN) inspired by the structure and function of the brain. The accuracy of predicting a task has tremendously improved with the implementation of deep neural networks, which in turn incorporate deep layers into the model allowing the system to learn complex data. This chapter intends to give a straightforward manual for the complexities of Google's Keras framework that is easy to understand. The basic steps for the installation of Anaconda, CUDA, along with deep learning libraries, specifically Keras and Tensorflow, are discussed. A practical approach towards solving deep learning problems in order to identify objects in CIFAR 10 dataset is explained in detail. This will help the audience in understanding deep learning through substantial practical examples to perceive algorithms instead of theory discussions.

Anmol Chaudhary, Government Engineering College, Ajmer, India
Kuldeep Singh Chouhan, Government Engineering College, Ajmer, India
Jyoti Gajrani, Malviya National Institute of Technology, India
Bhavna Sharma, JECRC University, Jaipur, India

In the last decade, deep learning has seen exponential growth due to rise in computational power as a result of graphics processing units (GPUs) and a large amount of data due to the democratization of the internet and smartphones. This chapter aims to throw light on both the theoretical aspects of deep learning and its practical aspects using PyTorch. The chapter primarily discusses new technologies using deep learning and PyTorch in detail. The chapter discusses the advantages of using PyTorch compared to other deep learning libraries. The chapter discusses some of the practical applications like image classification and machine translation. The chapter also discusses the various frameworks built with the help of PyTorch. PyTorch consists of various models that increases its flexibility and accessibility to a greater extent. As a result, many frameworks built on top of PyTorch are discussed in this chapter. The authors believe that this chapter will help readers in getting a better understanding of deep learning making neural networks using PyTorch.

Shahina Anwarul, Department of Systemics, School of Computer Science, University of
    Petroleum and Energy Studies (UPES), India
Deepa Joshi, Department of Systemics, School of Computer Science, University of Petroleum
    and Energy Studies (UPES), India

This chapter aims to acquaint the users with key parts of TensorFlow and some basic ideas about deep learning. In particular, users will figure out how to perform fundamental calculations in TensorFlow and implementation of deep learning using TensorFlow. This chapter intends to gives a straightforward manual for the complexities of Google's TensorFlow framework that is easy to understand. The basic steps for the installation and setup of TensorFlow will also be discussed. Starting with a simple "Hello World" example, a practical implementation of deep learning problem to identify the handwritten digits will be discussed using MNIST dataset. It is only possible to understand deep learning through substantial practical examples. For that reason, the authors have included practical implementation of deep learning problems that motivates the readers to plunge deeply into these examples and to get their hands grimy trying different things with their own ideas using TensorFlow because it is never adequate to perceive algorithms only theoretically.

#### Chapter 5

In any industry, attrition is a big problem, whether it is about employee attrition of an organization or customer attrition of an e-commerce site. If we can accurately predict which customer or employee will leave their current company or organization, then it will save much time, effort, and cost of the employer and help them to hire or acquire substitutes in advance, and it would not create a problem in the ongoing progress of an organization. In this chapter, a comparative analysis between various machine learning approaches such as Naïve Bayes, SVM, decision tree, random forest, and logistic regression is presented. The presented result will help us in identifying the behavior of employees who can be attired over the next time. Experimental results reveal that the logistic regression approach can reach up to 86% accuracy over other machine learning approaches.

Computational biology is the research area that contributes to the analysis of biological information. The selection of the subset of cancer-related genes is one amongst the foremost promising clinical research of gene expression data. Since a gene can take the role of various biological pathways that in turn can be active only under specific experimental conditions, the stacked denoising auto-encoder(SDAE) and the genetic algorithm were combined to perform biclustering of cancer genes from huge dimensional microarray gene expression data. The Genetic-SDAE proved superior to recently proposed biclustering methods and better to determine the maximum similarity of a set of biclusters of gene expression data with lower MSR and higher gene variance. This work also assesses the results with respect to the discovered genes and spot that the extracted set of biclusters are supported by biological evidence, such as enrichment of gene functions and biological processes.

#### Chapter 7

The field of audio forensics has seen a huge advancement in recent years with an increasing number of techniques used for the analysis of the audio recordings submitted as evidence in legal investigations. Audio forensics involves authentication of the evidentiary audio recordings, which is an important procedure to verify the integrity of audio recordings. This chapter focuses two audio authentication procedures, namely acoustic environment identification and tampering detection. The authors provide a framework for the above-mentioned procedures discussing in detail the methodology and feature sets used in the two tasks. The main objective of this chapter is to introduce the readers to different machine learning algorithms that can be used for environment identification and forgery detection. The authors also provide some promising results that prove the utility of machine learning algorithms in this interesting field.

#### Chapter 8

Breast cancer is one of the main causes of cancer death worldwide, and early diagnostics significantly increases the chances of correct treatment and survival, but this process is tedious. The relevance and potential of automatic classification algorithms using Hematoxylin-Eosin stained histopathological images have already been demonstrated, but the reported results are still sub-optimal for clinical use. Deep learning-based computer-aided diagnosis (CAD) has been gaining popularity for analyzing histopathological images. Based on the predominant cancer type, the goal is to classify images into four categories of normal, benign, in situ carcinoma, and invasive carcinoma. The convolutional neural networks (CNN) is proposed to retrieve information at different scales, including both nuclei and overall tissue organization. This chapter utilizes several deep neural network architectures and gradient boosted trees classifier to classify the histology images among four classes. Hence, this approach has outperformed existing approaches in terms of accuracy and implementation complexity.

The goodness measure of any institute lies in minimising the dropouts and targeting good placements. So, predicting students' performance is very interesting and an important task for educational information systems. Machine learning and deep learning are the emerging areas that truly entice more research practices. This research focuses on applying the deep learning methods to educational data for classification and prediction. The educational data of students from engineering domain with cognitive and non-cognitive parameters is considered. The hybrid model with support vector machine (SVM) and deep belief network (DBN) is devised. The SVM predicts class labels from preprocessed data. These class labels and actual class labels acts as input to the DBN to perform final classification. The hybrid model is further optimised using cuckoo search with Levy flight. The results clearly show that the proposed model SVM-LCDBN gives better performance as compared to simple hybrid model and hybrid model with traditional cuckoo search.

#### Chapter 10

Malaria is a disease caused when a female Anopheles mosquito bites. There are over 200 million cases recorded per year with more than 400,000 deaths. Current methods of diagnosis are effective; however, they work on technologies that do not produce higher accuracy results. Henceforth, to improve the prediction rate of the disease, modern technologies need to be performed for obtain accurate results. Deep learning algorithms are developed to detect, learn, and determine the containing parasites from the red blood smears. This chapter shows the implementation of a deep learning algorithm to identify the malaria parasites with higher accuracy.

Chapter 11

Wazir Muhammad, Electrical Engineering Department, BUET, Khuzdar, Pakistan
Irfan Ullah, Department of Electrical Engineering, Chulalongkorn University, Bangkok,
Thailand
Mohammad Ashfaq, School of Life Sciences, B. S. Abdur Rahman Crescent Institute of
Science and Technology, Chennai, India

Deep learning (DL) is the new buzzword for researchers in the research area of computer vision that unlocked the doors to solving complex problems. With the assistance of Keras library, machine learning (ML)-based DL and various complicated or unresolved issues such as face recognition and voice recognition might be resolved easily. This chapter focuses on the basic concept of Keras-based framework DL library to handle the different real-life problems. The authors discuss the codes of previous libraries and same code run on Keras library and assess the performance on Google Colab Cloud Graphics Processing Units (GPUs). The goal of this chapter is to provide you with the newer concept, algorithm, and technology to solve the real-life problems with the help of Keras framework. Moreover, they discuss how to write the code of standard convolutional neural network (CNN) architectures using Keras libraries. Finally, the codes of validation and training data set to start the training procedure are explored.

Chapter 12

Anju Yadav, Manipal University Jaipur, India
Venkatesh Gauri Shankar, Manipal University Jaipur, India
Vivek Kumar Verma, Manipal University Jaipur, India

In this chapter, machine learning application on facial expression recognition (FER) is studied for seven emotional states (disgust, joy, surprise, anger, sadness, contempt, and fear) based on FER describing coefficient. FER has many practical importance in various area like social network, robotics, healthcare, etc. Further, a literature review of existing machine learning approaches for FER is discussed, and a novel approach for FER is given for static and dynamic images. Then the results are compared with the other existing approaches. The chapter also covers additional related issues of applications, various challenges, and opportunities in future FER. For security-based face detection systems that can identify an individual, in any form of expression he introduces himself. Doctors will use this system to find the intensity of illness or pain of a deaf and dumb patient. The proposed model is based on machine learning application with three types of prototypes, which are pre-trained model, single layer augmented model, and multi-layered augmented model, having a combined accuracy of approx. 99%.

Chapter 13

Priti P. Rege, College of Engineering, Pune, India

Shaheera Akhter, Government College of Engineering, Pune, India

Text separation in document image analysis is an important preprocessing step before executing an optical character recognition (OCR) task. It is necessary to improve the accuracy of an OCR system. Traditionally, for separating text from a document, different feature extraction processes have been used that require handcrafting of the features. However, deep learning-based methods are excellent feature extractors that learn features from the training data automatically. Deep learning gives state-of-the-art results on various computer vision, image classification, segmentation, image captioning, object detection, and recognition tasks. This chapter compares various traditional as well as deep-learning techniques and uses a semantic segmentation method for separating text from Devanagari document images using U-Net and ResU-Net models. These models are further fine-tuned for transfer learning to get more precise results. The final results show that deep learning methods give more accurate results compared with conventional methods of image processing for Devanagari text extraction.

Foreword

Our lives are inundated with data. The popular quote coined in 2006 "data is the new oil" appropriately describes its profound importance in all aspects of human life. In its resemblance to oil the data is valuable but most of it is not directly usable by humans. The data needs to be broken down, analyzed, and converted into insights that are appropriate for consumption in human activities and to create a valuable entity that drives profitable activity.

Through machine learning, we enable computers to process, learn from, and draw actionable conclusions out of the structured and unstructured data that possess the *volume*, *variety*, and *velocity* dimensions. Deep learning – practically a subset of machine learning – functions in a similar way, however, its capabilities are different. Machine learning models progressively become accurate and useful at whatever their function is as more training data is provided. With a deep learning model, an algorithm can determine on its own if a prediction is accurate or not through its own neural network. Machine learning – as well as deep learning, natural language processing and cognitive computing – are driving innovations in wide variety of fields such as image identification, computer vision, document analysis and summarization, urban data science, prediction models for disease spread, and navigating the self-driving car. Most of the popular artificial intelligence (AI) breakthroughs that you hear about in the media are based on deep learning. As a result, whether you are researcher working on big data, businesses interested in improving sales or process efficiency, health care professional in diagnosing diseases, or law enforcement officials in predicting threats, it is important for you to have an understanding and working knowledge of deep learning.

How can I use deep learning to take a glimpse into the unknown, model human immune system, predict employee attrition in a business, conduct gene analysis to detect anomalies, recognize facial expressions, or just find out what the Internet at large thinks about my favorite book? All of this and more will be covered in the following chapters edited by my friend and collaborator, Professor Mehul Mahrishi and his peers. The book takes a very practical and effective approach in my view. The focus of the first part of the book is to enable student and faculty researchers in academic institutions, researchers in industrial labs as well as practitioners to gain an understanding of what deep learning is, how it works, and what tools and frameworks are available to develop applications based on it. State of the art frameworks – Keras, PyTorch, TensorFlow are covered in depth and follow a hands-on approach. The second part of the book covers seceral real life deep learning applications. Each application area is covered in details including domain-specific data samples, deep learning model development, and actionable insights gained from them. From my teaching experience, I have found that the approach this books adopts very effective. Deep learning is a collection of algorithms and models that tend to be mathematical in nature. In addition to a walk through mathematical concepts in clear and concise fashion it is important to introduce hand-on tools and bring in real life success stories.

Owing to their collective expertise in this field, I am confident that insights editors and chapter authors into the world of deep learning will be invaluable to users of all experience levels. I wholeheartedly recommend this book to anyone looking to gain a broader and more practical understanding of deep learning. This book is a good step in that direction.

Naveen Sharma
Department of Software Engineering, Golisano College of Computing and Information Sciences,
Rochester Institute of Technology, USA

Preface

The currently applied Artificial Intelligence techniques are penetrating into every domain and reaching its limits. We might not be noticing, but we keep accumulating intelligent agents and AI bots around us now and then. One of the most exciting tools that have entered in recent years is Machine/Deep Learning. There are several real time-applications of machine and deep learning in the field of higher education, medicals, manufacturing, marketing, finance, and particularly for making predictions; machine and deep learning algorithms used in lots of places in exciting ways. This collection of statistical methods and the availability of large datasets combined with the improvement in algorithms has already proved to be capable of considerably speeding up both fundamental and applied research and led to an unparalleled surge of interest in the topic of machine learning.

Machine Learning paradigms defined in two types, namely supervised learning (SL) and unsupervised learning (UL). In Supervised Learning, objects in a given collection are classified using a set of attributes or features. The classification process is a set of rules that prescribe assignments or allocations of objects to unique classes based on values of features. The objective of supervised learning is to design a reliable system that is able to precisely predict the class group membership of new objects based on the available attributes or features. Whereas in unsupervised learning (UL), all the data are unlabeled, and the learning process consists of both defining the labels and associating objects with them.

Deep learning paradigms are defined in different ways of apprehension. For example, deep learning is used to realize a functionality containing huge number of parameters. Deep learning is also a complex system of equations that uses different mathematical functions to produce trained output. Deep learning is essentially an advanced technique for classifying data patterns having higher order multiple layers neural networks.

The objective of this book is to introduce the reader to the Challenges and applications in the area of Machine Learning and Deep Learning. In particular, the book looks into the use of Machine Learning techniques and Artificial Intelligence to model various technical problems of the real world.

ORGANIZATION OF THE BOOK

The book is organized in 13 chapters written by researchers, scholars and professors from prestigious laboratories and educational institution across the globe. A brief description of each of the chapters in this section given below.

Chapter 1, "Obtaining Deep Learning Models for Automatic Classification of Leukocytes," classifies leukocyte images using pretrained neural networks and train the model in order to select the ones that achieve the best performance for the intended task. The analysis of the results takes into account the amount of training required, the regularization techniques used, the training time and the accuracy in image classification.

Chapter 2, "Deep Leaning Using Keras," introduces Google's Keras framework. The chapter discusses installation challenges, CUDA along with deep learning libraries specifically Keras and Tensorflow etc. For better understanding of Deep Learning concepts among the readers, CIFAR 10 dataset is explained through examples.

Chapter 3, "Deep Learning With PyTorch," throws light on both the theoretical aspects of deep learning and its practical aspects using PyTorch. The chapter discusses new technologies using deep learning and PyTorch, advantages of using PyTorch compared to other deep learning libraries and practical applications like image classification and machine translation. The chapter will help readers in getting a better understanding of deep learning making neural networks using PyTorch.

Chapter 4, "Deep Learning With TensorFlow," aims to acquaint the users with key parts of TensorFlow and some basic idea about deep learning. For better understanding of users, a practical implementation of deep learning problem to identify the handwritten digits is also discussed using MNIST dataset.

Chapter 5, "Employee's Attrition Prediction Using Machine Learning Approaches," addresses the problem identifying the behavior of employees who can be attired over the next time. The chapter also included a comparative analysis between various machine learning approaches such as Naïve Bayes, SVM, decision tree, random forest, and logistic regression.

Chapter 6, "A Novel Deep Learning Method for Identification of Cancer Genes From Gene Expression Dataset," presents the concept of computational Biology using Deep Learning. The chapter implemented Stacked denoising auto-encoder (SDAE) and the genetic algorithm to perform bi-clustering of cancer genes from huge dimensional microarray gene expression data. This work also assesses the results with respect to the discovered genes and spot that extracted set of bi-clusters are supported by biological evidence.

Chapter 7, "Machine Learning in Authentication of Digital Audio Recordings," introduces the readers to novel application of machine learning algorithms which can be used for environment identification and forgery detection. The chapter focuses two audio authentication procedures namely: Acoustic Environment Identification and Tampering Detection.

Chapter 8, "Deep Convolutional Neural Network-Based Analysis for Breast Cancer Histology Images," discusses the problem of Breast cancer which is one of the main causes of cancer death worldwide. The chapter proposes Convolutional Neural Networks (CNN) based Computer-Aided Diagnosis (CAD) for analyzing histopathological images. This chapter utilizes several deep neural network architectures and gradient boosted trees classifier to classify the histology images among four classes.

Chapter 9, "Deep Learning in Engineering Education: Performance Prediction Using Cuckoo-Based Hybrid Classification," applies the deep learning model on educational data for classification and prediction. The hybrid model with Support Vector Machine (SVM) and Deep Belief Network (DBN) is devised to track the performance of a student.

Chapter 10, "Malaria Detection System Using Convolutional Neural Network Algorithm," showcases the implementation of deep learning algorithm to identify the malaria parasites with higher accuracy. It is also evident that to improve the prediction rate of the disease, algorithms can be developed to detect, learn and determine the containing parasites from the red blood smears.

Chapter 11, "An Introduction to Deep Convolutional Neural Networks With Keras," analyzes the basic concept of Keras based framework DL library to handle the different real-life problems. The chapter also discusses new concept, algorithm, and technologies to solve the real-life problems with the help of Keras framework.

Chapter 12, "Emotion Recognition With Facial Expression Using Machine Learning for Social Network and Healthcare," studies Machine Learning Application on Facial Expression Recognition (FER) for seven emotional state (disgust, joy, surprise, anger, sadness, contempt, and fear) based on FER describing coefficient. The application has a very important medical usage as doctors can use this system to find the intensity of illness or pain of a deaf and dumb patient.

Chapter 13, "Text Separation From Document Images: A Deep Learning Approach," compares various deep-learning techniques and uses a semantic segmentation method for separating text from Devanagari document images using U-Net and ResU-Net models. These models are further fine-tuned for transfer learning to get more precise results.

Acknowledgment

It is very important to acknowledge the tireless support and endless contributions received from many people in completing this work. This book would not have been a reality without the support of IGI Global. We are grateful to the team from IGI Global, specially *Maria, Josh* and *Jan* for giving this wonderful opportunity and been extremely cooperative right from the inception of the idea of this book. Their unique contributions, advices, expertise and relentless efforts made this book a reality.

With earnest gratitude and profound thanks, we would like to acknowledge the continuous guidance of Dr. Sudha Morwal (Banasthali Vidhyapeeth), Dr, Naveen Sharma (Rochester Institute of Technology, New York) for their time, dedication, expertise and continuous support. Special thanks to Prof. Anders Henten, Prof. Kund Erik Skouby, Prof. Reza Tadayoni, Prof. Lene Tolstrup Sørensen, Anette Bysøe, Center for Communication, Media and Information Technologies (CMI), Aalborg University, Copenhagen, Denmark for providing in-depth scientific knowledge.

Our sincere thank goes to our organizations, Swami Keshvanand Institute of Technology Jaipur, Rajasthan and Sir Padampat Singhania University (SPSU), Udaipur, Rajasthan, India, Central University of Rajasthan and Pandit Deendayal Petroleum Universiy, Gandhinagar, Gujrat for providing a healthy academic and research environment during my consistent work.

We are truly moved by the gesture and constant support shown by all the members of Editorial Advisory Board since the beginning of the idea of the edited book. The editors would like to acknowledge the help of all the people involved in this project and, more specifically, to each author and reviewer who took part in the review process. Without their support, this book would not have become a reality.

The completion of this book could not have been possible without the contribution and support we got from our family, friends and colleagues. It is a pleasant aspect and we express our gratitude for all of them.

Mehul Mahrishi
Swami Keshvanand Institute of Technology, India

Kamal Kant Hiran
Aalborg University, Denmark

Gaurav Meena
Central University of Rajasthan, India

Paawan Sharma
Pandit Deendayal Petroleum University, India

Chapter 1
Obtaining Deep Learning Models for Automatic Classification of Leukocytes

Pedro João Rodrigues
https://orcid.org/0000-0002-0555-2029

CeDRI, Research Centre in Digitalization and Intelligent Robotics, Instituto Politécnico de Bragança, Portugal

Getúlio Peixoto Igrejas
https://orcid.org/0000-0002-6820-8858

CeDRI, Research Centre in Digitalization and Intelligent Robotics, Instituto Politécnico de Bragança, Portugal

Romeu Ferreira Beato
Instituto Politécnico de Bragança, Portugal

ABSTRACT

In this work, the authors classify leukocyte images using the neural network architectures that won the annual ILSVRC competition. The classification of leukocytes is made using pretrained networks and the same networks trained from scratch in order to select the ones that achieve the best performance for the intended task. The categories used are eosinophils, lymphocytes, monocytes, and neutrophils. The analysis of the results takes into account the amount of training required, the regularization techniques used, the training time, and the accuracy in image classification. The best classification results, on the order of 98%, suggest that it is possible, considering a competent preprocessing, to train a network like the DenseNet with 169 or 201 layers, in about 100 epochs, to classify leukocytes in microscopy images.

DOI: 10.4018/978-1-7998-3095-5.ch001

INTRODUCTION

The number of leukocytes presdataent in the blood, also known as white blood cells, provides important information regarding the state of the immune system, allowing to evaluate potential health risks. A significant change in the number of leukocytes, relative to reference values, is usually a sign that the body is affected by some type of antigen. Moreover, the variation in a particular white blood cell type is generally correlated with a specific type of antigen.

White blood cells are generally classified into 5 categories: lymphocytes, monocytes, neutrophils, eosinophils, and basophils. There is also the band designation for a specific form of the nucleus. Figure 1 shows examples of these categories.

Figure 1. Leukocyte types (from left to right): Neutrophil, Eosinophil, Basophil, Lymphocyte, and Monocyte (Noble, 2019)

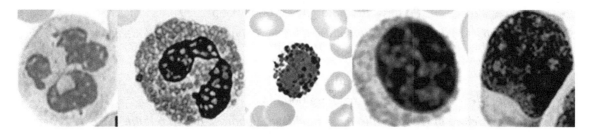

The preparation and analysis of blood samples are usually affected by deviations naturally introduced by manual operations. These difficulties can be minimized when performed by highly trained technicians. However, these tasks are labor-intensive and time-consuming and always subject to error. For these reasons, there is interest in having systems that can automatically classify with high specificity and high sensitivity.

The evolution of techniques for counting and identifying leukocytes (and blood cells in general) began in the mid-nineteenth century with the use of capillaries and slides. Over the years, several types of devices designed to count blood cells have appeared, which would later enable their classification.

The classification of blood cells has always been done by human specialists until the 1960's, since when emerged the possibility of automating this task. Firstly, through the use of optical and impedance methods and later through algorithms developed specifically for this purpose from microscopy images within the scope of computer vision and, in the last two decades, using neural networks.

Several researchers have presented papers for leukocyte identification and counting. Techniques that use classic machine learning models, in opposite to deep learning models, are built on manually selected characteristics. This approach can use shallow neuronal networks (Rezatofighi & Soltanian-Zadeh, 2011; Nazlibilek et al., 2014), Support Vector machines (SVM) (Rezatofighi & Soltanian-Zadeh, 2011; Putzu et al., 2014; Agaian et al., 2014; Alférez et al., 2016; MoradiAmin et al., 2016), Bayes classifier (Stathonikos et al., 2013; Prinyakupt & Pluempitiwiriyawej, 2015), etc. The manipulation of characteristics, prior to the classification model, may involve segmentation (Chaira, 2014), extraction and selection of features that describe the leukocyte defining region (Alférez et al., 2016). Thus, we can divide these classic processes into three main stages: segmentation, feature extraction, and classification. These approaches have the advantage of allowing the use of relatively small datasets, as the segmentation and the features uscd reduce the variability of the patterns delivered to the classification models. On the other hand, the segmentation performance and the lack of universality of the descriptors can limit the result achieved by the classification models. An example of this approach is found in Dan et al. (López-Puigdollers et al., 2020), where features such as SIFT (Lowe, 2004) are employed. However, the assertiveness of the classification is not very high.

The use of deep learning models tends to solve the problems presented in the approach described above, provided that the dataset is sufficiently representative of the pattern variability, associated with leukocyte optical visualization, or a transfer learning approach is employed, as is the case of the present work.

Recognition models based on convolutional neuronal networks (CNNs) have performed well in many applications. In this sense, studies appear in the literature where the use of CNNs is applied to leukocyte detection and recognition (Zhao et al., 2016). However, the accuracy presented in that paper for the identification of five base leukocytes is not high (eosinophil 70% and lymphocyte 75%). Other authors (Shahin et al., 2019), who also use CNNs to classify rather than detect the five base leukocytes, show results that exceed the classical approach (accuracy: 96%), so it can be deduced that the separation between detection and classification is beneficial for the problem-solving. Most methods using CNNs require leukocytes to be already segmented/detected (Shahin et al., 2019; Choi et al., 2017; Jiang et al., 2018; Qin et al., 2018; Rehman et al., 2018 and Tiwari et al., 2018). In this context, there are various approaches to CNNs: (e.g.) Regions with CNN features (R-CNN) (Girshick et al., 2020), Faster R-CNN (Ren et al., 2017), based on architectures that simultaneously integrate both tasks -detection and classification-. These architectures start from a preprocessing step where regions of interest are estimated for subsequent unification through a CNN-based training step and further classification.

Other architectures are one-stage and fully integrate detection and classification: e.g., You Only Look Once (YOLO) (Redmon et al., 2020), YOLOv2 (Redmon & Farhadi, 2020), YOLOv3 (Redmon & Farhadi, 2020) and Single Shot Multibox Detector (SSD) (Liu et al., 2020). Wang et al. used SSD and YOLOv3 models for the detection and classification of leukocytes, reaching a mean average precision of 93% (Wang et al., 2019). This value is noteworthy since this work shows the classification of eleven types of leukocytes, while most works use the five base leukocytes.

In the present work, the proposal is the classification of leukocyte images using the winning network architectures (with the exception of one) of the annual ILSVRC (ImageNet Large Scale Visual Recognition Challenge) software competition where programs compete to detect and classify objects and scenarios (Russakovsky, et al., 2015). The identification of leukocytes is made using pre-trained networks and these same network architectures trained from scratch in order to select the best network and the best approach for the intended task.

BACKGROUND

The difficulty of pattern recognition in images becomes apparent when we try to write a computer program that recognizes leukocytes in microscopy images. When we look for a set of precise rules for the recognition of forms, we quickly lose ourselves in an immensity of exceptions and special cases. Neural networks (NN) approach this type of situation differently (Nielsen, 2017). In the most common type of feedforward networks - MLP (multilayer perceptron) - neurons are organized in layers that have one-way links between them. Different connectivities produce different behaviors. Generally speaking, the feedforward networks are static, and they produce only one type of output value instead of a sequence of values of a given input. So, they don't have memory in the sense that their response is independent of the previous state of the network. Recurrent networks, on the other hand, are dynamic systems. Due to the feedback paths, the inputs of each neuron are modified, which causes the neural network to enter a new state dependent on the past states.

Neural Network Architectures

Neural Networks architecture includes several layers organization. Usually, they have one input layer that receives the feature dataset, one or more hidden layers and one output layer. The number of neurons included in each layer can vary and is defined by a trial and error scheme. For example, the four-layer NN of Figure 2 has two hidden layers:

Figure 2. Neural network with an input layer, two hidden layers and output layer

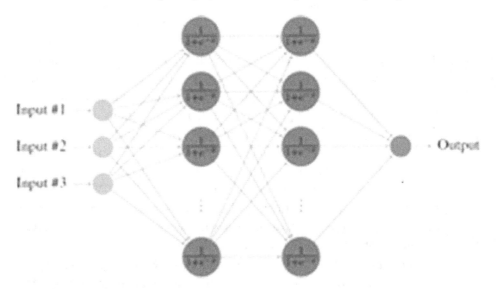

Training

At the beginning of the neural network training, the weights or values of the filters must be set at random, using very small values (but different from each other). At this stage, the filters of the initial layers don't know how to look for edges and curves in images, nor the ones of the higher layers know how to look for legs or nozzles.

The idea of providing an image with a label is related to the training process through which convolutional neural networks (CNN) pass. So, we have a training set that has thousands of images of the classes that we want to identify, and each of the images has a label of the respective category (Deshpande, 2016). For example, a training image of a handwritten digit enters a CNN, a 32×32×3 matrix that passes through the entire network. In the first training example, with all the weights or filter values randomly initialized, the output will probably be something like [.1 .1 .1 .1 .1 .1 .1 .1 .1]. Basically, it gives an output that does not give preference to any particular number. Let's say the first training image entered was a "4". The image label would be [0000100000]. Here we have to calculate the loss function, which can be defined in many different ways, such as the MSE (mean square error). If the MSE is used, the loss is given by (1).

$$E_{total} = \sum 1/2 \left(target - output \right)^2 \tag{1}$$

During the training, the value of each weight, w, is updated according to the negative direction of the E gradient, until E becomes sufficiently small. Here, the parameter η is the learning rate, and w is updated with (2) (Zhang & Devabhaktuni, 2003).

$$w = w - \cdot \frac{\partial E}{\partial w} \tag{2}$$

The learning rate is defined or chosen at random. A high learning rate means that larger steps are used in weight updates, and thus it may take less time for the model to converge to an ideal set of weights. However, a very high learning rate can result in jumps that are too large and not accurate enough to reach the ideal point.

All these steps constitute a training iteration. The program will repeat this process for a fixed number of iterations for each set of batch training images. After finishing the parameter update in the last training example, the network is expected to be trained, meaning that the weights of the layers are adjusted correctly (Deshpande, 2016).

Activation Functions

Neural networks can use various types of activation functions. The selection of the activation function is an important issue since it has a direct impact on the processing of input information. The activation functions used in this project were the ReLU and Softmax.

ReLU

In 2010 Teh and Hinton introduced the ReLU (Rectified Linear Unit), which, despite its simplicity, is a good choice for hidden layers. The advantage of ReLU (shown in Figure 3) lies, partly, in that it is linear and unsaturated. Unlike the sigmoid and hyperbolic tangent functions, the ReLU does not saturate in the positive domain, although it saturates in the negative domain. A saturation function tends to move to a certain value (Nascimento, 2016).

The neuroscience literature indicates that cortical neurons are rarely in their maximum saturation regime and suggest that their activation function can be approximated by a rectifier (Bush & Sejnowski, 1996).

After uniform initialization of the weights, about 50% of the continuous output values of the hidden layers are real zeros, and this fraction can easily increase with the sparsity-induced regularization (relative to the number of connections between a neuron with other, which is to be minimized), being biologically more plausible than many other activation functions (Glorot, Bordes, & Bengio, 2011)

Figure 3. Plot of rectified linear unit (ReLU) function

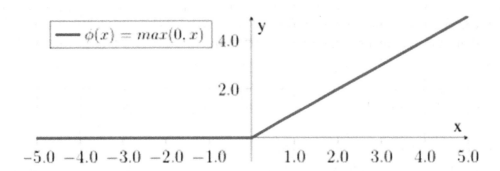

Softmax

Along with the linear function, softmax is usually found in the output layer of a neural network. The activation function softmax forces the output of the neural network to represent the probability of the input is inserted into each of the classes. Without the softmax, the outputs are simply numerical values, being the largest indicative of the winning class. When we insert information into the neural network by applying the activation function softmax, we get the probability that that input can be categorized according to predefined classes. The formula is shown in (3).

$$\varnothing_i = \frac{e^{z_i}}{\sum_{j \in group} e^{z_j}} \tag{3}$$

where *i* represents the index of the output node, and *j* represents the indexes of all the nodes in the group or level. The variable *z* designates the vector of the output nodes. It is important to note that the softmax function is calculated differently from the other activation functions provided. When using softmax, the output of a single node depends on the other output nodes. In the previous equation, the output of the other output nodes is contained in the *z* variable, unlike the other activation functions (Kloss, 2015).

Feedforward

As seen before, the networks in which the output of a neuron is used as the input of the neuron of the next layer are called feedforward neural networks. This means that there are no loops or cycles in the network, information is always passed, and there is no feedback (Nielsen, 2017). Given the inputs $x = [x_1, x_2, \ldots, x_n]^T$ and the weights *w*, a feedforward network is used to calculate outputs $y = [y_1, y_2, \ldots, y_m]^T$ of a network MLP. In the feedforward process, external inputs feed the neurons of input (first layer). The outputs of the input neurons feed the hidden neurons of the second layer, and so on, and finally the outputs of the layer L^{-1} feed the neurons of the last layer (*L*) (Zhang & Devabhaktuni, 2003). The calculation is given by (4) and (5)

$$z_i^l = x_i, \quad i = 1, 2, \ldots, N_1, N_1 \tag{4}$$

$$z_i^l = \sigma\left(\sum_{j=0}^{N_{l-1}} w_{ij}^l z_j^{l-1}\right), \quad i = 1, 2, \ldots, N_l, \quad l = 2, 3, \ldots, L. \tag{5}$$

where σ is the activation function. The outputs of the NN are extracted from the output neurons, as in (6).

$$y_i = z_i^L, \quad i = 1, 2, \ldots, N_L, \quad N_L = M \tag{6}$$

Backpropagation

The goal in developing neural models is to find an optimal set of weights w, so that $y = y(x, w)$ approaches the original behavior of a problem. This is achieved through the training process (that is, spatial optimization - w). A set of training data is presented to the neural network, consisting of pairs of (x_k, d_k), $k = 1, 2, \ldots, P$ where d_k is the desired output in the model for the inputs x_k and P is the total number of training examples.

During training, the performance of the neural network is evaluated by calculating the difference between your outputs and the desired output for all training examples. The difference, also known as error, could be quantified by (7).

$$E_{T_r}(w) = \frac{1}{2} \sum_{k \in T_r} \sum_{j=1}^{m} \left(y_j(x_k, w) - d_{jk}\right)^2 \tag{7}$$

where d_{jk} is the element j of d_k, $(y_j(x_k, w))$ is the output j of the neural network for the input x_k and T_r is an index of the training set. The weights w are adjusted during training so that this error is minimized. In 1986, Rumelhart, Hinton, and Williams proposed a systematic approach to NN training. One of the most significant contributions of their work is the backpropagation algorithm (Zhang & Devabhaktuni, 2003).

Optimization Methods

The term optimization refers to the search for minimum or maximum values for a given function, through a systematic choice of variable values within a viable set. It is intended, therefore, to find an optimal solution to a problem, which results in the best possible system performance.

Some of the most commonly used NN optimization methods are Stochastic Gradient Descent (SGD), Nesterov Accelerated Gradient (NAG), Adaptive Moment Estimation (Adam), and Root Mean Square Propagation (RMSprop). In the present study, the Stochastic Gradient Descent (SGD) was used because it leads to fast convergence and it doesn´t require memory storing of all the training data, which makes it appropriate for large datasets.

SGD

In the backpropagation algorithm, the gradient must be calculated in many iterations to adjust the weights of the neural network. When the training set is very large, in general, calculating the gradient for the whole set is impractical in terms of required computational resources. Considering this issue, the stochastic descending gradient is calculated with some examples iteratively (instead of the entire training base). Another advantage of using the SGD is the ability to reduce the occurrence of local minima in high dimensional error spaces. Batches are used because they reduce variance in learning and therefore have a more stable convergence, provided that the distribution of the examples is random. With the high computational power of GPU, mini-batches can also be processed quickly, since the operation is easily parallelized (Nascimento, 2016). Equation (8) shows the step of updating the SGD.

$$\theta = \theta - \alpha * \sum_{k=i}^{i+m} \nabla_\theta J\left(\theta; x^{(k)}, y^{(k)}\right) \qquad (8)$$

where θ is the parameter to update, α is the learning rate, and m is the size of the batch.

Data Augmentation

It is a fact that the larger and diverse the amount of data a machine learning algorithm has access to, the more effective it will tend to be.

Data augmentation is presented as a way to reduce overfitting in ML models, where data diversity is increased by using information that exists only in the available dataset.

A common practice to increase a set of images is to perform transformations at the level of their color and geometry, such as reflection, cropping, color palette changes, and image translation. Traditional transformation techniques (Figure 4) consist of using combinations of related transformations to manipulate training data. For each image, a "duplicate" image is generated that is shifted, enlarged/reduced, rotated, inverted, distorted or shaded with a tint. The image and its duplicate are then supplied to the neural network (Perez & Wang, 2017).

Figure 4. Four examples of morphological transformations performed on one cell image for the purpose of data augmentation

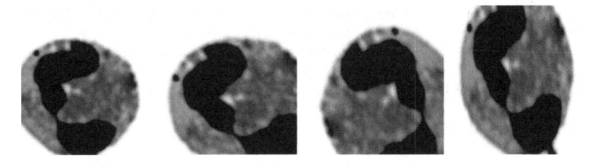

Fine-Tuning

Fine-tuning is a procedure based on the concept of transfer learning. It begins by training a network to learn characteristics for a broad domain with a classification function aimed at minimizing the error in that domain. Then, the classification function is replaced, and the network is optimized again to minimize the error in another more specific domain. Under this configuration, the characteristics and parameters of the broad domain network are transferred to a more specific one.

Assume a unique network in which the final classification function is the softmax (and a couple of dense layers), which calculates the probability in 1000 classes on the ImageNet dataset. To begin the fine-tuning procedure, this classifier component is removed, and another one is initialized with random values. The final classifier is then trained from scratch using the backpropagation algorithm with information relative to, for example, leukocyte classification.

In order to start the backpropagation for fine-tuning, it is necessary to define the learning rates of each layer appropriately. The classification layer requires a high learning rate due to its recent initialization. The rest of the layers require relatively small (or null) learning rates since it is intended to preserve the previous network parameters to transfer the knowledge to the new network (Reyes, Juan, & Camargo1, 2015).

One of the major difficulties in applying CNNs to cell images lies in the scarcity of labeled data. In this sense, the importance of the reuse of trained models in different tasks has already been demonstrated. However, the ability to transfer resources depends on the distance between the base task and the destination task. Booting a network with pre-trained resources improves its generalization capability (Kensert, Harrison, & Spjuth, 2018).

Convolutional Neural Networks

CNNs are useful in a large number of applications, especially those related to images, such as classification, segmentation, and object detection (Wu, 2017).

Let's say we have an image of a leucocyte in PNG format with size 480×480. The representative matrix will be 480×480×3. Each of these numbers receives a value from 0 to 255 that describes the pixel intensity at that point. The idea is to provide the computer with this array of numbers. With the output, one obtains the probability of the image belonging to a specific category (for example, 0.80 for neutrophil, 0.15 for monocyte, 0.05 for basophil). Similar to humans, the computer is able to perform image classification based on low-level features such as edges and curves, then constructing more abstract concepts through a series of convolutional layers. This is an overview of what a CNN does (Deshpande, 2016).

First Layer: Convolution

The first layer on CNN is always a convolutional layer. In this type of networks, a filter is used, which is in practice an array of numbers (weights or parameters) with the same depth of the input image, for example, 5×5×3 for 32×32×3 (RGB image).

The filter will slide, or convolve, around the input image, multiplying the values in the filter by the pixel values of the original image. A single representative number of each position of the filter is thus obtained throughout the convolution process, which gives rise to a new matrix 28×28, thus being smaller than the original matrix. If two 5×5×3 filters are used instead of one, the output volume will be

28×28×2. By using more filters, one can better preserve the spatial dimensions/directions. Each of these filters can be considered as identifying features such as borders, straight lines, simple colors and curves.

The output of the convolution layer is an activation map. The higher the value obtained, the greater the probability. The more filters you use, the greater the depth of the activation map, and consequently, more information about the input volume will exist.

For tensors of order 3, the convolution operation is done in a manner similar to that used for order 2 tensors. Assuming that the input in the ith layer is a tensor of order 3 with size H^1*D, the convolution kernel will also be a 3-order tensor with size $H*W*D^l$. When the kernel is placed on top of the input tensor at the spatial location (0,0,0), the products of the corresponding elements are calculated on all the channels D^l, and summed to the products of $H*W*D^l$ to obtain the convolution result in this spatial location (Wu, 2017). Although there are other ways of treating tensors (channels), this is the most common.

Pooling

Pooling is a process of data reduction. In general, the maximum or mean of a small region of the input data is calculated. The main advantage of pooling is the speed increase in the network due to interlayer downsampling, reducing the amount of data to be processed and making "the curse of dimensionality" less intense (Nascimento, 2016).

The purpose of pooling layers is also to achieve spatial invariance by reducing the resolution of feature maps. Each map corresponds to a characteristic map of the previous layer. Its units combine the input of small fragments(patches). These pooling windows can be of arbitrary size. The max-pooling consists in calculating the highest value present in a patch, normally, of four elements. Thus, those four elements are replaced by that value. The result is a lower-resolution feature map (Scherer, Muller, & Behnke, 2010).

Deeper Layers of the CNN

CNN are representatives of the multi-stage Hubel-Wiesel architecture, which extract local characteristics at high resolution and combine them successively into more complex features at lower resolutions. The loss of spatial information is offset by an increasing number of resource maps in the higher layers.

The general architecture is shown in Figure 5.

Figure 5. CNN architecture with convolution, pooling and fully-connected layers (Scherer, Muller, & Behnke, 2010)

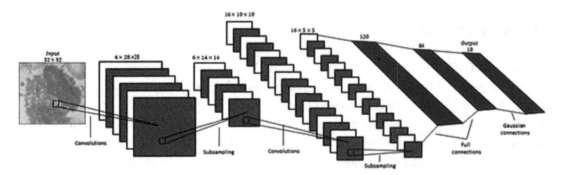

Each entry layer describes locations in the original image where certain low-level features appear. When you apply a filter set to this information, the output will represent higher-level features. The types of these characteristics can be semicircles or squares. As you go through more layers of convolution, you get activation maps that represent increasing aggregations of complex resources (Deshpande, 2016).

Fully-Connected Layer

A fully-connected layer is useful at the end of a multi-layered CNN model. For example, if after multiple layers of convolution, ReLU, and pooling, the output of the current layer contains distributed representations for the input image; one wants to use all these features in the fully-connected layers to create the right responses at the final stage. A fully connected layer is useful for this purpose. Assuming that the input of a layer x^l has size $H^l*W^l*D^l$, if one uses convolution kernels with size $H^l*W^l*D^l$, then the D cores form a tensor of order 4 in $H^l*W^l*D^l*D$. The output is $y \in \mathbb{R}^D$. It is obvious that to calculate any element in y, one needs to use all elements in the input x^l. Therefore, this layer is a fully-connected layer but is implemented as the convolution layer it is, so it is not necessary to derive learning rules for a fully-connected layer separately (Wu, 2017).

IMPLEMENTATION

Frameworks, Programming Languages and Equipment Used

The Jupyter Notebook using Python and the Keras API (using the TensorFlow as backend) were used for the construction and implementation of the leukocyte classification project.

The machine used to implement the NNS has the following characteristics: Intel Core i7 5930K @ 3.7GHz with 32 GB RAM and 2 * GTX 1080 Ti 11 GB GPUs.

Data Pre-Processing

The dataset used initially in the development of the program contains 598 leukocytes (stained) images. Most of the images (approximately 352) come from a repository on GitHub (available at https://github.com/dhruvp/wbc-classification/tree/master/Original_Images). The remaining images were obtained through a search performed on Google according to specific terminology, namely *'monocyte'*, *'leucocyte'*, *'lymphocyte'* and *'neutrophil'*. Basophils were excluded because of the poor representativeness in the blood, which was reflected in the difficulty of finding images in amounts similar to those obtained for the remaining leukocytes. For similar reasons, band leukocytes were also excluded. The dimensions of the dataset images vary according to their provenance.

A big part of the focus of this work was the dataset preprocessing. It was necessary to label each of the collected images according to the 4 categories to be classified. Subsequently, each image was manually segmented in order to provide the NN with a register, as specific as possible, of the framing of the cell whose classification was intended. GIMP (GNU Image Manipulation Program), a popular image editor with several tools that facilitate graphics editing tasks was used to segment all images manually. Figure 6 exemplifies the manual segmentation process performed.

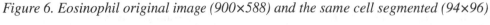

Figure 6. Eosinophil original image (900×588) and the same cell segmented (94×96)

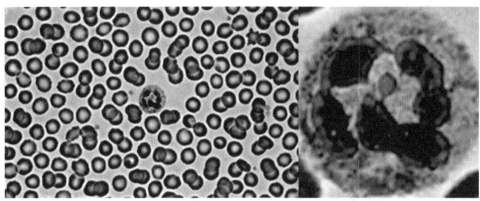

Starting from this initial set of images, data augmentation was implemented, leading to a total of 10466 images distributed as follows:

- Eosinophils: 2610 training images, 215 validation and 215 test images;
- Lymphocytes: 2628 training images, 213 validation and 213 test images;
- Monocytes: 2604 training images, 211 validation and 211 test images;
- Neutrophils: 2624 training images, 218 validation and 218 test images;

The data augmentation consisted essentially of morphological transformations such as:

- Random rotations up to a limit of 20°;
- Completion of points outside the input limits (image border padding), according to the selected mode (constant, near, reflect, and wrap). The selection of the mode in Keras translates into the extension of the limits of the morphology (color and shape) of the original image to the limits of the new image, that is, the maintenance of the color and shape of the boundary objects;
- Variations in the input area captured in the longitudinal and transverse axes by up to 10%, which means that the image may have been moved according to these axes;
- Inversions of the image in the horizontal and vertical axes;
- Changes in color.

The application of these transformations (exemplified in Figure 4) allowed the passage of the 598 initial images to the 10466 used in the training, validation, and test of the neural networks.

Due to the unsatisfactory results obtained after the training of the different networks, it was necessary to re-classify and segment all the leukocytes images as the leukocytes regions on the previous dataset were not segmented in a precise way. In this sense, the images were separated and categorized and all the images that raised doubts were eliminated and others were added, which allowed labeling with a higher level of confidence. A new segmentation was made using Paint 3D (the latest version of the popular paint editor usually found on Windows 10). This software allowed the creation of three-dimensional models and allowed the separation of the cell's foreground from the rest of the image background, as can be seen in Figure 7.

Figure 7. Original segmented eosinophil image (left) and the same image segmented with Paint3D, with the background eliminated (right)

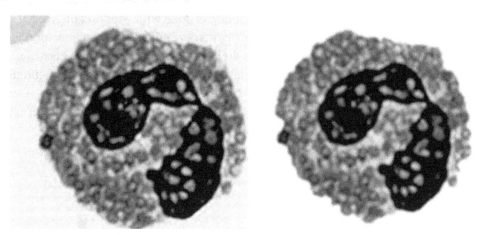

From this second selection and segmentation procedure were obtained 100 training images, 10 validation images, and 10 test images, for each of the 4 categories. After a new process of data augmentation, 4394 training images, 440 validation images and 440 test images were distributed uniformly across the four categories.

NN Models Used

Keras offers some deep learning models under the topology of the application on its documentation, as well as some weights (pre-trained in the Imagenet database) capable of classifying up to 1000 categories. In the list of available models are: Xception, VGG16, VGG19, ResNet50, InceptionV3, Inception-ResNetV2, MobileNet, DenseNet, NASNet and MobileNetV2.

Next, it is presented a brief description of the models used in this project.

VGG16 and VGG19

The second place in the ILSVRC 2014 competition was given to the VGGNet, developed by Simonyan and Zisserman. The VGGNet consists of 16 convolutional layers and presents a very uniform architecture. Similar to the AlexNet, only with 3×3 convolutions, but many filters. It was trained in 4 GPUs for 2 to 3 weeks. It is currently one of the preferred choices for extracting features from images. The weight configuration of the VGGNet is publicly available and has been used in many applications and challenges as a base resource extractor (Das, 2018).

The input for the ConvNets VGG (Visual Geometry Group), shown in Figure 8, are RGB images with dimensions 224×224. The only pre-processing performed during its implementation in ILSVRC was the subtraction of the average of the RGB value calculated in the training dataset in each pixel. The image is then passed through a set of convolutional layers, where filters with a very small receiver field are used: 3×3 (which is the smallest that allows capturing notions left/right, up/down, and center). In one of the configurations, filters of 1×1 were also used, which can be seen as linear transformations of the input channels (followed by non-linearities). The convolution step is 1 pixel; the spatial fill of the convolution layer is such that it allows the resolution to be preserved after the convolution, for example, the fill is 1 pixel for convolution layers with 3*3. Spatial grouping is accomplished with 5 layers of max-pooling, which follow some of the convolution layers. Max-pooling is done with windows of 2×2and step of 2.

The set of convolution layers (which have different depths depending on the architecture) is followed by three fully-connected layers: the first two contain 4096 channels each, the third classifies the 1000 classes (with one channel for each class). The final layer is a softmax layer. The configuration of the fully-connected layers was the same in all networks tested.

All concealed layers were equipped with the ReLU activation function (Simonyan & Zisserman, 2014).

Figure 8. Visualization of the VGG general architecture (Rosebrock, 2017)

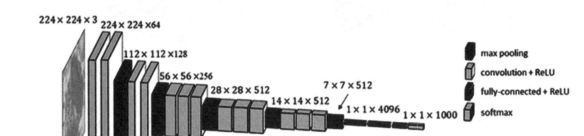

The numbers 16 and 19 represent the number of layers with weights in the network. Some disadvantages of VGGNet are the slowness of training and the width of the weight architecture. Due to its depth and number of fully-connected nodes, VGG16 is more than 533MB, and VGG19 is more than 574MB, which makes deploying these networks complicated.

InceptionV3

The winner of the ILSVRC 2014 contest was GoogLeNet (Inception V1) from Google. It achieved a top-5 error rate of 6.67%, very close to the human-level performance, also rated by the organizers.

The network used a LeNet-inspired CNN but implemented a new element called the Inception module (represented in Figure 9). It used batch normalization, image distortions and optimizer RMSprop. Its architecture consisted of a deep 22-layer CNN but reduced the number of parameters from 60 million (from AlexNet) to 4 million (Das, 2018).

The use of average pooling allows for easy adaptation and fine-tuning for other labels. The authors came to the conclusion that switching from fully-connected layers to average pooling layers improved the top-1 results by about 0.61%, with the use of dropout.

Given the large size of the network, the ability to propagate the gradient across all layers was a concern. Adding intermediate layered classifiers enabled discrimination at lower stages of the classifier, by increasing the propagated gradient signal back and providing additional regularization. These classifiers are in the form of small convolutional networks placed at the top of the Inception modules (additional pooling paths). During training, the loss is added to the total loss of the network with a weight discount. At the inference, these auxiliary networks are discarded (Szegedy, et al., 2014).

Figure 9. Original inception module used on GoogLeNet (Szegedy, et al., 2014)

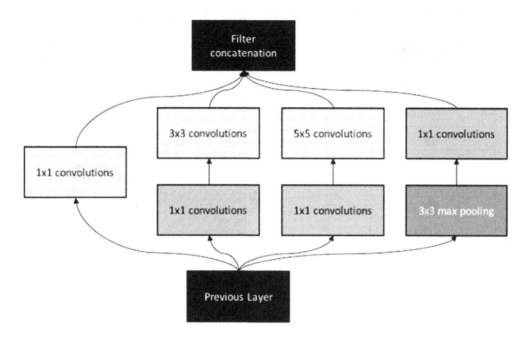

The Inception V3 architecture included in Keras comes from the paper *Rethinking the Inception Architecture for Computer Vision* from 2015. The size (or memory space required) of Inception V3 is lower to VGG and ResNet, leaving it at 96MB (Rosebrock, 2017).

Xception

The Xception was proposed by the creator of Keras, François Chollet, and is an extension of the Inception architecture that replaces the Inception modules with separable convolutions by depth, Figure 10.

ResNet50

In ILSVRC 2015, the Residual Neural Network (ResNet), by Kaiming He et al., presented a new architecture with non-consecutive connections (skipped connections) and the strong use of batch normalization. Ignored connections are also known as blocked units or gated recurrent units and have a strong resemblance to recently applied success factors in RNNs. Thanks to this technique, it is possible to train a NN with 152 layers, although with complexity inferior to a VGGNet. ResNet achieves a 3.57% Top-5 error rate, surpassing the human performance level (He, et al., 2015).

The authors of the ResNet were inspired by VGG networks. The convolution layers used have mainly 3×3 filters and follow two simple rules: (i) for the same map size of features, the layers have the same number of filters and (ii) if the filter map has its size reduced by half, the number of filters doubles in order to preserve the temporal complexity per layer. Downsampling is performed directly by the 2-pixel step convolutional layers, and the network terminates with a global mean pooling fully-connected with softmax.

Figure 10. Xception architecture. The data enters the entry flow and goes by the middle flow which is repeated eight times, and lastly by the exit flow (Chollet, 2016)

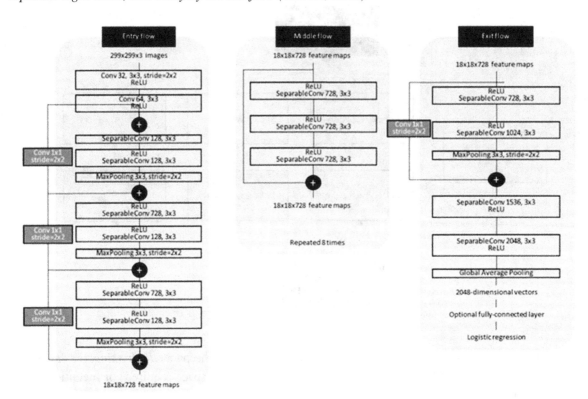

This model has fewer filters and complexity than VGG networks. A 34-layer network is equivalent to 3.6 billion FLOPs, which represents 18% VGG-19 (19.6 billion).

Based on the previous base network, the authors inserted shortcut links by transforming this network into its residual counterpart version. The identity shortcuts can be used directly when the input and output are of the same dimensions (represented with a solid trace in Figure 11).

When the dimensions increase, two options are considered: (A) The shortcut binding performs identity mapping, with zero fill entries to increase the dimensions. This option does not induce any extra parameters; (B) The projection shortcut link is used to match the dimensions (with convolutions 1×1). For both options, when shortcut links traverse feature-sized maps of two sizes, they are made with a step size of 2 (He et al., 2015).

So, the ResNet has an architecture based on micro-architecture modules (network-in-network architectures). This network has demonstrated that it is possible to train extremely deep networks using standard SGD through the use of residual modules. The implementation of ResNet50 in Keras is based on the original article of 2015. Although ResNet is much deeper than VGG, the model size is substantially lower (102MB) because of the greater abundance of pooling rather than layers fully-connected (Rosebrock, 2017).

Figure 11. ResNet residual module as originally proposed (Rosebrock, 2017)

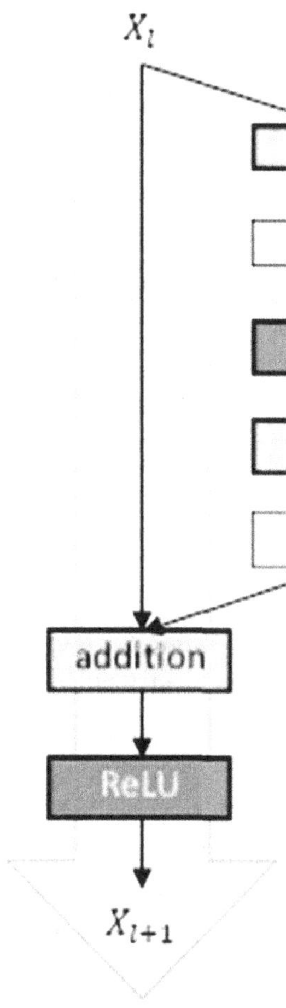

Densenet 121, 169 and 201

Generally, the ResNet architecture has a fundamental block structure, and in each of them, an anterior layer with a future layer is attached. In contrast, the DenseNet architecture proposes to concatenate the outputs of previous layers in a block.

The DenseNet architecture explicitly differentiates between information added to the network and preserved information. DenseNet layers are very narrow (for example, 12 feature-maps per layer), adding only a small set of resource maps to the "collective knowledge" of the network, keeping the resource maps unchanged and the final classifier makes a decision based on all network resource maps.

One of the great advantages of the DenseNet (Figure 12) is the improved flow of information and gradients across the network, which facilitates training. Each layer has direct access to the gradients of the loss function and the original input signal. This helps train deeper network architectures (Huang, Liu, Maaten, & Weinberger, 2016).

Figure 12. Over-simplified example of a DenseNet-121. Measures under each volume represent the width and depth and the numbers on the top of the feature map dimension. D represents dense blocks that perform operations with dense layers, T represents transition blocks performing 1x1 and 2x2 (with a stride of 2) convolutions (Ruiz, 2018).

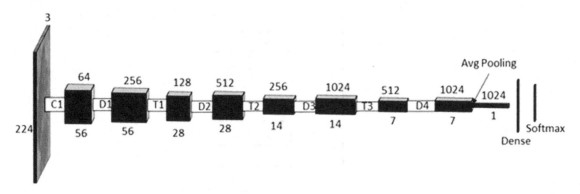

RESULTS

Implementing a model in a new set of data is a highly complex task whose evaluation depends on the innumerable factors inherent in the type, data source (as well as the level of pre-processing of data), the network architecture used, the hardware and frameworks used, among others. Some metrics not evaluated in this work are: transfer rate, utilization of GPU computing, use of FP32, CPU usage and memory consumption (Zhu, et al., 2016).

In the classification of leucocytes intended in this work are used open-source implementations available on the Internet and provided by its developers and, in this case, mediated by the Keras library.

The analysis of the project results mainly focuses on the accuracy and loss of training and validation of a set of models subsequently tested in the classification of four categories of leukocytes based on microscopic images. In the test dataset, which has different training and validation images, the percentage of the correctness of each of the models used (with and without transfer learning) is given, taking into account the time required to perform the training.

For the value of the loss, the lower it is, the better the model in question (unless it is overfitting on the training dataset). The loss is calculated during the training and validation processes, and its interpretation tells us how good the performance in these datasets is. Unlike accuracy, a loss is not a percentage value, but the sum of the errors for each training example (using the term cost for a set of examples or batch) in the training and validation sets.

In the case of the neural networks, the loss is usually given by the negative logarithm of the probability (softmax) of obtaining the number of categories. The main purpose of the model implementation is to reduce or minimize the loss function by changing the network weights using different optimization methods. The value of the loss gives an idea of the behavior of the model after each optimization iteration. Ideally, a reduction in this value should be expected after one or several iterations.

Although accuracy can be verified after each iteration, in the case of training, this value is only a reference for the correctness percentage of the model. The final precision value, obtained after learning all the parameters with the conclusion of the training, is the one that should be taken as correct. After the training, the test images are supplied to the network and the network forecasts are compared with the actual image labels, and the error percentage is usually calculated.

In this work, the comparative study was carried out between some models while training using transfer learning and without using this technique, that is, training or not the networks from scratch in the classification of leukocytes.

Models Trained with Transfer Learning

In the case of the training with transfer learning, the original top of the networks was excluded. That way it is possible to use the weights from previous training with Imagenet, that is, the knowledge of some characteristics of objects applicable to the identification of leukocytes. A small network with three layers was then created (the new top), a dense layer with the ReLU activation, a dropout layer and an output layer with the function softmax for 4 categories. The code needed to program this network in Keras is as follows:

```
model = models.Sequential()
model.add(layers.Dense(256, activation='relu', input_dim=7*7*512))
model.add(layers.Dropout(0.5))
model.add(layers.Dense(4, activation='softmax'))
```

The network received the weights related to pre-training features and was then trained to classify leukocytes in 4 categories. The initial training lasted 100 epochs, and a batch size of 16 examples was used. The average training time of the 8 NN (*'resnet50', 'vgg16', 'vgg19', 'inceptionV3', 'xception', 'densenet121', 'densenet169', 'densenet201'*) for 100 epochs was 9 minutes and 59 seconds on the computational architecture referred previously. The fastest network, VGG19, completed the training in 5 minutes and 47 seconds, and the slowest, Xception, took 16 minutes and 57 seconds. The results obtained in terms of loss are presented in the graph of Figure 13.

The networks that achieved the best results with lower loss values were the Xception, the Densenet201, the Densenet169, the Densenet121 and InceptionV3. The network that converged faster to (approximately) 0 was the Xception. The worst results were obtained by the VGG and the Resnet50 networks.

Although the networks were initially presented by their authors to operate with certain optimizers, in this work, all the training used the SGD optimizer, for comparing purposes (with the conscient possibility of penalizing the performance of some of the networks used), with a learning rate of 1^{-5} and decay of 0.001.

Figure 14 shows that the accuracy is closely related to loss, and the models that obtained the best accuracies were the same ones that had obtained the losses with lower values, logically. Thus, the Xception network was the one that converged faster to 1 (with possible overfitting), and the ResNet50 was the one that obtained the worst results with a training accuracy of about 40%. The poor ResNet results may be related to the use of SGD.

The results for the validation process are close to the ones obtained during the training, with the losses being slightly lower (and the accuracies slightly higher) on the training accuracies as expected.

In the case of transfer learning, the ResNet50 would be expected to perform better, because it is one of the newer networks, with an error of only 3.57% in ILSVRC'15. However, under the established training conditions, it was not able to track the networks with better results.

Figure 13. Loss registered on the training dataset by the set of models trained with transfer learning for 100 epochs

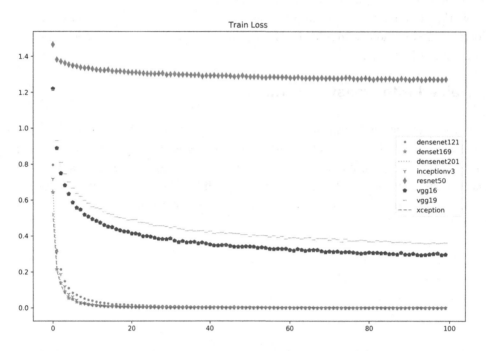

Figure 14. Accuracy registered on the training dataset by the set of models trained with transfer learning for 100 epochs

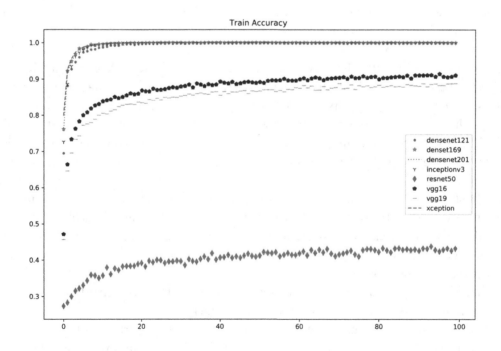

In general, the percentage of correctness for each of the categories has similar values, with the exception of the ResNet50, where some discrepancy in the classification process can be verified.

Models Trained From Scratch

In the models trained from scratch, it was necessary to train the entire network, being indispensable the specification of the number of classes or categories. The fact that it is necessary to train the whole network makes this training much more time consuming than training with transfer learning. Thus, the training of the eight networks took about 18 hours on the computational architecture used (referred previously). Each network took an average of 2 hours and 14 minutes to train for 100 epochs. The fastest network was VGG16 with 1 hour and 15 minutes and the slowest was the Xception with 3 hours and 24 minutes. Figure 15 shows the behavior of the models in terms of losses.

As shown in Figure 15, the models that obtained lower loss values were the Xception and the Densenet201, with ResNet50 having the highest loss.

Figure 15. Loss registered on the training dataset by the set of models trained from scratch for 100 epochs

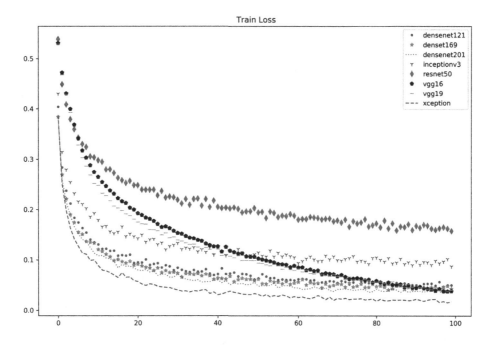

The training accuracies reflect the losses previously presented with results, similar to the losses and accuracies in the validation dataset.

Some variation in the hit percentages in each of the categories indicating that the models are not properly trained, given the number of training examples for each category being very similar.

Models Trained With Transfer Learning vs. Models Trained From Scratch

In order to get a general idea of the performance of the set of trained models with transfer learning and models trained from scratch, the graph of Figure 16 shows the mean of the values of loss obtained by the set of models in training and validation datasets.

This graph reveals lower values of the loss values of the models trained from scratch when compared to the models with transfer learning, implying a better performance in both the training and validation dataset. The values of loss for models trained without transfer learning are, after 100 epochs, below 0.15, converging to 0 in the case of the training dataset. The models with transfer learning have mean values of loss of about 0.4 for the validation dataset and about 0.3 for the training dataset.

Figure 16. Average training and validation losses obtained with the set of models trained for 100 epochs from scratch and with transfer learning

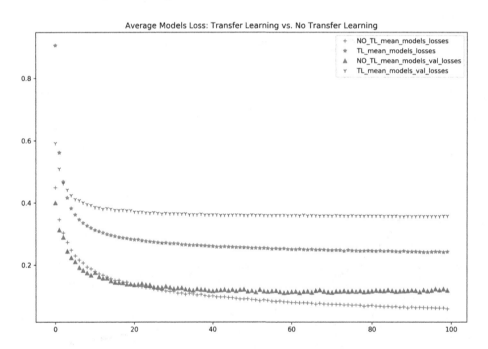

Higher accuracies were also obtained with the models trained from scratch, with values above 95% in both training and validation sets. The models trained with transfer learning got results below 90% in the two datasets referred previously.

The reduction of the value of the loss is associated with several factors. The fact that the results show very low values for this metric may be indicative of the existence of overfitting, meaning that the model "memorized" the training examples, with the possibility of having become inefficient in the test dataset. Overfitting also happens when regularization is not applied in very complex models (where the number of parameters W, the set of weights is large) or the number of data N (number of examples) is too low. In the case of models trained from scratch, no regularization method was used because there were no modifications made to the models supplied by Keras API. In the models with transfer learning, a layer of dropout (dropout = 0.5) was used at the network's top.

Table 1 shows the results obtained by the models trained from scratch. At the end of the training, these models were tested in a dataset with images different from those images used during the training and validation processes. From its observation, it is possible to verify that the percentage of correctness is very low. On average, the set of models trained from scratch achieve an accuracy of 26.31% for the 4 categories of leukocytes, which means that the process has results similar to a random classification.

Table 1. Classification accuracy percentages on the test dataset for each of the neural networks trained from scratch for 100 epochs, on four types of leukocytes

	Eosinophils	**Lymphocytes**	**Monocytes**	**Neutrophils**
Densenet121	19,09	18,18	29,09	27,27
Densenet121	20,91	29,09	20,00	25,45
Densenet121	24,55	24,55	22,73	28,18
InceptionV3	25,45	19,09	22,73	19,09
Resnet50	20,91	24,55	26,36	20,91
VGG16	26,36	23,64	21,82	27,27
VGG19	26,36	24,55	21,82	28,18
Xception	25,45	26,00	30,00	30,91

From this, it is possible to deduce the high probability of overfitting during training since the training and validation results are very good, but the models cannot perform with high precision classifications (or accuracy) in images different from those that were used in training.

Table 2 shows the results obtained by the models with transfer learning in the test dataset. Some models, such as the DenseNet, achieved average hit percentages (in all 4 categories) above 97%. The worst-performing model was the ResNet50 with only 46.4% hit. This value is due to the choice of the optimizer, the need for regularization, or the need for a higher number of training emphases. The networks

Table 2. Classification accuracy percentages on the test dataset for each of the neural networks trained with transfer learning for 100 epochs, on four types of leukocytes

	Eosinophils	**Lymphocytes**	**Monocytes**	**Neutrophils**
Densenet121	96,36	98,18	99,09	98,18
Densenet121	96,36	99,09	98,18	99,09
Densenet121	97,27	99,09	98,18	98,18
InceptionV3	91,82	97,27	93,64	97,27
Resnet50	34,18	82,73	40,91	23,64
VGG16	78,18	86,36	86,36	90,00
VGG19	81,82	90,00	80,00	88,18
Xception	95,45	97,27	96,36	97,27

VGG16 and VGG19 obtained results of approximately 85% on 100 epochs of training. InceptionV3 and Xception achieved 95% and 96.6% respectively.

From the observation of the obtained results, it is possible to realize that in spite of the initial indication that the models trained from scratch would obtain better performance (based on the best values of loss obtained during the training) that didn't happen in the test dataset. This can be explained by the large complexity of the models compared to the dataset images diversity. In addition to much less time-consuming workouts, the models trained with transfer learning were more successful being able to perform more correct ranks in the test dataset, with an overall hit rate of 87.8%, compared to 26.3% of the models trained from scratch.

Training of Models With Transfer Learning for 5000 Epochs

In an attempt to improve the performances of the models with transfer learning in the test dataset, new training of the same models was done for 5000 epochs. Given that the percentage of correctness was already quite high in some models, it was verified that the training increased the percentage of the correctness of these networks slightly. The training of all models for 5000 epochs took 69 hours and 2 minutes (while for the 100 epochs, all models took 1 hour and 20 minutes). The network that took less time to train was the VGG16 with 4 hours and 56 minutes and the one that took the most time to train was the Xception with 14 hours and 32 minutes.

Overall, the mean increase in the percentage of network set-up between the set of trained models for 100 and 5000 epochs was 1.68%, going from 87.81% in 100 training epochs to 89.49% in 5000 epochs of training.

The networks that had already achieved hit percentages above 96% obtained minor improvements, although they should not be neglected. The DenseNet121 achieved slightly lower results than those obtained after training for 100 epochs.

The networks that most benefited from the increase in the number of training epochs were the VGG16, the VGG19, and the ResNet50 with increases between 3% and 5%, although the ResNet50 maintained very low hit percentages. There was a tendency to increase the validation loss in most of the models, which suggests that the models are performing overfitting, remarkable also for the high accuracy of training (very close to 1). One could use a higher dropout value, increase decay and decrease the learning rate as a way to prevent overfitting.

Comparably to what verified in training by 100 epochs, that in general, the hit percentage for each of the categories has similar values, with the exception of the ResNet50 where one can see some discrepancy in the classification process.

In general, given the simplicity of the methodology used, the results are quite encouraging, even when compared with similar recent works. In 2016 Sajjad *et al.* created a mobile framework in the cloud to segment and classify leukocytes and achieved a 98.6% hit percentage using k-means algorithms to segment images and morphological operations to remove unwanted components. For the classification, they used an EMC-SVM (Sajjad, Khan, & Jan, 2016).

In 2018 Habidzadeh *et al.* used the ResNet50 V1, ResNet152 V1, and Resnet101 networks, trained by 3000 epochs, with 11200 training examples and 1244 test samples, having obtained results above 99% for 5 categories of leukocytes (Habibzadeh, Jannesari, Rezaei, & Totonchi, 2018).

Also, in 2018, Bhadauria *et al.* classified four categories of leukocytes, with an accuracy of 95% (Bhadauria, Devgun, Virmani, & Rawat, 2018).

However, it is not possible to make reliable comparisons between this and other works because the datasets used in this are not the same as the ones used in the other authors referred works, and some may have more visual quality than others.

FUTURE RESEARCH DIRECTIONS

Among some interesting proposals in terms of neural networks, in the last couple of years, the following articles are highlighted:

- *Identity mappings in deep Residual Networks* (He, et al., 2016) proposes an improvement of ResNet's block design. A more direct path has been created to propagate information across the network (it moves the activation to the residual path) performance.
- *Aggregated Residual Transformations for Deep Neural Networks* (RestNExt) (Xie, et al., 2017), from the creators of ResNet, presents an increase in the width of the residual blocks through of multiple parallel pathways ("cardinality") similar to the Inception modules.
- *Deep Networks with Stochastic Depth* (Huang, et al., 2016) aims to reduce the vanishing gradients and the training time through the use of short networks during the train. They do not use sets of layers, chosen at random, during a training pass. They bypass the identity function but use the network complete at the time of testing.
- *FractalNet: Ultra-Deep Neural networks without Residuals* (Larsson, et al., 2017) args that the key to good performance 'and the ability to make the transition between different network formats. They use fractal architectures that have little and a lot of depths up to the output. They are trained to omit some paths. The complete network is used during the test.
- *SqueezeNet: AlexNet-level accuracy with 50x fewer parameters and <0.5MB model size* (Iandola, et al., 2016) presents modules that consist in a 'squeeze' layer with 1×1 and 3×3 filters. The authors are able to accuracy at the level of an AlexNet in ImageNet with 50× fewer parameters. The network is compressed to a size 510× smaller than Alexnet (0.5 MB).

In the domain of cell identification and classification and microorganisms in general, it is expected to see an increase of AI techniques applied in hospitals and laboratories. In this specific case, the use of technology is dependent on the way the microscopy images are obtained. So, one hopes that this side of the equation sees an equal technological improvement, as the quality of the results depends directly on the quality of the images acquired, the speed of acquisition (as well as the efficiency of the pre-processing techniques).

CONCLUSION

The primary purpose of this document is the description of the implementation project of a set of neural networks in the classification of white blood cells or leukocytes. Open-source implementations were used with the Keras framework, with most implementations being available from ILSVRC winning networks. The Keras models used were the ResNet50, the VGG16, the VGG19, the InceptionV3, the Xception, the Densenet121, the Densenet169 and the Densenet201.

All the models were trained in two different ways: using transfer learning and training from scratch. Transfer learning allows transferring the values of the weights acquired in a previous training (in this case, with 1000 categories in the ImageNet) being necessary to train only the top of the network to recognize specific characteristics and set the number of categories to sort.

Training from scratch involves training the entire network, which is usually initialized at random and is a significantly more extended process.

The dataset is usually preprocessed and, in the case of this work, consisted in the selection, classification and segmentation of images containing eosinophils, lymphocytes, monocytes and neutrophils - basophils and band leucocytes were excluded due to the difficulty in finding images in equivalent number to the other categories. This process of preprocessing is also subject to human error, but it is the starting point for the automated classification performed by neural networks. The data augmentation was done to move from 110 images in each category to a total of 4394 training images, 440 validation, and 440 test images.

The training was performed for 100 epochs for both training approaches. In spite of the high accuracy and low loss of the models trained from scratch, it was found that these networks were overfitting, not achieving test scores with an accuracy above the random result to the number of categories concerned.

The networks with transfer learning have, on the whole, achieved classification accuracies of 87.8% versus 26.3% of the models trained from scratch. The best performing networks were the DenseNet169 and the DenseNet201, both with 98.2% accuracy. In addition, the average training time of the models with transfer learning was 9 minutes and 59 seconds, while, on average, it was needed 2 hours and 14 minutes to train a model from scratch.

The solution for the improvement of the results in the models trained from scratch should pass by the use of regularization, which introduces slight modifications in the learning algorithm in order to allow a better capacity of generalization, which translates into an improvement of the performance of the network. Some common regularization techniques are L2 and L1 regularization, dropout and early stopping. In spite of this issue, another approach would be formed by the usage of a larger and more diverse dataset.

Considering that it was intended to compare the performances with and without transfer learning, no changes were made to networks trained from scratch.

In the attempt to improve the performance of the networks and at the same time, perceive the effect given by the number of epochs on the functional performance, the training of the models with transfer learning was carried out for 5000 epochs. The results show an increase of 1.68%, on average, in the percentage of the correctness of these networks, when tested. There has also been a growing tendency for overfitting due to the scarce number of training examples used for a significant increase in the number of training epochs. Also, in this case, it would be advisable to use regularization techniques or a more suited dataset.

The good results obtained with some deep learning models are directly related to the pre-processing work done in the images. The absence of background in the images allowed the networks to extract more easily the pertinent features for the classification process. During the first preprocessing or segmentation process, there was only an approximate area containing the cell to be classified, and the test results in the test dataset were significantly lower than those obtained after leukocyte 'isolation' of the background. In this sense, it is understood the importance of data processing before providing it to neural networks for training (as well as for the test phase).

The analysis of the results must be made taking into account the limitations, mainly in the number of images used. The use of a dataset composed of more cell images (with an increase of two or three orders of magnitude) would be extremely important as a way of corroborating with greater confidence the results obtained and would certainly allow the development with more practical applicability (because only 4 categories were used).

Although there is some variability in the morphology of the images, the segmentation carried out caused that the different lighting conditions, and microscopy did not weigh too much on the final result. The existence of images from different sources was a way to increase the generalization power of the networks.

With this work, it was possible to implement a set of networks in the classification of 4 categories of leukocytes with percentages above 98% in the available dataset. It is highly probable that with a significantly larger set of images and the coupling of a computational mechanism for identification and segmentation of images (and this could also be a neural network) it could be possible to automate the identification and counting of all types of leukocytes existing from microscopy blood cell images.

Compared to state of the art, this work has higher levels of accuracy (98%). It should, however, be emphasized that the dataset used is not the same as that used in works leading to state of the art, so it is risky to make comparisons. In addition, the leukocytes used belong to the set of five base leukocytes. On the other hand, in some studies, leukocyte detection and classification are performed simultaneously, which may reduce the accuracy of classification. In the present work, we tested the performance of CNNs in relation to the classification process, but the detection was performed manually. Future work will analyze the performance of dedicated leukocyte detectors. With the use of these two methods, detection and classification, as they are separately trained methods, it is expected to achieve higher performances than achieved with hybrid methods.

REFERENCES

Agaian, S., Madhukar, M., & Chronopoulos, A. (2014). Automated Screening System for Acute Myelogenous Leukemia Detection in Blood Microscopic Images. *IEEE Systems Journal*, 8(3), 995–1004. doi:10.1109/JSYST.2014.2308452

Alférez, S., Merino, A., Bigorra, L., & Rodellar, J. (2016). Characterization and automatic screening of reactive and abnormal neoplastic B lymphoid cells from peripheral blood. *International Journal of Laboratory Hematology*, 38(2), 209–219. doi:10.1111/ijlh.12473 PMID:26995648

Bhadauria, H. S., Devgun, J. S., Virmani, J., & Rawat, J. (2018, January). Application of ensemble artificial neural network for the classification of white blood cells using microscopic blood images. *International Journal of Computational Systems Engineering*, 202–216.

Bush, P., & Sejnowski, T. (1996). Inhibition synchronizes sparsely connected cortical neurons within and between columns in realistic network models. *Journal of Computational Neuroscience*, 3(2), 91–110. doi:10.1007/BF00160806 PMID:8840227

Chaira, T. (2014). Accurate segmentation of leukocyte in blood cell images using Atanassov's intuitionistic fuzzy and interval Type II fuzzy set theory. *Micron (Oxford, England)*, 61, 1–8. doi:10.1016/j.micron.2014.01.004 PMID:24792441

Choi, J., Ku, Y., Yoo, B., Kim, J., Lee, D., Chai, Y., ... Kim, H. C. (2017). White blood cell differential count of maturation stages in bone marrow smear using dual-stage convolutional neural networks. *PLoS One*, *12*(12), e0189259. doi:10.1371/journal.pone.0189259 PMID:29228051

Chollet, F. (2016, October 7). Xception: Deep Learning with Depthwise Separable Convolutions. *CVPR*, *2017*, 5–6.

Das, S. (2018, July 23). *CNN Architectures: LeNet, AlexNet, VGG, GoogLeNet, ResNet and more....* Retrieved from Medium: https://medium.com/@sidereal/cnns-architectures-lenet-alexnet-vgg-googlenet-resnet-and-more-666091488df5

Deshpande, A. (2016). *A Beginner's Guide To Understanding Convolutional Neural Networks*. Retrieved from A Beginner's Guide To Understanding Convolutional Neural Networks: https://adeshpande3.github.io/A-Beginner%27s-Guide-To-Understanding-Convolutional-Neural-Networks/

Girshick, R., Donahue, J., Darrell, T., & Malik, J. (2020). *Rich feature hierarchies for accurate object detection and semantic segmentation*. ArXiv.

Glorot, X., Bordes, A., & Bengio, Y. (2011). Deep Sparse Rectifier Neural Networks. *Proceedings of the Fourteenth International Conference on Artificial Intelligence and Statistics*, 315-323.

Habibzadeh, M., Jannesari, M., Rezaei, Z., & Totonchi, M. (2018, April). Automatic white blood cell classification using pre-trained deep learning models. *Tenth International Conference on Machine Vision (ICMV 2017)*. 10.1117/12.2311282

He, K., Zhang, X., Ren, S., & Sun, J. (2015, December). 2015). Deep Residual Learning for Image Recognition. *CVPR*, *2015*, 6–8.

He, K., Zhang, X., Ren, S., & Sun, J. (2016, March 16). Identity Mappings in Deep Residual Networks. *CVPR*.

Huang, G., Liu, Z., Maaten, L. v., & Weinberger, K. Q. (2016, August 25). Densely Connected Convolutional Networks. *CVPR*, 4.

Huang, G., Sun, Y., Liu, Z., Sedra, D., & Weinberger, K. (2016, July). Deep Networks with Stochastic Depth. *Machine Learning*.

Iandola, F. N., Han, S., Moskewicz, M. W., Ashraf, K., Dally, W. J., & Keutzer, K. (2016, November 4). SqueezeNet: AlexNet-level accuracy with 50x fewer parameters and <0.5MB model size. *CVPR*.

Jiang, M., Cheng, L., Qin, F., Du, L., & Zhang, M. (2018). White Blood Cells Classification with Deep Convolutional Neural Networks. *International Journal of Pattern Recognition and Artificial Intelligence*, *32*(09), 1857006. doi:10.1142/S0218001418570069

Kensert, A., Harrison, P. J., & Spjuth, P. (2018, June 14). Transfer learning with deep convolutional neural network for classifying cellular morphological changes. *SLAS Discovery: Advancing Life Sciences R&D*, 8.

Kloss, A. (2015). *Object Detection Using Deep Learning - Learning where to search using visual attention*. Tübingen: Eberhard Karls Universitat Tubingen.

Larsson, G., Maire, M., & Shakhnarovich, G. (2017, May 24). FractalNet: Ultra-Deep Neural Networks without Residuals. *CVPR*.

Liu, W., Anguelov, D., Erhan, D., Szegedy, C., Reed, S., Fu, C., & Berg, A. (2020). *SSD: Single Shot MultiBox Detector*. arXiv.

López-Puigdollers, D., Javier Traver, V., & Pla, F. (2020). Recognizing white blood cells with local image descriptors. *Expert Systems with Applications, 115*, 695–708. doi:10.1016/j.eswa.2018.08.029

Lowe, D. (2004). Distinctive Image Features from Scale-Invariant Keypoints. *International Journal of Computer Vision, 60*(2), 91–110. doi:10.1023/B:VISI.0000029664.99615.94

MoradiAmin, M., Memari, A., Samadzadehaghdam, N., Kermani, S., & Talebi, A.MoradiAmin. (2016). Computer aided detection and classification of acute lymphoblastic leukemia cell subtypes based on microscopic image analysis. *Microscopy Research and Technique, 79*(10), 908–916. doi:10.1002/jemt.22718 PMID:27406956

Nascimento, P. P. (2016). *Applications of Deep Learning Techniques on NILM*. Rio de Janeiro: Academic Press.

Nazlibilek, S., Karacor, D., Ercan, T., Sazli, M., Kalender, O., & Ege, Y. (2014). Automatic segmentation, counting, size determination and classification of white blood cells. *Measurement, 55*, 58–65. doi:10.1016/j.measurement.2014.04.008

Nielsen, M. (2017). *Neural Networks and Deep Learning*. Retrieved from neuralnetworksanddeeplearning.com: http://neuralnetworksanddeeplearning.com/

NobleR. (2019). *Leucocytes*. Retrieved from Pinterest: https://www.pinterest.pt/pin/83457399321177163

Perez, L., & Wang, J. (2017, December). *The Effectiveness of Data Augmentation in Image Classification using Deep Learning*. ArXiv.

Prinyakupt, J., & Pluempitiwiriyawej, C. (2015). Segmentation of white blood cells and comparison of cell morphology by linear and naïve Bayes classifiers. *Biomedical Engineering Online, 14*(1), 63. doi:10.118612938-015-0037-1 PMID:26123131

Putzu, L., Caocci, G., & Di Ruberto, C. (2014). Leucocyte classification for leukaemia detection using image processing techniques. *Artificial Intelligence in Medicine, 62*(3), 179–191. doi:10.1016/j.artmed.2014.09.002 PMID:25241903

Qin, F., Gao, N., Peng, Y., Wu, Z., Shen, S., & Grudtsin, A. (2018). Fine-grained leukocyte classification with deep residual learning for microscopic images. *Computer Methods and Programs in Biomedicine, 162*, 243–252. doi:10.1016/j.cmpb.2018.05.024 PMID:29903491

Redmon, J., Divvala, S., Girshick, R., & Farhadi, A. (2020). *You Only Look Once: Unified, Real-Time Object Detection*. arXiv.

Redmon, J., & Farhadi, A. (2020). *YOLO9000: Better, Faster, Stronger*. arXiv.

Redmon, J., & Farhadi, A. (2020). *YOLOv3: An Incremental Improvement*. arXiv

Rehman, A., Abbas, N., Saba, T., Rahman, S., Mehmood, Z., & Kolivand, H. (2018). Classification of acute lymphoblastic leukemia using deep learning. *Microscopy Research and Technique, 81*(11), 1310–1317. doi:10.1002/jemt.23139 PMID:30351463

Ren, S., He, K., Girshick, R., & Sun, J. (2017). Faster R-CNN: Towards Real-Time Object Detection with Region Proposal Networks. *IEEE Transactions on Pattern Analysis and Machine Intelligence, 39*(6), 1137–1149. doi:10.1109/TPAMI.2016.2577031 PMID:27295650

Reyes, A. K., J. C., & Camargo1, J. E. (2015). Fine-tuning Deep Convolutional Networks for plant recognition. *CLEF 2015.*

Rezatofighi, S., & Soltanian-Zadeh, H. (2011). Automatic recognition of five types of white blood cells in peripheral blood. *Computerized Medical Imaging and Graphics, 35*(4), 333–343. doi:10.1016/j.compmedimag.2011.01.003 PMID:21300521

Rosebrock, A. (2017, March 20). *ImageNet: VGGNet, ResNet, Inception, and Xception with Keras.* Retrieved from pyimagesearch: https://www.pyimagesearch.com/2017/03/20/imagenet-vggnet-resnet-inception-xception-keras/

Ruiz, P. (2018, October 10). *Understanding and visualizing DenseNets.* Retrieved from Medium: https://towardsdatascience.com/understanding-and-visualizing-densenets-7f688092391a

Russakovsky, O., Jia Deng, H. S., Krause, J., Satheesh, S., Ma, S., Huang, Z., ... Fei-Fei, L. (2015). ImageNet Large Scale Visual Recognition Challenge. *International Journal of Computer Vision, 115*(3), 211–252. doi:10.100711263-015-0816-y

Sajjad, M., Khan, S., & Jan, Z. (2016, December). Leukocytes Classification and Segmentation in Microscopic Blood Smear: A Resource-Aware Healthcare Service in Smart Cities. *IEEE Access: Practical Innovations, Open Solutions,* 3475–3489.

Scherer, D., Muller, A., & Behnke, S. (2010, September). Evaluation of Pooling Operations. *20th International Conference on Artificial Neural Networks (ICANN),* 4.

Shahin, A., Guo, Y., Amin, K., & Sharawi, A. (2019). White blood cells identification system based on convolutional deep neural learning networks. *Computer Methods and Programs in Biomedicine, 168,* 69–80. doi:10.1016/j.cmpb.2017.11.015 PMID:29173802

Simonyan, K., & Zisserman, A. (2014, September 4). Very Deep Convolutional Networks for Large-Scale Image Recognition. *ILCR, 2015,* 2–4.

Stathonikos, N., Veta, M., Huisman, A., & van Diest, P. (2013). Going fully digital: Perspective of a Dutch academic pathology lab. *Journal of Pathology Informatics, 4*(1), 15. doi:10.4103/2153-3539.114206 PMID:23858390

Szegedy, C., Liu, W., Jia, Y., Sermanet, P., Reed, S., Anguelov, D., ... Rabinovich, A. (2014, September 17). Going Deeper with Convolutions. *CVPR, 2015,* 4.

Tiwari, P., Qian, J., Li, Q., Wang, B., Gupta, D., Khanna, A., ... de Albuquerque, V. H. C. (2018). Detection of subtype blood cells using deep learning. *Cognitive Systems Research, 52,* 1036–1044. doi:10.1016/j.cogsys.2018.08.022

Wang, Q., Bi, S., Sun, M., Wang, Y., Wang, D., & Yang, S. (2019). Deep learning approach to peripheral leukocyte recognition. *PLoS One, 14*(6), e0218808. doi:10.1371/journal.pone.0218808 PMID:31237896

Wu, J. (2017, May 1). Introduction to Convolutional Neural Networks. *National Key Lab for Novel Software Technology,* 5-8.

Xie, S., Girshick, R., Dollár, P., Tu, Z., & He, K. (2017, April 11). Aggregated Residual Transformations for Deep Neural Networks. *CVPR.*

Zhang, Q.-J., & Devabhaktuni, V. K. (2003, APRIL). *Artificial Neural Networks for RF and Microwave.* IEEE.

Zhao, J., Zhang, M., Zhou, Z., Chu, J., & Cao, F. (2016). Automatic detection and classification of leukocytes using convolutional neural networks. *Medical & Biological Engineering & Computing, 55*(8), 1287–1301. doi:10.100711517-016-1590-x PMID:27822698

Zhu, H., Zheng, M. A., Pelegris, A., Jayarajan, A., Phanishayee, A., Shroeder, B., & Pekhimenko, G. (2016, April 14). Benchmarking and Analyzing Deep Neural Network. In *2018 IEEE International Symposium on Workload Characterization (IISWC),* (pp. 13-15). IEEE.

ADDITIONAL READING

Bayramoglu, N., & Heikkila, J. (2016). Transfer learning for cell nuclei classification in histopathology images. *European Conference on Computer Vision*, pp. 532–539. Springer.

Bhagavathi, S., & Thomas Niba, S. (2016). An automatic system for detecting and counting rbc and wbc using fuzzy logic. *Journal of Engineering and Applied Sciences (Asian Research Publishing Network), 11*(11), 6891–6894.

Lawrence, S., Giles, C. L., & Tsoi, A. C. (1997). Lessons in neural network training: Overfitting may be harder than expected. AAAI/IAAI, pp. 540–545.

Othman, M. Z., Mohammed, T. S., & Ali, A. B. (2017). Neural network classification of white blood cell using microscopic images. *International Journal of Advanced Computer Science and Applications, 8*(5), 99–104.

Ruder, S. (2016). An overview of gradient descent optimization algorithms. *arXiv*:1609.04747.

Srivastava, N., Hinton, G. E., Krizhevsky, A., Sutskever, I., & Salakhutdinov, R. (2014). Dropout: A simple way to prevent neural networks from overfitting. *Journal of Machine Learning Research, 15*(1), 1929–1958.

KEY TERMS AND DEFINITIONS

Data Augmentation: Allows to increase the diversity on the dataset creating new patterns from small variations on the original dataset patterns.

Eosinophil: Type of leukocyte responsible for combating parasites and infection in vertebrates.

Features Maps: Are the output activations for a given filter produced by the convolution operator between the filter weights and the input signals.

Leukocyte: Also known as white blood cell, are involved in the protection of the body against foreign invaders and deseases.

Lymphocyte: Type of leukocyte found on the lymph. They include T and B cells as well as natural killer cells.

Monocyte: They are the largest type of leukocyte, being responsible for phagocytosis, antigen presentation and cytokine production.

Neutrophil: The most prevalent type of leukocyte, is a type of phagocyte normally found on the bloodstream.

Overfitting: Analysis that is too close to a specific dataset, that tends to fail to predict future observations or to fit additional data.

Pre-Processing: Includes processes like selection, cleaning, normalization, transformation feature extraction and transformation in order to obtain data that is more easily treatable.

Training: Determination of the best set of weights for maximizing a neural network's accuracy.

Chapter 2
Deep Learning Using Keras

Deepa Joshi

Department of Systemics, School of Computer Science, University of Petroleum & Energy Studies (UPES), India

Shahina Anwarul

Department of Systemics, School of Computer Science, University of Petroleum & Energy Studies (UPES), India

Vidyanand Mishra

Department of Systemics, School of Computer Science, University of Petroleum & Energy Studies (UPES), India

ABSTRACT

A branch of artificial intelligence (AI) known as deep learning consists of statistical analysis algorithms known as artificial neural networks (ANN) inspired by the structure and function of the brain. The accuracy of predicting a task has tremendously improved with the implementation of deep neural networks, which in turn incorporate deep layers into the model allowing the system to learn complex data. This chapter intends to give a straightforward manual for the complexities of Google's Keras framework that is easy to understand. The basic steps for the installation of Anaconda, CUDA, along with deep learning libraries, specifically Keras and Tensorflow, are discussed. A practical approach towards solving deep learning problems in order to identify objects in CIFAR 10 dataset is explained in detail. This will help the audience in understanding deep learning through substantial practical examples to perceive algorithms instead of theory discussions.

KERAS

Keras is an open source machine-learning library written in python and developed by a Google engineer named François Chollet for quickly building deep learning models by only writing few lines of code. It is a high-level API that runs on top of Tensorflow, Theano, and CNTK and wraps up extensive complex numerical computation to perform activities like objects identification, image labeling, sentiment analysis, automated car driving etc. keras provides a convenient solution to deep learning problems by replacing

DOI: 10.4018/978-1-7998-3095-5.ch002

hundreds of lines of conventional code with only few lines of codes. It removes the effort of building a complex network that could be challenging to build through conventional approaches that might take hours or days to hand code in Python or other languages. Both industry and research community has a stronger adoption of keras API as compared to other deep learning libraries. tf.keras module is the official frontend of TensorFlow, which is the most popular API among other deep learning libraries. Keras is used in Netflix, Yelp, Uber, Square, Instacart, Zocdoc, and many others. In addition, it takes 2nd place in terms of research article published by preprint arXiv.org and is adopted by researchers at large scientific organizations such as NASA and CERN.

Figure 1. Deep learning framework power scores 2018 (Chollet, 2015)

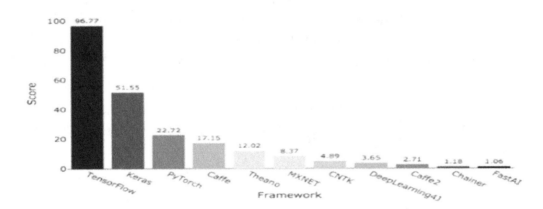

ARTIFICIAL INTELLIGENCE VS MACHINE LEARNING VS DEEP LEARNING

Artificial Intelligence is a far-reaching research domain, wherein the basic idea revolves around devices and machines exhibiting cognitive capabilities such as interaction with the environment, computer vision, handwriting and speech recognition, problem analysis and solving, comprehensive learning, perception and various other imperative applications (Russell and Norvig, 2016). Artificial Intelligence aims at imparting human intelligence and instincts to a computer, and a perfect blend of mathematics, statistics, and science makes this practicable.

A sub-branch of AI, Machine Learning (ML) focuses on imparting these capabilities contemporaneously, by teaching the computers, instead of training and programming them for specific tasks (Bishop, 2006). ML serves the purpose by creating algorithms, using which the computers can then make predictions for similar tasks and situations. The machines are provided with data and its desired output and thus are trained on these examples for future unseen data and problems. This is termed as supervised learning. Under unsupervised learning, only the input data is provided to the machine and it is expected to develop an output by itself, without supervision.

There is another learning field called reinforcement learning, where the machine interacts with its surroundings and trains itself seeing how the environment reacts to the machine's actions. The science behind this cognitive learning; computer vision revolves around artificial neural networks. The algorithms are inspired by the human brain that learns using large amounts of data sets so as to clone the human instincts a close as possible. This is referred to as Deep Learning (DL). The term deep, refers to the layers present in these artificial neural networks. Initially low, the requirement of number of layers present, to be considered "deep" is now hundreds. The algorithms in DL have superior accuracy, even surpassing human level in some tasks. It is due to the developer's brilliant and sagacious techniques that these relatively smaller number of algorithms have a commendable impact over a broad set of domains, including texts, images, speech and video. The availability of huge amounts of data sets to train the models has proved to be an essential part of the success. Companies like Google (Google Lens, Google Photos - Face, object and scene recognition, and Google Maps), Apple and Facebook extensively use these techniques to analyze, process, and work on their data at a daily basis. This field, and the algorithms and techniques associated with it, knows no bounds when it comes to research and development. DL is ever evolving and spreading its roots to several domains, hence extending its reach solely from the industrial or academic point of view. With the exception of being a Python programmer, this paper does not require the reader to be of a mathematical background or have any prior knowledge of a specific field.

Neural Network Foundation

The human visual system can effortlessly identify the patterns in a scene because of the presence of series of visual cortex v_1, v_2,.., in each hemisphere of our brain. Each visual cortex consists of billions of 140 million interconnected neurons capable of executing complex image processing tasks. The human brain itself is a supercomputer that has evolved in hundreds of millions of years and tremendously adapted to understand the visual world. The intricacy of visual pattern recognition is perceivable when we write a computer program to identify these patterns. Identifying different shapes in a pattern (For example "9") such as a vertical stroke in the bottom right and a loop at the top is quite difficult to express algorithmically. It becomes even more difficult in a labyrinth of exceptions, caveats and special cases. However, the approach of neural network in solving such problem is different from conventional approaches. It takes a large number of input of such handwritten digits termed as training samples (Figure 2) and creates a system to automatically derive rules for identifying the digits by constantly learning patterns from those training samples.

Furthermore, the accuracy of such models can be improved by including more training samples (Goodfellow, Bengio and Courville, 2016). The key concept behind developing a neural network is a "perceptron". A perceptron is inspired by the human nervous system, where each network consists of various interconnected neurons that communicates with each other. The concept of perceptron was introduced in 1950 by Frank Rosenblatt (Rosenblatt, 1958). A perceptron takes various binary inputs, such as x1, x2, and x3 and produces a single binary output as shown in the Figure 3.

Rosenblatt introduced the concept of weights w_1, w_2, and w_3 that represents importance of the respective inputs to the outputs and derived a mathematical rule to compute the output of the perceptron. If the weighted sum $\sum_i w_j x_j$ is less than or equals to a threshold value, the output generated is 0 otherwise the output is 1.

Figure 2. Random training samples of handwritten digits

Figure 3. A neuron depicting inputs and their corresponding weights along with a bias 'b'. The activation function f is then applied to the weighted sum of the inputs (Abhigoku, 2018).

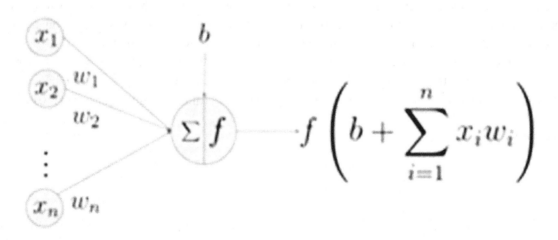

$$\text{Output=}\begin{cases} 0 \ \ if \ \ \sum_{j} w_j x_j \leq threshold \\ 1 \ \ if \ \ \sum_{j} w_j x_j > threshold \end{cases} \tag{1}$$

We can obtain different set of outputs or decision-making models by varying weights and threshold. The equation is further simplified by representing the above equation in a simpler form by rewriting $\sum_{i} w_j x_j$ as the dot product of weights and inputs w.x = $\sum_{i} w_j x_j$. In addition, threshold is moved to the other side of inequality and is replaced by a bias, b≡−threshold.

$$\text{Output=}\begin{cases} 0 \ \ if \ \ w.x + b \leq 0 \\ 1 \ \ if \ \ w.x + b > 0 \end{cases} \tag{2}$$

A network consisting of a perceptron utilizes a fact that if we could make a small change in weight or bias, a small change in the output also occurs that could lead to the accurate perdition of a digit. If the network mistakenly classifies a "9" as "8", we could repeat the process of modifying the weights and biases repeatedly to produce much better results. However, this small change can sometimes cause the output to completely flip from say 0 to 1 because of presence of perceptrons in our network. The entire behavior of the network can become unpredictable on all other images because it is difficult to analyze how to gradually change the weights and biases so that the network gets close to the desired output. A new type of artificial neuron known as "sigmoid neuron" was introduced to overcome this problem. Sigmoid neurons are modified in such a way that small change in the weights ad biases causes only a small change in its output unlike perceptrons.

Figure 4. A sigmoid neuron (Goodfellow, Bengio, and Courville, 2016)

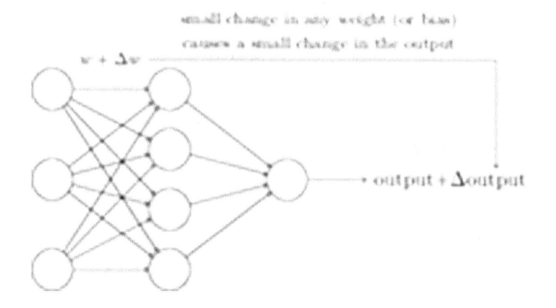

A sigmoid neuron (Figure 4) can have inputs ranging from 0 to 1, for instance 0.748 is a valid input for a sigmoid neuron. The output from the sigmoid neuron is σ(w·x+b) unlike perceptron where the output was either 0 or 1 when some weights w_1, w_2, w_3… are assigned corresponding to each input along with an overall bias 'b'. The sigmoid function is defined as:

$$\sigma(z) = \frac{1}{1+e^{-z}}$$

(3)

OR

$$\sigma(z) = \frac{1}{1+\exp\left(-\sum_j w_j x_j - b\right)}$$

(4)

The behavior of a sigmoid neuron is in close association with a perceptron. The similarity between a perceptron and sigmoid model can be understood by taking a large positive number of $z=w.x+b$. If z is a large positive number then output from sigmoid function is approximately 1 as $e^{-z}\sim 0$. Similarly, for a very large negative value of z, the sigmoid output becomes approximately 0 as $e^{-z}\sim\infty$. It is only when is of modest size that there is much deviation from the perceptron model.

Neural Network Architecture

A four-layer neural network with two hidden layers, one input later and one output layer is represented in Figure 5. Historically such multiple layer networks are also called multilayer perceptrons *or* MLPs but consisting of sigmoid neurons, instead of perceptrons. If the input image size 28*28 then we would have 784=28×28 input neurons to the network, with the intensities scaled appropriately between 0 and 1. The output layer will contain ten neurons, depicting probabilities of having a class (0-9). The concept was further extended in late 1960s with the introduction of backpropagation technique (Werbos, 1990) and almost 30 years later popularized by Rumelhart, Hinton and Williams (Rumelhart, Hinton, and Williams, 1986). Backpropagation algorithm is probably the most fundamental building block in a neural network. This technique helps in effectively train a neural network through adjusting model parameters via chain rule.

The algorithm of training a "N" layer neural network is described below:

1. Initialize the parameters of a N layer neural network.
2. Implement the forward propagation module:

$$W = \begin{bmatrix} j & k & l \\ m & n & o \\ p & q & r \end{bmatrix} X \begin{bmatrix} a & b & c \\ d & e & f \\ g & h & i \end{bmatrix} b = \begin{bmatrix} s \\ t \\ u \end{bmatrix}$$

Then WX + b will be:

Figure 5. Input layer, hidden layer and output layer in digit recognition model

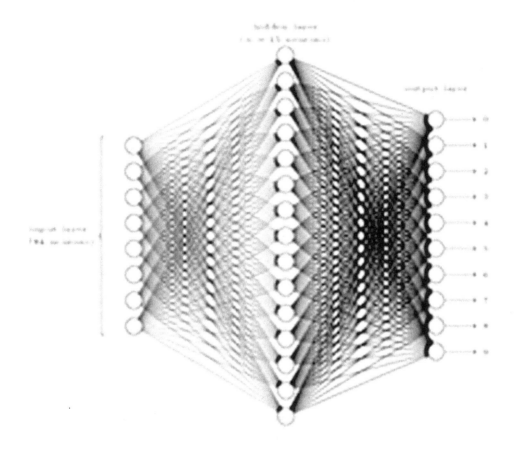

$$WX + b = \begin{bmatrix} \left(ja + kd + \mathrm{l}g\right) + s & \left(jb + ke + lh\right) + s & \left(jc + kf + li\right) + s \\ \left(ma + nd + og\right) + t & \left(mb + ne + oh\right) + t & \left(mc + nf + oi\right) + t \\ \left(pa + qd + rg\right) + u & \left(pb + qe + rh\right) + u & \left(pc + qf + ri\right) + u \end{bmatrix}$$

$$Z^{[l]} = W^{[l]}A^{[l-1]} + b^{[l]}$$

$$\sigma\left(Z\right) = \sigma\left(WA + b\right) = \frac{1}{1 + e^{-\left(WA+b\right)}}$$

3. Compute the loss,

Error$_{B}$= Actual Output – Desired Output

4. Implement the backward propagation module: Travel back from the output layer to the hidden layer to adjust the weights such that the error is decreased.

The three outputs $\left(dW^{[l]}, db^{[l]}, dA^{[l]}\right)$ are computed using the input $dZ^{[l]}$. Here are the formulas you need:

$$dW^{[l]} = \frac{\partial L}{\partial W^{[l]}} = \frac{1}{m} dZ^{[l]} A^{[l-1]T}$$
$$db^{[l]} = \frac{\partial L}{\partial b^{[l]}} = \frac{1}{m} \sum_{i=1}^{m} dZ^{[l](i)}$$
$$dA^{[l-1]} = \frac{\partial L}{\partial A^{[l-1]}} = W^{[l]T} dZ^{[l]}$$

Parameters are updated as:

$$W^{[l]} = W^{[l]} - \alpha \ dW^{[l]}$$
$$b^{[l]} = b^{[l]} - \alpha \ db^{[l]}$$

Where α is the learning rate

5.   Keep repeating the process until the desired output is achieved

Computer Vision has allowed us to achieve things in the areas such as healthcare, autonomous driving or retail which, until recently were nearly impossible. The application of computer vision can be found everywhere from unlocking our smartphone phone with our face to automatically retouch photos before posting them on social media. The most crucial building blocks behind this huge success are Convolutional Neural Networks. Various layers of CNN are discussed in detail with the help of CIFAR dataset in the next section.

SETUP A PYTHON ENVIRONMENT FOR MACHINE LEARNING AND DEEP LEARNING

This section provides commands for installing backend engines (TensorFlow, Theano, CNTK) of keras followed by commands for installing keras. Keras has two choices of backend engines: Tensorflow and Theano. This step will guide you to install keras for deep learning with Tensorflow backend, which provides distributed computing as oppose to Theano. It provides flexibility to deploy the network computations to multiple CPUs, GPUs, servers or even to mobile systems.

Background

A CPU can handle general computations while a GPU is worthy of handling specialized computations and is much faster at computation except for few cases. Its speed depends on the type of computation being performed and is highly suitable when computation is done in parallel. In parallel computing, a large task is broken down into smaller independent code depending on the number of cores available on the GPU, each of these tasks are then evaluated simultaneously and their results are combined or synchronized to generate the output. A CPU comprises of 4-16 cores in general, optimized for sequential serial processing while a GPU has massively parallel architecture that can have thousands of efficient cores, which make them well suitable for parallel computations. Traditional software were written for serial computation where instructions are executed one after the other whereas there are some algorithms that can be framed to utilize parallel computation. Matrix operations for deep learning can easily be parallelized. Millions of parameters in a DNN (Deep Neural Networks) can be trained at a much faster rate by utilizing GPUs. There are several programming frameworks available that allows programmers harness GPU cores such as OpenCL, OpenACC and most popular NVidia CUDA (Compute Unified Device Architecture). CUDA is a toolkit that access an extension of C with its own programming model that lets programmer run their code on NVidia's GPU. The cuDNN built on top of CUDA specifically for deep learning is used by every single major framework for Tensoflow, Pytorch, etc.

Python Environment for Machine Learning and Deep Learning

We can easily setup a python environment on our system. The installation steps in this section are targeting windows operating system. However, it is also applicable for Ubuntu & Linux users. The steps involved are:

Downloading and Installing Anaconda

Anaconda can be freely download from https://www.anaconda.com/distribution/ by selecting underlying operating system and with Python version (Python 3.7 is recommended). After downloading the setup, it can be installed that automatically install Python and some basic libraries along with it.

Figure 6.

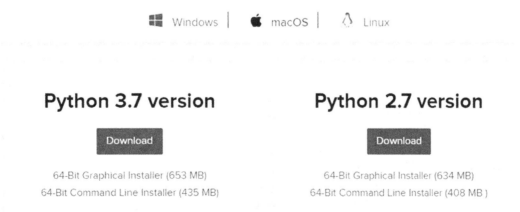

Updating Anaconda

Open Anaconda Prompt and type the following command(s) to update anaconda.

    conda update conda
    conda update –all

Installing CUDA

Once we have NVidia GPU, we can download CUDA toolkit from NVidia website. (https://developer. nvidia.com/cuda-downloads) by selecting package corresponding to the underlying operating system followed by extracting the packages.

Figure 7.

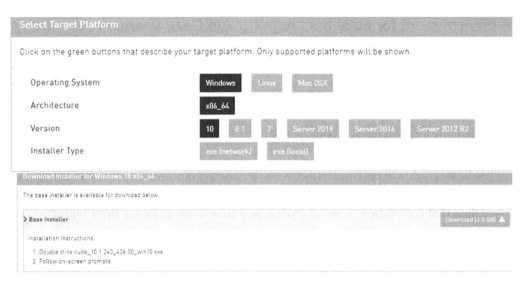

Downloading cuDNN

Download the latest version of cuDNN. Choose your version depending on your Operating System and CUDA. Membership registration is required.

    https://developer.nvidia.com/cudnn
    Put your unzipped folder in C drive

Adding cuDNN to Environment Path

- Open Run dialogue using (*Win + R)* and run the command sysdm.cpl
- In Window-10 System Properties, please select the Tab Advanced.
- Select Environment Variables and add the following path in your Environment add the following command to environment path

Figure 8.

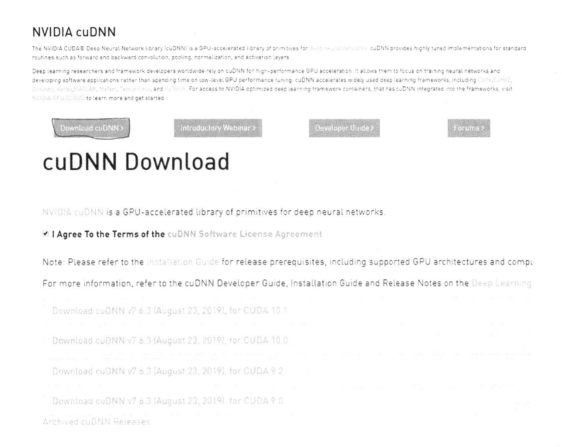

Figure 9.

$$C:\verb|\|cudnn-9.0-windows10-x64-v7$$

C:\cudnn-9.0-windows10-x64-v7\cuda\bin

Creating Anaconda Environment

Create a conda environment named "new_env" (you can change the name) by invoking the following command- conda create -n new_env pip python=3.7

Now, activate the conda environment by issuing the following command:

activate new_env

(new_env)C:> # Your prompt should change according to the new environment.

Installing Deep Learning Libraries

Now we will install Python libraries used for deep learning, including TensorFlow and Keras.

Installing TensorFlow

Open Anaconda Prompt and type the following commands.

To install the GPU version of TensorFlow:

C:\> pip install tensorflow-gpu

If your machine or system is the only CPU supported then use the below command for installing CPU-only version of TensorFlow:

C:\> pip install tensorflow

Now we test the installation by running this program on shell:

>>> import tensorflow as tf

If there is no error, it means tensorflow is successfully installed.

Installing keras

Open Anaconda Prompt to type the following commands.

pip install keras

DATASETS WITHIN KERAS

Finding the right dataset is a challenging and most common problem in building and testing a predictive model. Keras provides a seven publicly available standard datasets for building machine learning applications. List of popular datasets are:

- Boston Housing (regression)
- MNIST (classification of 10 digits)
- Fashion-MNIST (classification of 10 fashion categories)
- CIFAR10 (classification of 10 image labels)
- CIFAR100 (classification of 100 image labels)
- IMDB Movie Reviews (binary text classification)
- Reuters News (multiclass text classification)

BUILDING A DEEP NEURAL NETWORK USING SEQUENTIAL APPROACH FOR OBJECT DETECTION USING CIFAR DATASET

What is CIFAR-10?

CIFAR-10 (Canadian Institute for Advanced Research) dataset shown in Figure 10 is a classical computer-vision dataset comprising of 60,000 colored images of 32x32 dimension each and having 10 different category of objects such as automobile, cat, dog, airplane, etc. Alex Krizhevsky, Vinod Nair, and Geoffrey Hinton prepared the dataset (Krizhevsky, Nair and Hinton, 2014) covering the task of object detection in the images intended for computer vision research.

Figure 10. Example of images in CIFAR10 dataset (Kaggle, 2019)

Step 1. Loading the CIFAR10 dataset

Keras datasets package provides cifar10.load_data() function which can be used to download the dataset automatically instead of independently downloading and installing it in a directory. It comprises of training and testing dataset with 50,000 and 10,000 colored images (channel=3) having 32*32 pixel dimensions respectively. The actual label for the train and test set is stored in y_train and y_test arrays and we acquire the size of the datasets and their labels using shape attribute.

Figure 11.

```
import numpy as np
from keras.datasets import cifar10

(X_train, Y_train), (X_test, Y_test) = cifar10.load_data()
print(X_train.shape, Y_train.shape)
print(X_test.shape, Y_test.shape)


Using TensorFlow backend.
Downloading data from https://www.cs.toronto.edu/~kriz/cifar-10-python.tar.gz
170500096/170498071 [==============================] - 3s 0us/step
(50000, 32, 32, 3) (50000, 1)
(10000, 32, 32, 3) (10000, 1)
```

Step 2. Visualizing the Dataset

The first 10 training images will be displayed using matplotlib library.

Figure 12.

```
import matplotlib.pyplot as plt
img_rows, img_cols , channels= 32,32,3
for i in range(0,9):
    plt.subplot(330 + 1 + i)
    plt.imshow(X_train[i])
plt.show()
```

Figure 13.

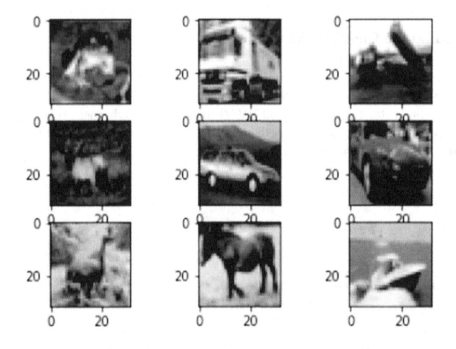

Step 3. Normalization

The images can be rescaled from 0-255 (pixel range) to 0-1 (pixel range) by subtracting each pixel value with the mean and dividing it by standard deviation of all pixel values in the image. It is useful to remove distortions caused by lights and shadows in an image.

Figure 14.

```
x_train=X_train.astype("float32")
x_train = (x_train - x_train.mean(axis=0)) / (x_train.std(axis=0))
x_test=X_test.astype("float32")
x_test = (x_test - x_test.mean(axis=0)) / (x_test.std(axis=0))
```

Step 4. One Hot Encoding

The actual output or label of the images are provided as integer numbers in the dataset. We have to convert these integer values into arrays using to_categorical() functions. The output of this function is shown in Figure 15.

Figure 15. Actual label vs hot encoded label data (Chansung, 2018)

index	label
0	airplane (0)
1	automobile (1)
2	bird (2)
3	cat (3)
4	deer (4)
5	dog (5)
6	frog (6)
7	horse (7)
8	ship (8)
9	truck (9)
...	...
...	...

original label data

label	index											
	0	1	2	3	4	5	6	7	8	9	...	...
airplane	1	0	0	0	0	0	0	0	0	0	...	...
automobile	0	1	0	0	0	0	0	0	0	0	...	...
bird	0	0	1	0	0	0	0	0	0	0	...	...
cat	0	0	0	1	0	0	0	0	0	0	...	...
deer	0	0	0	0	1	0	0	0	0	0	...	...
dog	0	0	0	0	0	1	0	0	0	0	...	...
frog	0	0	0	0	0	0	1	0	0	0	...	...
horse	0	0	0	0	0	0	0	1	0	0	...	...
ship	0	0	0	0	0	0	0	0	1	0	...	...
truck	0	0	0	0	0	0	0	0	0	1	...	...

one-hot-encoded label data

Figure 16.

```
num_classes=10
from keras import utils as np_utils
y_train = np_utils.to_categorical(Y_train, num_classes)
y_test = np_utils.to_categorical(Y_test, num_classes)
```

Step 5. Building a Sequential Model From Scratch

The convolution layer comprises of a set of independent filters where each filter allows us to find pattern or features in the image (Figure 17). A random weight is assigned to all filters initially which will be subsequently learned during backpropagation. 32 filters (size 3*3*3) are convolved over the input image (size 32*32*3) independently in the first convolution layer resulting in feature map of 30*30*32 dimension using the formula (n-f+1, n-f+1) where, n is input image dimension and f is the filter size. However, the image can shrink down to 1 by 1 dimension if we continue this process for a few more layers. In addition, pixel values on every corner of the image is used only once by these filters while it is overlapped many times in the middle. To overcome these problems of **shrinking output** and **data loss** from the edges, we have used "same" padding in our example. Padding helps us adding border around the image. These convolution layers are added sequentially in the layers followed by activation, max pool and dropout layers.

Activation Layer

We do not use linear activation/identity function for the activation map (output of convolution layer) as the images are highly non-linear in nature and using non-linear activation function such as ReLu is valuable after a linear convolution operation.

Maxpool Layer

Pooling layers operates on each feature map (output of convolution layer) independently in the network. It helps in gradually reducing the number of parameters and computational power of the network. A filter size of 2*2 and stride of 2*2 is used to reduce network parameters in this example.

Batch Normalization and Dropout Layer

Batch normalization is used for improving the speed, performance, and stability of neural networks while dropout prevents the network from overfitting. Dropout randomly turn off some of the nodes in the layers of the network by setting some amount of probability of eliminating a node in the neural network. We are eliminating 25%, 25% and 50% of the nodes in layer 1, layer 2 and layer 3 respectively.

Fully Connected Layer-

The entire network in CNN is divided into two parts: feature extraction and classification. The convolution layers are accountable for extracting meaningful complex features from the images while fully connected layers serves the purpose of predicting the class probability.

A baseline model using CNN is used to create network architecture for our task consisting of layers described below:

*Figure 17. Typical architecture of CNN (*Pokharna, 2016*)*

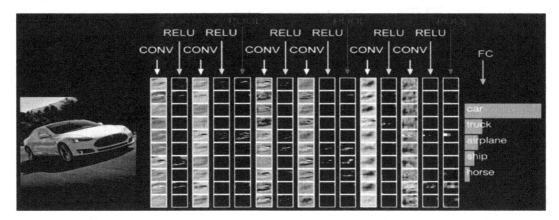

Figure 18.

```
#Importing the necessary libraries
from keras.models import Sequential
from keras.layers import Conv2D, Activation, BatchNormalization, MaxPooling2D, Dropout, Flatten, Dense
from keras import regularizers

weight_decay = 1e-4
model = Sequential()
model.add(Conv2D(32, (3,3), padding='same', kernel_regularizer=regularizers.l2(weight_decay),
                 input_shape=x_train.shape[1:]))
model.add(Activation('relu'))
model.add(BatchNormalization())
model.add(Conv2D(32, (3,3), padding='same', kernel_regularizer=regularizers.l2(weight_decay)))
model.add(Activation('relu'))
model.add(BatchNormalization())
model.add(MaxPooling2D(pool_size=(2,2)))
model.add(Dropout(0.3))

model.add(Conv2D(64, (3,3), padding='same', kernel_regularizer=regularizers.l2(weight_decay)))
model.add(Activation('relu'))
model.add(BatchNormalization())
model.add(Conv2D(64, (3,3), padding='same', kernel_regularizer=regularizers.l2(weight_decay)))
model.add(Activation('relu'))
model.add(BatchNormalization())
model.add(MaxPooling2D(pool_size=(2,2)))
model.add(Dropout(0.3))

model.add(Conv2D(128, (3,3), padding='same', kernel_regularizer=regularizers.l2(weight_decay)))
model.add(Activation('relu'))
model.add(BatchNormalization())
model.add(Conv2D(128, (3,3), padding='same', kernel_regularizer=regularizers.l2(weight_decay)))
model.add(Activation('relu'))
model.add(BatchNormalization())
model.add(MaxPooling2D(pool_size=(2,2)))

model.add(Dropout(0.5))
model.add(Flatten())
model.add(Dense(num_classes, activation='softmax'))
```

Step 6. Compilation

Compilation is performed before training the model. We use model.compile() method to initiate the training process in sequential approach by configuring the learning process. It receives three arguments-

Loss: Loss function helps in evaluating how well our model is performing on the given data by analyzing the actual label and predicted label during forward propagation. There are two category of loss function based on regression and classification problem. Since we are focusing on classification problem in our example, we will use Categorical_crossentropy as the loss function.

It is a popular classification loss function, which is used for multi-class classification problem where the number of output nodes is equals to the number of classes.

Optimizer: An optimizer helps in gradually decreasing the error in the loss function. It minimizes the objective (or loss) function by tuning the hyperparameters such as weights, biases, learning rate etc. in a neural network to produce slightly improved and faster results. These parameters are modified using optimizers, which updates the model parameters based on the loss function during each iteration of backpropagation. Gradient Descent, Stochastic gradient Descent, Adam, RMSprop, Adagrad are some examples of popular optimizers available in keras.

Metrics: The neural network evaluates the training, validation and test data on the list of metrics supplied by this parameter.

Figure 19.

```
import keras
# opt_rms = keras.optimizers.rmsprop(lr=0.001,decay=1e-6)
model.compile(loss='categorical_crossentropy', optimizer= 'adam',
              metrics=['accuracy'])
```

Step 7. Callbacks

A set of functions applied during training a neural network in order to view the internal states and statistics of the model is known as callbacks. A list of parameters can be passes to the fit() method of the sequential or Model classes to initiate this functionality.

ModelCheckpoint: It is used to save the model after every epoch. We can save the weights of the best model (i.e. the model with minimum loss) by setting save_best_only to True.

EarlyStopping: It stops training the model when the monitored quantity has stopped improving for a 'patience' number of epochs.

reduce_lr: It reduces the learning rate when a metric stops improving during the training. Models often benefit from reducing the learning rate by a factor of 2-10 once learning stagnates. It reduces the learning rate when the monitored quantity has stopped improving for a 'patience' number of epochs by a quantity known as 'factor', where a new learning rate is given by the formula new_lr = lr * factor

Figure 20.

```
import os
save_dir = os.path.join(os.getcwd(), 'saved_models')
model_name = 'keras_cifar10_trained_model.h5'

from keras.callbacks import ModelCheckpoint, ReduceLROnPlateau, TensorBoard, EarlyStopping

checkpoints =ModelCheckpoint(filepath= save_dir+model_name, monitor='val_loss', verbose=0, save_best_only=True,
                             save_weights_only=False)
early_stopping = EarlyStopping(monitor='val_loss', patience=5, verbose=0)
reduce_lr = ReduceLROnPlateau(monitor='val_loss', factor=0.2, patience=5, min_lr=0.001)
```

Step 8. Training

The two forms of training exists in keras are:

Standard Training With no Augmentation

It uses Keras fit method for training a model. It does not work with batches of data a_dirnd the functionality for data augmentation is not provided by this function. This function is used when the datasets are not very challenging and thus not require any data augmentation.

Training with Augmented Data

It uses Keras fit generator method for training a model. It is used when the size of dataset is large and it is too big to fit into the memory when taken as a whole. It provides functionality for data augmentation thus solving the problem of overfitting.

Initiate the Train and Test Generators With Data Augmentation

Image data augmentation is a technique utilized to artificially create modified version of the training data by applying shift, flip, rotation, brightness, zoom functions etc. Keras provides this capability via the ImageDataGenerator class with the intension to improve the accuracy of the model and reduce overfitting. However, we do not apply any random transformation in validation and test set because they are used to evaluate the model.

We can use both fit or fit_generator method by setting data_augmentation equals to 'True' for training the model in our code. However, we would be using both fit and fit_generator to understand the real-world dataset problems.

Without Using Data Augmentation

Refer to Figure 21 for illustration.

Using Data Augmentation

Refer to Figure 22 for illustration.

Step 9. Evaluating the Model on Test set

No Augmentation

Refer to Figure 23 for illustration.

Figure 21.

```
from keras.preprocessing.image import ImageDataGenerator
epochs= 40
batch_size= 64
data_augmentation = False

if not data_augmentation:
    print('Not using data augmentation.')
    history= model.fit(x_train, y_train, batch_size = batch_size,
                                  validation_data=(x_test, y_test),
                                  epochs=epochs,
                                  shuffle=True,
                                  verbose=2, callbacks=[checkpoints])
Epoch 35/40
 - 27s - loss: 0.5207 - acc: 0.8820 - val_loss: 0.6356 - val_acc: 0.8567
Epoch 36/40
 - 27s - loss: 0.5137 - acc: 0.8850 - val_loss: 0.6593 - val_acc: 0.8488
Epoch 37/40
 - 27s - loss: 0.5197 - acc: 0.8813 - val_loss: 0.6410 - val_acc: 0.8487
Epoch 38/40
 - 27s - loss: 0.5117 - acc: 0.8858 - val_loss: 0.6636 - val_acc: 0.8487
Epoch 39/40
 - 27s - loss: 0.5110 - acc: 0.8872 - val_loss: 0.6483 - val_acc: 0.8553
Epoch 40/40
 - 27s - loss: 0.5069 - acc: 0.8891 - val_loss: 0.6343 - val_acc: 0.8589
```

Data Augmentation

The accuracy of the model on train and test set is 88.9% and 85.8% respectively in the basic architecture with no data augmentation whereas the accuracy of the model on train and test set is 82.3% and 83.9% respectively while applying real time data augmentation. It is observed that the overfitting problem is reduced after applying augmentation in same dataset.

Step 10. Plotting Loss and Accuracy

The cross entropy loss and accuracy of the model (no augmentation) is plotted using matplotlib.

Note: Splitting the Dataset into Train, Validation and Test set

We can alternately solve the given problem using validation set. The downloaded dataset comprises of train and test set having 50,000 and 10,000 images respectively. The train set can be divided into train (75%) and validation test (25%) leaving test set aside for final assessment of the model. A sample of data chosen for training/fitting the model is known as train set and a sample of data selected from training set for analyzing the performance of the model during hyper parameter tuning is known as validation set. An unbiased evaluation of a model (already trained on train images) is offered by validation set using this approach. Test set is kept separate from training and validation set, offering final assessment of complete model once the model is entirely trained.

Figure 22.

```
else:
    print('Using real-time data augmentation.')
    # This will do preprocessing and realtime data augmentation:
    datagen =  ImageDataGenerator(
        featurewise_center=False,  # set input mean to 0 over the dataset
        samplewise_center=False,  # set each sample mean to 0
        featurewise_std_normalization=False,  # divide inputs by std of the dataset
        samplewise_std_normalization=False,  # divide each input by its std
        zca_whitening=False,  # apply ZCA whitening
        zca_epsilon=1e-06,  # epsilon for ZCA whitening
        rotation_range=0,  # randomly rotate images in the range (degrees, 0 to 180)
        # randomly shift images horizontally (fraction of total width)
        width_shift_range=0.1,
        # randomly shift images vertically (fraction of total height)
        height_shift_range=0.1,
        shear_range=0.,  # set range for random shear
        zoom_range=0.,  # set range for random zoom
        channel_shift_range=0.,  # set range for random channel shifts
        # set mode for filling points outside the input boundaries
        fill_mode='nearest',
        cval=0.,  # value used for fill_mode = "constant"
        horizontal_flip=True,  # randomly flip images
        vertical_flip=False,  # randomly flip images
        # set rescaling factor (applied before any other transformation)
        rescale=None,
        # set function that will be applied on each input
        preprocessing_function=None,
        # image data format, either "channels_first" or "channels_last"
        data_format=None,
        # fraction of images reserved for validation (strictly between 0 and 1)
        validation_split=0.0)
    datagen.fit(x_train)

    # Fit the model on the batches generated by datagen.flow().
    history= model.fit_generator(datagen.flow(x_train, y_train, batch_size = batch_size),
                        steps_per_epoch=len(x_train) // batch_size,
                        epochs=epochs,
                        validation_data=(x_test, y_test),
                        validation_steps=x_test.shape[0] // batch_size,
                        verbose=2, callbacks=[checkpoints])

  - 40s - loss: 0.7026 - acc: 0.8110 - val_loss: 0.7372 - val_acc: 0.8090
Epoch 34/40
  - 39s - loss: 0.6973 - acc: 0.8104 - val_loss: 0.6470 - val_acc: 0.8320
Epoch 35/40
  - 39s - loss: 0.6896 - acc: 0.8149 - val_loss: 0.6792 - val_acc: 0.8235
Epoch 36/40
  - 38s - loss: 0.6876 - acc: 0.8148 - val_loss: 0.6513 - val_acc: 0.8345
Epoch 37/40
  - 37s - loss: 0.6850 - acc: 0.8182 - val_loss: 0.6328 - val_acc: 0.8356
Epoch 38/40
  - 39s - loss: 0.6737 - acc: 0.8211 - val_loss: 0.6754 - val_acc: 0.8303
Epoch 39/40
  - 39s - loss: 0.6737 - acc: 0.8207 - val_loss: 0.6381 - val_acc: 0.8390
Epoch 40/40
  - 38s - loss: 0.6702 - acc: 0.8233 - val_loss: 0.6355 - val_acc: 0.8398
```

Figure 23.

```
# evaluate model
scores = model.evaluate(x_test, y_test, verbose=1)
print('Test loss:', scores[0])
print('Test accuracy:', scores[1])


10000/10000 [==============================] - 2s 232us/step
Test loss: 0.634319428062439
Test accuracy: 0.8589
```

Figure 24.

```
# evaluate model
scores = model.evaluate(x_test, y_test, verbose=1)
print('Test loss:', scores[0])
print('Test accuracy:', scores[1])


10000/10000 [==============================] - 2s 236us/step
Test loss: 0.635534990310669
Test accuracy: 0.8398
```

Figure 25.

```
import keras
from matplotlib import pyplot as plt
plt.plot(history.history['acc'])
plt.plot(history.history['val_acc'])
plt.title('model accuracy')
plt.ylabel('accuracy')
plt.xlabel('epoch')
plt.legend(['train', 'val'], loc='upper left')
plt.show()
```

```
plt.plot(history.history['loss'])
plt.plot(history.history['val_loss'])
plt.title('model loss')
plt.ylabel('loss')
plt.xlabel('epoch')
plt.legend(['train', 'val'], loc='upper left')
plt.show()
```

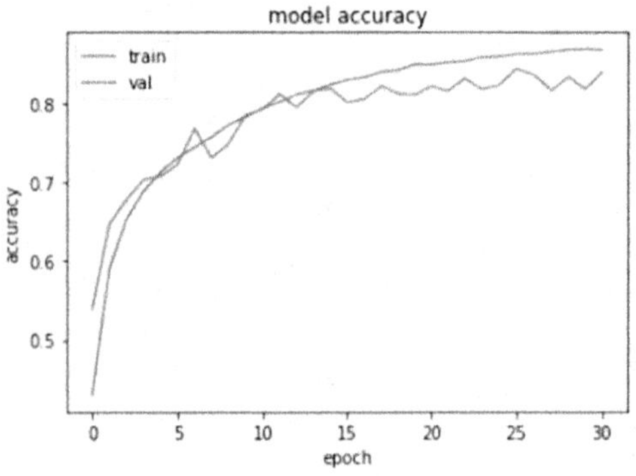

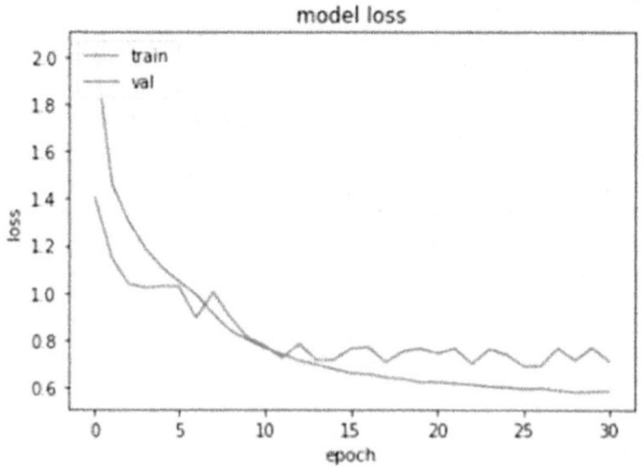

Figure 26.

```
from sklearn.model_selection import train_test_split
x_train, x_valid, y_train, y_valid = train_test_split(x_train, y_train, test_size=0.25, shuffle= True,  random_state=42)
print(x_train.shape, y_train.shape)
print(x_valid.shape, y_valid.shape)
print(x_test.shape, y_test.shape)

(37500, 32, 32, 3) (37500, 10)
(12500, 32, 32, 3) (12500, 10)
(10000, 32, 32, 3) (10000, 10)
```

Number of images after splitting of the dataset is given below:

Training set= 37500, Validation set= 12500, Testing set= 10000

PRE-TRAINED MODELS AVAILABLE WITH KERAS API

A model that is trained on a large benchmark dataset to solve a problem similar to the one that we want to solve is known as pre-trained model. It is a common practice to import these pre-trained model that are already trained on very large standard datasets due to the unavailability of computational resources for training a model from scratch that could take days or even months to finish training. A list of such pre-trained models based on deep convolutional neural networks (DCNN) available within keras library are listed in Figure 27.

Figure 27. Pre-trained models available in Keras (Chollet, 2015)

- Xception
- VGG16
- VGG19
- ResNet, ResNetV2, ResNeXt
- InceptionV3
- InceptionResNetV2
- MobileNet
- MobileNetV2
- DenseNet
- NASNet

TRANSFER LEARNING WITH KERAS AND DEEP LEARNING

Instead of training a model from scratch (as done in previous sections), transfer learning can be effectively utilized to leverage a pre-trained model that has demonstrated state-of-the-art performance in object classification tasks. Popular models like VGG16 or 19, InceptionV3, ResNet50 etc. are available with keras application API that are trained on ImageNet dataset which comprises of 1.2 million images with 1000 general purpose image categories. We can directly download the weights of any chosen pre-trained model and use it to fine-tune our model. In general, there are three ways to fine tune the model.

Feature Extraction

The output layer of a pre-trained network predicts one of the objects out of the 1000 categories. In feature extraction mechanism, the output layer of the pre-trained model is replaced by a new layer with number of classes our model wants to predict thereby acting as a fixed feature extractor for the new data set. It is useful in cases where we have:

- Limited resources to train the model from scratch, and/or
- Unavailability of larger datasets, and/or
- Dataset used to train the pre-trained model is similar to the one we are using to solve our problem.

Training the Entire Model Using Architecture of the Pre-Trained Model

The architecture of the pre-trained model is utilized to train the model from scratch in our dataset by randomly initializing all the weights. It is useful in cases when we have:

- A lot of computational power to train the model from scratch and
- Availability of larger datasets.

Training Some Layers While Freezing Others

Another way to use a pre-trained model is to train is partially. Low level layers of a network represents general features such as horizontal lines, vertical lines, curves, etc. while high level features represents more specific features. We can retrain only the higher layers of the network by freezing low-level layers whose weights do not change during training using this approach.

STEPS TO PERFORM TRANSFER LEARNING IN KERAS

We have already trained a model using sequential approach in the previous section of this chapter. Now, we will try to improve the accuracy of the model using transfer learning in Keras. The steps required to be followed are given below:

Step 1. Load the Necessary Libraries

Figure 28.

```
from tensorflow.keras.applications.resnet50 import ResNet50, preprocess_input
import tensorflow.keras as keras
from tensorflow.keras import models
from tensorflow.keras import layers
from tensorflow.keras import optimizers
import tensorflow as tf
from keras.utils import np_utils
from keras.models import load_model
from keras.datasets import cifar10
from keras.preprocessing import image
import numpy as np
import matplotlib.pyplot as plt
from PIL import Image
import cv2
```

Step 2. Load the Pre-Trained Model

The ResNet50 model is chosen in this example for the task of object classification in CIFAR dataset. In this step, we import ResNet50 model from keras.applications API. Since ResNet is trained on ImageNet dataset which comprises of 1000 different category of objects, we set *'include_top = False'*. It removes the fully connected layers of the pre-trained network towards the end.

Figure 29.

```
# Model creation
conv_base = ResNet50(weights='imagenet', include_top=False, input_shape=(200, 200, 3))

import numpy as np
from keras.datasets import cifar10

(X_train, Y_train), (X_test, Y_test) = cifar10.load_data()
print(X_train.shape, Y_train.shape)
print(X_test.shape, Y_test.shape)

Downloading data from https://www.cs.toronto.edu/~kriz/cifar-10-python.tar.gz
170500096/170498071 [==============================] - 6s 0us/step
(50000, 32, 32, 3) (50000, 1)
(10000, 32, 32, 3) (10000, 1)

x_train=X_train.astype("float32")
x_train = (x_train - x_train.mean(axis=0)) / (x_train.std(axis=0))
x_test=X_test.astype("float32")
x_test = (x_test - x_test.mean(axis=0)) / (x_test.std(axis=0))

num_classes=10
from keras import utils as np_utils
y_train = np_utils.to_categorical(Y_train, num_classes)
y_test = np_utils.to_categorical(Y_test, num_classes)
```

Step 3. Fine-Tuning the Model

Now, we add two fully connected layers followed by softmax layer towards the end of the ResNet architecture, which classifies the object into 10 categories instead of 1000. To begin with, the input image of Cifar10 needs to be scale up three times before we can pass it through the ResNet layers. Now, the output of the ResNet layer is taken, flattened and passed through two dense layers (with 128 and 64 neurons respectively). After training the model for only 5 epochs, we achieve the accuracy of 98% which is higher than creating a model from scratch as described in previous section.

Figure 30.

```
model = models.Sequential()
model.add(layers.UpSampling2D((2,2)))
model.add(layers.UpSampling2D((2,2)))
model.add(layers.UpSampling2D((2,2)))
model.add(conv_base)
model.add(layers.Flatten())
model.add(layers.BatchNormalization())
model.add(layers.Dense(128, activation='relu'))
model.add(layers.Dropout(0.5))
model.add(layers.BatchNormalization())
model.add(layers.Dense(64, activation='relu'))
model.add(layers.Dropout(0.5))
model.add(layers.BatchNormalization())
model.add(layers.Dense(10, activation='softmax'))

model.compile(optimizer=optimizers.RMSprop(lr=2e-5), loss='binary_crossentropy', metrics=['acc'])

history = model.fit(x_train, y_train, epochs=5, batch_size=20, validation_data=(x_test, y_test))
```

```
Epoch 1/5
50000/50000 [==============================] - 1889s 38ms/sample - loss: 0.2429 - acc: 0.9142 - val_loss: 0.1090 - val_acc: 0.9601
Epoch 2/5
50000/50000 [==============================] - 1874s 37ms/sample - loss: 0.1574 - acc: 0.9434 - val_loss: 0.0720 - val_acc: 0.9756
Epoch 3/5
50000/50000 [==============================] - 1874s 37ms/sample - loss: 0.1197 - acc: 0.9589 - val_loss: 0.0509 - val_acc: 0.9831
Epoch 4/5
50000/50000 [==============================] - 1868s 37ms/sample - loss: 0.0941 - acc: 0.9694 - val_loss: 0.0417 - val_acc: 0.9865
Epoch 5/5
50000/50000 [==============================] - 1875s 38ms/sample - loss: 0.0756 - acc: 0.9765 - val_loss: 0.0395 - val_acc: 0.9868
```

Step 4. Evaluating the Model

It can be clearly observed that test accuracy is tremendously improved from **85.8% to 98.6%** by using transfer learning in the same dataset.

Figure 31.

```
model.evaluate(x_test, y_test)
```

```
10000/10000 [==============================] - 92s 9ms/sample - loss: 0.0395 - acc: 0.9868
[0.039482792516052724, 0.9867798]
```

Step 5. Plotting the Loss and Accuracy

Figure 32.

```
history_dict = history.history
loss_values = history_dict['loss']
val_loss_values = history_dict['val_loss']
epochs = range(1, len(loss_values) + 1)
plt.figure(figsize=(14, 4))
plt.subplot(1,2,1)
plt.plot(epochs, loss_values, 'bo', label='Training Loss')
plt.plot(epochs, val_loss_values, 'b', label='Validation Loss')
plt.title('Training and Validation Loss')
plt.xlabel('Epochs')
plt.ylabel('Loss')
plt.legend()
acc = history_dict['acc']
val_acc = history_dict['val_acc']
epochs = range(1, len(loss_values) + 1)
plt.subplot(1,2,2)
plt.plot(epochs, acc, 'bo', label='Training Accuracy', c='orange')
plt.plot(epochs, val_acc, 'b', label='Validation Accuracy', c='orange')
plt.title('Training and Validation Accuracy')
plt.xlabel('Epochs')
plt.ylabel('Accuracy')
plt.legend()
```

Figure 33.

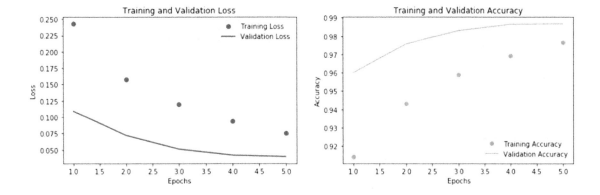

TENSORFLOW VS. KERAS

TensorFlow and Keras both are framework in data science domain which included different libraries and inbuilt packages (Figure 1). TensorFlow is open source framework that is used basically in machine learning algorithm while Keras is neural network library written in python that work on top of TensorFlow. Keras is more user friendly, easy to use and easy to extend for debug and use. Keras provide more abstraction where TensorFlow is more flexible to modification. In terms of performance, keras is comparatively slower than Tensorflow.

REFERENCES

Abhigoku. (2018). *Activation functions and its Types in Artificial Neural network*. Retrieved January 11, 2020, from https://medium.com/@abhigoku10/activation-functions-and-its-types-in-artifical-neural-network-14511f3080a8

Bishop, C. M. (2006). *Pattern recognition and machine learning*. Springer.

Chansung, P. (2018). *CIFAR-10 Image Classification in TensorFlow*. Retrieved September 7, 2019, from https://towardsdatascience.com/cifar-10-image-classification-in-tensorflow-5b501f7dc77c

Chollet, F. (2015). *Keras documentation*. Retrieved August 28, 2019, from https://keras.io/why-use-keras/

Goodfellow, I., Bengio, Y., & Courville, A. (2016). *Deep learning*. MIT Press.

Kaggle. (n.d.). Retrieved September 10, 2019, from https://www.kaggle.com/c/cifar-10

Krizhevsky, A., Nair, V., & Hinton, G. (2014). *The cifar-10 dataset*. http://www.cs.toronto.edu/kriz/cifar.html

Pokharna, H. (2016). *The best explanation of Convolutional Neural Networks on the Internet!* Retrieved August 12, 2019, from https://medium.com/technologymadeeasy/the-best-explanation-of-convolutional-neural-networks-on-the-internet-fbb8b1ad5df8

Rosenblatt, F. (1958). The perceptron: A probabilistic model for information storage and organization in the brain. *Psychological Review*, *65*(6), 386–408. doi:10.1037/h0042519 PMID:13602029

Rumelhart, D. E., Hinton, G. E., & Williams, R. J. (1986). Learning representations by back-propagating errors. *Nature, 323*(6088), 533-536.

Russell, S. J., & Norvig, P. (2016). *Artificial intelligence: a modern approach*. Malaysia: Pearson Education Limited.

Werbos, P. J. (1990). Backpropagation through time: What it does and how to do it. *Proceedings of the IEEE*, *78*(10), 1550–1560. doi:10.1109/5.58337

Chapter 3
Deep Learning With PyTorch

Anmol Chaudhary
Government Engineering College, Ajmer, India

Jyoti Gajrani
Malviya National Institute of Technology, India

Kuldeep Singh Chouhan
Government Engineering College, Ajmer, India

Bhavna Sharma
JECRC University, Jaipur, India

ABSTRACT

In the last decade, deep learning has seen exponential growth due to rise in computational power as a result of graphics processing units (GPUs) and a large amount of data due to the democratization of the internet and smartphones. This chapter aims to throw light on both the theoretical aspects of deep learning and its practical aspects using PyTorch. The chapter primarily discusses new technologies using deep learning and PyTorch in detail. The chapter discusses the advantages of using PyTorch compared to other deep learning libraries. The chapter discusses some of the practical applications like image classification and machine translation. The chapter also discusses the various frameworks built with the help of PyTorch. PyTorch consists of various models that increases its flexibility and accessibility to a greater extent. As a result, many frameworks built on top of PyTorch are discussed in this chapter. The authors believe that this chapter will help readers in getting a better understanding of deep learning making neural networks using PyTorch.

INTRODUCTION

Deep learning is a field of Artificial Intelligence in which a large amount of data is used to train computers to accomplish tasks that cannot be done by simple programming algorithms. With the rise of computational power due to GPUs, which can perform significantly more number of calculations in parallel as compared to traditional CPUs; and the rise of data generated due to the internet in the last decade deep learning techniques have become highly successful to solve problems that were up till now unsolvable by computers.

Deep learning has enabled computers to comprehend and better understand human languages, to understand the content in images and even learn from the environment in a similar fashion that humans do. Traditional machine learning enables the computers to learn and predict from data but deep learning

DOI: 10.4018/978-1-7998-3095-5.ch003

takes it one step forward. Although the foundation of theory and mathematics behind deep learning has existed even long before computers existed but it has become a reality in the 2010s due to computers having enough computational power.

Deep learning has given rise to several new technological innovations like interactive chatbots, better and natural translations, face detection, classifying images for diseases etc.

The field of deep learning is moving at a rapidly fast rate. As per the Artificial Intelligence index 2018 annual report AI papers in Scopus have increased by 7 times since 1996. In the same period, CS papers increased by 5 times. (Shoham, Yoav, et al., 2018) Every few years or even every few months, new neural network architecture or a new deep learning model replaces the previous state of the art.

The same holds for deep learning frameworks. The most commonly used framework is Tensorflow (Abadi et al., 2016) that is developed by Google and launched in 2015. Other frameworks that are less commonly used are Caffe (Jia et al., 2014), MXNet (Apache MXNet, 2017), etc. The recent addition to this is PyTorch (Paszke et al., 2017).

PyTorch is an open-source, python-based deep learning framework developed and backed by Facebook AI Research with strong support for GPU accelerated computations of deep learning models. It is based on Torch, which is written in the Lua programming language (Ierusalimschy et al., 1996). Due to its dynamic nature of computation graphs and close integration with python, it is gaining a lot of attention in the research community.

The pythonic nature of PyTorch allows us to use native python code and other python libraries like Numpy (NumPY 2018) and Scipy (Jones, 2001) to easily integrate with PyTorch code as compared to other deep learning libraries where library-specific methods are used to execute the same task.

The dynamic nature of graphs allows PyTorch to build its deep learning applications to be executed at runtime, as compared to other popular deep learning frameworks that rely on static graphs that have to be built before running the model.

A computational graph is a directed graph in which the nodes correspond to operations or variables. Variables can feed their values into operations, and operations can feed their output into other operations. In this way, each node in the graph defines a function of the variables. The values fed into the nodes and come out of the nodes are called tensors, which is a multi-dimensional array. Hence, it comprises scalars, vectors, and matrices as well as tensors of a higher rank.

The dynamic nature of computation graphs allows the creation and execution of the graph at the same time. This allows easy debugging of a neural network. The ease of debugging becomes even more prominent as the size of the neural network model increases. The dynamic nature also allows for changing the graph at run time which is particularly helpful in sequence modeling where the size of inputs is different. However, dynamic computational graphs do not offer optimization of computations nor static analysis which static computational graphs offer.

This has allowed deep learning researchers and practitioners to quickly create and evaluate new neural network architecture and approaches easily rather than waiting for the entire model to compile and run.

You might have also heard the term machine learning, sometimes even used interchangeably with deep learning. The two terms are although a subset of AI and try to achieve a similar task of making machines intelligent is quite different.

In machine learning, the engineer has to first create numerous features specific to the problem and then extract those features from the data. These features are then fed to a machine learning algorithm. This technique is called feature extraction. Where as in deep learning there is no need for feature extraction. In deep learning, a large amount of labeled data is provided to the neural network architecture and it can extract relevant information to perform the given task.

For example, in the case of breast cancer detection, the engineer needs to extract specific features in the image and use those features to train a classifier, whereas in deep learning they just need to provide the labeled image.

Comparison with State-of-the-Art

Ketkar, Nikhil. "Introduction to PyTorch." (Ketkar et al., 2017) discusses only the basics of PyTorch library methods along with a brief introduction of PyTorch with no focus on practical applications.

The authors of this chapter discuss not only the basic methods and features of PyTorch but also explains how deep learning works by discussing the mathematical expressions behind the algorithms. The authors explain PyTorch with real-life examples. The chapter in overall is a complete discussion of deep learning using PyTorch that will be insightful to those who are just starting with deep learning but also those who already have some previous knowledge on the topic.

PyTorch: An imperative style, high-performance deep learning library (Paszke et al., 2019) discusses in detail the architecture and ideology of PyTorch. The paper discusses the low level inner workings of PyTorch along with benchmarks which might be too much details for a beginner. Similarly it ignores the concepts of deep learning, hence not suitable for beginners.

Automatic differentiation in PyTorch (Paszke et al., 2017) is the original paper published with PyTorch that discusses the automatic differentiation module of PyTorch. *Introduction to PyTorch, Tensors, and Tensor Operations* (Mishra, 2019) discusses the basic operations on tensors in PyTorch.

PyTorch Vs Deep Learning Libraries

Over the past couple of years, several deep learning frameworks have emerged, each having its own set of methods to implement neural network models. Most of the major frameworks support GPU acceleration. Some even use optimized libraries for GPU support such as CUDA (Nvidia C.U.D.A, 2007).

Deep Learning libraries have abstracted the process of neural network creation so that the engineer can focus more on creating new neural network architectures rather than implement lower-level mathematical functions every time.

The frameworks also optimize the neural networks to be more efficient and less resource-intensive. This section discusses some of the deep learning frameworks and libraries.

Tensorflow

Tensorflow is the most widely used deep learning library that is developed by Google. Tensorflow allows the creation of neural network models by constructing static graphs that take data in runtime and are executed. The use of static graphs allows room for more optimizations. Tensorflow can train and infer deep learning models on CPU, GPU and TPU (Tensor processing unit), which is specialized hardware developed by Google to specifically train neural networks. Tensorflow model can also be inferred on low power devices like smartphones with the help of Tensorflow Lite. Tensorflow also supports high-level API like Keras (Chollet, 2015) which simplifies the process of creating simple models.

Creating advanced network architectures with Tensorflow using lower-level API is difficult and static graphs make it more difficult to code a neural network.

Advantages
- ○ Better support and documentation.
- ○ Availability of Tensorboard with makes it easier to visualize the training loss and accuracy.
- ○ High demand in industry due to better support.

Disadvantages
- ○ Poor performance as compared to MXNet and PyTorch.
- ○ No support for dynamic computational graphs.
- ○ Difficult learning curve.

MXNet

MXNet is a deep learning framework that is designed to be fast, flexible and scalable. To ease the process of making neural networks, MXNet allows combined use of both symbolic and imperative programming. MXNet can support multiple GPUs to train models, making it fast and also scalable. MxNet auto parallelize all operations using a dynamic dependency scheduler.

Advantages
- ○ Good performance.
- ○ Easily scalable.
- ○ Trained models can be run on any device.

Disadvantages
- ○ Smaller support

PyTorch

PyTorch is written in C++ and Python and uses optimized libraries from Nvidia like cuDNN (Chetlur, 2014) and NCCL (Nvidia, 2017) making it optimized to Create neural networks. The dynamic nature of computational graphs helps in sequence modeling tasks and simplifies the process of developing new models without much effort. Due to the above reasons and its close integration with python and other data science libraries like Numpy and Scipy, PyTorch has become a go-to language in the research community.

Advantages
- ○ Easy learning curve due to Dynamic computational graphs.
- ○ Models can be easily created using traditional Object Oriented Programming Paradigm.
- ○ Can be integrated with other Python libraries easily.

Disadvantages
- ○ It is not as good as other libraries to create production ready applications.
- ○ Less support as its not widely used.

CNTK (Seide et al., 2016)

The Microsoft Cognitive Toolkit was previously known as CNTK. It is an open source library developed by Microsoft research. CNTK consists of both a low level API that is beneficial for the research community to develop new neural network architectures, and a high level API that is beneficial to produce production ready applications.

CNTK can also be used with C# and Java to make it easy to develop apps that uses deep learning.

Advantages
- ○ Good performance and scalable.
- ○ Efficient resource management.
- ○ Good for both research and production.

Disadvantages
- ○ Small community and low support.

Caffe (Jia et al., 2014)

Caffe is another popular deep learning library that has now been merged with PyTorch. It is implemented in C++ with interface on Python. The second version of Caffe called Caffe2 was highly production ready. It is used to deploy mobile and large scale applications.

Advantages
- ○ Optimized implementation of several neural network architectures.
- ○ Scalable and also light weight to work on mobile devices.

Disadvantages
- ○ Less frequently optimized and updated as it is not supported by any large organization.

PyTorch Basics

In this section, the authors discuss some basics of PyTorch. How PyTorch can be used as an alternative to Numpy for creating Ndarrays (called Tensors). How PyTorch creates computational graphs using Autograd package, which is essential for neural network training.

The authors also discuss some optimization methods that are essential for efficient and fast training of neural networks and their implementation in PyTorch.

torch.Tensor Package

The torch.Tensor package is used to create multi-dimensional matrices called 'tensors'. Unlike its counterpart, NumPy; PyTorch can initialize these tensors on a CPU as well as on a GPU. The benefit is that deep learning at its base is just a huge number of operations on tensors and manipulation of data in tensors. This means that essentially, by storing tensors on a GPU a significantly more number of calculations can be performed due to high parallelism.

Table 1. An overview of the differences between deep learning frameworks

Framework	Initial Release	Software Licence	Open Source	Core Language	Interface language	CUDA support	Automatic differentiation	Pretrained models
Tensorflow	2015	Apache 2.0	yes	C++, Python	Python, C++, JavaScript, Java, Go, R, Julia	yes	Yes, with static computational graphs	yes
MXNet	2015	Apache 2.0	yes	C++	C++, Python, Julia, JavaScript, Go, R, Scala, Perl	yes	yes	yes
Pytorch	2016	BSD	yes	C, C++, Python	Python, C++	yes	Yes, with dynamic computational graphs	yes
Caffe	2013	BSD	yes	C++	Python, C++, Matlab	yes	yes	yes
CNTK	2016	MIT licence	yes	C++	Python, C#, Java	yes	yes	yes

Below some of these operations are discussed:

First import torch:

>>>import torch

torch.tensor(list object)

This creates a tensor right from data. The data is given in the form of python list.

Example:
>>> torch.tensor(((4.3, 3.2), (3.2,7.6)))
tensor(((4.3000, 3.2000),
(3.2000, 7.6000)))

torch.zeros(dimension)

This creates a tensor populated with zeros of a given dimension.

Example:
>>> torch.zeros(2, 3, 4)
tensor(((((0., 0., 0., 0.),
(0., 0., 0., 0.),
(0., 0., 0., 0.)),
((0., 0., 0., 0.),

(0., 0., 0., 0.),
(0., 0., 0., 0.))))

torch.ones(dimension)

This creates a tensor populated with ones of a given dimension.

Example:
>>> torch.ones(2, 3)
tensor(((1., 1., 1.),
(1., 1., 1.)))

torch.rand(dimension)

This creates a tensor populated with random digits of given dimension.

Example:
>>> torch.rand(2, 3)
tensor((((0.3273, 0.1834, 0.5345),
(0.2946, 0.4208, 0.7635)))

The default data type of tensors is torch.float32, which is generally used in deep learning to store information without loss. To change the default data type, an extra parameter is passed as dtype=<data_type>

Example:
>>> torch.rand(2,3, dtype=torch.float64)
tensor((((0.3187, 0.7623, 0.3013),
(0.1027, 0.4982, 0.1452)), dtype=torch.float64)

<tensor>.size()

This is used to get the dimension of a declared tensor.

Example:
>>> x = torch.rand(2, 3)
>>> x.size()
torch.Size((2, 3))

Integration with NumPy

Conversion between NumPy and PyTorch tensors is shown below:

Converting Torch Tensor to NumPy ndarray

```
>>> x = torch.rand(2, 3)
>>> x
tensor(((0.2778, 0.0672, 0.2158),
(0.4721, 0.5770, 0.4593)))
>>> y = x.numpy()
>>> y
array(((0.27776885, 0.06715792, 0.21575862),
(0.47211725, 0.57698375, 0.45925605)), dtype=float32)
```

Converting NumPy ndarray to Torch Tensor

```
>>> import torch
>>> import numpy as np
>>> x = np.random.rand(2, 3)
>>> x
array(((0.52806884, 0.18309049, 0.54891401),
(0.55006161, 0.09836883, 0.71446342)))
>>> y = torch.from_numpy(x)
>>> y
tensor(((0.5281, 0.1831, 0.5489),
(0.5501, 0.0984, 0.7145)), dtype=torch.float64)
```

Shifting Tensor from CPU to GPU

```
>>> import torch
>>> if torch.cuda.is_available(): #checks if cuda enabled gpu is available
... device = torch.device("cuda")
>>> x = torch.rand(2, 3, device=device)
>>> x
tensor(((0.9473, 0.4240, 0.4758),
(0.5120, 0.0520, 0.4360)), device='cuda:0') #directly initializing tensor in GPU
>>> y = torch.rand(2, 3)
>>> y = y.to(device) #shifting tensor from CPU to GPU
>>> y
tensor(((0.9082, 0.8258, 0.5843),
(0.8274, 0.1618, 0.6526)), device='cuda:0')
```

Computational Graphs and Autograd Package

The Autograd package in PyTorch is the backbone of the whole framework. It is responsible for calculating derivatives of tensors automatically using the chain rule. Autograd does this by creating computational graphs under the hood. These graphs are created on run time and can be different on each iteration depending on how the code is run.

To understand Autograd, first a neural network is discussed and later it is discussed how to train it.

Neural Network

A neural network is a type of mathematical algorithm that learns the patterns in data and can predict the output when shown new data on its own. The brain loosely inspired the design of a neural network.

Figure 1. A simple neural network (Fadja et al., 2018)

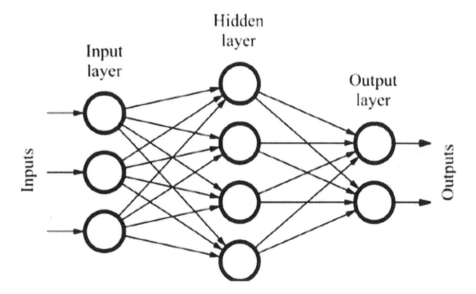

Each circle in figure 1 is called a node or neuron. The arrows connecting nodes of one layer to the nodes of another layer are called weights. These weights are the parameters that the neural network learns to predict the output.

A neural network has three types of layers: input, hidden, and output. The input layer takes in data. The output layer gives the predicted output. The number of nodes in the output layer determines the number of possible outcomes. The hidden layer is the intermediary layer that learns the complex functions. There can be several hidden layers depending on the size of the data.

In Figure 2, the value of a node is determined by the sum of values of previous nodes multiplied by its corresponding weight.

$$z = \Sigma w_i * x_i + b \, . \, a{=}f(z). \tag{1}$$

z is then passed through a non-linearity function f. also known as activation function, such as Relu, sigmoid, or softmax, so that the neural network can learn complex functions and not just linear functions.

Figure 2. A single node of a neural network (CS231n)

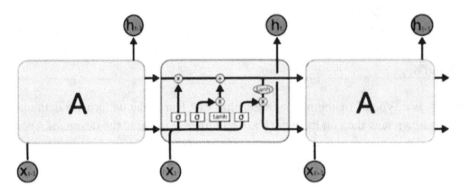

To put simply, a single node in the neural network acts as a simple logistic regression unit. Put together several of these units and the result is neural network learning more complex functions. Hence, more number of nodes and layers result in better learning, given enough data.

The bigger neural network does not always mean better prediction. If a large neural network architecture is given a small amount of data, then the result is overfitting - a condition in which the neural network learns the specific features of training data rather than general features that help in classifying new cases. The result is, neural networks performing very well on training data and giving very high accuracy but performing very poorly on test data that it was not trained, giving wrong predictions.

At the output layer, loss is calculated by comparing the actual output in the dataset with the predicted output of the neural network.

The process described above is called forward propagation. In short, forward propagation is just multiplying weights with node values to calculate the value of nodes further in the networks. The flow of direction is forward.

But how does a neural network learn? How are these "weights" updated and set to optimal values so that our neural network can predict the correct output? The answer is **backpropagation**.

Backpropagation (Rumelhart et al., 1988) (Karpathy)

Backpropagation is a process by which a neural network learns to output the desired result. It works by reducing the loss using the principle of gradient descent. The error (loss) is backtracked through the network by taking derivatives of error with respect to the weights of different layers. The weights are updated by subtracting weight derivative from previous weight values.

This cycle of forward propagation, calculating loss, backpropagation, and updating weights is an iterative process in which each of these steps is repeated several times. After several iterations, the weights reach an optimal value such that the loss is minimized. This results in the neural network outputting the correct output when it is shown new data.

Figure 3 shows loss with respect to single weight for the sake of simplicity. In reality, there are several weights (in order of thousands or millions), which cannot be projected onto a 2D or 3D graph.

Figure 3. Gradient Descent (gradient descent)

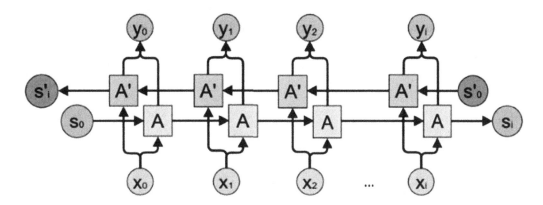

There is a local minima for which a value of weight minimizes the loss. This is achieved by taking a derivative of loss with respect to weight, $\dfrac{\partial loss}{\partial w}$. This is the slope of the curve in fig 3. By taking small steps along the slope the weight reaches an optimum local minima which reduces the loss.

$$w_{new} = w_{old} - \frac{\alpha * \partial loss}{\partial w}. \tag{2}$$

Here, α is the learning rate, which is the size of one step to be taken while going down the slope. α is a hyperparameter - a parameter that is determined by the trial and error process. If α is too small, the training time increases, as reaching the minima takes a lot of steps. On the other hand, too large learning rates result in overshooting and optimum value is never achieved.

Figure 4. Forward and Backward propagation expanded view graph (CS224n)

Stochastic Gradient Descent

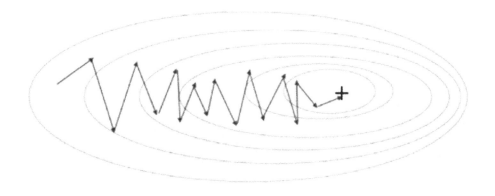

In figure 4, the Blue arrows are called error signals, because they are derivatives of error, e with respect to other values in the graph.

The derivative of error calculated with respect to other values is done through chain rule.

Figure 5 shows how $\dfrac{\partial e}{\partial b}$ is calculated:

$$\frac{\partial e}{\partial w} = \frac{\dfrac{\dfrac{\dfrac{\dfrac{\partial e}{\partial a} * \partial a}{\partial z} * \partial z}{\partial wx} * \partial wx}{\partial w}}{}. \tag{3}$$

Figure 5. Chain Rule in backpropagation (CS224n)

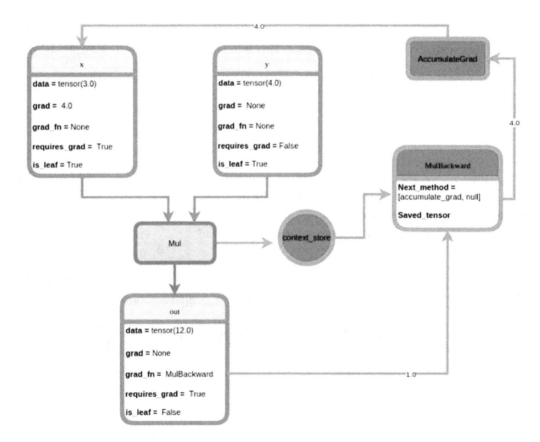

Now let's come back to the original question: What is a computational graph and how does autograd create these computational graphs?

A computational graph is a map or graph of all the calculations that will be performed in the process of training a neural network. As PyTorch creates dynamic graphs, these graphs are initialized and run at runtime as compared to static graphs in which the user lays out the graph and at run time data is passed in the already defined graph and run.

First initialize two tensors, as seen in Table 2. For the sake of simplicity, take them as scaler tensors.

Table 2. Creating Computational Graph

```
x = torch.tensor(3.0)
y = torch.tensor(4.0)
Out = x.mul(y)
```

These two tensors are multiplied and the output is saved in another tensor called out:

Figure 6. Computational graph

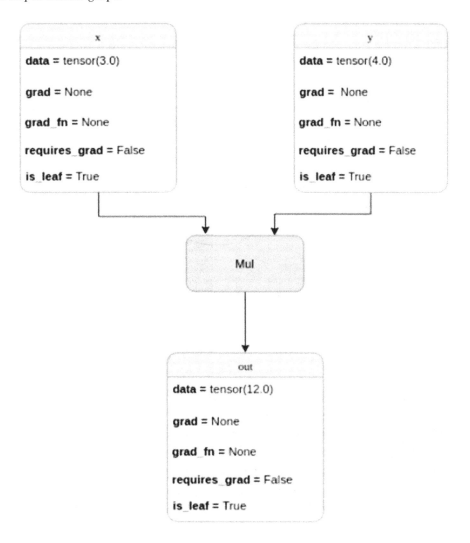

Every tensor object has attributes: data, grad, grad_fn, requires_grad, is_leaf.

Data attribute stores the data of tensor, requires_grad specifies if the gradient is to be calculated in the backward graph, grad_fn stores the backward propagation function, grad stores the gradient value passed in backpropagation, is_leaf specifies if a node in the graph a leaf or is an intermediary node.

In figure 6, both x.requires_grad and y.requires_grad are set to False. Therefore out.requires_grad is False too. Since requires_grad is False in all three tensors, no backward graph is created, and grad and grad_fn are None.

If even one of the tensors' requires_grad attributes is set to True, then autograd creates a backward graph in the background and starts tracking derivatives in backward graph.

x and y are initialized as scalar tensors with x.requires_grad as True as seen in table 3:

Table 3. code to initiate backward computational graph

```
x = torch.tensor(3.0, requires_grad=True)
y = torch.tensor(4.0)
Z = x.mul(y)
z.backward()
```

Figure 7. Backward Computational Graph

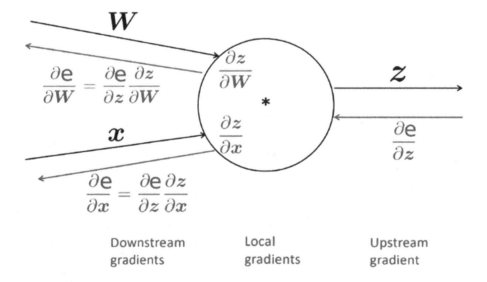

In the above graph, x.required_grad is set to True, therefore, in this case, a backward graph is created and the derivative of output tensor is calculated with respect to x by using the chain rule. In Figure 7, the green-colored nodes are part of the backward graph. Since x.requires_grad is True, therefore, out. requires_grad will also be True.

Context_store may store some intermediary values required to calculate the gradient in case of bigger and complex computational graphs and pass it to the saved_tensor of MulBackward. Next_method of MulBackward points out to the method where gradient would be passed.

Here for x gradient is passed to AccumulateGrad. Since y.requires_grad is set to False, Next_method for y is set to Null.

Note that since the backward graph is created in the background, the code for it is written in C++, and no Class like MulBackward, AccumulateGrad or attributes in backward graph exist in python code. They are for representational purposes.

Optimization Package

An optimization algorithm is an algorithm that minimizes the loss function and brings the loss down by updating the parameters. The simplest optimization algorithm- **Gradient descent** has already been discussed in the previous section. But the problem with gradient descent is that it considers every single example in the dataset to compute one single step of parameter updation. A typical deep learning data-set contains examples in the order of millions. Thus gradient descent considers all of these millions of examples to take just one step down the weight-loss curve. This leads to very slow training of neural networks or may even lead to memory overflow and terminate without updating the parameters.

But what if one decides to take a single example or a small batch of examples to calculate one step of gradient descent? This is precisely what stochastic gradient descent (SGD) and mini-batch gradient descent do.

SGD takes a single example in the dataset and use it to compute loss by forward propagation, and update the parameters by backpropagation in order to reduce loss. Mini-batch gradient descent works in a similar manner, but rather than using a single example to take one step down the curve, it uses a small group of examples in the dataset.

In general, mini-batch gradient descent is used because a GPU is good in doing parallel computations and PyTorch (and other deep learning frameworks) can exploit the parallel computation to use several examples at once for computing steps of gradient descent.

Table 4. shows how to use SGD in PyTorch:

Table 4. Stochastic Gradient Descent

```
optimizer = optim.SGD(model.parameters(), lr=0.01)
for input, target in batch_iter(dataset, batch_size):
optimizer.zero_grad()
output = model(input)
loss = loss_fn(output, target)
loss.backward()
optimizer.step()
```

A user-defined function batch_iter divides the dataset into several batches of given batch_size and returns every batch generated. The loop iterates over every batch, calculates loss, uses gradient descent to update parameter, and reduces loss. Each batch contributes to one step of gradient descent. For SGD, batch_size is 1. Typically batch_size is 32 to 128 depending on the memory size of the machine used.

optimizer.zero_grad() resets the grad values to zero for the new grad value. optimizer.step() takes updates the parameters.

SGD and mini-batch gradient descent approach have solved memory overflow and slow step updation problem. But a new problem arises in these optimization algorithms. The parameters, rather than reaching closer to local minima with every step of optimization, oscillates. Some batch rather than reducing loss may increase loss, and others may reduce loss as expected. The result is, parameters converging down to local minima in a zig-zag motion. This leads to slow training.

Figure 8. Contour graph showing how parameters converge to local minima in SGD. '+' is the local minima

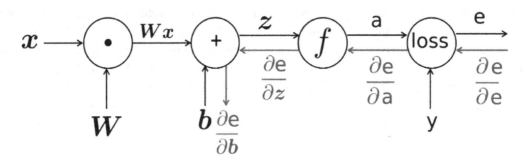

To solve this problem of parameter converging to local minima in an inefficient zig-zag manner, there are several optimization algorithms. These algorithms make the parameter convergence smoother. The next subsections discuss some of the important ones.

Momentum

In this approach, oscillations in wrong directions are smoothed and make the parameters converge in the right direction by using past gradients. In figure 8, where there are only two directions (for the sake of simplicity), this can be thought of like a car moving in a zig-zag motion to its destination. Momentum approach reduces the velocity in the y-direction and increases in the x-direction, so that the motion becomes more smooth and the destination is reached faster.

$$V = \beta V + (1 - \beta)dW. \tag{4}$$

$$W = W - \alpha V. \tag{5}$$

β is also a hyperparameter. Generally, the value of β is 0.9
   In PyTorch:

Table 5. defining an Optimizer in PyTorch

Optimizer=torch.optim.SGD(model.parameters(), lr=0.01, momentum=0.9)

Adam

Adam is one of the most efficient and most widely used optimization algorithm. Adam combines the approach of both RMS prop and momentum.

$$V_{dW} = \frac{\beta_1 V_{dw} + (1 - \beta_1) dW}{} \quad S_{dw} = \beta_2 S_{dW} + (1 - \beta_2) \quad W = W - \alpha \frac{V_{dW}}{\sqrt{}} \ldots \text{ In PyTorch:} \tag{6}$$

Table 6. Defining Adam Optimizer

Optimizer = torch.optim.Adam(params, lr=0.001, betas=(0.9, 0.999), eps=1e-08, weight_decay=0, amsgrad=**False**)

Practical Applications

In this section, the authors discuss some practical applications of deep learning in the real world. The authors will also show how to create a very simple image and language models using PyTorch.

Image Processing and Deep Learning in Medical Image Understanding (Litjens et al., 2017)

Deep Learning has proved to be immensely helpful in image analysis. Image analysis using Deep Learning is playing a key role in self-driving cars, face recognition systems, mining industry, survey for natural resources, traffic management, etc. One of the key industries where image analysis using deep learning is proving to be extremely useful in the medical industry.

Deep learning has been able to correctly classify tumors, Alzheimer's by analyzing x-ray scans of patients with better accuracy than a panel of doctors.

In the machine learning era, medical images were analyzed and classified using feature engineering. The machine learning engineer needed to have a good understanding of the classifying task. For example, in the case of brain tumor scan analysis, the engineer needed to have the knowledge and a good understanding to classify the scan as a tumor as well as a trained doctor. The engineer would then manually design and extract some key features that helped in classification and feed them to a machine learning classifier to predict if the patient has a brain tumor or not. Even then, after developing several features, machine learning algorithms did not perform as well.

In the deep learning era; medical image analysis, more generally image analysis tasks, are done with the help of a neural network architecture called the Convolutional Neural Network (CNN).

Convolutional Neural Network (CNN) (LeCun et al., 1988)

A fundamental and intuitive idea on which a convolutional neural network operates is edge detection and pattern recognition by using convolutional operations. A convolutional operation is a mathematical operation on two functions to determine how these two functions affect the other. In the case of image

Figure 9. 2D Convolution operation between source image and kernel (Goodfellow et al., 2016)

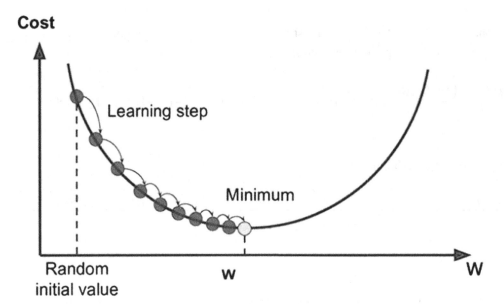

analysis, these two functions are the source image tensor and the filter (also called kernel) tensor. The result generated is called a feature map.

Figure 9 depicts how a convolutional operation is applied between an image and a kernel to create a feature map. The kernel slides through the image, and the corresponding pixel value of the kernel is multiplied with the corresponding pixel value of the image in a boundary of kernel size. These values are then added together to create a single value of the feature map. The kernel strides through all the windows, and this process is repeated for all windows. This results in the formation of the feature map.

Figure 10. Detecting different edges

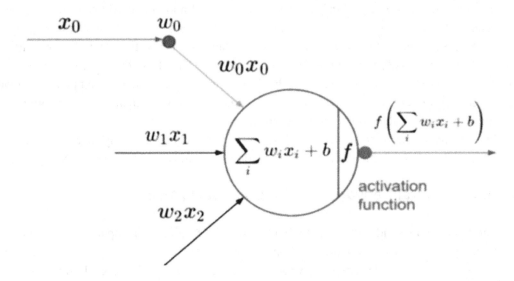

In figure 10, the first filter can detect vertical edges, and the other one detects horizontal edges.

There can be different filters to detect edges at different angles. If these filters are assigned as weights in the neural networks, then the neural network can learn these weights and identify edges at different angles. A combination of learning several filters helps in identifying patterns that are specific to a particular category of images.

This is essentially what a Convolutional Neural Network does. By learning several filters, it can identify certain patterns that are specific to a class of image and correctly identify it.

But, why is a CNN better than a simple feedforward neural network?

In a feedforward architecture, each pixel is fed as an input to the network. This leads to a considerable number of weights that the model has to learn. Consider an example of an image of resolution 28*28, which is the size of a single image in the MNIST dataset. Consider the hidden layer size of a single layer feed forward neural network to be h = 300. The number of weights to be trained would be (28*28)*300, which is 235,200 weights. Now in a CNN if there are 10 filters of size 6*6, then the number of weights would be 10*(6*6), which is 360 weights. This property of a CNN is called a **sparse connection** as all the input nodes do not interact with all the output nodes, thus leading to sparse interactions.

The small filter scans through the entire large image and detects edges in these small portions one by one, thus eventually scanning the whole image. This means that the same weights are shared among several inputs. This property is called **parameter sharing**.

These two properties help in making a CNN much more efficient for image analysis as compared to a vanilla feed forward neural network.

Padding

In a CNN, as the filter strides through the image, it encounters pixels several times, with most encounters towards the center of the image, and least in the corners. Thus if an object of interest is in the corner of the image then CNN may not be able to detect it as it was not trained well to consider corners.

To solve this problem, the image is padded with empty pixels so that the corner pixels are also encountered by a filter several times, and the CNN classifier is trained well to classify objects at the corner.

Stride

Stride is used to define how much the filter should shift every time during scanning. By default, stride is 1, which means that the filter will shift through either one row or column in every stride. A stride of 2 means that the filter will shift through two rows or columns.

Pooling

A convolutional neural network architecture typically involves a pooling layer that is used to generalize the patterns learned by the filters. Our classifier does not need to learn specific features of an image but rather general features to classify new unseen cases correctly too. Thus pooling helps in generalizing the classification task.

The most widely used form of pooling is called max pooling. In max-pooling, the maximum pixel value is chosen from a grid of pixels.

Transfer Learning (Pan et al., 2009)

In the real world, it is not always possible to train a model for image analysis from scratch due to a lack of data. A good classifier requires a dataset in the order of 10s of millions. Such large datasets are not easily available for every task. So how to train an image classifier? The answer is transfer learning.

Transfer Learning is a technique that became popular in 2012 with the imagenet competition. In this technique pre-trained models are used, that have been trained to perform some tasks and fine-tune them to train them to classify objects that need to be classified. This technique works well with small datasets.

How do pre-trained models produce good results? It was shown in the paper "Visualizing and understanding convolutional networks" (Zeiler et al., 2014), that the early layers in CNN models start identifying some fundamental patterns that are common in all types of objects. The first layer identifies lines and edges at various angles. The second layer stats is identifying some basic shapes like circles, gradients, and slightly complicated features. By the third layer, it starts identifying patterns of specific objects like tires, people, etc. This pattern recognition becomes more sophisticated and starts identifying objects of interest as the layers progress.

As lines and basic shapes are common to every object, one can use the early layers of a pre-trained model and train the further layers to our requirements using the small dataset.

Figure 11. Visualizing patterns detected by different layers of a CNN (Zeiler et al., 2014)

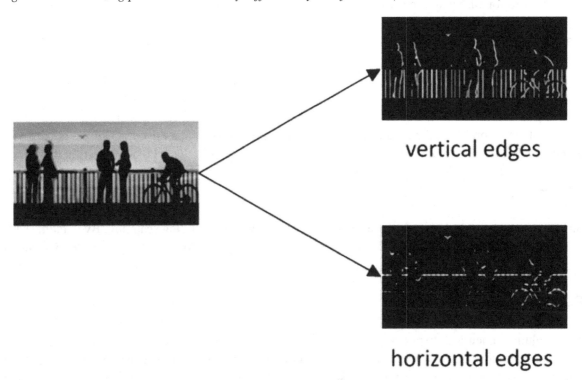

vertical edges

horizontal edges

Pneumonia Detection (Shouno et al., 2015)

Image classification has made a big impact in healthcare by detecting several health issues like cancer and alzheimer in patients early on and has very good promises in the future too. One such case is detection of Pneumonia from X-ray scans of chest.

Pneumonia is an inflammatory infection of the lungs caused by a bacteria, virus or fungi. It is a life threatening condition which generally affects children and old people. In severe cases the lungs are inflamed with fluid which results in problems in breathing.

According to the world health organization pneumonia results in deaths of 15 percent of children under the age of 5. It resulted in the deaths of almost 1 million children in 2017, especially in developing countries due to lack of medical practitioners and medical facilities. Deep learning provides a solution to detection of pneumonia using x ray scans of lungs and thus gives the chance of early detection of pneumonia.

Pneumonia can be easily be detected from chest x ray scans by training a Convolutional Neural Network on a labeled dataset of pneumonia.

Figure 12. sample image from dataset of chest x-rays

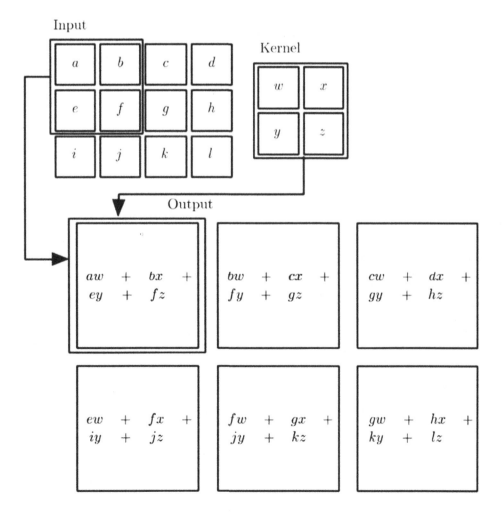

The dataset can be found on kaggle which contains labeled images of x-ray scans of chest.

Table 7. Preprocessing Dataset

```
batch_size = 32
data_dir = { 'train': '/chest_xray/test', 'test': '/chest_xray/test', 'valid': '/chest_xray/val'}
data_transforms = {
'train': transforms.Compose((
transforms.Resize((224, 224)),
transforms.CenterCrop(224),
transforms.RandomHorizontalFlip(), # randomly flip and rotate
transforms.RandomRotation(10),
transforms.ToTensor(),
transforms.Normalize((0.485, 0.456, 0.406), (0.229, 0.224, 0.225)),
)),
'test': transforms.Compose((
transforms.Resize((224,224)),
transforms.ToTensor(),
transforms.Normalize((0.485, 0.456, 0.406), (0.229, 0.224, 0.225)),
)),
'valid': transforms.Compose((
transforms.Resize((224,224)),
transforms.ToTensor(),
transforms.Normalize((0.485, 0.456, 0.406), (0.229, 0.224, 0.225)),
))
}
# Loading datasets with ImageFolder
data_set={
'train':torchvision.datasets.ImageFolder(data_dir('train'),data_transforms('train')),
'test':torchvision.datasets.ImageFolder(data_dir('test'),data_transforms('test')),
'valid':torchvision.datasets.ImageFolder(data_dir('valid'),data_transforms('valid')),
}
# Using the image datasets and the transforms, define the data loaders
data_loader={
'train': torch.utils.data.DataLoader(data_set('train'), batch_size=batch_size,shuffle=True),
'test': torch.utils.data.DataLoader(data_set('test'), batch_size=batch_size,shuffle=True),
'valid': torch.utils.data.DataLoader(data_set('test'), batch_size=batch_size,shuffle=True),
}
_ = data_set('valid').class_to_idx
cat_to_name = {_(i): i for i in list(_.keys())}
```

The given raw dataset cannot be used directly to train a model. The images can be of different sizes, and therefore, the first need to be cropped to a fixed size so that they can be fed to train the model. First, some data transformations are defined as seen in table 7 that will be applied to the train, test and validation set of images like resizing, cropping, and flipping randomly.

Then batches are created using torch.utils.data.DataLoader

Table 8. Defining a pre trained model for transfer learning

```
model = models.densenet121(pretrained=True) # using densenet121 and only retraining last layer.
for param in model.parameters():
param.requires_grad = True
model.classifier = nn.Sequential(OrderedDict((
('fcl1', nn.Linear(1024,256)),
('dp1', nn.Dropout(0.3)),
('r1', nn.ReLU()),
('fcl2', nn.Linear(256,32)),
('dp2', nn.Dropout(0.3)),
('r2', nn.ReLU()),
('fcl3', nn.Linear(32,2)),
('out', nn.LogSoftmax(dim=1)),
)))
```

PyTorch has various pre trained models saved. densenet121 model as seen in table 8 is used and it fine tuned to detect pneumonia. model.parameters() has all the trainable parameters of the model. By setting param.requires_grad = True all layers are first unfreezed and become trainable. In the train function, all other layers except the last are frozen for transfer learning.

A classifier is defined that is fully connected layers to classify the scans at the end.

Here if a CNN classifier would have been trained from scratch then the model would have needed a dataset much bigger than the current dataset to train the lower layers too. Using a pretrained model like densenet makes it possible to fine tune the higher layers only; in order to achieve the specific task, as the lower layers are already good at detecting basic patterns.

Table 9. Defining a train function

```
def train_function(model, train_loader, valid_loader, criterion, optimizer, scheduler=None,
train_on_gpu=False, n_epochs=30, save_file='model.pth'):
if train_on_gpu:
model.cuda()
for epoch in range(1, n_epochs + 1):
if epoch == n_epochs // 2:
model.load_state_dict(torch.load(save_file))
for param in model.features.parameters():
param.requires_grad = False
train_loss = 0.0
valid_loss = 0.0
if scheduler != None:
scheduler.step()
model.train()
for data, target in train_loader:
if train_on_gpu:
data, target = data.cuda(), target.cuda()
optimizer.zero_grad()
output = model(data)
loss = criterion(output, target)
loss.backward()
optimizer.step()
train_loss += loss.item() * data.size(0)
train_on_gpu = torch.cuda.is_available()
criterion = nn.NLLLoss()
optimizer = optim.Adadelta(model.parameters())
```

Natural Language Processing and Machine Translation (Collobert et al., 2011) (Jurafsky et al., 2000)

Another area where deep learning has impacted is language processing for computers. This has resulted in a better speech to text systems, intelligent agents like chatbots, more accurate translations. The techniques used for understanding natural language are also applied to generate music.

Before deep learning speech to text system did not perform well at all, chatbots were a bunch of if-else statements, hardcoded to understand specific sentences that were predefined using complex dialog trees, and translations were performed using statistical techniques that required feature engineering (called statistical machine translation or SMT). All these applications changed with deep learning and started performing well.

Recurrent Neural Network (RNN) (Mikolov et al., 2010)

Recurrent Neural Networks or RNN are used to keep track of a sequence of data like text, audio, etc. For example, a sentence is a sequence of words. The meaning contained in the sentence not just depends on a single word but the words before and after it.

In an RNN, all nodes in a layer are also connected to each other so that the sequence of words can be processed. These nodes in RNN are referred to as time steps.

Figure 13. A layer of RNN (Colah, 2015)

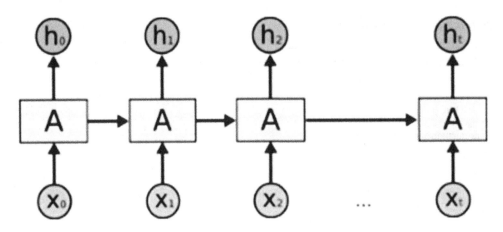

This architecture results in an output that depends on the previous sequence. But it only accounts for sequence in the forward direction.

Bi-Directional RNN

A bi-directional RNN accounts for the sequence in both forward and backward directions.

It is important because the meaning of a sentence or phrase can depend not only on what is before but also on what comes after. A bi-directional RNN accounts for this.

Long Short Term Memory Networks (LSTM) (Hochreiter et al., 1997)

A simple RNN does not work well for a big sequence as it forgets key information that was much earlier in the sequence.

To solve this, LSTM, RNN are used. LSTM, RNN are almost always used instead of the simple vanilla RNN as they produce very good results.

Vanilla RNNs make changes to existing information when they encounter new information, but an LSTM RNN does not make changes to the complete information but only a part of it. This way, the LSTM RNN can remember important information that was encountered long ago in the sequence.

An LSTM produces a cell state C along with a hidden state h. There are many gates that help in ordering information, what old information to be forgotten, what new information to be kept.

Figure 14. Bi-directional RNN (Colah, 2015)

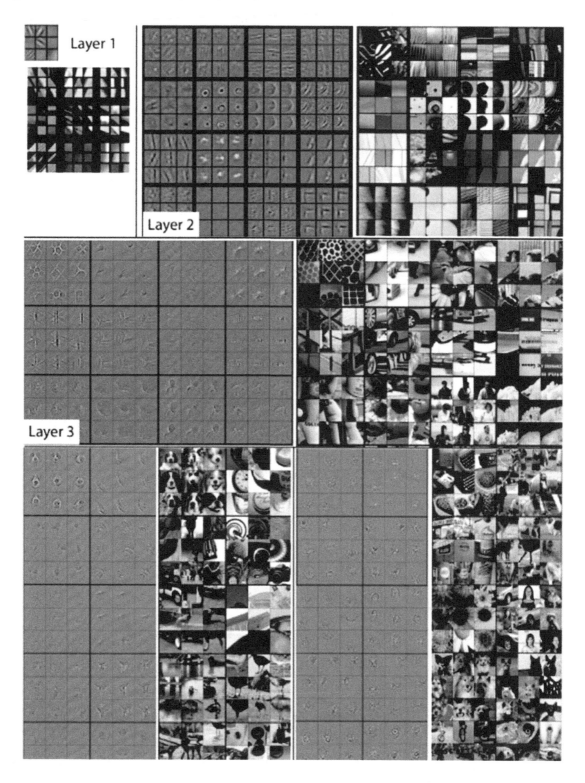

Figure 15. Architecture of LSTM RNN (Colah, 2015)

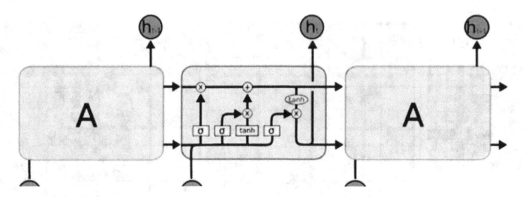

Forget Gate

The forget gate produces a value between 0 and 1 that is produced with previous cells hidden state h_{t-1} and the current input x_t. The value produced by the forget gate determines how much of the previous cell state C_{t-1} is to be kept.

$$f_t = \sigma\left(W_f x_t + U_f h_{t-1} + b_f\right). \tag{7}$$

Where W_f and U_f are both Weights to be learned by the network.

Input Gate

The input gate helps in calculating the new information to be stored in cell state.

$$i_t = \sigma\left(W_i x_t + U_i h_{t-1} + b_i\right) \quad C' = tanh\left(W_c h_{t-1} + U_c x_t + b_c\right). \tag{8}$$

New Cell State

Using forget and input gates new cell state is calculated.

$$C_t = f_t * C_{t-1} + i_t * C'. \tag{9}$$

New Hidden State

First, calculate output state that determines what to be output. Using the output gate and cell state the hidden state is determined.

$$o_t = \sigma\left(W_o x_t + U_o h_{t-1} + b_o\right) \quad h_t = tanh\left(C_t\right) * o_t. \tag{10}$$

Machine Translation

Translations between various languages is important for exchange of ideas and information between populations of different linguistic backgrounds.

Deep learning play makes it easier to translate between different languages without the need of a human interpreter.

This section shows how to use recurrent neural networks for translating from one language to another. As every language involves complex grammar rules specific to their own, merely translating each individual words does not make any sense.

When a deep learning algorithm, called **sequence-to-sequence**, is fed a lot of parallel text data, with the same sentence or phrase in the two languages, the algorithm starts understanding these language semantics and is able to translate between the two languages.

Next, the working of sequence-to-sequence is discussed.

Sequence-to-Sequence (Sutskever et al., 2014)

A sequence-to-sequence model is made up of two recurrent neural networks called, **encoder** and **decoder**. The encoder takes in the input sequence and creates a fixed size vector that contains the encoded information of the sequence. The decoder uses this vector to create a new sequence, in this case, a translation.

Table 10 shows how to define a Neural Machine Translation model with encoder and decoder.

In the init constructor method of class NMT the two LSTM layers corresponding to encoder and decoder are defined along with linear layers. The forward method is an overloaded method of nn.Module class that is run to create the model and forward propagate.

Source_padded and target_padded are padded tensors that contain index of the words of every sentence in the vocabulary. The source_padded tensor is passed to the encoder LSTM layer that is defined as encode method. The encode method returns hidden states of sentences, enc_hid and a tensor containing all the information of the source sentence that is fed to the decoder LSTM, dec_init_state. These tensors are used by the decoder to generate a translation to the target language.

Malware Detection (Yuan et al., 2014) (Pascanu et al., 2015)

Deep learning helps in detecting malware more efficiently in applications that may be disastrous for a user by stealing their personal information, deleting important files, etc.

Using RNN and CNN, the code sequence of an application is analyzed, and the application is labeled as malicious or benign. By showing codes of several malicious and benign applications, the deep learning model starts understanding if a particular application contains some malicious code even if it has not seen that exact same malicious code before in training data.

This problem is still under research as attackers find new methods to fool previous counter methods. Since it is a research problem so using PyTorch to develop models is very effective as they are easy to debug and new methods can easily be implemented.

Table 10. Defining an NMT model in PyTorch (Pencheng)

```python
import sys
import torch
from torch.nn.utils.rnn import pad_packed_sequence, pack_padded_sequence
import torch.nn as nn
import torch.nn.utils
import torch.nn.functional as F
class NMT(nn.Module):
  def __init__(self, embed_size, hid_size, vocab dropout_rate=0.2):
    super().__init__()
    self.dropout_rate = dropout_rate
    self.hid_size = hid_size
    self.vocab = vocab #vocab object creates a vocabulary of target and source sentences
    # model
    self.encoder = nn.LSTM(embed_size, self.hid_size, bias=True, bidirectional=True)
    self.decoder = nn.LSTMCell(embed_size+self.hid_size, self.hid_size, bias=True)
    self.h_proj = nn.Linear(2*self.hid_size, self.hid_size, bias=False)
    self.c_proj = nn.Linear(2*self.hid_size, self.hid_size, bias=False)
    self.att_proj = nn.Linear(2*self.hid_size, self.hid_size, bias=False)
    self.combined_output_proj = nn.Linear(3*self.hid_size, self.hid_size, bias=False)
    self.target_vocab_proj = nn.Linear(self.hid_size, len(self.vocab.tgt))
    self.dropout = nn.Dropout(self.dropout_rate)
  def forward(self, source, target, source_padded, target_padded):
    #source_padded is a tensor of all source language sentences padded to a fixed length
    #target_padded is a tensor of all source language sentences padded to a fixed length
    source_lengths = (len(s) for s in source) #source sentence Lengths
    enc_hid, dec_init_state = self.encode(source_padded, source_lengths)
    enc_masks = torch.zeros(enc_hid.size(0), enc_hid.size(1), dtype=torch.float)
    for e_id, src_len in enumerate(source_lengths):
    enc_masks(e_id, src_len:) = 1
    enc_masks.to(self.device)
    combined_outputs = self.decode(enc_hid, enc_masks, dec_init_state, target_padded)
    P = F.log_softmax(self.target_vocab_proj(combined_outputs), dim=-1)
    # Removing words that contribute to total loss for which there is nothing in the target text
    target_masks = (target_padded != self.vocab.tgt('<pad>')).float()
    # Compute log probability of generating true target words
    target_gold_words_log_prob = torch.gather(P, index=target_padded(1:).unsqueeze(-1), dim=-1).squeeze(-1) * target_masks(1:)
    scores = target_gold_words_log_prob.sum(dim=0)
    return scores
  def encode(self, source_padded, source_length):
    enc_hid, dec_init_state = None, None
    X = nn.Embedding(len(self.vocab.src), self.embed_size, self.vocab.src('<pad>'))
    X = pack_padded_sequence(X, source_lengths)
    enc_hid, (last_hid, last_cell) = self.encoder(X)
    enc_hid, _ = pad_packed_sequence(enc_hid)
    enc_hid = enc_hid.transpose(0, 1)
    last_hid = torch.cat((last_hid(0), last_hid(1)),1)
    init_decoder_hid = self.h_proj(last_hid)
    last_cell = torch.cat((last_cell(0), last_cell(1)), 1)
    init_decoder_cell = self.c_proj(last_cell)
    dec_init_state = (init_decoder_hid, init_decoder_cell)
    return enc_hid, dec_init_state
  def decode(self, enc_hid, enc_masks, dec_init_state, target_padded):
    # Chop of the <END> token for max length sentences.
    target_padded = target_padded(:-1)
    # Initialize the decoder state (hid and cell)
    dec_state = dec_init_state
    # Initialize previous combined output vector o_{t-1} as zero
    batch_size = enc_hid.size(0)
    o_prev = torch.zeros(batch_size, self.hid_size, device=self.device)
    # Initialize a list that will be used to collect the combined output o_t on each step
    combined_outputs = ()
    enc_hid_proj = self.att_proj(enc_hid)
    Y = nn.Embedding(len(self.vocab.tgt), self.embed_size, self.vocab.tgt('<pad>'))
    for Y_t in torch.split(Y, 1, 0): #(1, b, e)
    squeeze = torch.squeeze(Y_t, 0) #(b, e)
    Ybar_t = torch.cat((squeeze, o_prev), dim=1) #(b, e+h)
    dec_state, o_t, _ = self.step(Ybar_t, dec_state, enc_hid, enc_hid_proj, enc_masks)
    combined_outputs.append(o_t)
    o_prev = o_t
    combined_outputs = torch.stack(tuple(combined_outputs), dim=0)
    return combined_outputs
  def step(self, Ybar_t: torch.Tensor,
    dec_state: Tuple(torch.Tensor, torch.Tensor),
    enc_hid: torch.Tensor,
    enc_hid_proj: torch.Tensor,
    enc_masks: torch.Tensor) -> Tuple(Tuple, torch.Tensor, torch.Tensor):
    """ Computes a single step of decoder"""
    combined_output = None
    dec_state = self.decoder(Ybar_t, dec_state)
    (dec_hid, dec_cell) = dec_state
    e_t = enc_hid_proj.bmm(dec_hid.unsqueeze(2)).squeeze(2)
    # Set e_t to -inf where enc_masks has 1
    if enc_masks is not None:
    e_t.data.masked_fill_(enc_masks.byte(), -float('inf'))
    alpha_t = F.softmax(e_t, dim=1)
    att_t = torch.unsqueeze(alpha_t,1)
    a_t = torch.bmm(att_t, enc_hid).squeeze(1)
    U_t = torch.cat((dec_hid, a_t), 1)
    V_t = self.combined_output_proj(U_t)
    O_t = self.dropout(torch.tanh(V_t))
    combined_output = O_t
    return dec_state, combined_output, e_t
```

Internet of Things (Mohammadi et al., 2018)

Deep learning helps in analyzing the massive data that is generated by IoT devices and find optimal solutions to the problems. Deep learning can analyze problems that may arise in a photovoltaic cell by analyzing the data generated by the IoT sensors on the photovoltaic cell. Deep learning can analyze the routing information between IoT devices and can find a more secure and optimized way to route the information.

Frameworks Built on top of PyTorch

This section discusses the frameworks which have been developed on top of PyTorch. Each subsection discusses a different framework.

MemCNN (van de Leemput et al, 2018)

This framework is made for developing memory-efficient invertible convolution neural networks. By removing the need to store input activations and instead reconstructing them on demand have helped researchers to reduce memory footprint. But for this approach, there is a need to write custom backpropagation every time. MemCNN is a PyTorch based framework that removes this need of writing a custom backpropagation every time. MemCNN resulted in similar accuracy to state of the art model on CIFAR dataset with faster training time.

MedicalTorch (Perone et al., 2018)

MedicalTorch is an open-source framework based on PyTorch. It contains various medical datasets, preprocessed models, and tools that help in simplifying the process of neural network building for medical image analysis.

Modular Deep Reinforcement Learning Framework in PyTorch (Keng et al., 2017)

Reinforcement Learning is a type of machine learning technique that is used to make the system learn by making it interact with its environment using a reward system.

The SLM (simulated laboratory module) is developed in PyTorch with the objective of making reinforcement learning research easier and more accessible by designing it to correspond to the way papers discuss reinforcement learning closely.

PyTorch-Kaldi Speech Recognition Toolkit (Ravanelli et al., 2019)

PyTorch-Kaldi Speech Recognition Toolkit is an open-source repository that helps in developing state-of-the-art deep neural network/hidden Markov model (DNN/HMM) speech recognition systems.

The DNN part is managed by PyTorch, while feature extraction, label computation, and decoding are performed with the Kaldi toolkit.

The latest version of PyTorch-Kaldi toolkit have various features like easy interface and plug-in, flexible configuration files, several pre-implemented models (MLP, CNN, RNN, LSTM, GRU, Li-GRU, SincNet), Natural implementation of complex models based on multiple features, labels, and neural architectures, Automatic recovery from the last processed chunk, Automatic chunking and context expansions of the input features, Multi-GPU training, Designed to work locally or on high performance computing (HPC) clusters, Tutorials on TIMIT and Librispeech Datasets.

UBER Pyro (Bingham et al., 2019)

Pyro is a universal probabilistic programming language developed by Uber. It is written in Python and supported by PyTorch. Pyro helps in simplifying the testing of deep learning models

Future of Deep Learning and PyTorch

Deep learning is changing the way how the technology works, making every aspect of it smart, along with our lives. This section discusses the impact deep learning could have in the future.

Self-Driving Cars (Bojarski et al., 2016)

Self-driving cars or autonomous vehicles are cars that can drive themselves without the need of a human driver. A self-driving car consists of various sensors like Lidar, GPS, and a camera that provides raw data, which is then processed by a deep learning algorithm to determine the position and helps in navigation. It also helps in understanding the environment, like detecting pedestrians, traffic signals, traffic signs, lane markings, etc. The deep learning algorithm understands all this information and makes a decision to steer the car. This process is currently far from perfect and is prone to several errors. This makes fully autonomous vehicles unsafe to be used in everyday life. Research is under progress from various companies like Google, Tesla, Nissan, Mercedes, etc.

Google's self-driving car division Waymo has driven 10 million miles in the real world, and 10 billion miles in simulation and they plan to soon release a self-driving taxi service.

Tesla has included a full self-driving mode that can self-drive Tesla cars on certain roads. Tesla develops their deep learning models using PyTorch. Because of the flexibility provided by PyTorch the engineers at Tesla were able to develop efficient custom models that run on custom developed hardware. The model can detect several objects like traffic lights, road markings, moving and stationary objects in real time from all the different camera feeds of the car.

Traffic Control (Lv et al., 2014)

The traffic management systems can help in managing a large amount of traffic using Deep learning. This will help in lowering the chances of traffic jams. The system could also more efficiently detect traffic law violators. This would also help the traffic police. By using traffic data, a system can be trained that can control the traffic lights more effectively. A real-time video analyzer system could be trained to detect traffic laws violations and by reading the violater's license plate a fine can be sent directly without any human intervention.

A system like this has been implemented in some cities in China. This has resulted in an increase of traffic speed by 15 percent and traffic laws violations were reported with 92 percent accuracy.

Biomedicine (Mamoshina et al., 2016)

Applying Deep learning in the field of Biomedicine can help in better understanding diseases and finding better ways to counter them more efficiently. By using deep learning in gene analysis, scientists can understand genes that cause cancer and autoimmune disorders. The research is already going on currently.

Researchers at princeton University have developed a library called Selene(Chen et al., 2019), which is based on PyTorch and is used to develop deep learning models to analyse biological sequential data.

Economic Effect

Deep learning holds a lot of potential to change every single industry vastly. From healthcare, energy, satellite mapping, manufacturing to a better transport system as a result of a combination of self-driving cars and smart traffic control systems. PricewaterhouseCoopers estimates that AI will be responsible for $15.7 trillion of global GDP growth by 2030. According to World Economic Forum's (WEF) report called "The Future of Jobs 2018", it is expected that the field will create 58 million new jobs by 2022. Many of the traditional industries and professions like cab and truck drivers will be obsolete and new industries like robotics will emerge. Deep Learning will enhance make almost every industry: In healthcare deep learning will assist doctors to make better decisions regarding the diagnosis of a particular disease and providing correct medication to the patients. In law, deep learning will help to catch law offenders easily and help lawyers and judges to take better decisions in the court. Smart assistants will make it easier to schedule and manage appointments. The applications of Deep Learning are endless and it will prove to be an essential tool for the progress of human society if administered correctly.

CONCLUSION

Deep learning is a field of Artificial Intelligence that learns to find patterns in problems by analyzing large amounts of data. It is capable of solving problems like image analysis and accurate translations that are not possible using conventional programming techniques. To make deep learning easy and optimum to implement, there are several deep learning frameworks. One of them is PyTorch.

PyTorch is a deep learning framework that is used for research and commercial purposes. PyTorch differs from other deep learning frameworks due to the pythonic nature and its ability to construct a dynamic computational graph at run time, which makes it more flexible and easy to understand. Tensors are the building blocks of the PyTorch framework, and the autograd package is the backbone of the whole framework that helps in computing derivatives of tensors for backpropagation by constructing a computational graph at run time. PyTorch has many practical applications like image analysis that can be used to analyze and classify medical images among other uses, natural language processing, and machine translation and many more.

PyTorch consists of various models such as RNN, CNN, LSTM, MLP, GRU, Li-GRU, etc. which increases its flexibility and accessibility to a greater extent. As a result, many frameworks are built on top of PyTorch such as MemCNN, MedicalTorch, Modular Deep Reinforcement Learning, PyTorch-Kaldi toolkit, etc.

Deep learning holds the ability to transform every industry in the future and lead to a significant boost of the global economy. Some of the future applications of deep learning are self-driving cars, traffic control systems, biomedicine.

REFERENCES

Abadi, M., Agarwal, A., Barham, P., Brevdo, E., Chen, Z., Citro, C., . . . Ghemawat, S. (2016). *Tensorflow: Large-scale machine learning on heterogeneous distributed systems.* arXiv preprint arXiv:1603.04467

Bingham, E., Chen, J. P., Jankowiak, M., Obermeyer, F., Pradhan, N., Karaletsos, T., ... Goodman, N. D. (2019). Pyro: Deep universal probabilistic programming. *Journal of Machine Learning Research*, *20*(1), 973–978.

Bojarski, M., Del Testa, D., Dworakowski, D., Firner, B., Flepp, B., Goyal, P., . . . Zhang, X. (2016). *End to end learning for self-driving cars.* arXiv preprint arXiv:1604.07316

CS224n, Stanford. (n.d.). Retrieved 2019, from http://web.stanford.edu/class/cs224n/slides/cs224n-2019-lecture04-backprop.pdf

CS231n, Stanford. (n.d.). Retrieved 2019, from http://cs231n.github.io/neural-networks-1/

Chen, K. M., Cofer, E. M., Zhou, J., & Troyanskaya, O. G. (2019). Selene: A PyTorch-based deep learning library for sequence data. *Nature Methods*, *16*(4), 315–318. doi:10.103841592-019-0360-8 PMID:30923381

Chetlur, S., Woolley, C., Vandermersch, P., Cohen, J., Tran, J., Catanzaro, B., & Shelhamer, E. (2014). *cudnn: Efficient primitives for deep learning.* arXiv preprint arXiv:1410.0759

Chollet, F. (2005). *Keras: Deep learning library for theano and tensorflow.* https://keras. io/k

Colah. (2015). *Understanding LSTM.* Retrieved 2019, from http://colah.github.io/posts/2015-08-Understanding-LSTMs/

Collobert, R., Weston, J., Bottou, L., Karlen, M., Kavukcuoglu, K., & Kuksa, P. (2011). Natural language processing (almost) from scratch. *Journal of Machine Learning Research*, *12*(Aug), 2493–2537.

Fadja, A. N., Lamma, E., & Riguzzi, F. (2018). Vision Inspection with Neural Networks. RiCeRcA@ AI* IA.

Goodfellow, I., Bengio, Y., & Courville, A. (2016). *Deep learning.* MIT Press.

Gradient Descent. (n.d.). Retrieved 2019, from https://saugatbhattarai.com.np/what-is-gradient-descent-in-machine-learning/

Hochreiter, S., & Schmidhuber, J. (1997). Long short-term memory. *Neural Computation*, *9*(8), 1735–1780. doi:10.1162/neco.1997.9.8.1735 PMID:9377276

Ierusalimschy, R., De Figueiredo, L. H., & Filho, W. C. (1996). Lua—An extensible extension language. *Software, Practice & Experience, 26*(6), 635–652. doi:10.1002/(SICI)1097-024X(199606)26:6<635::AID-SPE26>3.0.CO;2-P

Jia, Y., Shelhamer, E., Donahue, J., Karayev, S., Long, J., Girshick, R., ... Darrell, T. (2014, November). Caffe: Convolutional architecture for fast feature embedding. In *Proceedings of the 22nd ACM international conference on Multimedia* (pp. 675-678). ACM.

Jia, Y., Shelhamer, E., Donahue, J., Karayev, S., Long, J., Girshick, R., ... Darrell, T. (2014, November). Caffe: Convolutional architecture for fast feature embedding. In *Proceedings of the 22nd ACM international conference on Multimedia* (pp. 675-678). ACM. 10.1145/2647868.2654889

JonesE.OliphantT.PetersonP. (2001). https://www.scipy. Org

Jurafsky, D. (2000). *Speech & language processing.* Pearson Education India.

Keng, W. L., & Graesser, L. (2017). *"SLM Lab", kengz/SLM-Lab.* GitHub.

Ketkar, N. (2017). Introduction to PyTorch. In *Deep learning with python* (pp. 195–208). Berkeley, CA: Apress. doi:10.1007/978-1-4842-2766-4_12

LeCun, Y., Bottou, L., Bengio, Y., & Haffner, P. (1998). Gradient-based learning applied to document recognition. *Proceedings of the IEEE, 86*(11), 2278–2324. doi:10.1109/5.726791

Litjens, G., Kooi, T., Bejnordi, B. E., Setio, A. A. A., Ciompi, F., Ghafoorian, M., ... Sánchez, C. I. (2017). A survey on deep learning in medical image analysis. *Medical Image Analysis, 42,* 60–88. doi:10.1016/j.media.2017.07.005 PMID:28778026

Lv, Y., Duan, Y., Kang, W., Li, Z., & Wang, F. Y. (2014). Traffic flow prediction with big data: A deep learning approach. *IEEE Transactions on Intelligent Transportation Systems, 16*(2), 865–873. doi:10.1109/TITS.2014.2345663

Mamoshina, P., Vieira, A., Putin, E., & Zhavoronkov, A. (2016). Applications of deep learning in biomedicine. *Molecular Pharmaceutics, 13*(5), 1445–1454. doi:10.1021/acs.molpharmaceut.5b00982 PMID:27007977

Mikolov, T., Karafiát, M., Burget, L., Černocký, J., & Khudanpur, S. (2010). Recurrent neural network based language model. *Eleventh annual conference of the international speech communication association.*

Mishra, P. (2019). Introduction to PyTorch, Tensors, and Tensor Operations. In PyTorch Recipes (pp. 1-27). Apress.

Mohammadi, M., Al-Fuqaha, A., Sorour, S., & Guizani, M. (2018). Deep learning for IoT big data and streaming analytics: A survey. *IEEE Communications Surveys and Tutorials, 20*(4), 2923–2960. doi:10.1109/COMST.2018.2844341

MXNet. (2017). *A flexible and efficient library for deep learning.* Author.

Nguyen, G., Dlugolinsky, S., Bobák, M., Tran, V., García, Á. L., Heredia, I., ... Hluchý, L. (2019). Machine Learning and Deep Learning frameworks and libraries for large-scale data mining: A survey. *Artificial Intelligence Review, 52*(1), 77–124. doi:10.100710462-018-09679-z

NumPy. (2018). *NumPy—the fundamental package for scientific computing with Python*. Retrieved 2019, from http://www.numpy. org/

NVIDIA. (2017). *NVIDIA Collective Communications Library (NCCL)*. Author.

Nvidia CUDA. (2007). *Compute unified device architecture programming guide*. Author.

Pan, S. J., & Yang, Q. (2009). A survey on transfer learning. *IEEE Transactions on Knowledge and Data Engineering*, *22*(10), 1345–1359. doi:10.1109/TKDE.2009.191

Pascanu, R., Stokes, J. W., Sanossian, H., Marinescu, M., & Thomas, A. (2015, April). Malware classification with recurrent networks. In *2015 IEEE International Conference on Acoustics, Speech and Signal Processing (ICASSP)* (pp. 1916-1920). IEEE. 10.1109/ICASSP.2015.7178304

Paszke, A., Gross, S., Chintala, S., Chanan, G., Yang, E., DeVito, Z., & Lerer, A. (2017). *Automatic differentiation in PyTorch*. Academic Press.

Paszke, A., Gross, S., Massa, F., Lerer, A., Bradbury, J., Chanan, G., . . . Desmaison, A. (2019). PyTorch: An imperative style, high-performance deep learning library. In Advances in Neural Information Processing Systems (pp. 8024-8035). Academic Press.

Perone, C.S., Saravia, E., Ballester, P., & Tare, M. (2018, November 24). *perone/medicaltorch: Release v0.2* (Version v0.2). Zenodo. doi:10.5281/zenodo.1495335

Ravanelli, M., Parcollet, T., & Bengio, Y. (2019, May). The pytorch-kaldi speech recognition toolkit. In *ICASSP 2019-2019 IEEE International Conference on Acoustics, Speech and Signal Processing (ICASSP)* (pp. 6465-6469). IEEE. 10.1109/ICASSP.2019.8683713

Rumelhart, D. E., Hinton, G. E., & Williams, R. J. (1988). Learning representations by back-propagating errors. *Cognitive Modeling, 5*(3), 1.

Seide, F., & Agarwal, A. (2016, August). CNTK: Microsoft's open-source deep-learning toolkit. In *Proceedings of the 22nd ACM SIGKDD International Conference on Knowledge Discovery and Data Mining* (pp. 2135-2135). ACM. 10.1145/2939672.2945397

Shoham, Y. (2018). The AI Index 2018 Annual Report. *AI Index Steering Committee, Human-Centered AI Initiative, Stanford University*. Available at http://cdn.aiindex.org/2018/AI%20Index%202018%20 Annual%20Report.pdf

Shouno, H., Suzuki, S., & Kido, S. (2015, November). A transfer learning method with deep convolutional neural network for diffuse lung disease classification. In *International Conference on Neural Information Processing* (pp. 199-207). Springer. 10.1007/978-3-319-26532-2_22

Sutskever, I., Vinyals, O., & Le, Q. V. (2014). Sequence to sequence learning with neural networks. In Advances in neural information processing systems (pp. 3104-3112). Academic Press.

van de Leemput, S. C., Teuwen, J., & Manniesing, R. (2018). *MemCNN: a Framework for Developing Memory Efficient Deep Invertible Networks*. Academic Press.

Yes you should understand backprop. (n.d.). *Karpathy*. retrieved 2019, from https://medium.com/@karpathy/yes-you-should-understand-backprop-e2f06eab496b

Yuan, Z., Lu, Y., Wang, Z., & Xue, Y. (2014, August). Droid-sec: Deep learning in android malware detection. *Computer Communication Review*, *44*(4), 371–372. doi:10.1145/2740070.2631434

Zeiler, M. D., & Fergus, R. (2014, September). Visualizing and understanding convolutional networks. In *European conference on computer vision* (pp. 818-833). Springer.

Chapter 4
Deep Learning With TensorFlow

Shahina Anwarul

Department of Systemics, School of Computer Science, University of Petroleum & Energy Studies (UPES), India

Deepa Joshi

Department of Systemics, School of Computer Science, University of Petroleum & Energy Studies (UPES), India

ABSTRACT

This chapter aims to acquaint the users with key parts of TensorFlow and some basic ideas about deep learning. In particular, users will figure out how to perform fundamental calculations in TensorFlow and implementation of deep learning using TensorFlow. This chapter intends to gives a straightforward manual for the complexities of Google's TensorFlow framework that is easy to understand. The basic steps for the installation and setup of TensorFlow will also be discussed. Starting with a simple "Hello World" example, a practical implementation of deep learning problem to identify the handwritten digits will be discussed using MNIST dataset. It is only possible to understand deep learning through substantial practical examples. For that reason, the authors have included practical implementation of deep learning problems that motivates the readers to plunge deeply into these examples and to get their hands grimy trying different things with their own ideas using TensorFlow because it is never adequate to perceive algorithms only theoretically.

DEEP LEARNING

Deep learning is a subset of machine learning in Artificial Intelligence (AI) that has networks capable of learning in a supervised, unsupervised or semi-supervised manner given in Figure 1. It is also known as deep structured learning and hierarchical learning (Jason, 2019). The core component of deep learning is a neural network. Most of the deep learning models are predicated on Artificial Neural Networks. Conventional neural networks consist of a single input layer, a single hidden layer, and one output layer. Deep learning networks are different from these conventional neural networks comprise more hidden layers as given in Figure 2. They consist of more depths, that is the reason to known as deep networks. These kinds of networks are proficient in exploring hidden structures from unlabeled and unstructured data.

DOI: 10.4018/978-1-7998-3095-5.ch004

Figure 1. Relation between Artificial Intelligence, Machine Learning, and Deep Learning

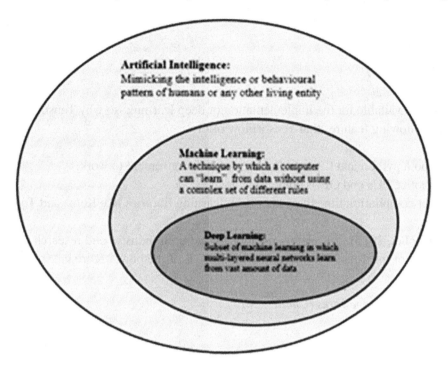

Figure 2. a) Conventional Neural Network, b) Deep Neural Network

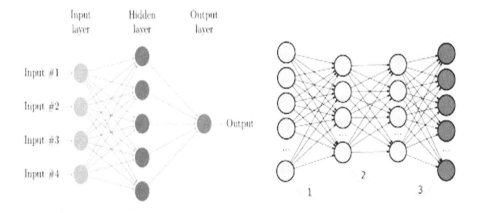

TENSORFLOW

This chapter, entitled "Deep learning with TensorFlow," emphasizes TensorFlow. It is one of the best open-source software library that is employed for the implementation of deep learning developed by Google. This framework is used for numerical computations using data flow graphs that have nodes and edges. TensorFlow is nothing; it is like numpy with a twist. In the event that you have worked with numpy, working with TensorFlow will be simple. The huge distinction among numpy and TensorFlow is that TensorFlow pursues a lazy programming paradigm. It can do all that typically would do in numpy! It's suitably called "numpy on steroids."

WHY TENSORFLOW?

Several libraries are available for the implementation of deep learning, so why TensorFlow?
These are the following features that TensorFlow offers:

a)   It provides both python and C++ API's that makes it convenient to work.
b)   It supports both CPUs and GPUs computing devices.
c)   It has a faster compilation time than other deep learning libraries like Keras and Torch.

In Figure 3 (Chollet, 2015), it is clearly mentioned that both industry and research community has the highest adoption of the TensorFlow library with 96.77% of the power score in 2018.

Figure 3. Deep learning frameworks (Chollet, 2015)

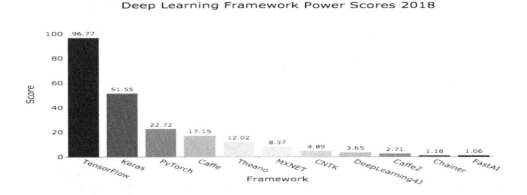

TENSOR

Tensor is a generalization of vectors and matrices of potentially higher dimensions. It is the standard way of representing data in deep learning. In simple terms, tensor is a matrix or an array of data with different dimensions and ranks that are supplied as input to the neural network. Figures 4 and 5 represent different dimensions and ranks of tensors respectively.

Rank of tensors: It is defined as a quantity of dimensions in which the tensors live.

\# Rank 0 is equivalent to scalar
\# Rank 1 is equivalent to vector
\# Rank 2 is equivalent to 2D matrix
\# Rank 3 is equivalent to 3D matrix

Figure 4. Different dimensions of Tensors; Tensor of dimension 1 Tensor of dimension 2 Tensor of dimension 3

Figure 5. Rank of Tensors: Rank 0, Rank 1, Rank 2, Rank 3

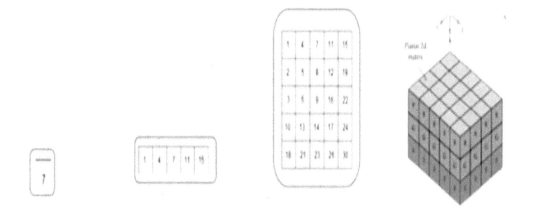

Rank of Tensors

There are two sections in TensorFlow library:

1) Tensor: It is used to convert the data in terms of numerical value representation for computation.
2) Flow: It describes the flow of operations.

DATAFLOW GRAPH

A computational graph or dataflow graph is a sequence of TensorFlow operations arranged into a graph of nodes and edges given in Figure 6 (TensorFlow, 2016). It consists of two types of objects:

- tf.Operation: Nodes in the computational graph represent the operations. It defines calculations that consume and generate tensors.

- tf.Tensor: Edges in the computational graph represent the values (tensors) that will pass through the graph on which the operations are performed.

Figure 6. Dataflow graph (TensorFlow, 2016)

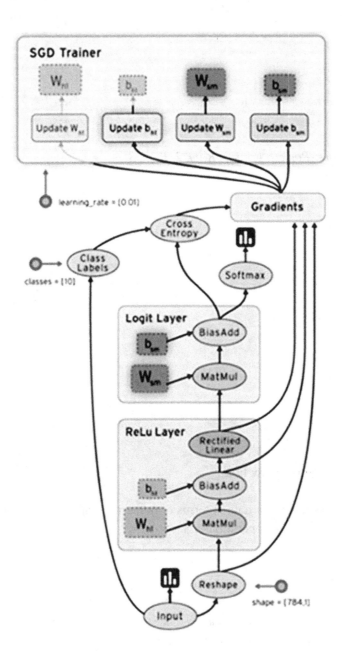

BASICS OF CODING IN TENSORFLOW

The main object of the TensorFlow program is the tf.Tensor that manipulate and pass around. A tf.Tensor has the following characteristics:

- A data type (for example int32, float32, or string)
- A shape

The data type of each element in the tensor should be the same and is always known. The shape (i.e., the number of dimensions and the size of each dimension) might be partially known. Some special kinds of tensors are as follows that will be discussed in the next section of this chapter:

- tf.Variable
- tf.constant
- tf.placeholder

TensorFlow core program consists of two distinct sections

- Building the computational graph
- Running the computational graph

Building the computational graph (using tf.Graph): TensorFlow uses a dataflow graph or computational graph to denote the computation in terms of association between individual operations. In this step, tf.Operation (node) and tf.Tensor (edge) objects are constructed using TensorFlow API functions and add them to tf.Graph instance.

For example: tf.constant (32.0) creates a tf.Operation that produces the value 32.0 and added to the default graph, and returns a tf.Tensor that represents the value of the defined constant.

Let's understand with the help of python code. Here, a and b are two floating-point constants:

Figure 7. Python code to add two TensorFlow constants

```
import tensorflow as tf
a = tf.constant(3.0, dtype=tf.float32)
b = tf.constant(4.0) # also tf.float32 implicitly
total = a + b
print(a)
print(b)
print(total)
```

The output of the above code is:

Figure 8.

```
Tensor("Const:0", shape=(), dtype=float32)
Tensor("Const_1:0", shape=(), dtype=float32)
Tensor("add:0", shape=(), dtype=float32)
```

Note that the above tensors do not print the values 3.0, 4.0, and 7.0 that you might expect. It only builds the computational graph. A unique name is assigned to each operation in a graph. This name is independent of the names of the objects that assigned to Python. Tensors are named after the operation that produces them followed by an output index, as in "add:0" above.

Running the computational graph (using tf.Session): In TensorFlow, everything has to be run within a session. We have to explicitly tell the program to run the command or object within the TensorFlow session. We can run the computational graph with the help of session in two ways:

Method 1

Figure 9.

```
import tensorflow as tf
hello_constant=tf.constant('Hello World')

#Run the session
with tf.Session() as sess:
    output=(sess.run(hello_constant).decode())
    print(output)
```

```
Hello World
```

Method II

If we are specifying the session by this particular fashion, then we have to close the session at the end explicitly. If we are not closing the session, it may create a problem at runtime to provide the results.

Figure 10. Model II

```
import tensorflow as tf
hello_constant=tf.constant('Hello World')

#Run the session
sess=tf.Session()
print(sess.run(hello_constant))
sess.close()

b'Hello World'
```

TYPES OF DATA IN TENSORFLOW

There are three types of data in TensorFlow:

1) Constant
2) Placeholder
3) Variable

Constant: If the data object is specified as a constant, then its value will remain the same across the program. We use tf.constant() command to define a constant.

Example: Multiply two constants (figure 11)

Placeholder: Placeholders are used to assign the data to a TensorFlow graph. The value of the data object is assigned later in a placeholder. We use tf.placeholder() command to define a placeholder. Final values of placeholder objects will always be assigned using feed_dict (feed dictionary).

Example: Addition of two placeholders (figure 12)

Variable: It allows us to add trainable parameters to a computational graph. We use tf.Variable() command to define a variable. In this type of data, any value is assigned initially, but during the program, the values are changed as per the requirements. Whenever we are assigning the value to the TensorFlow variable, we need to initialize the variable using **tf.global_variables_initializer()** function.

INSTALLATION OF TENSORFLOW IN ANACONDA DISTRIBUTION

General Considerations

1) Two variations of TensorFlow can be installed on whether you would like to run TensorFlow on your CPU or GPU (If you have your own Nvidia graphics card).

Figure 11.

```
#Example: Multiply two constants
#import tensorflow library
import tensorflow as tf
#Initialize TensorFlow constant
a=tf.constant(4.0)
b=tf.constant(5.0)
c=a*b

#Run the session
sess=tf.Session()
print(sess.run(c))
sess.close()
```

20.0

Figure 12.

```
#Example: Placeholder
#import tensorflow library
import tensorflow as tf
a=tf.placeholder(tf.float32)
b=tf.placeholder(tf.float32)
add=a+b

#Run the session
sess=tf.Session()
print(sess.run(add,feed_dict={a:[1,2,7], b:[3,20,2]}))
```

[4. 22.   9.]

Figure 13.

```
#Example: Variables
#import tensorflow library
import tensorflow as tf

# Assignment of value to a tensorflow variable
W1=tf.Variable([0.5],tf.float32)
#important: need to run below code to initialize the variables
init=tf.global_variables_initializer()

#Run the session
sess=tf.Session()
sess.run(init)
print(sess.run(W1))
```

[0.5]

2) It is a suggestion to create a different (virtual) environment if you wish to install both TensorFlow variations on your machine. Without making virtual environments, it will either end up failing or when you later start running code, there will consistently be incertitude about which variation is being utilized to execute your code.

Installation Steps

Step 1: The first step is to install Anaconda Python 3.7. It is optional, any python framework can be used but the authors would suggest using Anaconda because of its instinctive way of managing packages and setting up new virtual environments. Anaconda distribution can be downloaded from the given link:
https://www.anaconda.com/download/

Step 2: Installation of TensorFlow CPU

It directly runs on the CPU of your machine. In some cases, you will feel the degradation of performance in comparison to TensorFlow GPU. It can be done in 3 simple steps:

2. 1) Create a new Conda virtual environment (Optional)

a) Open Anaconda/ Prompt window

Figure 14.

b) Type the following command given below:

Figure 15.

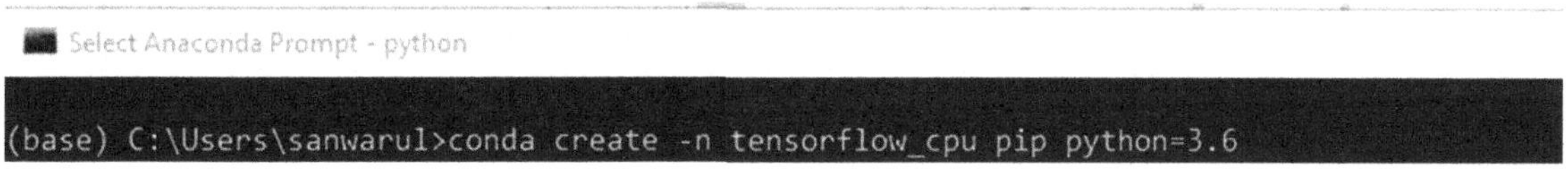

The above command will create a new virtual environment with name tensorflow_cpu

c)   Activate the created virtual environment using the following command:

Figure 16.

d)   After activating the virtual environment, the name of the environment will be displayed at the beginning of the cmd path specifier within brackets:

Figure 17.

2. 2) Install TensorFlow CPU for Python

a)   Open Anaconda/ Prompt window and activate the tensorflow_cpu environment (If you have not done earlier).
b)   Type the following command on cmd and wait for the installation to finish.

Figure 18.

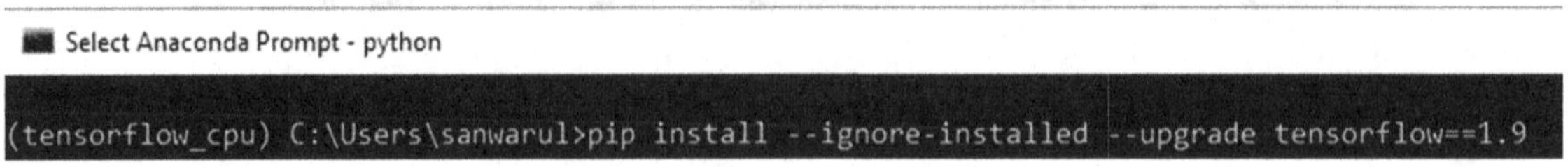

Select Anaconda Prompt - python

```
(tensorflow_cpu) C:\Users\sanwarul>pip install --ignore-installed --upgrade tensorflow==1.9
```

2. 3) Testing of installation

a)   Start python interpreter by typing the command

Figure 19.

b) Run below code to check whether TensorFlow is successfully installed or not:

Figure 20.

c) For the sake of the completion of testing the installation, check the output by typing 'Hello TensorFlow'

Figure 21.

TENSORBOARD

TensorBoard is a utility provided by the TensorFlow. It helps to visualize the computational graph. In other terms, it helps to visualize the training parameters, metrics, hyperparameters, or any statistics of neural networks. It provides a set of web applications that help us to understand the flow of the computational graph. It provides five types of visualizations:

- Scalars
- Images
- Audio
- Histograms
- Graphs

The visualization of the TensorBoard window is given in Figure 22 (Aryan, 2018).

Figure 22. TensorBoard Window (Aryan, 2018)

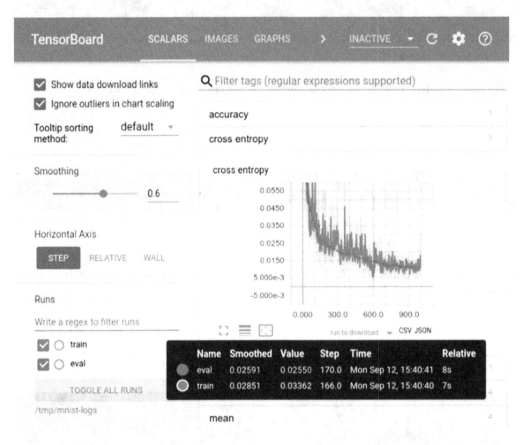

The first step to visualize the graph with TensorBorad is to write the logs of the program. For this, we need to create a writer for those logs using below line of code:

Figure 23.

```
writer = tf.summary.FileWriter([logdir], [graph])
```

Where logdir is the directory where we want to store the log file, the second argument is the graph of the program on which we will work. There are two methods to get the graph:

- Creating the writer out of the session using tf.get_default_graph() function, which returns the default graph of the program.
- Creating the writer inside the session using sess.graph, which returns the graph of the session.

Python code to visualize the graph using TensorBoard is given below:

Figure 24.

```
# import tensorflow library
import tensorflow as tf
tf.reset_default_graph()    # To clear the defined variables and operations of the previous cell
# create graph
a = tf.constant(2)
b = tf.constant(3)
c = tf.add(a, b)
# creating the writer out of the session
# writer = tf.summary.FileWriter('./graphs', tf.get_default_graph())
# launch the graph in a session
with tf.Session() as sess:
    # or creating the writer inside the session
    writer = tf.summary.FileWriter('./graphs1', sess.graph)
    print(sess.run(c))

5
```

After the execution of the above code, it creates a directory with the name 'graphs1' in the current working directory that contains the event file, as you can see below.

Figure 25.

Now, open anaconda prompt and make sure that you are in a current working directory where the python code is running. If not, change the working directory using the cd command (figure 26).

Then run below command to display the graph with TensorBoard (figure 27).

You can replace the name of the directory "./graphs1" if you choose another name. It will generate the link on the command prompt (http://Sanwarul-ltp:6006/), copy this link and open it on a web browser. The link will redirect you to the TensorBoard page that looks similar to the below image (figure 28).

Figure 26.

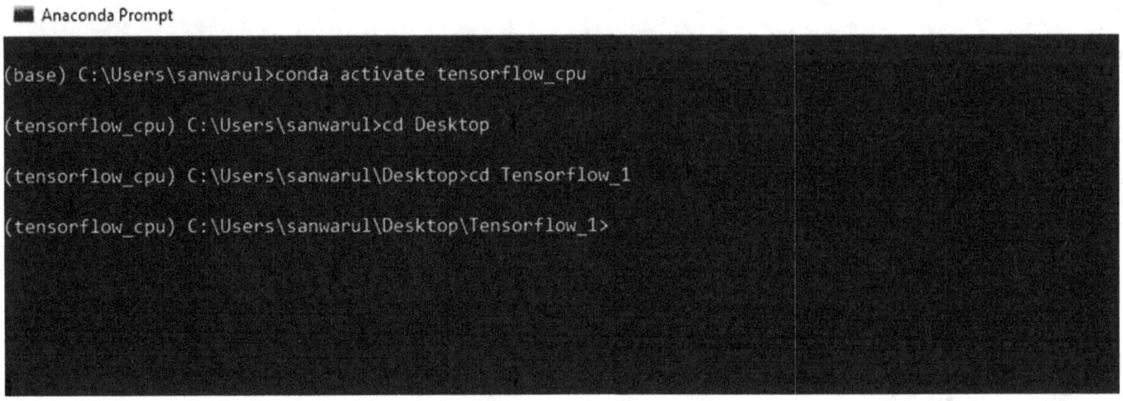

```
■ Anaconda Prompt

(base) C:\Users\sanwarul>conda activate tensorflow_cpu

(tensorflow_cpu) C:\Users\sanwarul>cd Desktop

(tensorflow_cpu) C:\Users\sanwarul\Desktop>cd Tensorflow_1

(tensorflow_cpu) C:\Users\sanwarul\Desktop\Tensorflow_1>
```

Figure 27.

Figure 28.

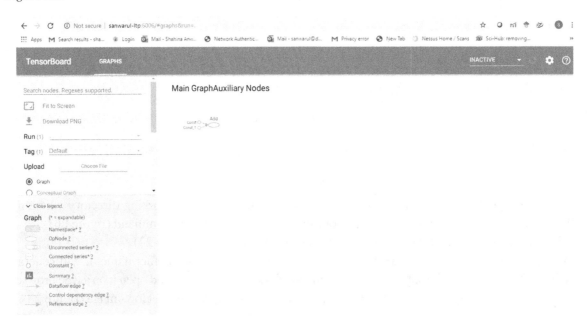

TensorBoard uses a web browser to display the visualization of the code. The above graph represents the different parts of the used model. Const and const_1 represent a and b respectively and the node Add represents c.

IMPLEMENTATION

Simple hello world code in python using TensorFlow. Either you can use Jupyter notebook, Spyder, Pycharm framework for writing the code, or you can open a python interpreter in cmd.

Figure 29.

The output of the above code snippet is b'hello world!', here b represents byte strings rather than Unicode strings. You can use **Print(sess.run(hello).decode**()) to remove b from the output.

DATASETS AVAILABLE WITH TENSORFLOW

In TensorFlow, there are 29 well-known datasets available such as MNIST; the Large Movie Reviews Dataset, the 1 Billion Word Language Model Benchmark and Street View House Numbers, etc. (Introducing TensorFlow Datasets, 2019).

You can check the detailed explanation of available datasets with TensorFlow under different categories in given link:

https://www.tensorflow.org/datasets/catalog/overview

You can install all the datasets using the below command:

Figure 30.

Command to Check the List of Available Datasets

Once datasets have been installed, import tensorflow_datasets as tfds

Figure 31.

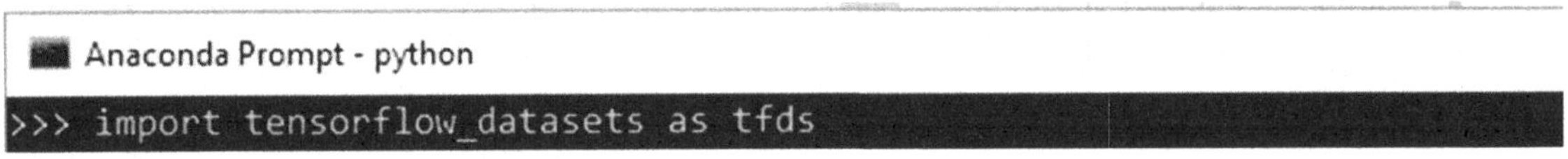

After importing the datasets, you can check the list of available datasets using **tfds.list_builders()**

Figure 32.

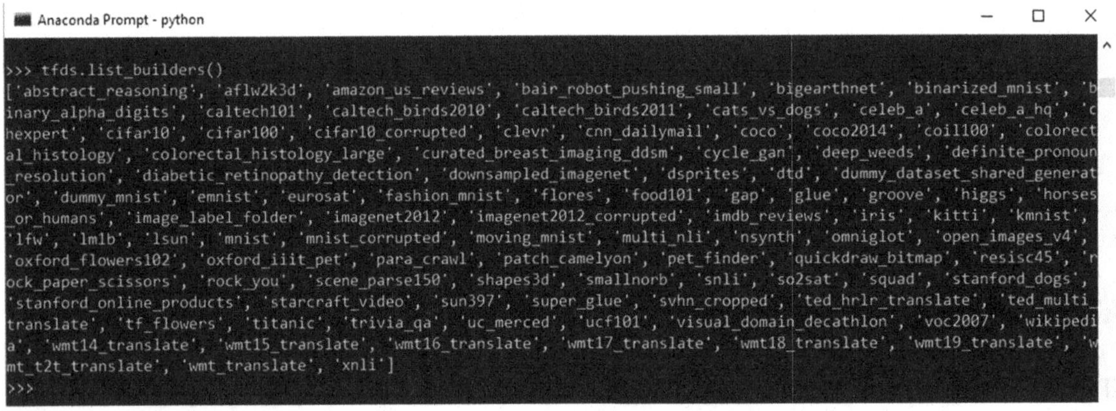

A PRACTICAL IMPLEMENTATION OF DEEP LEARNING PROBLEM TO IDENTIFY THE HANDWRITTEN DIGITS USING MNIST DATASET

In this practical implementation of the Deep Learning problem in Python, the authors are using the MNIST dataset (LeCun, Cortes & Burges, 1998). This dataset consists of images of handwritten digits of 28*28 pixels in size as given in Figure 33.

Figure 33. MNIST Dataset (LeCun, Cortes & Burges, 1998)

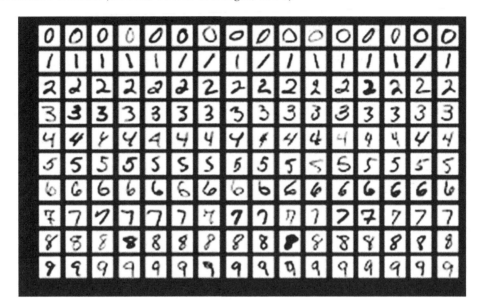

Step 1: Importing the Dataset

First, import the TensorFlow library and then add the above code to import the MNIST dataset that stores the image data in mnist variable. Here, one-hot-encoding is used to depict the labels. It uses a vector of binary values to render numeric or categorical values. The vector includes ten values, one for each possible digit as we have numbers from 0-9. To represent any particular digit, the value of the vector at that index will be 1 and the rest will be 0. For example, the digit 4 is represented using the vector [0,0,0,0,1,0,0,0,0,0]. Now, the images of 28*28 pixels are converted into a 1D vector of 784 pixels in size. Each 784 pixels contain the value between 0 and 255 because we have a grayscale image. In black and white images, 255 represents a black pixel and white pixel is represented by 0.

Figure 34.

```
#Import tensorflow library
import tensorflow as tf
#Import dataset
from tensorflow.examples.tutorials.mnist import input_data
mnist = input_data.read_data_sets("MNIST_data/", one_hot=True)  # y labels are oh-encoded
```

Step 2: Division of Dataset for Training and Testing

mnist variable is used to check the size of the divided datasets for training and testing. Using the below lines of code, it can be determined that the dataset has been split into 55000 images for training, 5000 for validation and 10000 for testing.

Now, the dataset has been imported, it is a time to define the architecture of Neural Network.

Figure 35.

```
n_train = mnist.train.num_examples        # Images for training
n_validation = mnist.validation.num_examples   # Images for cross_validation
n_test = mnist.test.num_examples          # Images for testing
```

Figure 36.

```
print(n_train)
print(n_validation)
print(n_test)
```

```
55000
5000
10000
```

Step 3: Defining the Architecture of Neural Network

As the authors have discussed in the above section that deep neural network consists of a single input layer, multiple hidden layers and a single output layer. The architecture of the human brain highly inspires the architecture of a neural network. In the human brain, neurons are responsible for passing signals around the brain. Similarly, units are responsible for taking the inputs, perform computations and then passing the values to the other units in neural networks.

Add below lines of code to define the number of units per layer. The authors have taken 784 units in the input layer to represent each pixel of the 1D vector as discussed above. Ten units of the output layer represents the digits from 0 to 9.

Figure 37.

```
n_input = 784   # input layer (28x28 pixels)
n_hidden1 = 512  # 1st hidden layer
n_hidden2 = 256  # 2nd hidden layer
n_hidden3 = 128  # 3rd hidden layer
n_output = 10   # output layer (0-9 digits)
```

Figure 38 represents the visualization of the defined architecture of the neural network.

The hyperparameters need to be defined here, whose values will remain constant throughout the implementation.

The learning_rate variable defines how much the parameters will amend at each pass of the learning process. After each pass of the learning process, we tune the weights to reduce the loss. Here, n_iterations defines the number of iterations that represent how many times we go through the training step.

Figure 38. The architecture of Deep Neural Network

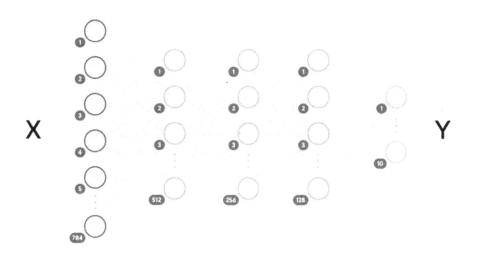

Figure 39.

```
learning_rate = 1e-4
n_iterations = 1000
batch_size = 128
dropout = 0.5
```

Batch size represents how many images are processing at each training step. The dropout variable is used to represent the threshold to eliminate some units at random. Dropout will be used in the final hidden layer to give a 50% chance to each unit from being eliminated at every training step. This prevents overfitting. The above-discussed hyperparameters affect the learning process. Now, the next step is to build the TensorFlow graph.

Step 4: Building the TensorFlow graph

The first step for the execution in TensorFlow is to build the computational graph. Tensor is the core concept of TensorFlow, a data structure similar to an array or list. Below lines of code defines three tensors as placeholders whose values will be assigned later. The dropout rate will be controlled by Keep_prob tensor.

Figure 40.

```
X = tf.placeholder("float", [None, n_input])
Y = tf.placeholder("float", [None, n_output])
keep_prob = tf.placeholder(tf.float32)
```

The parameters that will be updated in the network during the training process are weights and bias. Bias should be initialized with small constant value to activate the tensors in the initial stages.

Figure 41.

```
weights = {
    'w1': tf.Variable(tf.truncated_normal([n_input, n_hidden1], stddev=0.1)),
    'w2': tf.Variable(tf.truncated_normal([n_hidden1, n_hidden2], stddev=0.1)),
    'w3': tf.Variable(tf.truncated_normal([n_hidden2, n_hidden3], stddev=0.1)),
    'out': tf.Variable(tf.truncated_normal([n_hidden3, n_output], stddev=0.1)),
}
biases = {
    'b1': tf.Variable(tf.constant(0.1, shape=[n_hidden1])),
    'b2': tf.Variable(tf.constant(0.1, shape=[n_hidden2])),
    'b3': tf.Variable(tf.constant(0.1, shape=[n_hidden3])),
    'out': tf.Variable(tf.constant(0.1, shape=[n_output]))
}
```

Now, the next step is to set up the layers in the network by defining the operations to manipulate the tensors.

Figure 42.

```
layer_1 = tf.add(tf.matmul(X, weights['w1']), biases['b1'])
layer_2 = tf.add(tf.matmul(layer_1, weights['w2']), biases['b2'])
layer_3 = tf.add(tf.matmul(layer_2, weights['w3']), biases['b3'])
layer_drop = tf.nn.dropout(layer_3, keep_prob)
output_layer = tf.matmul(layer_3, weights['out']) + biases['out']
```

The final step in building the computational graph is to define the loss function that we want to optimize. Cross_entropy is the popular loss function in TensorFlow, which is also known as log-loss. There is a need for an optimization algorithm to minimize the loss function. The gradient descent optimization is a popular method to find the minimum of a function.

Figure 43.

```
cross_entropy = tf.reduce_mean(
    tf.nn.softmax_cross_entropy_with_logits(
        labels=Y, logits=output_layer
        ))
train_step = tf.train.AdamOptimizer(1e-4).minimize(cross_entropy)
```

The next step is to feed the input data to the computational graph for the training process.

Step 5: Training and Testing

Before starting the training process, define the method to evaluate the accuracy of mini-batches of data during the training. Then calculate the total accuracy score for the model.

Figure 44.

```
correct_pred = tf.equal(tf.argmax(output_layer, 1), tf.argmax(Y, 1))
accuracy = tf.reduce_mean(tf.cast(correct_pred, tf.float32))
```

Now, initialize the session to run the graph.

Figure 45.

```
init = tf.global_variables_initializer()
sess = tf.Session()
sess.run(init)
```

The main objective of the training process in deep learning is to optimize the loss function. Here, the authors are trying to minimize the difference between the predicted labels and the actual labels of the images. At each training step, parameters are adjusted in such a way that the loss is reduced for the next step (figure 46).

The output of the above lines of code is shown in figure 47.

Once the training is done, run the session on the test images. Now, the keep_prob dropout rate is 1.0 to ensure that all the units are active during the testing process (figure 48).

You can see that the accuracy of the above model is approximately equal to 92%. The proposed model can be tested on your hand-drawn number or any image of digit. One image can be downloaded from the given command (figure 49).

The above command will download the test image in the desired mentioned location.

Now, test the input image using below lines of code as seen in figure 50).

The output of the above code accurately determines that the given input image contains the image of digit 2.

Prediction for test image: 2

Figure 46.

```python
# train on mini batches
for i in range(n_iterations):
    batch_x, batch_y = mnist.train.next_batch(batch_size)
    sess.run(train_step, feed_dict={
        X: batch_x, Y: batch_y, keep_prob: dropout
        })

    # print loss and accuracy (per minibatch)
    if i % 100 == 0:
        minibatch_loss, minibatch_accuracy = sess.run(
            [cross_entropy, accuracy],
            feed_dict={X: batch_x, Y: batch_y, keep_prob: 1.0}
            )
        print(
            "Iteration",
            str(i),
            "\t| Loss =",
            str(minibatch_loss),
            "\t| Accuracy =",
            str(minibatch_accuracy)
            )
```

Figure 47.

```
Iteration 0      | Loss = 3.5653255    | Accuracy = 0.1328125
Iteration 100    | Loss = 0.5562477    | Accuracy = 0.84375
Iteration 200    | Loss = 0.29927945   | Accuracy = 0.8984375
Iteration 300    | Loss = 0.22969262   | Accuracy = 0.9375
Iteration 400    | Loss = 0.36258748   | Accuracy = 0.8828125
Iteration 500    | Loss = 0.41628528   | Accuracy = 0.8828125
Iteration 600    | Loss = 0.33859777   | Accuracy = 0.9140625
Iteration 700    | Loss = 0.34839442   | Accuracy = 0.921875
Iteration 800    | Loss = 0.27601948   | Accuracy = 0.9296875
Iteration 900    | Loss = 0.16266724   | Accuracy = 0.953125
```

Figure 48.

```python
test_accuracy = sess.run(accuracy, feed_dict={X: mnist.test.images, Y: mnist.test.labels, keep_prob: 1.0})
print("\nAccuracy on test set:", test_accuracy)
```

```
Accuracy on test set: 0.9179
```

Figure 49.

```
(tensorflow_cpu) C:\Users\sanwarul\Desktop>curl -O https://raw.githubusercontent.com/do-community/tensorflow-digit-recog
nition/master/test_img.png
  % Total    % Received % Xferd  Average Speed   Time    Time     Time  Current
                                 Dload  Upload   Total   Spent    Left  Speed
100   393  100   393    0     0    393      0  0:00:01 --:--:--  0:00:01   513
```

Figure 50.

```
import numpy as np
from PIL import Image
img = np.invert(Image.open("C:/Users/sanwarul/Desktop/test_img.png").convert('L')).ravel()
prediction = sess.run(tf.argmax(output_layer, 1), feed_dict={X: [img]})
print ("Prediction for test image:", np.squeeze(prediction))
```

ADVANTAGES AND DISADVANTAGES OF TENSORFLOW

Advantages

1) It is an open-source library so it is easily available free of cost.
2) It provides graph visualizations using TensorBoard for a better understanding of the model.
3) It supports both CPU and GPU.
4) It has excellent community support
5) It provides regular updates and frequent releases with new features.
6) Scalability

Disadvantages

1) It does not support windows operating system. If you are a window user, you can install it through anaconda or python package library.
2) Extra steps are required to run even a simple hello world program; we need to run the program using a session.
3) It supports only NVIDIA GPUs and has only full language support of python.
4) It has a unique structure so it is difficult to debug the TensorFlow program.

REFERENCES

Abadi, M., Agarwal, A., Barham, P., Brevdo, E., Chen, Z., Citro, C., . . . Ghemawat, S. (2016). *Tensorflow: Large-scale machine learning on heterogeneous distributed systems.* arXiv preprint arXiv:1603.04467

Aryan, M. (2018). *How to Use TensorBorad?* Retrieved 12 September 2019, from https://itnext.io/how-to-use-tensorboard-5d82f8654496

Chollet, F. (2015). Keras documentation. *keras.io.*

Introducing TensorFlow Datasets. (2019). Retrieved 8 September 2019, from https://medium.com/tensorflow/introducing-tensorflow-datasets-c7f01f7e19f3

Jason, B. (2019). *What is Deep Learning?* Retrieved 10 January 2020, from https://machinelearning-mastery.com/what-is-deep-learning/

LeCun, Y., Cortes, C., & Burges, C. J. (1998). *The MNIST database of handwritten digits, 1998.* http://yann. lecun. com/exdb/mnist

Ramsundar, B., & Zadeh, R. B. (2018). *TensorFlow for deep learning: from linear regression to reinforcement learning.* O'Reilly Media, Inc.

TensorFlow. (2016). Retrieved 4 September 2019, from https://www.tensorflow.org/guide/graphs

Zaccone, G., Karim, M. R., & Menshawy, A. (2017). *Deep Learning with TensorFlow.* Packt Publishing Ltd.

Chapter 5
Employee's Attrition Prediction Using Machine Learning Approaches

Krishna Kumar Mohbey

 https://orcid.org/0000-0002-7566-0703

Department of Computer Science, Central University of Rajasthan, India

ABSTRACT

In any industry, attrition is a big problem, whether it is about employee attrition of an organization or customer attrition of an e-commerce site. If we can accurately predict which customer or employee will leave their current company or organization, then it will save much time, effort, and cost of the employer and help them to hire or acquire substitutes in advance, and it would not create a problem in the ongoing progress of an organization. In this chapter, a comparative analysis between various machine learning approaches such as Naïve Bayes, SVM, decision tree, random forest, and logistic regression is presented. The presented result will help us in identifying the behavior of employees who can be attired over the next time. Experimental results reveal that the logistic regression approach can reach up to 86% accuracy over other machine learning approaches.

INTRODUCTION

Today attrition is one of the major problems faced by industry across the world. It is the most burning issue for the industry, and high attrition rates lead to many issues in the boundary of the organization like losing the talents and knowledge, cost related to training and administration, and recruitment. It is observed that many attributes lead to the attrition of an employee. Which includes working environment, job satisfaction, employer's behavior, job timing, and most important is salary or incentives. Also, the prediction model plays an essential role in finding the behavior of employees.

DOI: 10.4018/978-1-7998-3095-5.ch005

Timely delivery of any service or product is the primary goal of any organization in recent days due to high competition in industries. If a talented employee leaves unexpectedly, the company is not able to complete the task at defined times. It may become the reason for the loss of that company. Therefore, companies are interested in knowing the employee's attrition. They can make a proper substitute or arrangements earlier.

There may be various reasons for employee attrition, which include less salary, job satisfaction, personal reasons, or environmental issues if the employer terminates an employee for any reason. It is known as involuntary attrition (Kaur & Vijay, 2016). On the other hand, voluntary attrition is known as the left of an employee by their side. This kind of attrition is a loss for the company if he or she is a talented employee. In the present scenario, everyone wants a higher salary and job security. Therefore, employees leave jobs immediately if they got a better chance in other places.

In the recent era of computer science, machine learning approaches play an important role in employee attrition prediction. These approaches provide predictions based on historical information of the employee, such as age, experience, education, last promotion, and so on. Based on the prediction results HR department have prior knowledge about employee attrition. The HR department also has preplanned recruiting employees as a substitute for the employee who is interested in leaving in the coming days.

Various researches have also studied the performance of different machine learning approaches (Ajit, 2016; Sikaroudi et al., 2015). Kaur et al. (Kaur & Vijay, 2016) have discussed various reasons or factors that are involved in employee attrition. They have also investigated that talented employee replacement is a time-consuming and challenging task. It is also a significant factor in loss in business.

Compensation is one solution to decreasing the attrition rate. Moncaarz et al. (Moncarz et al., 2009) have discussed how attrition can be decreased by providing better compensation.

Punnoose and Ajit (Ajit, 2016) have provided a comparative analysis of various machine learning approaches for employee turnover. Tree-based approaches are also used to predict employee attrition (Alao & Adeyemo, 2013). Jantan et al. (Jantan et al., 2010) have compared tree-based methods with other traditional machine learning approaches. Radaideh and Nagi (Al-Radaideh & Al Nagi, 2012) uses the decision tree for employee attrition prediction. In their work, they have found that job title is an essential feature of attrition, whereas age is not a very important feature.

Saradhi (Saradhi & Palshikar, 2011) uses various machine learning approaches for employee attrition prediction. They have taken a database of 1575 records with 25 features of employee and applied various classification approaches to predict attrition. They have shown that SVM has higher accuracy, which is 84.12%.

Due to confidentiality and noisy HR data, sometimes prediction has higher accuracy. It is difficult to generalized predictions for different organizations and employee roles (Zhao et al., 2018).

Previous studies presented accuracy as a primary evaluation standard for attrition prediction. Various machine learning approaches are used and evaluated in different datasets. It is challenging to conclude that which model is best for attrition prediction. The rate of employee attrition is always less than the employee who stays in the organization. Therefore, datasets are always imbalanced. Accuracy measures are not reliable for imbalanced datasets (Sexton et al., 2005; Sikaroudi et al., 2015; Tzeng et al., 2004). So that it is desired to have an accurate model to enhance the prediction accuracy of the models. Which provides better results to employers. Based on the accurate prediction results employers and HR department know the behavior of their employees

The aim of this chapter is to provide a comparative analysis of different machine learning approaches for employee attrition prediction. Here we have significantly enhanced the training process to solve the imbalanced class problem.

Methodology

In this chapter, various supervised machine learning approaches are used. This section provides a general description of these approaches.

Naïve Bayes

It is a probabilistic approach that uses Bayes theorem to predict the posterior probability of a class. It computes the posterior probability of an event based on the prior knowledge of the related feature(Rane & Kumar, 2018). Equation 1 shows the computation of posterior probability.

$$P\left(\frac{Cl}{x}\right) = \frac{P\left(\frac{x}{Cl}\right).P(Cl)}{P(x)}$$

(1)

Where, Cl: specified class

x: review used for classification

$P(Cl)$ and $P(x)$: prior probabilities

$P\left(\dfrac{Cl}{x}\right)$: posterior probability

Support Vector Machine

It is a non-probabilistic supervised machine learning approaches used for classification and regression. It was initially proposed by Vapnik and cooper in 1995(Cortes & Vapnik, 1995). It assigns a new data member to one of two possible classes. It defines a hyperplane that separates n-dimensional data into two classes.

Logistic Regression

It is a traditional classification approach used to assign observations to a particular class. It transforms its output using a logistic sigmoid function to return a probability value that can be mapped to a class. It is a widely used classifier that is easy to implement and works well on linearly separable classes (Raschka, 2015).

Random Forest

It consists of many individual decision trees that are used to train data (Ho, 1995). Each tree in a random forest spits out a class prediction, and the class with the most votes becomes the model's prediction. It uses an ensemble approach that provides an improvement over basic tree structure. It combines various weak learners to form an active learner. Ensemble methods are based on the divide and conquer approach to improve performance.

Decision Tree

It is a supervised learning approach that builds a classification model in a tree structure. It makes classification rules by using the top-down approach. It makes sequences of rules which is used to determine the class of a new observation. It uses post pruning methods to handle overfitting problems (Morgan & Sonquist, 1963).

Dataset and Tools

In this work, we used a publicly available dataset of HR details. This dataset is a simulated dataset that is created by IBM Watson Analytics (McKinley Stacker, 2015). This dataset contained standard HR features such as attrition, age, gender, education, last promotion, job title, and so on. This dataset contained 1470 employee records with 38 features. In this dataset 237 employee has "yes" attrition category while 1233 employee was "no" attrition category. Here all non-numeric values were assigned numerical values. The data conversion was performed using label encoding via the Scikit-learn package in Python (Pedregosa et al., 2011). Furthermore, Python is used in this work to train and evaluate various machine learning approaches. The correlation of different features is a heatmap in figure 1. Figure 1 shows how different features of the HR dataset are correlated. It also shows poorly correlated features and highly correlated features.

Experiment Design

In this section, the results of various machine learning approaches are illustrated. All the approaches are evaluated on the precision, recall, accuracy, and AUC (Area Under ROC Curve). Various performance parameters are described below (Alduayj & Rajpoot, 2018; Powers, 2011).

$$\text{Accuracy} = \frac{TP+TN}{TP+TN+FP+FN} \tag{2}$$

$$\text{Precision} = \frac{TP}{TP+FP} \tag{3}$$

$$\text{Recall} = \frac{TP}{TP+FN} \tag{4}$$

$$F-\text{measure} = \frac{2*\text{Precision}*\text{Recall}}{\text{Precision}+\text{Recall}} \tag{5}$$

Figure 1. Correlation between various features

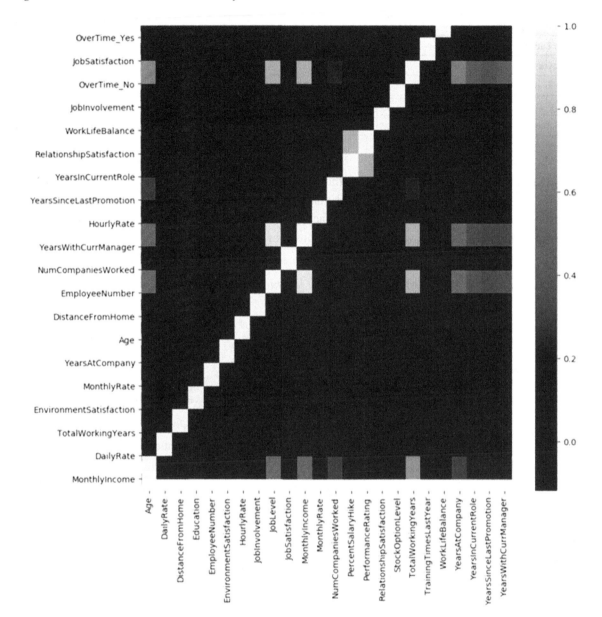

$$AUC = \frac{\left(Recall - \frac{FP}{FP+TN} + 1 \right)}{2} \qquad (6)$$

where TP is true positives values, TN is true negative, FP is false positives, and FN is the false negatives values.

Table 1 compares the performance of various machine learning approaches. It includes precision, recall, and accuracy of employee attrition prediction.

Table 1. Comparison of precision, recall and f1 score of a different approach

Approach	Precision	Recall	f1-score
Random Forest	0.84	0.85	0.80
Naïve Bayes	0.75	0.54	0.59
Logistic Regression	**0.87**	**0.86**	**0.83**
SVM	0.77	0.41	0.45
Decision Tree	0.79	0.80	0.79

Table 1 show that the logistic regression method has a higher f1-score over other compared approaches.

Figure 1 displays the accuracy of different machine learning approaches. It can be concluded that the logistic regression approach has better accuracy over other approaches on the HR dataset. Another comparison is made using AUC values, which is shown in figure 2.

Figure 2. Accuracy comparison of various machine learning approaches

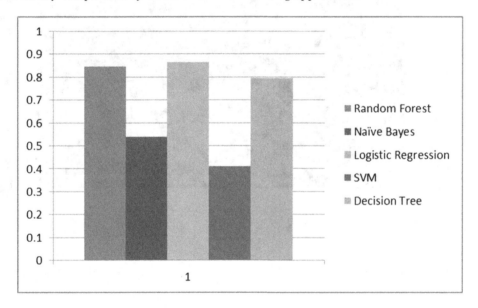

CONCLUSION

Employee attrition has been identified as a significant problem for any organization. High performance and talented employee attrition are considered as a loss for that organization. Finding a substitute for that employee is a time-consuming task. In this work, the performance of various machine learning approaches is evaluated on the HR dataset. Here five different approaches are compared. Based on the accuracy measurement, logistic regression well performed for this dataset. It has higher precision, recall, and accuracy. The result of the attrition prediction will be helpful for an organization to reduce the attrition rate of their company.

Figure 3. AUC comparison of various machine learning approaches

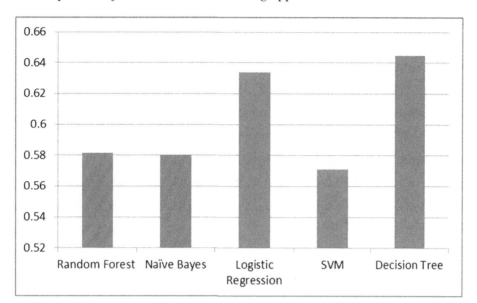

REFERENCES

Ajit, P. (2016). Prediction of employee turnover in organizations using machine learning algorithms. *Algorithms*, *4*(5), C5.

Al-Radaideh, Q. A., & Al Nagi, E. (2012). Using data mining techniques to build a classification model for predicting employees performance. *International Journal of Advanced Computer Science and Applications*, *3*(2).

Alao, D., & Adeyemo, A. B. (2013). Analyzing employee attrition using decision tree algorithms. *Computing, Information Systems, Development Informatics and Allied Research Journal, 4*.

Alduayj, S. S., & Rajpoot, K. (2018). Predicting Employee Attrition using Machine Learning. *2018 International Conference on Innovations in Information Technology (IIT)*, 93–98. 10.1109/INNOVATIONS.2018.8605976

Cortes, C., & Vapnik, V. (1995). Support-vector networks. *Machine Learning*, *20*(3), 273–297. doi:10.1007/BF00994018

Ho, T. K. (1995). Random decision forests. *Proceedings of 3rd International Conference on Document Analysis and Recognition*, *1*, 278–282.

Jantan, H., Hamdan, A. R., & Othman, Z. A. (2010). Human talent prediction in HRM using C4. 5 classification algorithm. *International Journal on Computer Science and Engineering*, *2*(8), 2526–2534.

Kaur, S., & Vijay, M. R. (2016). Job satisfaction-A major factor behind attrition of retention in retail industry. *Imperial Journal of Interdisciplinary Research*, *2*(8), 993–996.

McKinley Stacker, I. V. (2015). IBM waston analytics. Sample data: HR employee attrition and performance [Data file]. McKinley Stacker.

Moncarz, E., Zhao, J., & Kay, C. (2009). An exploratory study of US lodging properties' organizational practices on employee turnover and retention. *International Journal of Contemporary Hospitality Management*, *21*(4), 437–458. doi:10.1108/09596110910955695

Morgan, J. N., & Sonquist, J. A. (1963). Problems in the analysis of survey data, and a proposal. *Journal of the American Statistical Association*, *58*(302), 415–434. doi:10.1080/01621459.1963.10500855

Pedregosa, F., Varoquaux, G., Gramfort, A., Michel, V., Thirion, B., Grisel, O., & ... . (2011). Scikit-learn: Machine learning in Python. *Journal of Machine Learning Research*, *12*(Oct), 2825–2830.

Powers, D. M. (2011). *Evaluation: from precision, recall and F-measure to ROC, informedness, markedness and correlation*. Academic Press.

Rane, A., & Kumar, A. (2018, July). Sentiment Classification System of Twitter Data for {US} Airline Service Analysis. In *2018 {IEEE} 42nd Annual Computer Software and Applications Conference ({COMPSAC})*. IEEE. 10.1109/compsac.2018.00114

Raschka, S. (2015). *Python machine learning*. Packt Publishing Ltd.

Saradhi, V. V., & Palshikar, G. K. (2011). Employee churn prediction. *Expert Systems with Applications*, *38*(3), 1999–2006. doi:10.1016/j.eswa.2010.07.134

Sexton, R. S., McMurtrey, S., Michalopoulos, J. O., & Smith, A. M. (2005). Employee turnover: A neural network solution. *Computers & Operations Research*, *32*(10), 2635–2651. doi:10.1016/j.cor.2004.06.022

Sikaroudi, E., Mohammad, A., Ghousi, R., & Sikaroudi, A. (2015). A data mining approach to employee turnover prediction (case study: Arak automotive parts manufacturing). *Journal of Industrial and Systems Engineering*, *8*(4), 106–121.

Tzeng, H.-M., Hsieh, J.-G., & Lin, Y.-L. (2004). Predicting Nurses' Intention to Quit with a Support Vector Machine: A New Approach to Set up an Early Warning Mechanism in Human Resource Management. *CIN: Computers, Informatics, Nursing*, *22*(4), 232–242. PMID:15494654

Zhao, Y., Hryniewicki, M. K., Cheng, F., Fu, B., & Zhu, X. (2018). Employee turnover prediction with machine learning: A reliable approach. *Proceedings of SAI Intelligent Systems Conference*, 737–758.

Chapter 6

A Novel Deep Learning Method for Identification of Cancer Genes From Gene Expression Dataset

Pyingkodi Maran
Kongu Engineering College, India & Anna University, India

Thenmozhi K.
https://orcid.org/0000-0003-0934-2552
Selvam College of Technology, India

Shanthi S.
Kongu Engineering College, India

Hemalatha D.
Kongu Engineering College, India

Nanthini K.
Kongu Engineering College, India

ABSTRACT

Computational biology is the research area that contributes to the analysis of biological information. The selection of the subset of cancer-related genes is one amongst the foremost promising clinical research of gene expression data. Since a gene can take the role of various biological pathways that in turn can be active only under specific experimental conditions, the stacked denoising auto-encoder(SDAE) and the genetic algorithm were combined to perform biclustering of cancer genes from huge dimensional microarray gene expression data. The Genetic-SDAE proved superior to recently proposed biclustering methods and better to determine the maximum similarity of a set of biclusters of gene expression data with lower MSR and higher gene variance. This work also assesses the results with respect to the discovered genes and spot that the extracted set of biclusters are supported by biological evidence, such as enrichment of gene functions and biological processes.

DOI: 10.4018/978-1-7998-3095-5.ch006

INTRODUCTION

Bioinformatics is a multidisciplinary subject, related to area as diverse as Computer Science, Mathematics, Biology, Statistics and Information Technology. Cancer is featured by an irregular, unmanageable growth that may destroy and cause the neighboring healthy body tissues. In the past, cancer classification by medical practitioners and radiologists was based on clinical and morphological features and had limited diagnostic ability. It deals with different kinds of biological data. The dimension and complexity of raw gene expression data creates challenging data analysis and data management problems. The fundamental goal of microarray gene expression data analysis is to find the behaviourial patterns of genes.

Computational molecular biology deals with different kinds of biological data. Gene expression data is one among them. Hence Gene expression data are the basic data used in this paper. Gene expression is the process by which the information encoded in a gene is changed into an observable phenotype (protein). It is the degree to which a gene is active in certain tissues of the body, measured by the amount of Messenger Ribonucleic Acid (mRNA) in the tissue. Individual genes can be switched on (apply their effects) or switched off according to the needs and situations of the cell at a particular instance. Thus, abnormalities or deviations of gene expression may result in the death of cells, or their uncontrolled growth, such as cancer (Subramanian 2010).

Gene Expression Data

The gene expression matrix is a processed data obtained after the normalization. Each row in the matrix corresponds to a particular gene and each column could either correspond to an experimental condition or a specific time point at which expression of the genes has been measured (Tiwari *et al.* 2012). The expression level for a gene across different experimental conditions is cumulatively called the gene expression profile, and the expression level of each gene under an experimental condition is cumulatively called the sample expression profile (Androulakis *et al.* 2007). An expression profile of an experimental condition or a gene is thought of as a vector and can be represented in vector space. For example, an expression profile of a gene can be considered as a vector in n dimensional space where n is the number of conditions, and an expression profile of a condition with m genes can be considered as a vector in m dimensional space where m is the number of genes. Figure 1 shows the gene expression matrix A with m genes across n conditions is considered to be an $m \times n$ matrix. Each element a_{ij} of this matrix represents the expression level of a gene i under a specific condition j, and is represented by a real number.

SIGNIFICANCE OF CANCER DIAGNOSIS USING MICROARRAY

Current cancer classification includes more than 200 types of cancer (American Cancer Society). For any patient to receive proper therapy, the clinician must identify as accurately as possible the cancer type. Although analysis of morphologic characteristics of biopsy specimens is still the standard diagnostic method, it gives very limited information and clearly misses much important cancer aspects such as rate of proliferation, capacity for invasion and metastases, and development of resistance mechanisms to certain treatment agents. To appropriately classify cancer subtypes, therefore, molecular diagnostic methods are needed. The classical molecular methods look for the DNA, RNA or protein of a defined marker that is correlated with a specific type of tumor and may or may not give biological information

Figure 1. Gene expression matrix

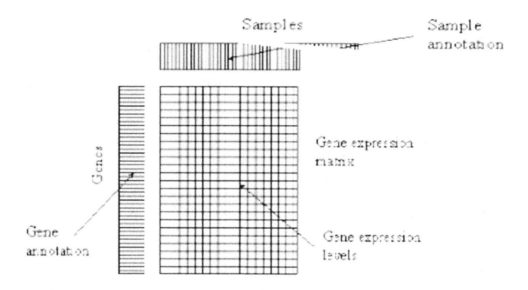

about cancer generation or progression. However, a major advantage of microarray is that huge amount of molecular information that can be extracted and integrated to find common patterns within a group of samples. The microarrays could be used in combination with other diagnostic methods to add more information about the cancer specimen by looking at thousands of genes concurrently. This new method is revolutionizing cancer diagnostics because it not only classifies cancer samples into known and new taxonomic categories, and discovers new diagnostic and therapeutic markers, but also identifies new subtypes that correlate with treatment outcome.

Biclustering

The clustering problem deals with gene similarities as reflected by their activity across all conditions is that all genes in the cluster share the exact same functions, and are therefore all affected by the same conditions. Actually, many gene products are known to have more than one function. This means that a group of genes displays similar expression behavior across some of the conditions (those related to the shared function), while displaying different properties when looking at conditions relating to functions not shared among all the genes in the group. The standard clustering approach is oversimplified to detect such cases, creating the need for a more refined, local, approach to biclustering. It should be noted that while the clustering problem always creates disjoint clusters that cover all the input set, biclusters may overlap, and they usually cover only a part of the matrix. This overlap is expected when assuming that each bicluster represents a function and that genes have more than one function.

Biclustering takes the input as huge dimensional gene expression dataset, and tries to find statistically significant sub-matrices in it, also called biclusters. These structures show a joint behavior of few genes under some conditions. While clustering techniques can be applied to either rows or columns of a data matrix separately, biclustering methods perform clustering in the two dimensions simultaneously are known as two-way clustering.

Review of Related Works

As we discussed in the introduction of this paper, the biclustering problem is a NP-hard Tany (2002). For that reason, meta-heuristic approaches are generally employ to the problem by finding suboptimal solutions.Cheng & Church (2000) were the first apply this concept on biclustering in gene expression data. Their objective is to select biclusters with a MSR value lower than a given threshold. Hence, authors arrived an iterative search procedure which deletes/adds rows/columns to the biclusters. The single node deletion method iteratively removes the row or column that has low quality according to MSR. This strategy succeeds in discovering biclusters with coherent values. Since, the method selects one bicluster at a time, repeated application of the method on a modified matrix is needed for finding multiple biclusters. This has the drawbacks that it overcomes in highly overlapping gene sets.

Most of biclustering methods of binary microarray data, including BiMax and GBC, fail to extract pertinent biclusters on sparse binary datasets. Therefore, recently (Saber & Elloumi 2015) presented BiBin Alter, BiBin Cons, BiBin Sim and BiBin Max for biclustering of binary microarray data. It starts with binarize thresholding function to transform the input gene expression data to a binary one. Ayadi *et al.* (2012) presented a Pattern Driven Neighborhood Search (PDNS) approach for the biclustering problem. PDNS first follows up a preprocessing step to transform the input data matrix to a behavior matrix and a dedicated neighborhood taking into account various patterns information. (Ayadi & Hao 2014) proposed a Memetic Biclustering Algorithm (MBA) which is able to detect negatively correlated biclusters. This method adopts population-based search and neighbourhood-based local search. It is generally consider that the population- based search framework provides more facilities for exploration while neighbourhood search offers more capabilities for exploitation.Huang *et al.* (2012) proposed a biclustering algorithm called Condition-Based Evolutionary Biclustering (CBEB) which is based on the use of an Evolutionary Algorithm (EA) combined with hierarchical clustering. In this technique, the conditions are isolated into a number of condition subsets, also called subspaces.Maatouk *et al.* (2014) proposed an Evolutionary Biclustering algorithm based on the new crossover method (EBACross). It applys a fast-local search method to generate an initial population with better quality. Yidong *et al.* (2016) present a novel biclustering algorithm, which is called Weighted Mutual Information Biclustering algorithm (WMIB) it discovers the local characteristics of gene expression data.

A supervised learning hidden Markov model (HMMs) was developed inThanh et al (2015) for performing the cancer classification with the help of gene expression profiles. But, an optimal subset of genes was not selected for classification. Kun-Huang et al (2014) proposed a particle swarm optimization technique associated with decision tree classifier was developed to select an efficient gene from thousands of candidate genes in cancers detection. However, the hybrid search algorithm was not minimizing the execution time. A several machine learning (ML) techniques was presented in Konstantina et al (2015) to select certain genes for cancer prediction. However it failed to perform better statistical analysis for obtaining more accurate results for cancer detection. A Hybrid search method Simulated Annealing with a Greedy Algorithm (SAGA) and Bayesian Networks was developed in Emmanuel et al (2015) for detecting the transcriptional regulatory correlations among the genes. However, the false discovery from true relationships was not improved. A new gene expressions based colon classification approach (GECC) was introduced in Saima et al(2014) for performing the classification using colon gene samples and obtained two output classes as normal and malignant. However, an efficient technique was not used to select optimal patterns from the gene. Support Vector Machine classifier was developed in (Heena et al 2017) for cancer classification with gene expression data. But the optimization was not carried out in bio informatics data analysis. Binary particle swarm optimization (BPSO) technique was developed in (Mohd 2011) for gene selection on gene expression datasets. However, it failed to produce optimal patterns from gene expression data. An evolutionary computation and multi objective optimization technique was introduced in [20] for solving the bioinformatics problem. However, cancer detection was not performed using optimized sequences. Different gene expression pattern associated to breast cancer was detected in (Zhenzhen, 2015) using Cancer Genome Atlas dataset. However, the performance of cancer detection rate was not improved.

A machine learning clustering and classification techniques were developed in (Shaurya et al 2014) for detecting the cancer with gene expression data. But, optimal patterns were not selected for diseases prediction. From the output of microarrays technology are gene expression data which consist of valuable Information of medical diagnostic and foretelling for investigator (Pyingkodi et al 2017). The author believe that stacked denoising auto encoders can extract good representations from this highdimensional data and enable the extraction of biologically meaningful information that can give cancer researchers a direction for further studies (Vıtor,2017)

(Jie et al, 2015) DAs were trained using the METABRIC dataset and evaluated on the TCGA dataset. DAs constructed a novel feature that was highly predictive of patient survival, and from this we uncovered a variety of biological processes enriched in that feature(Padideh, 2017) used stacked denoising autoencoders (SDAE) to transform high dimensional, noisy gene expression data to a lower dimensional, meaningful representation.Then used the new representations to classify breast cancer samples from the healthy control samples.We presented a deep learning method forgene expression inference that significantly outperforms LR on the GEO microarray data. With dropout as regularization, our deeplearning method also preserves cross platforms generalizability on the GTEx RNA-Seq data. In summary, deep learning provides a better model than LR for gene expression inference. The author believe thatit achieves more accurate predictions for target gene expressions of the LINCS dataset generated from the L1000 platform (Yifei et al 2016). considering 500 bp sequences, CNN outperforms all the other classififiers considering all the three performances score, demonstrating thatthe CNN network is the only algorithm that build a model that is able to generalize in order to correctly classify genomic sequences even in only a short fragmentis provided (Angelini et al 2016).The above said issues are overcome by introducing a new technique called Genetic Stacked Denoising Autoencoders .

GENETIC ALGORITHM FOR PERFORMING BICLUSTERING OPERATIONS

Given a two-dimensional gene expression matrix M with n columns and m rows, it consists of the expression level of m genes G = {I_1, I_2,…, I_m} over a series of n successive time-points or conditions C = {C_1, C_2,…, C_n} during a biological process. Each element M_{ij}denotes the expression level of the ith gene at the j^{th}time-point or Experimental conditions. A bicluster interpreted as a submatrix B(I, J) of expression matrix *M*, where I, J are subsets of genes set G and conditions set C respectively(I $\subseteq$ G and J $\subseteq$ C). A bicluster is encoded as a genetic chromosome that is represented by a fixed-size binary string collection of genes and experimental conditions. If a gene is available in a bicluster, the corresponding bit is set to 1, otherwise 0

a)   a fitness function to evaluate the solutions
b)   Genetic operators

Binary tournament is used as selection operator. The crossover operator used as two-point crossover operator. Crossover is separately performed on both of gene and time-point parts of each chromosome. For the gene segment, two crossover points are selected on each of two chosen parent chromosomes, and then the segments between these segments are swap over between two parents. For the conditions segment, it is performed similarly. Mutation operator is done as follows. For each bit of selected chromosome in both conditions and genes, it is functioned based on mutation probability rate.

STACKED DENOISING AUTOENCODER DEEP LEARNING TECHNIQUE FOR PATTERN SELECTION

The dataset contains a noisy gene expression data which has a number of sequence patterns. The identification of more suitable patterns from the gene sequences for cancer detection is a demanding issue by the reason of the high dimensionality and complexity since the patterns appears exactly once in each gene sequence. In order to reduce complexity and obtain the significant patterns for cancer detection is performed using stacked denoising autoencoder (SDA) deep learning technique. Autoencoder is a deep feed forward neural network based feature selection method for obtaining the significant features from the dataset for cancer detection. A typical neural network consists of three layers such as input, hidden and output. A deep learning approach is used to select functional features (i.e. patterns) for cancer detection from the high dimensional gene expression dataset using more than one hidden layers. In the deep learning architecture, autoencoders are stacked one layer over the other layer to learn gene sequences for cancer detection from the dataset. Denoising is used to reduce the sequence pattern from the gene regulatory sequences. The Stacked denoising autoencoder for significant pattern selection is shown in figure 2.

Figure 2. Stacked denoising autoencoder

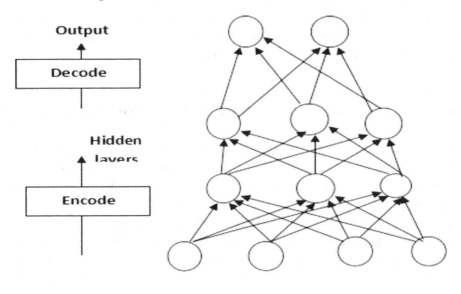

Construction of Denoising Autoencoders from Genomic Data

DAs provide a powerful means to analyze audio or image data where measurements are temporally or spatially linked.4,9Here we describe a technique that allowed construction of DAs from genomic data, which do not have temporal or spatial linkage. These DAs summarized the gene expression characteristics of both breast cancers and normal tissues to automatically extract biologically and clinically relevant features. The constructed DAnetworks contained three layers: an input layer, a hidden layer and a reconstructed layer (Figure.2). The hidden layer represented the constructed features, with each node corresponding to one feature. The reconstructed layer and the input layer had the same dimensions, and the objective function for the algorithm was to minimize the difference between the two layers. Noise was added to the input data during training to construct robust, high-quality features.6Here we describe the detailed training process for DAs from genome-wide transcriptome measurements. We define the term "sample" to represent the complete gene expression vector for each collected tissue biopsy. To facilitate training, samples were randomly grouped into batches, and the number of samples contained in a batch was termed the batch size. For each sample in a batch, a set of genes matching a defined proportion of genes (termed the corruption level) were randomly chosen. The expression values for these genes in this sample were set to zero. Like other feed-forward ANNs, the hidden layer y was constructed by multiplying one sample x with a weight matrix W. A bias vector, b, was added before transformation by the sigmoid function (Formula 1). The value contained in the hidden vector y for each node was termed the activity value of that node. The reconstructed layer was generated from the hidden layer in a similar manner (Formula 2). We used tied weights, which meant that the transpose of W was used for W'. Cross-entropy (Formula 3) was used to measure the difference between the input layer (x) and the reconstructed layer (z). Thus, the problem became fitting appropriate weights and bias terms to minimize the cross-entropy. This optimization was achieved by stochastic gradient descent using the Theano10 library, with weight and bias being updated after each batch and the size of each update is controlled by learning rate. Training proceeded through epochs, and samples were rebatched at the beginning of each epoch. Training was stopped after a specified number of epochs (termed epoch size) was reached.

Interpretation of Constructed Features

A major weakness of traditional ANNs has been the difficulty of interpreting the constructedmodels. DAs have largely been used in image processing, where these algorithms constructfeatures that recognize key components of images, for example diagonal lines. Unlike pixelsin image data, genes are not linked to their neighbors, and unlike audio data, they are notlinked temporally. Instead they are linked by their transcription factors, their pathwaymembership, and other biological properties. To address this interpretation challenge, wedeveloped strategies that allow constructed features to be linked to clinical and molecularfeatures of the underlying samples

SDAE Implementation

In this work a deep learning technique that obtain the significant gene expression relationships using SDAE. Next training the SDAE, it identified a layer that has both low-dimension and low validation error compared to other encoder stacks using a validation data set independent of both our training and test set. As a result, we selected an SDAE with four layers of dimensions of 15,000, 10,000, 2,000, and 500.

Consequently we used the selected layer as input features to the classification algorithms. The goal of our model is extracting a mapping that possibly decodes the original data as closely as possible without losing significant gene patterns.

We evaluated our approach for feature selection by feeding the SDAE-encoded features to a shallow artificial neural network (ANN) and an SVM model. Furthermore, we applied a similar approach with PCA and KPCA as a comparison Lastly, we used the SDAE weights from each layer to extract genes with strongly propagated influence on the reduced-dimension SDAE-encoding. These selected "deeply connected genes" (DCGs) are further tested and analyzed for pathway and Gene Ontology (GO) enrichment. The results from our analysis showed that in fact our approach can reveal a set ofbiomark for our analysis, we analyzed RNA-seq expression data from The Cancer Genome Atlas(TCGA) database for both tumor and healthy breast samples. These data consist of 1097breast cancer samples, and 113 healthy samples. To overcome the class imbalance of the data, we used synthetic minority over-sampling technique (SMOTE) to transform data into a more balanced representation for pre-training. We used the imbalanced-learn package for this transformation of the training data. Furthermore, we removed all genes that had zero expression across all samples.ers for the purpose of cancer diagnosis.

Dimensionality Reduction Using Stacked Denoising Autoencoder

An autoencoder (AE) is a feedforward neural network that produces the output layer as close as possible to its input layer using a lower dimensional representation (hidden layer). The autoencoder consists of an encoder and a decoder. The encoder is a nonlinear function, like a sigmoid, applied to an fine mapping of the input layer, which can be expressed as $f\theta(X) = \sigma(W x+b)$ with parameters $\theta = \{W, b\}$. The matrix W is of dimensions d0×d to go from a larger dimension of gene expression data d to a lower dimensional encoding corresponding to d0. The bias vector b is of dimension d0. This input layer encodes the data to generate a

PROPOSED METHOD

This algorithm improved the traditional method to resolve the two problems are population size selection no longer depends on the specific data and running effect. Since the nested is used, the algorithm will run at a higher speed. In order to take account of population scale and efficiency, this algorithm used the Nested implementation of genetic algorithm and SDAE to overcome the population problem. The SDAE- Genetic method has two important advantages. SDAE- Genetic algorithm will result in decreasing computation time and also the result is very accurate.

SDAE – Genetic Method For Biclustering Of Gene Data Expression

In general, the performances of the meta-heuristic algorithms are mainly dependent on two properties of the algorithm: diversification and intensification, also mentioned as exploration and exploitation (Yang *et al.* 2014). The stochastic search algorithms are known for their powerful ability to avoid local optimal solutions, especially after using some local search strategies. Therefore, they can converge quickly to the global optimal solution so that a huge number of every meaningful biclusters are found in the relevant work. However, due to the type and structure complexity of the biclusters, no biclustering algorithm can solve all the bicluster analysis problems, so the method based on the hybrid strategy is proposed to solve the biclustering gene expression matrix problems. Considering that the genetic algorithm can quickly jump out of the global optimal solution and has a local search ability to get a solution of high coverage and better quality, the algorithm has weak local search ability so that it is tedious to further maximize the quality of the solution. Compared with the CS algorithm, the GA algorithm has strong local search power but weak global search ability.

Based on the characteristics of the above two algorithms and in order to further discover more biclusters with better coverage and quality on the gene expression data, the work describes a hybrid optimization method based on CS and GA and applies it to biclustering analysis. Although the basic GA algorithm demonstrates good global optimal search ability in optimization applications, it has the problem of premature convergence. Therefore, the GA is improved by balanced intensification and diversification.

Nested implementation of deeplearning hybrid scheme: the program mainly about nesting Deeplearning algorithm in the GA algorithm. Specially, the two algorithms are used to perform two iterations respectively to obtain two new populations. Then, the best individual is selected from the above two groups to form the descendants by the tournament selection. Then, combine the nest discard strategy of the Stacked denoising algorithm and the elite retention strategy of GA algorithm to eliminate the poor offspring individuals. Since the starting biclusters are constructed randomly, it may include that some irrelevant genes and/or conditions get included in spite of their expression values lying far apart in the feature space. An analogous situation may also happen during crossover and mutation in every generation. The crossover and mutation operator are applied to form a new off-spring in each generation: Crossover operator like single point crossover is utilized in each part of the solution (rows part and columns part). Each part takes place crossover independently.

These genes and conditions, with dissimilar values, need to be eliminated deterministically. Furthermore, for best biclustering, some conditions and /or genes having similar expression values need to be combined as well. In such situations, local search strategies (genetic algorithm) can be employed to add or remove multiple genes and/or conditions. It was observed that, in the absence of local search, stand-alone single-objective or MOEAs could not generate satisfactory solutions. The algorithm starts with a specified bicluster and an initial gene expression array (G, C). The irrelevant genes or conditions contains mean squared residue above (or below) a particular threshold are now selectively eliminated (or added) employing the Fitness function.

EXPERIMENTAL RESULTS AND ANALYSIS

Dataset

Experiments are conducted on five well–known gene expression datasets. In this work, the cancer gene expression datasets from NCBI are used for experimental purpose. The Datasets are widely used in these works are preprocessed which enables them to be used directly. Datasets are downloaded from GEO Database publicly available Gene expression Datasets constructed by NCBI. In order to assess the performance of the proposed methods, five datasets are investigated.

Experimental Setup

The Deeplearning biclustering algorithm implemented in this work and all the biclustering algorithms used Matlab language programming and run in Matlab R2014b environment. In addition, the GO biological enrichment analysis of biclusters is based on the R language package Gostats. All of the codes in this work are running on a 64-bit Windows 7 OS, the CPU is Intel Xeon (R) E3- 1225 whose dominant frequency is 3.2 GHz and its main memory is 16 GB.

The nest size of genetic Algorithm is 50. The minimum fitness value is obtained for 20 biclusters with the stopping criterion is up to the maximum iteration 100. The parameters p_a, α and λ are set as 0.25, 1 and 1.5 respectively. Table 3.1 shows the parameter and its value used in this work.

BIOLOGICAL VALIDATION OF BICLUSTERS

Biological validation can qualitatively evaluate the capacity of an algorithm to extract meaningful biclusters from a biological point of viewTanay *et al.* (2002); Yang *et al.* (2011). If the discovered biclusters contain significant proportion of biologically similar genes, then it proves that the biclustering method produces biologically relevant results. The biological significance can be verified using Gene Ontology (GO) database. The enriched annotation GO terms associated with the large gene list will give important insights that allow investigators to understand the biological themes behind the large gene list. The GO project has developed three structured ontologies that describe gene products in terms of their associated biological processes, cellular components and molecular functions in a species- independent manner. The degree of enrichment is measured by p-values which use a cumulative hyper geometric distribution to compute the probability of observing the number of genes from a particular GO category (function, process and component) within each bicluster. A bicluster is said to be over represented in a functional category if the p-value is below a certain threshold. The probability p for finding at least k genes from a particular category within a cluster of size m is given in Equation (6.1).

$$p = 1 - \sum_{r=0}^{k-1} \frac{\binom{G}{r}\binom{M-G}{m-r}}{\binom{M}{m}} \tag{1}$$

Where G is the total number of genes within a category and M is the total number of genes within the genome. The p-value is the probability that the genes are selected into the cluster by random. When the p-value is very small, it means that the majority of genes in a cluster appear in one category. The annotations of genes for three ontologies including biological process, cellular component and molecular function are obtained.

$$Jac(BC_i, BC_b BC_i, BC_b) = Jac_{ij} = \frac{\left|BC_i \cap BC_j\right|}{\left|BC_i \cup BC_j\right|} \tag{2}$$

Bicluster Extraction for Human Lymphoma Dataset

Table 3.2 summarizes the best biclusters for lymphoma cancer dataset after 100 generations. The maximum sized bicluster is identified at MSR=226.43, with coherence index CI seen minimal and proves the goodness of the identified patterns. The minimum value of CI is 0. 0465 with a corresponding size of 4587 being the best in the Table 1 As mentioned earlier, a low mean squared residue indicates a maximum coherence of the founded biclusters.

Table 1. Extracted biclusters for lymphoma dataset

Bicluster	Genes	Conditions	Volume	MSR	Row Variance	CI
BC$_2$	208	8	1664	158.53	796.90	0.0898
BC27	304	6	1824	179.84	812.16	0.0878
BC52	372	8	2976	183.16	793.77	0.0576
BC74	389	9	3501	192.36	835.75	0.0517
BC83	417	11	4587	226.43	948.02	0.0465

Figure 3. Gene expression profile of the largest bicluster on lymphomadataset

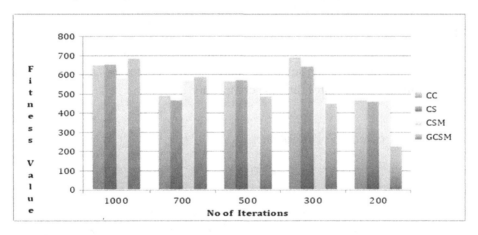

Figure 3 depicts the gene expression dataset of the maximum sized bicluster, corresponding to MSR=226.43. The gene expression values gives in the range 150 to 350 proves the highly dense profiles of the co regulated genes having few or no fluctuations under the selected conditions of the bicluster. It has the highest row variance is 948.02 whereas the MSR is 226.43. In terms of fitness, this is the most "interesting" bicluster which has largest volume 4587 with the lowest MSR. Moreover, GCSM tries to find highly row- variant biclusters instead of trivialbiclusters.

From Table 2 the fact can be seen that there is no difference between SDAE-Genetic algorithm and other heuristic Algorithm at the time and the number of iterations. But the algorithm willlose the space to speed up the algorithm. The maximum number of iteration in this algorithm always reached 1000 to terminate the algorithm.

Table 2. Number of iterations versus MSR on various

Number of Iterations	Fitness Value			
	CC (Cheng & Church 2000)	CS (Yang, S. Deb.)	CSM (Balamurugan)	SDAE(proposed)
1000	650	653	583	685
700	492	467	568	590
500	564	572	536	489
300	692	642	539	450
200	469	460	469	226

Table 3. Comparison of Average MSR Vs No. of Iteration Vs Time Complexity on various Algorithms

Method	Average MSR	No of Iterations	Iterative value in seconds (Time Complexity)
CC (Cheng & Church 2000)	204.29	543	1106
CS (Yang S. Deb.)	228.16	487	998
CSM(Balamurugan)	176.12	351	621
SDAE(proposed)	167.43	318	486

From Table 3 the Experimental results show that the proposed nested based SDAE genetic on biclustering of geneexpression data, can retrieve more significant marker subset of genes and conditions. It not only find out biclusters having low mean square redidue, but also it takes less number of iterations, meanwhile the proposed method can control the time complexity

Figure 4. Comparison of Fitness value Vs Algorithm

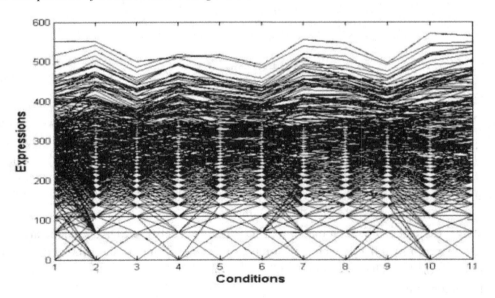

Figure 4 shows the results of the proposed method that are compared with CC (Cheng & Church 2000), CS(X. Yang, S. Deb.) and CSM(Balamurugan) on Colon tumor dataset. The high value of MSR depicts that the bicluster is weakly coherent while a low value MSR shows that it is highly coherent (SDAE). CS employs a herusitic approach to find biclusters of limited size. It is based on the initial choice of random seeds. Similarly CC algorithm gives a small size of biclusters because of random inference is involved. SDAE is able to locate large biclusters for minimum MSR compared with CS. The bicluster found by GCSM is interesting; however, it extracts very small size of bicluster for average MSR of 206.17. CC returns biclusters with large MSR. Next CS method returns largest bicluster, however average MSR of CS is larger than all other methods. In the case of SDAE, average MSR is better than the all other algorithms. Even so volume of bicluster is far better than the other algorithms. Thus, it can finds significant bicluster while maintain the maximum size of bicluster with lowMSR.

CONCLUSION AND FUTURE WORK

In this work SDAE algorithms for biclustering microarray gene expression data are proposed to speed up the convergence rate of CS algorithm. It focuses on finding coherent bicluster with lower MSR and higher row variance. In CSM uses the mutation operator instead of levy flight to generate a new solution. The proposed method improves the global search ability and prevents the basic CS algorithm into a local optimum. It increases the solution convergence easily. Moreover, the SDAE preserves the balanced exploitation and exploration via the process of mutation shuffling in the solution of the search space respectively. In particular the SDAE shows a high convergence rate to the true global minimum even problem at multi-dimensions. The proposed biclustering method is applied to two gene expression data sets. The coherent biclusters obtained using the proposed method reveal good biological meanings. Biological assessment of the identified genes within the biclusters are provided by publicly available GO consortium. This experimental study shows that SDAE algorithm competes satisfactorily compared to other popular biclustering algorithms to detect the coherent biclusters.

REFERENCES

Adabor, Acquaah-Mensah, & Oduro. (2015). SAGA: A hybrid search algorithm for Bayesian Network structure learning of transcriptional regulatory networks. *Journal of Biomedical Informatics, Elsevier, 53*, 27–35. doi:10.1016/j.jbi.2014.08.010

American Cancer Society. (2019). *Cancer Facts & Figures 2019*. Atlanta: American Cancer Society.

Androulakis, I. P., Yang, E., & Almon, R. R. (2007). Analysis of time-series gene expression data: Methods, challenges, and opportunities. *Annual Review of Biomedical Engineering, 9*(1), 205–228. doi:10.1146/annurev.bioeng.9.060906.151904 PMID:17341157

Angelini & Riccardo. (2016). Deep Learning Approach to DNA Sequence Classifification',Springer International Publishing Switzerland 2016,C. CIBB 2015. *LNBI, 9874*, 129–140.

Ayadi, W., Elloumi, M., & Hao, J. K. (2012). Pattern-Driven Neighborhood Search for Biclustering of Microarray Data. *BMC Bioinformatics, 13*(7), 1–15. doi:10.1186/1471-2105-13-S7-S11 PMID:22594997

Ayadi, W., & Hao, J. K. (2014). A Memetic Algorithm for Discovering Negative Correlation Biclusters of DNA Microarray Data. *Neurocomputing, 145*(7), 14–22. doi:10.1016/j.neucom.2014.05.074

Balamurugan. (2016). ' modified harmony search method for biclustering microarray gene expression data. *International Journal of Data Mining and Bioinformatics, 16*(4), 269 – 289.

Bhat, H. F. (2017). Evaluating SVM Algorithms for Bioinformatics Gene Expression Analysis. *International Journal on Computer Science and Engineering, 6*(02), 42–52.

Chen, K.-H. (2014). Gene selection for cancer identification: A decision tree model empowered by particle swarm optimization algorithm. *BMC Bioinformatics, 15*(49), 1–10.

Chen, Y., Li, Y., Narayan, R., Subramanian, A., & Xie, X. (2016). Gene expression inference with deep learning. *Bioinformatics (Oxford, England), 32*(12), 1832–1839. doi:10.1093/bioinformatics/btw074 PMID:26873929

Cheng, Y., & Church, G. M. (2000). Biclustering of Expression Data. *Proceedings of the Eighth International Conference on Intelligent Systems for Molecular Biology*, 93-103.

Fatimaezzahra, Loubna, Mohamed, & Abdelaziz. (2017). A Combined Cuckoo Search Algorithm and Genetic Algorithm for Parameter Optimization in Computer Vision. *International Journal of Applied Engineering Research, 12*(22), 12940-12954.

Houari, A., Ayadi, W., & Yahia, S. B. (2017). Mining Negative Correlation Biclusters from Gene Expression Data using Generic Association Rules. *Procedia Computer Science, 112*, 278–287. doi:10.1016/j.procs.2017.08.262

Huang, Q., Tao, D., Li, X., & Liew. (2012). Parallelized evolutionary learning for detection of biclusters in gene expression data. *IEEE/ACM Transaction Computational Biology and Bioinformatics, 9*(1), 560-570.

Huang, Z., Duan, H., & Li, H. (2015, Sept.). Identification of Gene Expression Pattern Related to Breast Cancer Survival Using Integrated TCGA Datasets and Genomic Tools. *BioMed Research International*, 1–10.

Jauhari, S., & Rizvi, S. A. M. (2014). Mining Gene Expression Data Focusing Cancer Therapeutics: A Digest. *IEEE/ACM Transactions on Computational Biology and Bioinformatics, 11*(3), 53. doi:10.1109/TCBB.2014.2312002 PMID:26356021

Khedidja. (2015). Using Multiobjective optimization for biclustering microarray data. *Applied Soft Computing, 33*, 239-249.

Kourou, K., Exarchos, T. P., Exarchos, K. P., Karamouzisc, M. V., & Fotiadis, D. I. (2015). Machine learning applications in cancer prognosis and prediction. *Computational and Structural Biotechnology Journal, Elsevier, 13*, 8–17. doi:10.1016/j.csbj.2014.11.005 PMID:25750696

Li, Y., Liu, W., Jia, Y., & Dong, H. (2016). A Weighted Mutual Information Biclustering Algorithm for Gene Expression Data. *Computer Science and Information Systems, 14*(3), 643–660. doi:10.2298/CSIS170301021Y

Maatouk, O., Ayadi, W., Bouziri, H., & Duval, B. (2014). Evolutionary Algorithm Based on New Crossover for the Biclustering of Gene Expression Data. Proceedings of the Pattern Recognition in Bioinformatics, 48-59. doi:10.1007/978-3-319-09192-1_5

Mohamad, M. S., Omatu, S., Deris, S., & Yoshioka, M. (2011). A Modified Binary Particle Swarm Optimization for Selecting the Small Subset of Informative Genes From Gene Expression Data. *IEEE Transactions on Information Technology in Biomedicine, 15*(6), 813–822. doi:10.1109/TITB.2011.2167756 PMID:21914573

Nesrine, A., Asma, M., & Sahbi, M. (2019). A comparative study of nonlinear Bayesian filtering algorithms for estimation ofgene expression time series data. *Turkish Journal of Electrical Engineering and Computer Sciences, 27*(4), 2648–2665. doi:10.3906/elk-1809-187

Nguyen, T., Khosravi, A., Creighton, D., & Nahavandi, S. (2015). Hidden Markov models for cancer classification using gene expression profiles. *Information Sciences, Elsevier, 316*, 293–307. doi:10.1016/j.ins.2015.04.012

Padideh. (2017). A Deep Learning Approach For Cancer Detection And Relevant Gene Identification. *Pacific Symposium on Biocomputing*, 219-229.

Pyingkodi, M., & Thangarajan, R. (2017, February). Meta-Analysis in Autism Gene Expression Dataset with Biclustering Methods using Random Cuckoo Search Algorithm. *Asian Journal of Research in Social Sciences and Humanities, 7*(2), 186–194. doi:10.5958/2249-7315.2017.00082.X

Rathore, S., Hussain, M., & Khan, A. (2014). GECC: Gene Expression Based Ensemble Classification of Colon Samples. *IEEE/ACM Transactions on Computational Biology and Bioinformatics, 11*(6), 1131–1145. doi:10.1109/TCBB.2014.2344655 PMID:26357050

Rengeswaran, B., Mathaiyan, N., & Kandasamy, P. (2017, May). Cuckoo Search with Mutation for Biclustering of Microarray Gene Expression Data. *The International Arab Journal of Information Technology, 14*(3).

Rubio-Largo, A., Vega-Rodriguez, M. A., & Gonzalez-Alvarez, D. L. (2016). Miguel A. Vega-Rodríguez, David L. González-Álvarez, 'A Hybrid Multiobjective Memetic Metaheuristic for Multiple Sequence Alignment'. *IEEE Transactions on Evolutionary Computation, 20*(4), 499–514. doi:10.1109/TEVC.2015.2469546

Saber, H. B., & Elloumi, M. (2015). Efficiently Mining Gene Expression Data via Novel Binary Biclustering Algorithms. *Journal of Proteomics & Bioinformatics, S9*(8).

Subramanian, J., & Simon, R. (2010). Gene expression-based prognostic signatures in lung cancer: Ready for clinical use? *Journal of the National Cancer Institute, 102*(7), 464–474. doi:10.1093/jnci/djq025 PMID:20233996

Tan. (2015). Unsupervised feature construction and knowledge extraction from genome-wide assays of breast cancer with denoising autoencoders. *Pacific Symposium on Biocomputing, 20*, 132–143. PMID:25592575

Tanya, A., Sharan, R., & Shamir, R. (2002). Discovering Statistically Significant Biclusters in Gene Expression Data. *BMC Bioinformatics*, *18*(Suppl 1), 136–144. doi:10.1093/bioinformatics/18.suppl_1.S136

Tiwari, M. (2012). An gene expression pattern. *Journal of Natural Science, Biology, and Medicine*, *3*(1), 12–18. doi:10.4103/0976-9668.95935 PMID:22690045

Vıtor. (2017). Learning inflfluential genes on cancer geneexpression data with stacked denoising autoencoders. *IEEE International Conference on Bioinformatics and Biomedicine*.

Xiaoshu. (2017). A multi-objective biclustering algorithm based on fuzzy mathematics. *Neurocomputing, 253*, 177–182.

Chapter 7
Machine Learning in Authentication of Digital Audio Recordings

Rashmika Kiran Patole
College of Engineering, Pune, India

Priti Paresh Rege
iD https://orcid.org/0000-0003-0584-5208
College of Engineering, Pune, India

ABSTRACT

The field of audio forensics has seen a huge advancement in recent years with an increasing number of techniques used for the analysis of the audio recordings submitted as evidence in legal investigations. Audio forensics involves authentication of the evidentiary audio recordings, which is an important procedure to verify the integrity of audio recordings. This chapter focuses two audio authentication procedures, namely acoustic environment identification and tampering detection. The authors provide a framework for the above-mentioned procedures discussing in detail the methodology and feature sets used in the two tasks. The main objective of this chapter is to introduce the readers to different machine learning algorithms that can be used for environment identification and forgery detection. The authors also provide some promising results that prove the utility of machine learning algorithms in this interesting field.

INTRODUCTION

Authentication of digital audio recordings is a complex process which determines whether the audio recording submitted as evidence is free from any tampering attacks. The digital era has made manipulating of digital media very easy with the availability of free, easy-to-use tools that can be used to make changes in the original file without any visible traces. This poses serious challenges for forensic experts to verify the integrity of the submitted audio recordings. To date, there is no 'cookbook' of steps that is involved in determining the authenticity of audio recordings. Therefore, there is a need for a standard

DOI: 10.4018/978-1-7998-3095-5.ch007

procedure for authentication containing scientific methods and computational tools that will help make logical interpretations of analyses and present unambiguous conclusions regarding the authenticity of recordings.

This section provides a brief introduction to the fundamentals of audio processing, the different formats of audio signals and the basics of an audio recording system. It also provides a discussion in the area of audio forensics and audio authentication. The practices followed by forensic experts in the examination and the analysis tools currently being used are presented as well. Tampering detection and Environment identification are the two procedures involved in the task of audio authentication that are explained, followed by a discussion on machine learning algorithms that can be used in these tasks.

Structure and Format of an Audio Signal

Digital audio is composed of a sequence of discrete samples taken from an analog audio signal. The sampling frequency and the bits per sample are important parameters related to an audio signal. A sampling frequency of 44.1 kHz and 16 bits per sample are common parameters that are used to obtain a sufficiently good quality audio signal. There are different audio formats available, which are employed depending upon the application. The uncompressed audio formats include PCM (Pulse Code Modulation), WAV (Waveform Audio File format) and AIFF (Audio Interchange File Format). MP3(MPEG-1 Audio Layer 3), AAC (Advanced Audio Coding) and WMA (Windows Media Audio) are lossy compressed audio file formats while FLAC (Free Lossless Audio Codec) and ALAC (Apple Lossless Audio Codec) belong to a category of lossless compressed file formats.

Audio Recording Set Up

The components of a digital audio recording setup are shown in Figure 1. It consists of a microphone, a preamplifier, an analog-digital converter and a digital recorder. The incoming sound is an analog signal which is converted into an electric signal by the microphone. There are different types of microphones available which can be chosen mainly depending upon the directional pattern (e.g. Omni-directional, cardioid and unidirectional). The output signal of a microphone is weak which is amplified by a preamplifier to a voltage of amplitude around 1.5V. The electrical signal up to this point is an analog signal which is converted into a digital signal by the A/D converter. This signal may be stored or played. The recorder converts the electrical signal of the A/D converter into a physical form which can be stored or played back. If the signal has to be played back, the player such as a loudspeaker converts the signal back into pressure waves.

Introduction to Audio Forensics and Audio Authentication

The field of audio forensics involves acquisition, analysis and evaluation of an audio recording that has to be presented as evidence in a court of law in case of a legal investigation. An audio forensic expert is involved in applying scientific methods to recover, evaluate, enhance and authenticate an audio recording submitted as evidence. According to the Scientific Working Group on Digital Evidence (SWGDE) definition, "an original recording is the first manifestation of sound in a recoverable stored format, be it a magnetic tape, digital device, voicemail file stored on a server, optical disk, or some other form". Digital audio authentication consists of container analysis and content analysis (Grigoras, Rappaport,

Figure 1. Components of an Audio Recording system

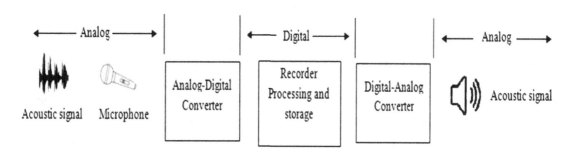

& Smith, 2012). Container analysis includes the investigation of the file structure, metadata, etc. Maintaining HASH calculations, MAC time stamps, review of the file format, sample rate, codec, bit rate, etc. are tasks involved in container analysis. Checking the header information and the hex data is also a part of container analysis. Content analysis deals with the analysis of the actual content of the audio file and also the acoustic events in the file. Below are the preliminary steps involved in any digital authentication procedure:

1. Critical listening: The first step after acquisition of the evidence and analyzing the structure of the audio file is critical listening. Not much can be inferred from critical listening, but it is an important step to form hypotheses that will be evaluated in the later stages of investigations. Critical listening involves study of background noises, any discontinuities present, identifying the number of speakers, in some cases the location of recording, etc.

2. Waveform Analysis: Similar to critical listening, waveform analysis is also a preliminary procedure followed by forensic analysts for audio authentication. By analyzing the high resolution waveform of the evidentiary audio recording, one can obtain information regarding any discontinuities, transients, presence of normalization, etc. Observing these parameters may give clues of possible tampering attacks in the audio recording.

3. Signal power and DC offset: If the power of the audio signal is computed on short analysis frames, missing acoustic information in the signal power can be an indication of tampering. Ideally there is no DC offset in an audio recording as the positive and negative amplitude values cancel out. But practically, a recording which has not been processed will have a slight positive or negative DC offset because of the addition of some direct current when the electrical signal from the microphone passes to the A/D converter. Therefore, if the DC offset is zero, it indicates that there has been some manipulation in the recording.

4. FFT spectrum: The spectrum of the audio signal can provide important information such as frequency limits and response of the recording device, frequencies of particular acoustic events, presence or absence of ENF, etc. Any inconsistency in the spectrum may be a possible attack on the audio file.

There are various other established methodologies that can be applied to identify the presence of editing such as ENF analysis, Butt splice detection, phase analysis, reverberation analysis, etc. The above-mentioned procedures are a few common methods used in authenticating an audio signal. However, every case will not employ each of these procedures as some of the procedures may not be applicable at all.

Introduction to Tampering Detection and Environment Identification

As stated previously, there are numerous tasks that a forensic expert needs to perform. The authentication of audio recordings involves verifying the integrity of the audio recording by finding any traces of forgery or tampering. Inconsistencies in artifacts embedded in the audio recording may provide clues of any tampering attacks. Obvious clicks, pops, discontinuities in the audio recording may also indicate forgery. Audio authentication also involves the task of Acoustic Environment Identification. This consists of identifying the environment in which the recording was made, or it may involve verifying whether the environment is the same as claimed. Moreover, the acoustic events in the audio recording can provide information regarding the environment in which the audio was recorded. It may so happen that the intruder may completely change the background of the recording so that the environmental clues are eliminated. For example, if there is some humming noise due to a fan in the recording environment, one can conclude that the recording was made in a particular room and the crime scene can be verified. But obvious background noise can also be changed or completely deleted eliminating the clues regarding the recording environment.

BACKGROUND

Over the past decade, several techniques for audio tampering detection have been proposed. A remarkable contribution in this field is the analysis of the Electric Network frequency embedded in the audio recording which has been used to detect traces of forgery as in (Grigoras, 2012). (Cuccovillo & Aichroth, 2016; Cuccovillo, Mann, Tagliasacchi, & Aichroth, 2013) discuss tampering detection via microphone classification and microphone frequency response. In (Seichter, Cuccovillo, & Aichroth, 2016; Gärtner, Dittmar, Aichroth, Cuccovillo, Mann, & Schuller, 2014), audio forgery detection has been done using encoding traces while (Grigoras, & Smith, 2017) discusses the framework for audio authentication using container metadata. A robust pitch tracking method has been proposed in (Yan, Yang, & Huang, 2015) for the detection of copy move forgery. In (Maksimovic, Cuccovillo, & Aichroth, 2019), the authors have presented a new approach for detecting and localizing copy-move forgeries in audio files based on audio fingerprinting and matching that does not require pre-segmentation of the audio recording, which is a conventional pre-processing task followed in a majority of the papers. These pre-processing tasks are prone to errors and contribute to computational overhead. The methodologies discussed in (Patole, Kore, & Rege, 2017; Bhangale, & Patole, 2019; Zhao, Chen, Wang, & Malik, 2017) employ environmental signatures like background noise and reverberation for tampering detection.

Similar to audio tampering detection, there has been a significant amount of research in the area of acoustic environment identification. In (Chaudhary, & Malik, 2010), the authors have employed Competitive Neural Networks for the classification of environments with the help of acoustic signatures like reverberation time and variance. These parameters have been estimated using Maximum Likelihood estimation. (Malik, 2013; Malik, & Farid, 2010; Zhao, & Malik, 2012) have used techniques such as particle filtering, inverse filtering and voiced activity detection to estimate the amount of reverberation embedded in the audio recordings which is further used for classification. Different features extracted from the reverberant component have been exploited for classification purposes as illustrated in (Patole, Kore, & Rege, 2017; Narkhede, & Patole, 2019)

Despite extensive research in the area of audio authentication, very few papers have actually discussed and illustrated the application of machine learning algorithms for the purpose of authentication. There has been a large proliferation of machine learning methodologies in image processing as compared to audio. Moreover, there is a need to make use of artifacts embedded in recordings which will provide clues of tampering and also aid in the identification of the acoustic environment. This chapter focuses on tampering detection and environment identification. The following sections provide a framework for the above two audio authentication procedures. The next sections discuss the framework for environment identification and tampering detection which will provide insights on database creation and feature extraction. Following this, different machine learning methodologies for audio authentication are explained with some important results and conclusions in the last section.

FRAMEWORK FOR ACOUSTIC ENVIRONMENT IDENTIFICATION

The first task considered under audio authentication is Acoustic Environment Identification. The environment in which the evidentiary audio was recorded is an important parameter for forensic investigations as forensic experts may need to identify the environment of the crime scene for further investigations. The audio recording that is submitted as evidence may provide clues regarding the environment in which it was recorded. There may be certain artifacts present in the recording which can help experts to obtain information about the acoustic environment. For example, the audio recording may contain obvious car horn sounds on the basis of which the forensic expert may come to the conclusion that the recording was made in a car. The Room Impulse Response (RIR) and the reverberation component are parameters that are embedded in the audio recording that provide information about the acoustic environment of the audio recording like geometry of the room, etc. This section first discusses the basics of RIR and reverberation followed by feature extraction and classification of environments using Machine Learning algorithms.

Room Impulse Response (RIR) and Reverberation

Consider an enclosed room consisting of a source of sound and a microphone placed in some fixed location in the room. The sound recorded at the microphone consists of two components,

(i)   Direct sound component which is the sound signal that reaches directly from the source to the microphone and
(ii) Wall Reflections which are the sound signals following the direct sound component that reach the microphone after hitting the walls of the room. These multiple reflections eventually decay with time. This phenomenon has been depicted in Figure 2.

The RIR is the transfer function which provides the properties of the environment in which the audio is recorded. The components of the RIR are shown in Figure 3. It shows the direct sound component and the reflections from the wall surfaces of the room. These reflections make up the reverberant component of the RIR and give information about the room geometry. As the RIR and the reverberation component provide information about the acoustic environment, these are the parameters that will be extracted and used in acoustic environment classification. The following section provides details of extracting the RIR and reverberation followed by feature extraction.

Figure 2. Direct and reflected paths of audio

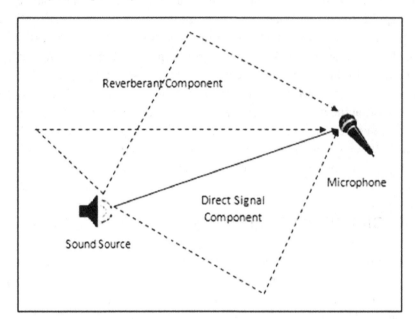

Figure 3. Components of RIR

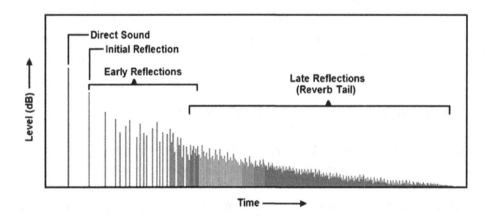

Extraction of Room Impulse Response

There are various methods in literature which can be employed to measure the RIR like Time-Stretched Pulses, inverse Repeated Sequences (IRS), Maximum Length Sequence (MLS) and Sine sweep (Stan, Embrechts, & Archambeau, 2002). The authors have adopted the sine sweep methodology as it gives a high Signal-to-Noise ratio compared to other methods of measurement of RIR. The steps involved with this method are shown in Figure 4.(Stan, Embrechts, & Archambeau, 2002)

For the generation of Room Impulse Response, there is first a need to generate a test sine sweep signal. Therefore, the first step is to generate a test signal using (1):

Figure 4. Extraction of RIR using Sine sweep method

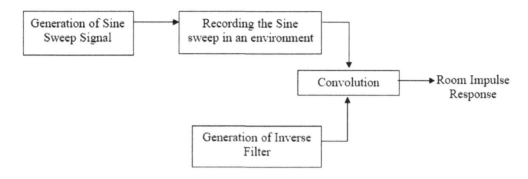

$$x(t) = \sin\left[\frac{\omega_1 T}{\ln\left(\frac{\omega_2}{\omega_1}\right)}\left(e^{\frac{t}{T}\ln\left(\frac{\omega_2}{\omega_1}\right)} - 1\right)\right] \tag{1}$$

where ω_1 is the angular start frequency of the sweep which is considered to be 20Hz and ω_2 is the angular stop frequency equal to 20 KHz. T is the duration of the sine sweep.

This generated sine sweep is now played and recorded in an environment. Therefore, the reverberation characteristics of the recorded environment are captured in the recorded signal. If the signal recorded at the microphone is represented by y(t) and the system's (environment's) response is h(t), let f(t) be an inverse filter which is just a time reversal of the test signal. The impulse response is obtained by the convolution of y(t) and f(t).

For the above experiment, sine sweep signals are synthetically generated as discussed in the previous section and convolved with the already available impulse responses from the Multichannel Acoustic Reverberation Database at York (MARDY) database. This gives an effect that the sweep signals are recorded in that particular environment.

Now from the obtained impulse response, features are extracted and applied to classifiers for classification.

Feature Extraction

This section discusses features that will be used for the classification of the acoustic environment. The popular Mel Frequency Cepstral Coefficients (MFCC) and the Reverberation time features are two sets of features which are used.

1. MFCCs

MFCCs are the most popular features used in many speech and audio processing applications, mainly in Automatic Speech and Speaker recognition systems. In this experiment, these features are extracted from the obtained RIR. The MFCCs take into consideration the human auditory response and therefore

Figure 5. Computation of MFCCCs

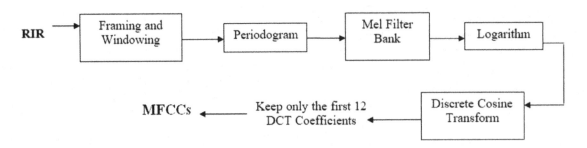

the recognition rate with MFCCs is better than other common features. The steps to compute the MFCC features can be summarized as in Figure 5.

The audio signal is framed into frames of size 25ms as the audio signal is stationary in this time duration. The frame step is taken to be 10ms where the frames overlap. For each frame the Discrete Fourier Transform is computed using equation (2)

$$S_i(k) = \sum_{n=1}^{N} S_i(n) h(n) e^{\frac{-j2\pi kn}{N}} \quad 1 \leq k \leq K \tag{2}$$

Where I is the number of frames, S(n) is the time domain signal. $S_i(k)$ is the complex DFT, h(n) is the analysis window which is usually Hamming. The periodogram $P_i(k)$ of the DFT signal is computed using equation (3).

$$P_i(k) = \frac{1}{N} \left| S_i(k) \right|^2 \tag{3}$$

The mel filter bank which is a set of 26 triangular filters is now applied to the periodogram. Equation (4) converts the frequency in Hertz to the Mel scale while equation (5) converts Mel scale back to Hertz.

$$M(f) = 1125 \ln\left(1 + \frac{f}{700}\right) \tag{4}$$

$$M^{-1}(m) = 700\left(\exp\left(\frac{m}{1125}\right) + 1\right) \tag{5}$$

Each filter bank is multiplied by the power spectrum and the coefficients are added to get the filter bank energies. This gives an idea about how much energy is present in each filter bank. Now, logarithm applied on these filter bank energies. The final step is to compute the Discrete Cosine Transform of the obtained energies.

If 26 filter banks are used then we get 26 coefficients. Out of these 26 coefficients, only 13 coefficients are chosen which are the final MFCC feature vectors.

Reverberation Time Features

The length of time it takes for sound to decay from its original level is called reverberation time. This reverberation time is an important parameter extracted from the RIR which characterizes a particular environment. Different reverberation times like RT60, RT30 and RT 20 are defined depending upon how much the sound energy decays after the source stops emitting the signal. RT 60 is the duration required for the sound energy to decay by 60dB after the source stops. Similarly, the time for the sound to decay from -5dB to -25dB and -5dB to -35 dB is RT20 and RT30 respectively. Apart from these, there are two more parameters that are extracted from the RIR: The Early Decay Time (EDT) and the Direct to Reverberant Ratio (DRR). EDT is the time required for the sound pressure level to drop from 0dB to -10dB. DRR is defined as the ratio of the sound energy level of a direct sound to the sound energy of the reverberant component. The methodology for computing the above reverberation parameters is given in The International Standards Organization (ISO) document 3382 (Measurement of Room Acoustic Parameters, Part 1, 2009).

FRAMEWORK FOR AUDIO PROCESSING SYSTEM WITH TAMPERING DETECTION

Tampering detection methods can be of two types: (a) Active Tampering detection and (b) Passive Tampering detection (Hua, Zhang, Goh, & Thing, 2016). In active tampering detection methods, fingerprints and watermarks are embedded in the original audio recording which provides clues of tampering. In passive detection methods, no a priori information about the recording is available. It is important to develop algorithms for the passive detection method because in active detection methods, embedding information in the original audio can degrade the quality of the audio. Also, in a forensic setting, the audio recordings which are available as evidences would not be embedded with any side information and therefore the detection of forgery is blind in a way. This section provides a detailed framework for tampering detection. Different types of tampering attacks are discussed followed by the creation of a database and feature extraction.

Types of Tampering Attacks

The types of tampering attacks considered in this chapter include:

1. **Insertion:** Here, one or more segments from other audio recording is inserted in the original audio recording
2. **Deletion:** Delete one or more segments from the original audio
3. **Splicing:** In this type of forgery, a part of an audio recording is copied and pasted over another audio recording i.e. audio segments from different audio recordings are concatenated.

4. **Copy-move forgery:** In copy-move forgery, a part of an audio recording is copied and pasted in the same recording at some other location. Here, source and destination audio is same as against splicing where source and destination are two different audio files.

Database Creation

As a standard database consisting of the original and its tampered version is not available, a synthetic database is created which includes audio recordings and their respective tampered versions. The above types of forgery attacks are applied on the original audio recordings to obtain the tampered versions. Tampering has to be done in such a manner that there should be no audible anomaly which can provide obvious clues of forgery. From a forger's point of view, the audio waveform should flow naturally and there should be no obvious abrupt changes of signal levels, background noise levels or multiple recording environments.

The original recordings are taken from Free Spoken Digit Database (Retrieved from https://github.com/Jakobovski/freespoken-digit-dataset). The database consists of recordings from 4 different speakers with 50 audio files from each speaker. There are 2000 total recordings of spoken digits recorded at 8 kHz. For creating copy move forged audio files, initially digits from 'zero' to 'nine' are concatenated together in a single audio file with some silence present between two digits. In this way, for each speaker numerous audio files are created which contain the utterances of the digits 'zero' to 'nine' with the digits in a random order; different for each audio file. Now, one digit utterance is copied from a particular location and moved to another location. This is copy move forgery. Figure 6 shows an example of a copy-move forged audio recording.

Figure 6. Original and Copy-Move forged Recording

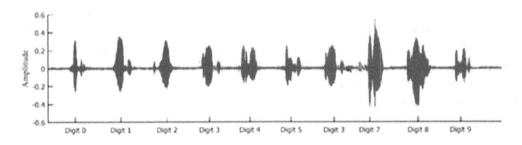

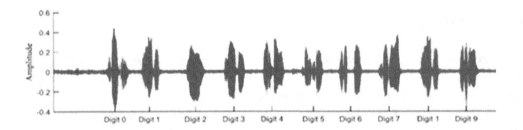

The waveform of an original recording consisting of digit utterances 'zero' to 'nine' is shown. The figure also shows a copy-move forged recording which is created by copying digit 'one' and moving it in place of digit 'eight'. As seen in the figure, this type of forgery is done on the same audio recording.

To create a database for Splicing, a digit utterance of one speaker is inserted into the audio recording of another speaker. In this type of forgery, one or more segments of audio from one recording are inserted into another recording. The spliced audio recording is as shown in the Figure 7.

Figure 7. Spliced Forged Audio

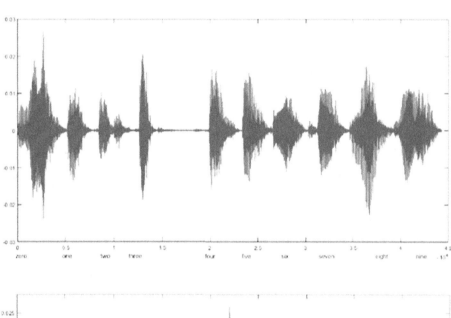

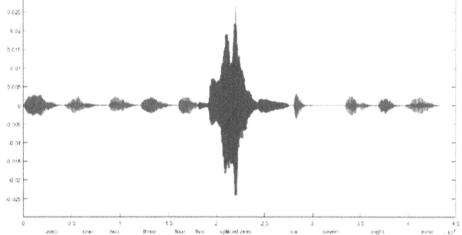

As shown in the figure, the original recording shown in 'orange' consists of utterances of digits from 'zero' to 'nine' of one speaker. The spliced audio is obtained by inserting digit utterances of one speaker into another speaker's audio file. Any random digit is selected and inserted in the other file. As shown, the digit 'zero' of one speaker's audio file is inserted between digit utterances 'four' and 'five' of another speaker's audio.

For Insertion type forgery, a digit utterance of one audio is replaced by another digit utterance from a different audio file as shown in Figure 8. Here digit 'four' from the original audio is replaced with digit 'four' of another audio file.

Figure 8. Insertion type forgery

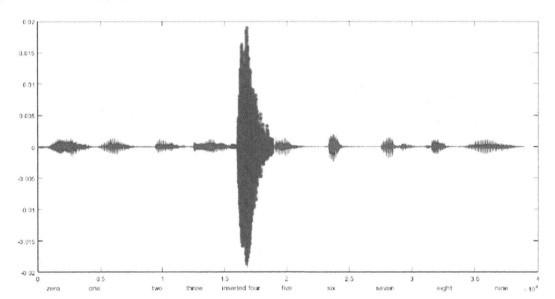

Methodology for Tampering Detection

As discussed in the previous section, we now have with us a database consisting of original audio recordings and the tampered versions obtained by manipulating the original recordings by copy-move, splicing and insertion type forgery. This section gives a framework for audio tampering detection and discusses the methodology adopted. Tampering detection for splicing and insertion type forgery will be discussed in this chapter. Similar methodology can be used for detecting copy move forgery.

As discussed in the case of environment identification, the conventional procedure to detect forgery is to first extract features from the original and tampered audio recordings and then provide these features as inputs to a machine learning classifier which will help classify the original recording and the tampered versions. Here, for detecting splicing and insertion type forgery, Convolutional Neural Network(CNN) has been used.

The methodology starts by creating a database consisting of original audio recordings and forged versions using splicing and insertion type forgery as discussed in the previous section. The audio files in the dataset first undergo pre-processing which is the conventional pre-processing which is done in all speech and audio processing applications. It involves dividing each audio file into overlapped frames of size 25 ms with 50% overlap. The frames are then windowed using a Hamming window followed by FFT computation of each windowed frame of the audio signal. This process is computing the Short time Fourier Transform (STFT) of the audio recordings. We represent the STFT of the frames in the form of an image of the spectrogram representation. Spectrograms are frequency representations of audio signals which are shown by different colors in an image. The horizontal axis represents time while the vertical axis gives information about the frequency content. The amplitude of a particular frequency is represented by different colors. Figure 9 shows an example of a spectrogram of an audio recording Therefore each audio file is now converted into an image. These spectrogram images are inputs to the CNN.

Figure 9. Spectrogram representation of an audio signal

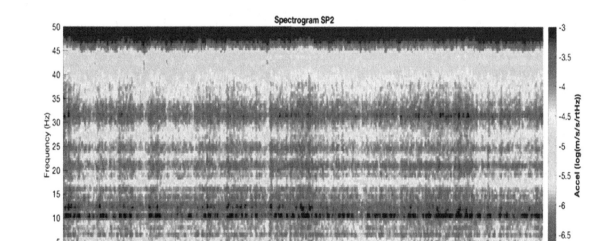

Figure 10. Framework for Tampering Detection

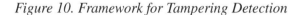

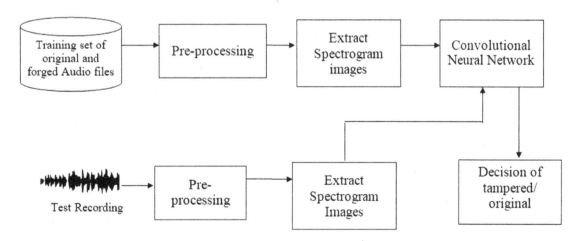

The framework and experimental set up is shown in the block diagram of Figure 10. A brief discussion on the architecture of a CNN has been given in the next section.

APPLICATIONS OF MACHINE LEARNING IN AUDIO AUTHENTICATION

Machine learning is a branch of Artificial Intelligence in which a machine learns from the input data, past experiences and observations and takes decisions based on these learnings. Machine Learning finds applications in almost all major areas like Healthcare, Social media, Transport, eCommerce, Financial services, Security, etc. Machine Learning tasks can be distinguished into supervised and unsupervised learning tasks. In a supervised learning method, the input and outputs are available and the machine learns based on the past experience. In an unsupervised learning task, it is necessary to find unknown patterns in the data. The task of audio authentication that this chapter focuses on is considered to be a supervised learning task. Figure 11 shows the pipeline of a typical supervised machine learning task.

Figure 11. Machine Learning Pipeline

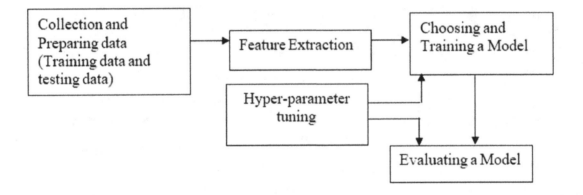

Any machine learning task starts with the collection of data which can be divided into training data and testing data. The training data in a supervised machine learning task consists of the input and the corresponding output which is used to train the machine. The testing data contains only the inputs. Outputs are unknown which the machine has to predict. After the data collection, one needs to choose an appropriate machine learning model which is further trained for classification, prediction or decision making. Once the training phase is completed, the model obtained is used on the testing data for obtaining the required output. Hyper-parameters are parameters which may not be learned from the data but are to be specified by the user. The tuning of hyper-parameters, i.e. finding an appropriate set of parameters, needs to be done for increasing the performance of the machine learning algorithm. There are numerous methods for tuning the hyper-parameters like gradient descent, randomized search, etc. which can be used.

The following machine learning algorithms have been deployed for the task of audio authentication. Subsequent sections give a brief description about the algorithms. Some sample results have also been discussed.

Support Vector Machines

Support Vector machines (SVMs) are a type of supervised machine learning method used for the tasks of classification and regression. SVMs have been popularly used in many different pattern recognition application areas such as face recognition, handwriting recognition, etc. The performance of SVMs is comparable to the sophisticated neural networks. SVMs can be used for a binary classification problem for linearly separable data, for classifying data which is not linearly separable and also in regression. SVM is a classifier that is defined by a separating hyperplane. The output is in the form of an optimum hyperplane which classifies new data points. Suppose the datapoints belong to separate labeled classes as in Figure 12.

Figure 12.

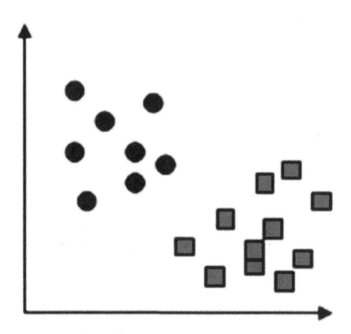

We can decide a separating line for these classes which separates the two classes fairly. Hence, the SVM finds out the line, i.e. hyperplane that separates the classes. In cases where the data points cannot be linearly separated we use different transformations called kernels that can separate the datapoints. This is shown as in Figure 13.

There may also be a scenario where the data points are overlapping as shown in Figure 14.

In such a case, the classification is non- linear and we have to define a hyperplane which classifies the data points with minimum classification errors. This is done by tuning the hyper parameters of the SVM namely, the regularization parameter and gamma. Appropriate choice of these parameters can achieve nonlinear classification with more accuracy. The classification can make use of a linear kernel or a non-linear kernel like polynomial, exponential, radial basis, etc.

Figure 13.

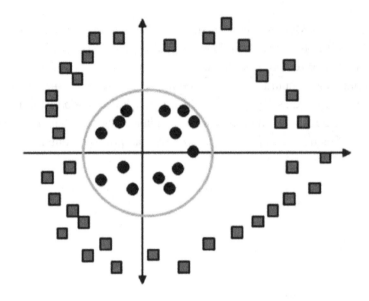

Figure 14.

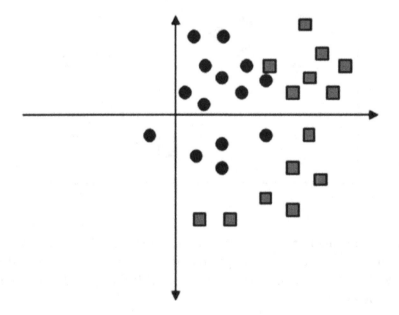

Artificial Neural Networks

Artificial neural networks (ANNs) are parallel processing systems that are analogous to the biological neural networks. The basic computational unit in a neural network is the neuron which is called a node. An ANN consists of inter connection of these nodes which receive input from some other nodes or external input and computes the output. The neural network has weights associated at each layer which

Figure 15. Architecture of ANN

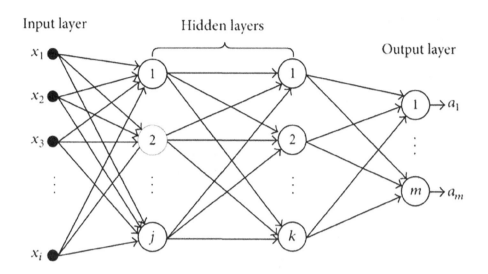

can be adjusted so that the network learns. Each node has a weight associated with it which specifies the importance of the inputs from the previous node. The highest weight is given to those inputs that contribute the most towards the next node. Figure 15 shows the general architecture of an Artificial Neural Network.

The components of an ANN are:

a. **Input nodes/ Input Layer:** The inputs are applied to these blocks of nodes called the input layer. This layer only passes information to the next layer. No computation is done.

b. **Hidden nodes/ Hidden Layer**: These sets of nodes form the intermediate layer where processing is done. A neural network may contain one or multiple hidden layers. The hidden layers perform computations and pass on the weights/information from input layer to the next hidden layer or to the output layer.

c. **Output Nodes/ Output Layer:** The output nodes use what is called the activation function to map to the desired output format. The information learned from the previous layers is transferred to the outer world by the output layer.

d. **Weights**: For each connection of neuron i to neuron j, a weight wij is assigned. The data received by the neurons is multiplied by the value of the weight assigned and the result is passed on to the next layer.

e. **Activation Function:** The output of a node is defined by the activation function of that node. The activation function decides whether a neuron has to be activated or not. It introduces non-linearity to the output of the neuron and decides whether a neuron should be activated or not.

There are different types of neural networks that use different principles with their own strengths. Following is a list of some popular neural networks:

1. Feedforward Neural Network
2. Radial Basis Function Neural Network
3. Multilayer Perceptron
4. Convolutional Neural Network
5. Recurrent Neural Network
6. Modular Neural Network
7. Sequence to sequence models

This chapter discusses the results of Support Vector Machines, Simple Feedforward Neural Network, Convolutional Neural Network (CNN) and Recurrent Neural Networks (RNN) for Audio Authentication. A brief introduction of CNN and RNN has been given next followed by some sample results of the algorithms implemented by the authors.

Convolutional Neural Networks

The CNN contains one or more convolutional layers which are either completely interconnected or pooled. A convolution operation is performed on the input of a layer before the result is passed to the next layer. Due to this, the network is deep with fewer parameters. The input of a CNN is usually an image where the network will assign certain weights and biases to the various characteristics of the image which will help differentiate one image from another. CNNs have the ability to learn the characteristics/ features of the input data directly without the need of evaluating hand-engineered features. The architecture of a CNN consists of Convolutional layer, Batch normalization layer, Activation Function and Pooling layer. The convolutional layer performs dot product between an array of input data and a two-dimensional array of weights called filter or kernel.

The first layer of the CNN extracts low-level features such as color from the input image. Additional convolutional layers of the network extract high level features such as edges from the input. The pooling layer reduces the size of the convolved feature which helps to decrease the computational power required to process the data. Max pooling and Average Pooling are the two types of Pooling where the former returns the maximum value of the portion of image covered by the kernel and the latter returns the average of all values of the image inside the kernel. After the convolution and pooling layers, the output is now fed to a regular neural network for classification using a softmax layer. A typical convolution neural network architecture is as shown in Figure 16.

Recurrent Neural Networks

RNNs are effective when the data is in the form of a time series sequence. For example, Text-to-speech conversion. The inputs and the outputs of a RNN can be of varying lengths. In a recurrent neural network, the output of a layer is saved and fed back to the input. For a particular time step, each node will remember some information from the previous time step. RNNs have feedback loops connected to take into account the previous output as against conventional feed forward networks which do not have any feedback loops. These feedback loops occur at every time step. The simplest architecture of a RNN can be shown in Figure 17.

Figure 16. Typical CNN Architecture

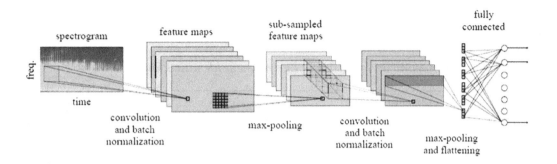

Figure 17. Architecture of RNN

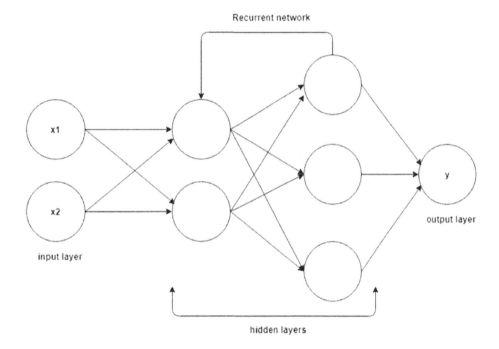

RESULTS

The authors have conducted two experiments for audio authentication:

a) Acoustic environment identification
b) Tampering detection

This section discusses the results obtained for the above two tasks using machine learning algorithms specified in the previous section.

Acoustic Environment Identification was performed using SVM and ANN. The results are shown for different types of SVMs: Linear, Quadratic and Cubic. For ANN, a learning rate of 10^{-4} and ReLU activation function were employed. The classification accuracy for MFCC, RT and MFCC+RT features has been summarized in Table I

Table 1. Classification Accuracies for Acoustic Environment Identification

Sr. No.	Classifier/ Features	Accuracy (%)		
		MFCC	RT	MFCC+RT
1.	Linear SVM	81.2%	84.8%	89.3%
2.	Quadratic SVM	86.3%	88.2%	92.4%
3.	Cubic SVM	84.7%	88.2%	90.8%
4.	Random Forest	89.4%	92.6%	97.1%
5.	ANN	**90.4%**	**94.5%**	**97.3%**

It can be seen that ANN outperforms SVM giving an accuracy of 97.3% when MFCC and RT features are used in combination. It can also be seen that Quadratic SVM performs better than Linear and Cubic SVM. The table also depicts the weightage of the feature sets. If MFCC features are used in isolation, the accuracy is less than with RT features alone. The addition of RT features increases the accuracy in each of the classifiers.

For Tampering detection, CNN and RNN have been employed to detect whether an audio is original or tampered. As discussed, CNN can be used for a classification which classifies the data directly without the need of giving features separately as in the case of other machine learning algorithms. The CNN architecture employed has two convolutional layers, two batch normalization layers, two ReLU, max pooling layer and softmax layer for classification. The MFCCs are given as features to the RNN architecture. Table II shows the classification accuracies for insertion and deletion type forgeries using CNN and RNN.

Table 2. Classification Accuracy for Tampering Detection

Sr. No.	Tampering attack/Classifier	Accuracy (%)	
		CNN	RNN
1.	Insertion	96.35	**99.73**
2	Splicing	97.6	**99.44**

As depicted in Table II, RNN outperforms CNN in classifying original and tampered audio recordings. The accuracy obtained using CNN is also comparable. This may be due to the fact that RNNs are more suitable for temporal data like audio and text. The experimentation for tampering detection can also be extended to take into account the length of the attack. The accuracy will definitely change if the length of the attack is different.

CONCLUSION

This chapter discusses the problem of audio authentication focusing on two authentication tasks, namely, Environment Identification and Tampering Detection. The authors have discussed a general framework for these two tasks describing the feature sets that can be used for classification purposes. Different machine learning algorithms have been used for computing the classification accuracies for the above two tasks. The chapter discusses in brief the architecture of the machine learning algorithms along with some sample results for the two tasks. However, readers are encouraged to read more literature about the algorithms if needed.

It can be concluded that ANN and RNN perform better than other classifiers for Environment identification and tampering detection respectively. Future work will focus on considering different environmental scenarios and tampering attacks. The effect of noise and compression on the classification accuracy also needs to be taken into account. The effect of tampering on the reverberant component and different feature sets which can help build a system which can perform the two tasks simultaneously can be an addition.

REFERENCES

Bhangale, T., & Patole, R. (2019). Tampering Detection in Digital Audio Recording Based on Statistical Reverberation Features. In *Soft Computing and Signal Processing* (pp. 583–591). Singapore: Springer. doi:10.1007/978-981-13-3600-3_55

Chaudhary, U. A., & Malik, H. (2010, November). Automatic recording environment identification using acoustic features. In *Audio Engineering Society Convention 129*. Audio Engineering Society.

Cuccovillo, L., & Aichroth, P. (2016, March). Open-set microphone classification via blind channel analysis. In *2016 IEEE International Conference on Acoustics, Speech and Signal Processing (ICASSP)* (pp. 2074-2078). IEEE. 10.1109/ICASSP.2016.7472042

Cuccovillo, L., Mann, S., Tagliasacchi, M., & Aichroth, P. (2013, September). Audio tampering detection via microphone classification. In *2013 IEEE 15th International Workshop on Multimedia Signal Processing (MMSP)* (pp. 177-182). IEEE. 10.1109/MMSP.2013.6659284

Free Spoken Digit Database. (n.d.). Retrieved from https://github.com/Jakobovski/freespoken-digit-dataset

Gärtner, D., Dittmar, C., Aichroth, P., Cuccovillo, L., Mann, S., & Schuller, G. (2014, April). Efficient cross-codec framing grid analysis for audio tampering detection. In *Audio Engineering Society Convention 136*. Audio Engineering Society.

Grigoras, C., Rappaport, D., & Smith, J. M. (2012, June). Analytical framework for digital audio authentication. In *Audio Engineering Society Conference: 46th International Conference: Audio Forensics*. Audio Engineering Society.

Grigoras, C., & Smith, J. (2017, June). Large scale test of digital audio file structure and format for forensic analysis. In *Audio Engineering Society Conference: 2017 AES International Conference on Audio Forensics*. Audio Engineering Society.

Grigoras, C., & Smith, J. M. (2012, June). Advances in ENF analysis for digital media authentication. In *Audio Engineering Society Conference: 46th International Conference: Audio Forensics*. Audio Engineering Society.

Hua, G., Zhang, Y., Goh, J., & Thing, V. L. (2016). Audio authentication by exploring the absolute-error-map of ENF signals. *IEEE Transactions on Information Forensics and Security, 11*(5), 1003–1016. doi:10.1109/TIFS.2016.2516824

ISO. (2009). *Measurement of room acoustic parameters part 1*. ISO Std.

Maksimovic, M., Cuccovillo, L., & Aichroth, P. (2019, June). Copy-Move Forgery Detection and Localization via Partial Audio Matching. In *Audio Engineering Society Conference: 2019 AES International Conference On Audio Forensics*. Audio Engineering Society.

Malik, H. (2013). Acoustic environment identification and its applications to audio forensics. *IEEE Transactions on Information Forensics and Security, 8*(11), 1827–1837. doi:10.1109/TIFS.2013.2280888

Malik, H., & Farid, H. (2010, March). Audio forensics from acoustic reverberation. In *2010 IEEE International Conference on Acoustics, Speech and Signal Processing* (pp. 1710-1713). IEEE. 10.1109/ICASSP.2010.5495479

Mardy (multichannel acoustic reverberation database at york) database a Speech and audio processing laboratory. (n.d.). Retrieved from http://commsp.ee.ic.ac.uk/~sap/resources/mardy-multichannel-acoustic-reverberation-database-at-york-database/

Narkhede, M., & Patole, R. (2019). Acoustic Scene Identification for Audio Authentication. In *Soft Computing and Signal Processing* (pp. 593–602). Singapore: Springer. doi:10.1007/978-981-13-3600-3_56

Patole, R., Kore, G., & Rege, P. (2017, June). Reverberation based tampering detection in audio recordings. In *Audio Engineering Society Conference: 2017 AES International Conference on Audio Forensics*. Audio Engineering Society.

Scientific Working Group on Digital Evidence. (2008, Jan.). *SWGDE Best Practices for Forensic Audio, Version 1.0*. Retrieved from https://www.swgde.org/documents

Seichter, D., Cuccovillo, L., & Aichroth, P. (2016, March). AAC encoding detection and bitrate estimation using a convolutional neural network. In *2016 IEEE International Conference on Acoustics, Speech and Signal Processing (ICASSP)* (pp. 2069-2073). IEEE. 10.1109/ICASSP.2016.7472041

Stan, G. B., Embrechts, J. J., & Archambeau, D. (2002). Comparison of different impulse response measurement techniques. *Journal of the Audio Engineering Society, 50*(4), 249–262.

Yan, Q., Yang, R., & Huang, J. (2015, April). Copy-move detection of audio recording with pitch similarity. In *2015 IEEE International Conference on Acoustics, Speech and Signal Processing (ICASSP)* (pp. 1782-1786). IEEE. 10.1109/ICASSP.2015.7178277

Zhao, H., Chen, Y., Wang, R., & Malik, H. (2017). Audio splicing detection and localization using environmental signature. *Multimedia Tools and Applications, 76*(12), 13897–13927. doi:10.100711042-016-3758-7

Zhao, H., & Malik, H. (2012, August). Audio forensics using acoustic environment traces. In 2012 IEEE Statistical Signal Processing Workshop (SSP) (pp. 373-376). IEEE. doi:10.1109/SSP.2012.6319707

Chapter 8
Deep Convolutional Neural Network–Based Analysis for Breast Cancer Histology Images

E. Sudheer Kumar

https://orcid.org/0000-0003-2752-0711

JNTUA College of Engineering, India

C. Shoba Bindu

https://orcid.org/0000-0002-3637-507X

JNTUA College of Engineering, India

Sirivella Madhu

JNTUA College of Engineering, India

ABSTRACT

Breast cancer is one of the main causes of cancer death worldwide, and early diagnostics significantly increases the chances of correct treatment and survival, but this process is tedious. The relevance and potential of automatic classification algorithms using Hematoxylin-Eosin stained histopathological images have already been demonstrated, but the reported results are still sub-optimal for clinical use. Deep learning-based computer-aided diagnosis (CAD) has been gaining popularity for analyzing histopathological images. Based on the predominant cancer type, the goal is to classify images into four categories of normal, benign, in situ carcinoma, and invasive carcinoma. The convolutional neural networks (CNN) is proposed to retrieve information at different scales, including both nuclei and overall tissue organization. This chapter utilizes several deep neural network architectures and gradient boosted trees classifier to classify the histology images among four classes. Hence, this approach has outperformed existing approaches in terms of accuracy and implementation complexity.

DOI: 10.4018/978-1-7998-3095-5.ch008

INTRODUCTION

Breast Cancer (BC) is the most routine cancer found in women. The growth of cancer ratio has been increasing over the last 10 to 15 years. The average age for these cancers is 50 to 69 years and it is the highest over 85 years of age. The rate of cancer is also higher in socioeconomic groups. The UK has a maximum rate of cancer incidence. BC is the most commonly occurring cancer in women, affecting 2.1 million women every year and that origin a massive number of cancer deaths among women. In 2018, expected that 6,27,000 women would die from BC about 15% of all cancer deaths among women (World Health Organization, 2018). Early diagnosis can significantly improve treatment very successfully. BC symptoms and signs may vary, and the diagnosis includes a physical examination, mammography, ultrasound examination, and biopsy.

Introduction to Breast Cancer

Early detection is an essential aspect of increasing the survival rate of BC. Two types of initial detection strategies are following they are early diagnosis and screening. Restricted resource settings with weaker health systems, more women being diagnosing in the final stages, so prioritizing the advanced diagnosis based on early signs and symptoms are important (Sree, Ng, Acharya, & Faust, 2011). The determination of BC by conventional methods is not a challenging task but these can be visualized on a traditional mammogram or ultrasound. A mammogram is the best method for detecting BC at the present stage. But the difficulty of using a mammogram is that the images of the mammogram itself are more complicated. So, by using image processing and feature extraction procedures can help the radiologist to detect a tumor much easier and faster. Symptoms extracted from areas not known in mammography images can help clinicians to detect tumor presence in real-time to speed up the process of treatment. Consequently, each cancer is different from other cancer that exists. In cancer treatment, a single drug may have a different reaction when administered to rare cancer and also can vary from person to person. Depending on one approach or an algorithm may not produce accurate results. The mammography image can also be compromised if the patient undergoes breast surgery. Various categories of imaging techniques are available in the current era to evaluate the human body without harming the body (Sudheer Kumar & Shoba Bindu, 2019). The different types of imaging modalities are shown in the below Figure 1.

Tumor cells differ in location (milk ducts or lobules) and how they look under the microscope, but they may be invasive or non-invasive. A breast biopsy is a procedure of taking a sample of breast tissue for laboratory testing and the results determine if there are cancer cells in the suspicious area of your breast or not. It provides a tissue sample used by doctors to detect abnormalities in cells. A lab report from a breast biopsy can help you decide whether if you need any additional surgery or other treatment. The natural history of BC begins with invasive carcinoma by hyperplasia and carcinoma in-situ with normal epithelial enlargement through clinical and pathological stages and is the pinnacle in metastatic disease. The mixture of Hematoxylin-Eosin (H&E) is the primary stain of tissue samples for the diagnosis of histopathological.

Introduction to Histopathology

Histopathology is the identification and interpretation of tissue diseases, and examination of tissue and/or cells under a microscopic examination. Histopathologists are responsible for assisting physicians in

Figure 1. Various Categories of Imaging Modalities

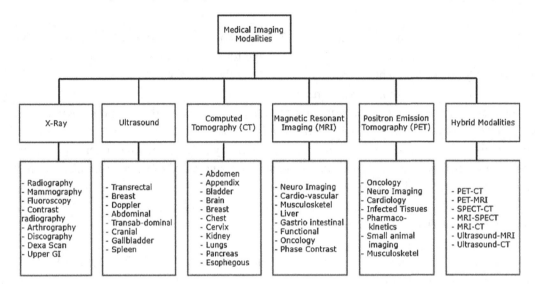

diagnosing tissue and looking after the patient. They examine the tissues under the microscope to identify that the changing cells affect the patient's illness. Figure 2 shows examples of various non-malignant and malignant lesions of the breast.

Although the early stages of tumor progression and the exact underlying mechanism have not fully elucidated, it is also known that almost all invasive breast cancers originate from in-situ carcinomas. Multiple pathological and biological features differentiate between in-situ carcinoma, invasive ductal carcinoma and benign breast lesions. Accurate diagnosis of breast enlargement disease is crucial in determining the optimal treatment plan. At present, the diagnosis of these conditions is largely based on careful examination of breast tissue sections under the pathologist's microscope. Histological procedures are direct to provide the best quality components for sensitive microscopic evaluation of human tissue changes in immediate or induced diseases. Typically, the tissue was fixed with paraffin, fixed with neutral formalin 10%, and then physically divided with a microtome to obtain 4-5μm thick paraffin sections. Dewoxed sections are marked with H&E and are used for several purposes (Slaoui & Fiette, 2011). These steps are usually performed by a Pathology Lab technician, who then sends the sample to a pathologist for clarification.

Figure 2. (a) Normal (b) Benign (c) In situ (d) Invasive

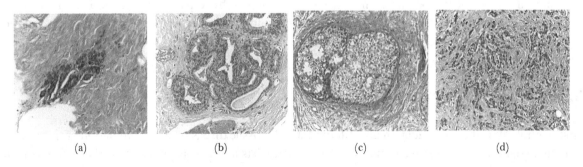

Staining is one of the most important steps in the preparation of tissue because most cells are colour-less and transparent. Therefore, histological sections should be stained to highlight important features of the tissue as well as to increase tissue contrast. Microscopic evaluation of such tissue sections provides invaluable information for pathologists to diagnose and classify various pathological conditions. H&E staining is the most commonly used staining technique in hematopathology. Hematoxylin stains the cell nuclei blue, and counterstain eosin cytoplasmic and non-nuclear components in various shades of pink. H&E staining is not specific because it stains most of the cells in the same way. Selective staining methods are those that select specific chemical groups or molecules in cells or tissues.

Histopathological analysis of breast tissue samples almost always begins with a careful examination of H&E stained specimens. Despite the introduction of powerful and highly specialized stain procedures over the last 40 years, H&E remains the most widely used tissue stain for determining the diagnosis and prognosis of breast cancer patients. The pathological classification of breast enlargement diseases depends on the molecular morphometric properties and structural patterns of cells and glands. In-vascular tumors are routinely classified based on the assessment of tubule/gland formation, nuclear pleomorphism, and mitotic count. Due to different pathological criteria, intervertebral variability, and differential tumor growth pattern, classification and grading are challenging due to time-consuming. Computerized analysis can solve the problem of inappropriate comments and subjectivity, and the lack of widespread access to robust solutions for digitizing glass slides has hindered the use of computerized analysis techniques.

Computer-Aided Diagnosis for Histopathology

Computer-aided detection (CADe) and computer-aided diagnosis (CADx) refer to the automated procedures that assist physicians in the interpretation of medical images. CADe and CADx were similarly referring to as CAD (Doi, 2007). An example of such a system would automatically discriminate between malignant and benign Whole Slide Imaging (WSI) of the breast sample. The application of CAD for histopathology has been classified into three main groups:

Detection, Segmentation, and Quantification of Important Tissue Structures:

The first use case for CAD in pathology refers to tedious routine diagnostic tasks that require much accuracy. Examples of these include:

- Identifying and dividing nuclei to analyze nuclear morphology as one of the hallmarks of cancer conditions (Kowal, Filipczuk, Obuchowicz, Korbicz, & Monczak, 2013).
- Analysis of glandular structures and the morphology of the gland is the main criterion for grading cancer (Sarmiento & Fondón, 2018).
- Identification of cancer metastases in lymph node segments (Bándi et al., 2019).

Classification of Histopathology Imagery Based on Grade or Lesion Type:

The Classification of histopathology imagery is often the ultimate goal in many diagnostic tasks, especially in cancer applications. The interpretation of pathology images for grading cancer or classifying wounds is subjective. The CAD may provide objective and accurate classification results to aid the pathologist's decision. Examples are:

- Gleason scoring for prostate cancer, and
- Classifying breast enlargement lesions into benign, DCIS and invasive cancer.

Disease Diagnosis and Prognosis:

Computerized instruments have relied on the assessment of micro sub-visual changes in the patterns of important structures in histopathological images, which are difficult to detect or detect in human eyes. It may lead to the early diagnosis and prognosis of the disease and facilitates the subsequent clinical management of patients (Schnitt, 2010).

Introduction to Deep Learning

Deep Learning (DL) (also known as Deep Structural Learning or Hierarchical Learning) is a sub-field of the Machine Learning (ML). Deep Belief Networks, Deep Neural Networks, Repetitive Neural Networks, and Convolutional Neural Networks (CNN) are various models used in computer vision, speech recognition, audio recognition, natural language processing, social network filtering, machine translation, bioinformatics, and medical image analysis. DL is a classification of ML algorithms that use multiple layers to extract high-level properties from raw input. For example, in image processing, the lower layers can detect or notice the edges, while the higher layer can identify human-meaning elements such as digits, letters, or faces. Recent DL models rely on artificial neural networks, specifically, CNN.

Mainly, the DL process can help you acquire what features to obtain (of course, this does not eliminate the need for hand-tuning; for example, different layers and layer sizes can provide various levels of abstraction). For supervised learning tasks, DL techniques remove feature engineering and get layered structures that remove idleness in representation by changing the data into compact, intermediate representations similar to the main components. Because of having more unlabeled data than labeled data, DL algorithms can also be applied to unsupervised learning tasks. Until 2011, CNNs has not played an essential role in computer vision meetings in June 2012, a document written on Max-pooling CNNs at a leading conference showed how to improve vision benchmark records. In October 2012, a close system by ImageNet (Alex Krizhevsky, Ilya Sutskever, & Geoffrey E. Hinton, 2012) won the contest on a large scale by a significant margin over shallow ML techniques. In November 2012, (Cireşan, Giusti, Gambardella, & Schmidhuber, 2013) won the ICPR Competition on the Analysis of Large Medical Images for Cancer Detection or Examination and won the MICCAI Grand Challenge on the same subject in the following year. Resulting in a similar trend in large-scale speech recognition, the error rate on image network classification tasks using DL decreased further in 2013 and 2014. In March 2019, Joshua Benzio, Geoffrey Hinton and Ann LeCun attended the Turing Award for their conceptual and engineering advances that have made deep neural networks a significant part of computing (Turing awards, 2018).

The objective of this chapter is to develop a 4-class classification system that performs analysis of histopathology images to identify BC. Also, it requires the development of robust and high throughput algorithms that can be performed at the WSI level as well. Analyzing histopathological images in particular to the WSI level is complicated for several reasons. First, histological stains show a considerable variation in their color and intensity. Such differences hamper the effectiveness of quantitative image analysis. Second, tissue preparation and digitization usually produce many artifacts that pose challenges to automated analysis. Finally, the large size of a WSI and the large number of different structures that need to be analyzed within the WSI, so it is a challenging task to develop an accurate and reliable CNN model for histopathology image analysis. Throughout this chapter, focuses on the evolution of deep CNNs for image classification, which can overcome challenges and operate at the WSI level. This approach uses in-depth scenarios for gradient enhanced trees for feature extraction and classification, and to our knowledge, this approach surpasses other identical solutions.

This chapter has a societal impact by providing the solution as a CAD tool, indeed helps to diagnose breast cancer at an early stage even from remote places and also can increase awareness about BC. The other sections of this chapter are structured as follows: In Section 2, we review the contributions to the classification of BC histology image. Then, the proposed technique is discussed in Section 3. Finally, the experimental results and conclusion of this chapter will be discussed in Sections 4 and 5, respectively.

LITERATURE SURVEY

In (George, Zayed, Roushdy, & Elbagoury, 2014) implemented an intelligent remote detection and diagnosis system for diagnosing BC based on cytological images. This approach has considered 12 features for the process of classification of tumour adequately. The dataset which was used in this approach has 92 breast cytological images which consist of 11502 nuclei. By using the backpropagation algorithm, support vector machines, probability neural network and learning vector quantization in the multilayer perceptron have used in this model. The performance metrics used for evaluation are error rate, sensitivity rate, correct rate, and specificity. This system performs pre-processing of data, cell nuclei detection, false finding elimination, cell nuclei segmentation, feature extraction and classification. The model results have stated that by using the Probability neural network and support vector machine, the model achieves reasonable specificity with 94.57 and 90.99 respectively. As specified, this approach can be improved by applying the hybrid clustering algorithms.

For the classification of H&E stained breast biopsy images, the approach (Araújo, T et al., 2017) utilizes CNN. A benign lesion, in situ carcinoma, normal tissue and invasive carcinoma are four class labels for the breast biopsy images which mainly of two class's non-carcinoma and carcinoma. The organization of the network is planned to obtain info on various scales, as well as the nucleus and whole tissue organization. This methodology allows the expansion of the planned system to full-slide histology images. Features collected by CNN has used to train SVM classification and achieved an accuracy of 77.8% for 4-class and 83.3% for 2-class.

Preliminary work in (Hou, L et al., 2016) proposed a model based on decision fusion to combine patch-level prediction specified by patch-level CNN. Besides, the researcher has designed a unique expectation-maximization (EM) that naturally detects differential patches using the spatial relationship of patches. This approach is appropriate for the classification of glioma and non-small cell lung carcinoma. The classification correctness of this approach is identical to the inter-observer deal between pathologists. In (Liu, Y et al., 2017) applies a framework for inevitably detecting and localizing small tumours of 100×100 pixels in gigapixel microscopy images in the range of 14000×1000 pixels. This approach takes benefit of the structure of CNNs and results in a challenging lesion-level tumour detection task in the Camelyon 16 dataset. In (Ehteshami Bejnordi, B et al., 2017) the performance of automated DL algorithms is based on the reflection of metastases in H&E stained tissue sections of the lymph nodes. The curve (AUC) for this algorithm is in between 0.556 to 0.994. The algorithm attained an injury-level, true-positive fraction similar to that of a pathologist WOTC (72.4% [95% CI, 64.3% -80.4%]) with a mean of 0.0125 false-positives for the normal WSI. In the WSI classification task, the best algorithm

(AUC, 0.994 [95% CI, 0.983-0.999]) showed that pathologists performed better than WOTC in diagnostic emulation (mean AUC, 0.810 [range, 0.738-0.884]; P <0.001). The performance of the algorithm can be distinguished from a skillful pathologist, who is inferring WSIs without time constraints.

In (Cruz-Roa, A et al., 2014) proposed a DL for automatic discovery and visual investigation of Invasive Ductal Carcinoma (IDC) tissue areas in WSIs of BC. The DL structure in this article extends several CNN visual semantic analyses of tumour areas to provide diagnostic support. This method has estimated the WSI data set from 162 patients with IDC. IDC in WSI is designed to measure the accuracy of the classifier in detecting tissue areas. The future work in this approach is to investigate the effects of CNN models with deeper structures (i.e. more layers and neurons) and justification on large coordinates. Nevertheless, the fascinating future direction is to learn and recognize visual features automatically related to histopathology architecture and morphology to acquire quantifiable meaning. In (Han, Z. et al., 2017) discussed about multiple classifications of BC based on histopathological images. The author proposed an approach with too many classifications of BC using a DL model. He conducted two training strategies. The first is "CSDCNN from scratch", which means direct CSDCNN training in the BreakHis data set. The second is constructed with transfer learning, which initially includes training before CSDCNN in Imagenet. Besides, the CSDCNN basic learning frequency is set to 0.01 and the number of training iterations is 5K, which is the best accuracy since validation and test suite.

A deep CNN based solution has been implemented in (Das, Karri, Roy, Chatterjee, & Sheet, 2017), which analyzes images from a random number of tissue sections at multiple magnifications without the need to enlarge the correspondence view. However, the majority voting approach is used to determine the level of the slide, i.e., the estimation of the posterior class of each view at a particular zoom with and after zoom, the specific posterior rating in random multiple views with multiple voting is filtered to ensure slide level confirmation. Experimentally evaluated performance using 5-fold cross-validation at patient level with 58 malignancies and an average of 24 benign cases of BC accuracy $94.67 \pm 14.60\%$, $96.00 \pm 8.94\%$ sensitivity, $92.00 \pm 17.85\%$ and result as $96.24 \pm 5.29\%$ when processing each view in 10ms. A method (Golatkar, Anand, & Sethi, 2018) of classifying H&E stained breast tissue images based on DL. This strategy involves extracting patches based on atomic density and discarding patches that are not high in the nucleus, e.g., from non-epithelial areas. An average of 85% is obtained in four classes and 93% for non-cancer patients (i.e. normal or benign) compared to malignancies (in situ or invasive cancer), which is an improvement over the previous comparative test.

In (Nazeri, Aminpour, & Ebrahimi, 2018), the goal is to split the images into four classes: general, benign, in situ and invasive cancer, depending on the primary type of cancer. Due to the large size of each image in the training data set, a patch-based method consisting of two consecutive neural networks is proposed. The first "patch" network acts as an auto coder that removes the most critical features of image patches, while the second "image" network classifies the entire image. The network is pre-trained and aims to collect local information, while the second network introduces global image information. Training networks using the ICIAR 2018 Grand Challenge on the set of breast cancer histology (BACH) The proposed method provides 95% accuracy in a validation set, compared with the 77% accuracy indicator previously described in the literature. In (Huang CH. et al., 2018) proposed an automated approach for the classification of pathological images to support the diagnosis of BC, e.g., classification of the image into general, benign, in situ and invasive categories. The proposed model consists of two parts: a Double Path Network (DPN) and a deep CNN for transformation RGB. The properties of a given input image on the probability map of each category: and secondly, the integration of noise and model as well as a fully integrated neural network can be used as a class, taking into account global and local characteristics to achieve better performance. Based on 10-fold cross-validation using a given training kit, the accuracy of this approach is ~ 91.75%.

In (Vang, Chen, & Xie, 2018) presents an in-depth learning framework for the multi-class classification of BC images at the International Meeting on Image Analysis and Recognition (ICIAR) 2018 a great challenge in the field of histological images of BACH. The author proposed a method using Inception V3 to classify the level of patches. The patch level estimates are passed by majority voting as part of a joint fusion, Gradient Enhancement Machine (GBM) and logistic regression to attain an image-level rating. This method can improve class sensitivity to regular and gentle classes by creating a DPN, which can be used as a feature extractor. The captured features are transferred to the second layer of the complicated forecast by means of GBM, logistic regression and the auxiliary vector machine to improve expectations. In (Sarmiento, & Fondón, 2018) provides a CAD tool for the classification task that uses color and textures features for classification. The color features are being estimated using k-means clustering. From the perspective of texture, all of these distributions are different textures occurring on the images. They have computed two sets of texture descriptors: fractal dimension and local binary patterns for extracting textural features and those features were applied to the different classifiers like SVM with the quadratic kernel which outperforms all other classifiers by providing high classification accuracy.

In (Nahid, Mehrabi, & Yinan, 2018) classifies biomedical BC images using the novel DNN methods guided by structural and statistical information obtained from images. Specifically, a combination of Long-Short-Term-Memory (LSTM) and CNN LSTimer proposed for BC Image Classification. SoftMax and SVM layers used for decision making after capturing features that make use of the proposed novel DNN models. The best accuracy value of 91.00% has achieved at 200x in this experiment. In (Adeshina, Adedigba, Adeniyi, & Aibinu, 2018) solved the intra-class problem, classification of breast histopathology images into eight classes of benign or malignant cells. This approach adopted the DCNN architecture in conjunction with the ensemble learning method using the TensorFlow framework with backpropagation and ReLU activation function achieved an precise automatic classification of these images. In (Jiang, Chen, Zhang, & Xiao, 2019) a novel CNN has been developed consisting of a convolutional layer, a small SE-ResNet module, and a fully connected layer. The problem of cell overlap and asymmetric color distribution in pathological images of BC obtained from various staining methods needs to be addressed.

In (Bardou, Zhang, & Ahmad, 2018) automatic classification of BC histology images as malignant & benign and malignant sub-classes. Experimented with augmentation techniques to improve the accuracy of the convoluted neural network as well as the handcrafted features with CNN. The achieved accuracy between 96.15% and 98.33% for binary classification and 83.31% and 88.23% for multi-class classification. In (Cuiru et al., 2019) implemented an automatic BC detection method based on hybrid features for pathological images. Due to the weak interaction between the H & E channels, the conformation of features for both the channels can be captured separately, which makes them more representative results. From multiple perspectives, morphological features, spatial structural features and texture characteristics are captured and combined. Using SVM, classification can be better generalized, the pathological picture is classified as benign or malignant on the basis of mitigation method for feature selection.

METHODOLOGY

Dataset

The collected dataset is an addition of the dataset to (Araújo, T et al. 2017) and consists of 400 H&E stain images, each of size 2048×1536 pixels downloaded from (ICIAR Grand Challenge, 2018). The entire images are of digitally acquired within the equivalent conditions, with an intensification level of 200× and $0.42\mu m \times 0.42\mu m$ of pixel size. Each image is labelled into one of four balanced classes: normal, benign, in situ carcinoma, and invasive carcinoma, where the class defined in the image is its cancer type.

Proposed Approach

Deep CNN architectures with millions of factors, such as VGG, Inception, and ResNet have resulted in many computer vision tasks (Christian, Sergey, Vincent, & Alexander, 2016). Still, a large number of images are essential to train these neural networks from scratch, whereas training on a small dataset is insufficient, that is, the inability to generalize knowledge which leads to either overfitting/underfitting. A common alleviate for these situations is the refinement of a portion of a pre-trained network to a new dataset. Conversely, in these experiments, the tuning method did not perform well on this task. Therefore, a different technique called deep convolutional feature representation (Yanming et al., 2016) has been considered in this work. The unsupervised dimensionality reduction phase considerably decreases the risk of overfitting in the future stage of supervised learning. With the usage of LightGBM which is a rapid, distributed, and elevated performance of gradient boosted trees for supervised classification. Gradient Boosting Models (GBM) are widely used in ML due to their speed, accuracy and rigidity against overfitting (Guolin et al., 2017).

Figure 3. Overall Pre-Processing Pipeline

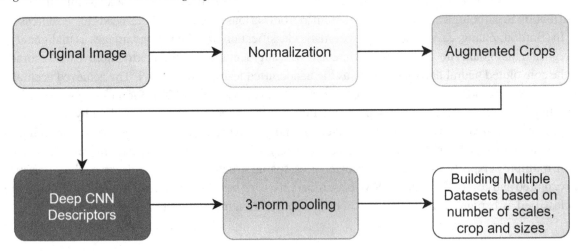

Data Pre-Processing and Augmentation

The extent of H&E on the tissue was normalized as described in Algorithm 1 (Macenko et al., 2009) to retrieve microscopy images which enables for better quantitative analysis and for all the images performing 50 random colour augments. Following (Ruifrok, & Johnston, 2001) the amount of H&E is accommodated by dissolving the RGB colour of the tissue into the H&E colour space, then multiplying the H&E size of each pixel's by two random uniform variables [0.7, 1.3]. Additionally, in early experiments, using diverse image criteria, the original 2048 × 1536 pixels would be reduced to half 1024 × 768 pixels. Extracting random crops of two sizes: 800 × 800 and 1300 × 1300 and the crops from downscaled images as 400 × 400 pixels and 650 × 650 pixels. Recently, it has been found that downscaled images are sufficient. So that each image is represented by 20 crops. Then the crops are encoded into 20 descriptors. Finally, a set of 20-descriptors is combined into a single descriptor by 3-norm pooling (Boureau, Ponce, & LeCun, 2010). The overall pre-processing pipeline is depicted in Figure 4. Figure 6 shows the output of the normalization.

Algorithm 1. Normalizing H&E stained on the tissue for obtaining stain vectors.
  Input: RGB Slide

1. Convert RGB to OD
2. Remove data with OD intensity less than β
3. Calculate SVD on the OD tuples
4. Create plane from the SVD directions corresponding to the two largest singular values
5. Project data onto the plane, and normalize to unit length
6. Calculate angle of each point wrt the first SVD direction
7. Find robust extremes $\left(\alpha^{th} and \left(100 - \alpha\right)^{th} percentiles\right)$ of the angle
8. Convert extreme values back to OD space

  Output: Optimal Stain Vectors

Figure 4. Process flow of Feature Extraction

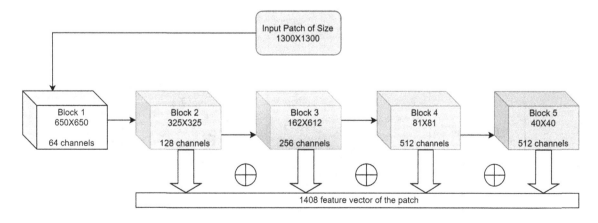

3.1 Process of Feature Extraction

For the features extraction process, this approach used a pre-trained Inception ResNet v2 network from Keras distribution. By removing fully connected layers from the model which will allow the model to make use of images of indiscriminate size. In the model, the GlobalAveragePooling operation is applied to four blocks 2,3,4,5 with 128, 256, 512 and 512 channels correspondingly. Finally, combining them into a 1408 vector, and this process will depict in the figure 5.

Figure 5. Normalization Output in Pre-Processing Pipeline

Type of Image	Original Image	Normalized Image
Normal	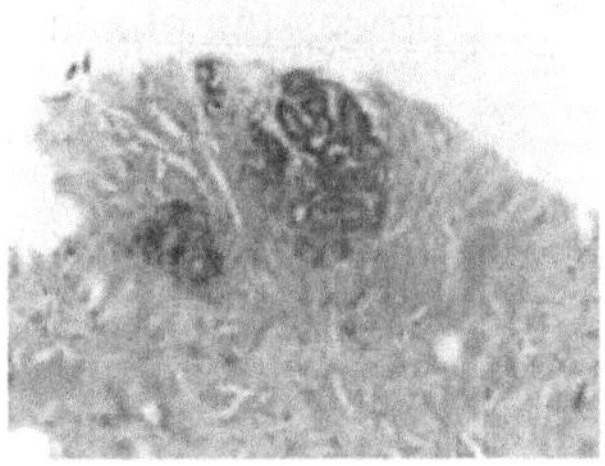	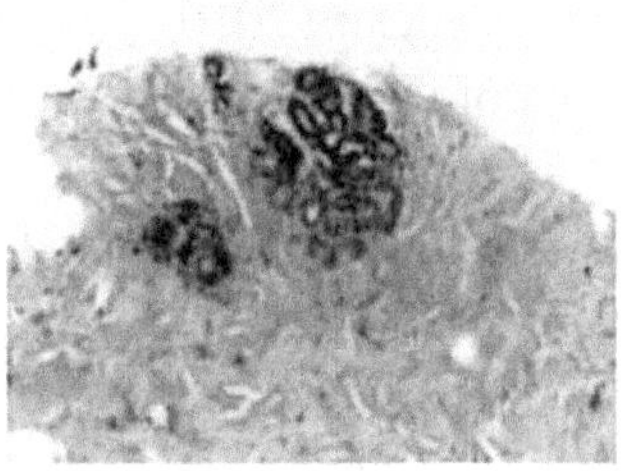
Benign	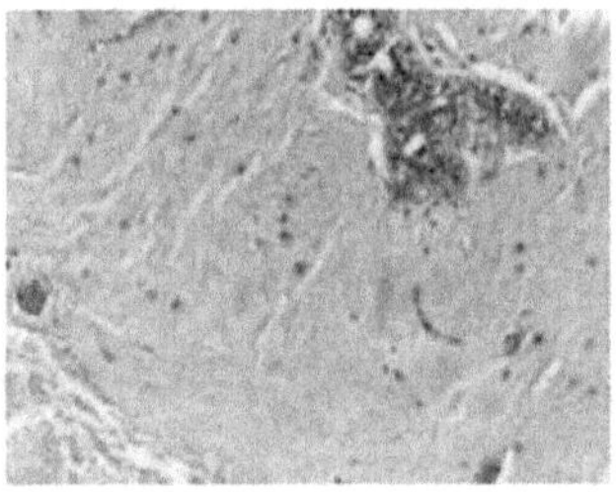	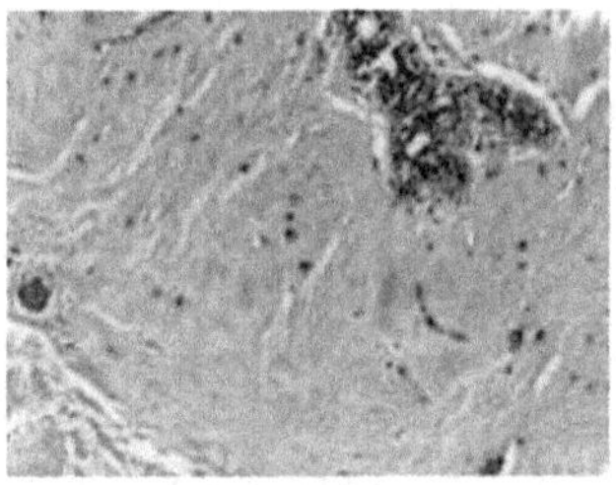
In situ	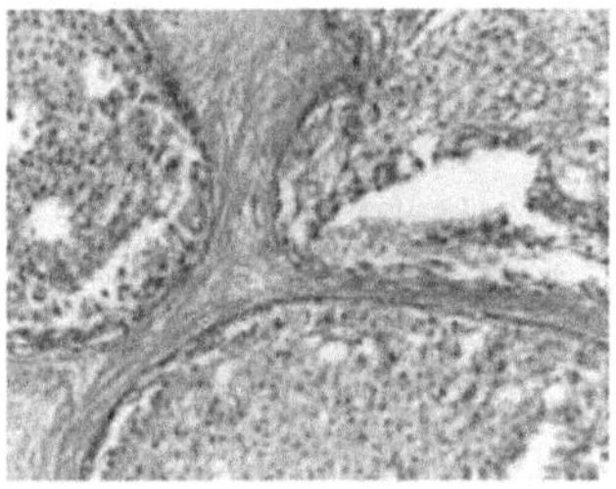	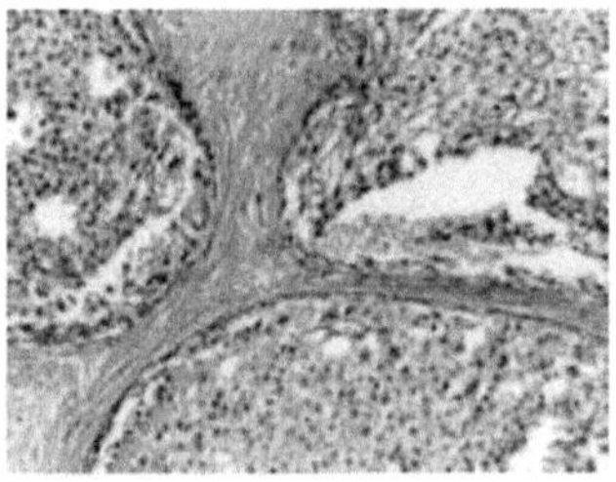
Invasive	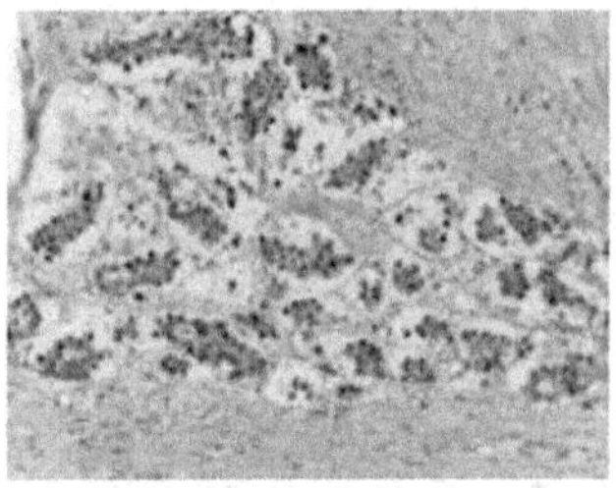	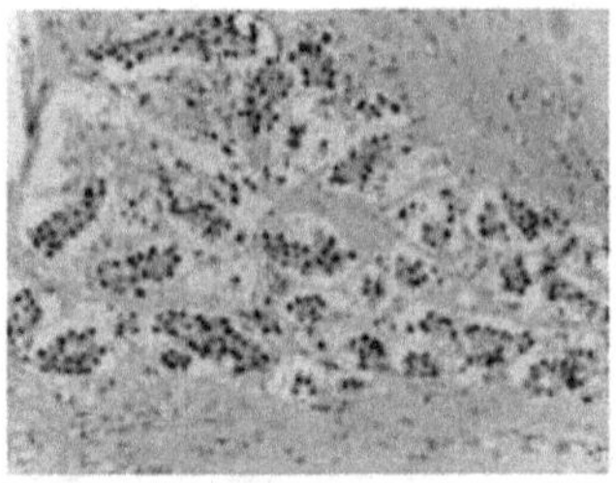

Training

To conserve the class distribution, data were divided into ten stratified folds. Augmentations will increase the size of the dataset by considering two patch sizes with one encoder and fifty colour/affine augmentations, so totally it gives 100. However, interpretations of a given image are interrelated. For training 10 GBMs along with ten times of cross-validation each blend of an encoder, crop size and scale was considered. Also, recycling each dataset five times with altered random seeds in LightGBM increases the augmentation of the model-level growth. As a consequence, by training ten folds with five seeds and two-scale with crop and with the encoder achieved 100 GBMs. In the cross-validation phase, each fold is evaluated only with untrained models on this fold. Extract 100 descriptors of each image for test data and use them with all models trained for a specific patch size and encoder. All Predictions are averaged for overall augmentations and models. Finally, the maximum likelihood score of the class predicted is defined.

This approach originated in Keras with Tensorflow backend and the language used is Python 3.6. Intel Core i7-8700 CPU @3.20 GHz ×12, memory 16GB, Radeon RX 550 series GPU, 64-bit processor with Ubuntu 18.04 LTS used for training and testing.

Figure 6. 2-class Classification ROC Curve

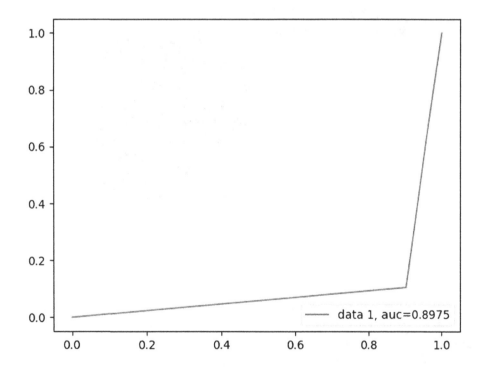

EXPERIMENTAL RESULTS

To validate the approach 10-fold cross-validation is considered. For 2-class, the classification accuracy is 89.7±1.8%, and for 4-class, the accuracy is 81.8±2.1% as shown in the below table 4.1. The area under the ROC curve for 2-class classification is depicted in the below figure 7. The Confusion matrix, without normalization, has been plotted in the below figure 8. The Vertical axis represents ground truth values and the horizontal axis represents predictions.

Figure 7. Confusion Matrix for 2-class Classification

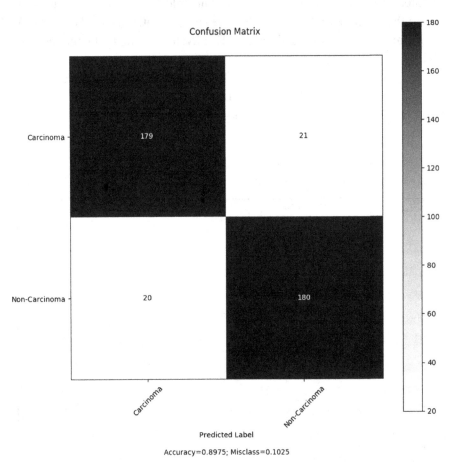

The below Table 1 depicts the 2-class and 4-class blended model with their corresponding 10-fold cross-validation values. Also the Tables 2 & 3 depicts the accuracy of 10 (no of folds) ×5 (no of seeds) ×2 (scaling and cropping) ×1 (encoder) with its Accuracy of all seeds and the parameters used for this evaluation are: learning_rate = 0.1, 70 steps, loss 0.63, accuracy 0.825, knobs num_leaves 191, feature_fraction 0.46, bagging_fraction 0.66, max_depth 7

Figure 8. Confusion Matrix for 4-class Classification

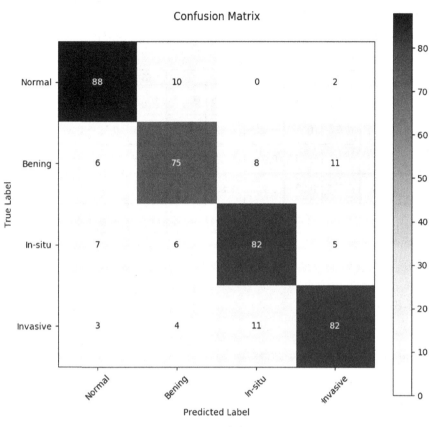

Accuracy=0.8175; Misclass=0.1825

Table 1. Calculated Mean and Standard Deviation across all folds for 2 & 4 classes

Class	f0	f1	f2	f3	f4	f5	f6	f7	f8	f9	Mean	Standard Deviation
2-class	0.975	0.925	0.825	0.925	0.9	0.9	0.85	0.9	0.95	0.825	**0.897**	0.048
4-class	0.9	0.775	0.775	0.925	0.85	0.725	0.775	0.825	0.85	0.775	**0.818**	0.0603

IncResNet-0.5-400

Table 2. Calculated Accuracy across all folds for both scaling (0.5) and crop size (400)

Seed No	f0	f1	f2	f3	f4	f5	f6	f7	f8	f9	mean
Seed 0: Accuracies:	0.85	0.825	0.8	0.9	0.875	0.725	0.75	0.8	0.825	0.75	0.81
Seed 1: Accuracies:	0.875	0.77	0.77	0.925	0.82	0.72	0.825	0.82	0.875	0.75	0.81
Seed 2: Accuracies:	0.825	0.77	0.775	0.925	0.85	0.77	0.825	0.8	0.85	0.75	0.815
Seed 3: Accuracies:	0.9	0.775	0.825	0.925	0.85	0.775	0.8	0.8	0.775	0.75	0.818
Seed 4: Accuracies:	0.825	0.75	0.8	0.925	0.85	0.75	0.8	0.8	0.825	0.75	0.807

Accuracy of all seeds: **0.814**

IncResNet-0.5-650

Table 3. Calculated Accuracy across all folds for both scaling (0.5) and crop size (650)

Seed No	f0	f1	f2	f3	f4	f5	f6	f7	f8	f9	mean
Seed 0: Accuracies:	0.925	0.725	0.725	0.9	0.85	0.725	0.8	0.85	0.8	0.8	0.81
Seed 1: Accuracies:	0.875	0.77	0.775	0.9	0.85	0.65	0.8	0.85	0.82	0.725	0.802
Seed 2: Accuracies:	0.95	0.8	0.775	0.925	0.85	0.7	0.8	0.825	0.8	0.7	0.812
Seed 3: Accuracies:	0.85	0.8	0.775	0.9	0.85	0.675	0.85	0.85	0.85	0.725	0.812
Seed 4: Accuracies:	0.875	0.8	0.725	0.9	0.85	0.7	0.85	0.85	0.825	0.75	0.812

Accuracy of all seeds: **0.81**

Table 4. Comparison of accuracy with the existing approach

Approach	2-class	4-class
Ara´ujo, T . ,	83.3%	77.8%
Proposed Approach	**89.7%**	**81.8%**

CONCLUSION

This chapter proposes a CNN framework to solve the four-class classification problem (normal, benign, in situ, and invasive) on H&E stained microscopic images by retrieving nuclei and tissue structure information. Recently, DL techniques have emerged to address many problems in the field of medical image processing. Proposing a classification scheme for BC tissue image classification based on deep CNNs. Convolutional networks are considered as state-of-the-art techniques for classification problems when the input is high-dimensional data such as images. These networks learn to extract local features from images and classify the input according to the extracted features. Using a robust data augmentation and deep convolutional feature extraction process at different scales with pre-trained CNNs on ImageNet can increase the visibility of classification. On top of that, the implementation of the gradient boosting algorithm is highly accurate. This approach achieved 89.7% and 81.8% of accuracies for 2-class and 4-class classification of histopathology BC. There is scope for improving classification performance by using better network design. The influence of other scales on the performance is also considerable future work. Furthermore, multiple instance learning-based approaches which work with weakly supervised data can also be attempted.

REFERENCES

Adeshina, S. A., Adedigba, A. P., Adeniyi, A. A., & Aibinu, A. M. (2018). Breast Cancer Histopathology Image Classification with Deep Convolutional Neural Networks. *Proceedings of 14th International Conference on Electronics Computer and Computation (ICECCO)*, 206-212. 10.1109/ICECCO.2018.8634690

Araújo, T., Aresta, G., Castro, E., Rouco, J., Aguiar, P., Eloy, C., ... Campilho, A. (2017). Classification of breast cancer histology images using Convolutional Neural Networks. *PLoS One*, *12*(6), e0177544. doi:10.1371/journal.pone.0177544 PMID:28570557

Bándi, P., Geessink, O., Manson, Q., Van Dijk, M., Balkenhol, M., Hermsen, M., ... Litjens, G. (2019). From Detection of Individual Metastases to Classification of Lymph Node Status at the Patient Level: The CAMELYON17 Challenge. *IEEE Transactions on Medical Imaging*, *38*(2), 550–560. doi:10.1109/TMI.2018.2867350 PMID:30716025

Bardou, D., Zhang, K., & Ahmad, S. (2018). Classification of Breast Cancer Based on Histology Images Using Convolutional Neural Networks. *IEEE Access*.

Boureau, Y., Ponce, J., & LeCun, Y. (2010). A theoretical analysis of feature pooling in visual recognition. *Proceedings of the 27th international conference on machine learning (ICML-10)*, 111-118.

Christian, S., Sergey, I., Vincent, V., & Alexander, A.A. (2016). *Inception-v4, inception-resnet and the impact of residual connections on learning*, ArXiv:1602.07261v2

Cireşan, D. C., Giusti, A., Gambardella, L. M., & Schmidhuber, J. (2013). Mitosis Detection in Breast Cancer Histology Images with Deep Neural Networks. In K. Mori, I. Sakuma, Y. Sato, C. Barillot, & N. Navab (Eds.), Lecture Notes in Computer Science: Vol. 8150. *Proceedings of Medical Image Computing and Computer-Assisted Intervention – MICCAI 2013*. Berlin: Springer. doi:10.1007/978-3-642-40763-5_51

Cruz-Roa, A. (2014). Automatic detection of invasive ductal carcinoma in whole slide images with convolutional neural networks. *SPIE Medical Imaging. International Society for Optics and Photonics*, *9041*, 904103.

Cuiru. (2019). Breast cancer classification in pathological images based on hybrid features. *Multimedia Tools and Applications*, *78*. doi:10.100711042-019-7468-9

Das, K., Karri, S. P. K., Roy, A. G., Chatterjee, J., & Sheet, D. (2017). Classifying histopathology whole-slides using fusion of decisions from deep convolutional network on a collection of random multi-views at multi-magnification. *Proceedings of IEEE 14th International Symposium on Biomedical Imaging (ISBI 2017)*, 1024–1027. 10.1109/ISBI.2017.7950690

Doi, K. (2007). Computer-aided diagnosis in medical imaging: historical review, current status and future potential. *Computerized Medical Imaging and Graphics: The Official Journal of the Computerized Medical Imaging Society*, *31*(4-5), 198–211.

Ehteshami Bejnordi, B., Veta, M., Johannes van Diest, P., van Ginneken, B., Karssemeijer, N., Litjens, G., ... Venâncio, R. (2017). Diagnostic Assessment of Deep Learning Algorithms for Detection of Lymph Node Metastases in Women with Breast Cancer. *Journal of the American Medical Association*, *318*(22), 2199–2210. doi:10.1001/jama.2017.14585 PMID:29234806

George, Y. M., Zayed, H. H., Roushdy, M. I., & Elbagoury, B. M. (2014). Remote computer aided breast cancer detection and diagnosis system based on cytological images. *IEEE Systems Journal*, *8*(3), 949–964. doi:10.1109/JSYST.2013.2279415

Golatkar, A., Anand, D., & Sethi, A. (2018). Classification of Breast Cancer Histology using Deep Learning. In A. Campilho, F. Karray, & B. ter Haar Romeny (Eds.), Lecture Notes in Computer Science: Vol. 10882. *Proceedings of Image Analysis and Recognition (ICIAR 2018)*. Cham: Springer. doi:10.1007/978-3-319-93000-8_95

Guolin, K. (2017). LightGBM: A highly efficient gradient boosting decision tree. *Advances in Neural Information Processing Systems*, 3149–3157.

Han, Z., Wei, B., Zheng, Y., Yin, Y., Li, K., & Li, S. (2017). Breast cancer multi-classification from histopathological images with structured deep learning model. *Scientific Reports*, *7*(1), 4172. doi:10.103841598-017-04075-z PMID:28646155

Hou, L. (2016). Patch-based convolutional neural network for whole slide tissue image classification. *Proceedings of the IEEE Conference on Computer Vision and Pattern Recognition*, 2424–2433. 10.1109/CVPR.2016.266

Huang, C. H., & ... . (2018). Automated Breast Cancer Image Classification Based on Integration of Noisy-And Model and Fully Connected Network. In A. Campilho, F. Karray, & B. ter Haar Romeny (Eds.), Lecture Notes in Computer Science: Vol. 10882. *Proceedings of Image Analysis and Recognition (ICIAR 2018)*. Cham: Springer. doi:10.1007/978-3-319-93000-8_105

ICIAR. (2018). *Grand Challenge on Breast Cancer Histology Images*. Retrieved from https://iciar2018-challenge.grand-challenge.org/

Jiang, Y., Chen, L., Zhang, H., & Xiao, X. (2019). Breast cancer histopathological image classification using convolutional neural networks with small SE-ResNet module. *PLoS One, 14*(3), e0214587. doi:10.1371/journal.pone.0214587 PMID:30925170

Kowal, M., Filipczuk, P., Obuchowicz, A., Korbicz, J., & Monczak, R. (2013). Computer aided diagnosis of breast cancer based on fine needle biopsy microscopic images. *Computers in Biology and Medicine, 43*(10), 1563–1572. doi:10.1016/j.compbiomed.2013.08.003 PMID:24034748

Krizhevsky, A., Sutskever, I., & Hinton, G. E. (2012). ImageNet classification with deep convolutional neural networks. *Proceedings of the 25th International Conference on Neural Information Processing Systems*, 1.

Liu, Y. (2017). *Detecting Cancer Metastases on Gigapixel Pathology Images.* ArXiv, abs/1703.02442

Macenko, M. (2009). A method for normalizing histology slides for quantitative analysis. *IEEE International Symposium on Biomedical Imaging: From Nano to Macro*, 1107-1110. 10.1109/ISBI.2009.5193250

Nahid, A.-A., Mehrabi, M. A., & Kong, Y. (2018). Histopathological Breast Cancer Image Classification by Deep Neural Network Techniques Guided by Local Clustering. *BioMed Research International, 2018*, 1–20. doi:10.1155/2018/2362108 PMID:29707566

Nazeri, K., Aminpour, A., & Ebrahimi, M. (2018). Two-Stage Convolutional Neural Network for Breast Cancer Histology Image Classification. In A. Campilho, F. Karray, & B. ter Haar Romeny (Eds.), Lecture Notes in Computer Science: Vol. 10882. *Proceedings of Image Analysis and Recognition (ICIAR 2018).* Cham: Springer. doi:10.1007/978-3-319-93000-8_81

Ruifrok, A., & Johnston, D. (2001). Quantification of histochemical staining by color deconvolution. *Analytical and Quantitative Cytology and Histology*, 23. PMID:11531144

Sarmiento, A., & Fondón, I. (2018). Automatic Breast Cancer Grading of Histological Images Based on Colour and Texture Descriptors. In A. Campilho, F. Karray, & B. ter Haar Romeny (Eds.), Lecture Notes in Computer Science: Vol. 10882. *Proceedings of Image Analysis and Recognition (ICIAR 2018).* Cham: Springer. doi:10.1007/978-3-319-93000-8_101

Sarmiento, A., & Fondón, I. (2018). Automatic Breast Cancer Grading of Histological Images Based on Colour and Texture Descriptors. In A. Campilho, F. Karray, & B. ter Haar Romeny (Eds.), Lecture Notes in Computer Science: Vol. 10882. *Proceedings of Image Analysis and Recognition (ICIAR 2018).* Cham: Springer. doi:10.1007/978-3-319-93000-8_101

Schnitt, S. (2010). Classification and prognosis of invasive breast cancer: From morphology to molecular taxonomy. *Modern Pathology, 23*(S2), S60–S64. doi:10.1038/modpathol.2010.33 PMID:20436504

Slaoui, M., & Fiette, L. (2011). Histopathology Procedures: From Tissue Sampling to Histopathological Evaluation. In J. C. Gautier (Ed.), *Drug Safety Evaluation. Methods in Molecular Biology (Methods and Protocols)* (Vol. 691). Humana Press. doi:10.1007/978-1-60761-849-2_4

Sree, S. V., Ng, E. Y., Acharya, R. U., & Faust, O. (2011). Breast imaging: A survey. *World Journal of Clinical Oncology, 2*(4), 171–178. doi:10.5306/wjco.v2.i4.171 PMID:21611093

Sudheer Kumar, E., & Shoba Bindu, C. (2019). Medical Image Analysis Using Deep Learning: A Systematic Literature Review. In Proceedings of Emerging Technologies in Computer Engineering: Microservices in Big Data Analytics (ICETCE 2019). Communications in Computer and Information Science (vol. 985, pp. 81-97). Springer. doi:10.1007/978-981-13-8300-7_8

Turing awards press note. (2018). Retrieved from https://awards.acm.org/binaries/content/assets/press-releases/2019/march/turing-award-2018.pdf

Vang, Y. S., Chen, Z., & Xie, X. (2018). Deep Learning Framework for Multi-class Breast Cancer Histology Image Classification. In A. Campilho, F. Karray, & B. ter Haar Romeny (Eds.), Lecture Notes in Computer Science: Vol. 10882. *Proceedings of Image Analysis and Recognition (ICIAR 2018)*. Cham: Springer. doi:10.1007/978-3-319-93000-8_104

World Health Organization breast cancer statistics. (2018). Retrieved from https://www.who.int/cancer/prevention/diagnosis-screening/breast-cancer/en/

Yanming, G. (2016). Deep learning for visual understanding: A review. *Neurocomputing, 187*, 27–48. doi:10.1016/j.neucom.2015.09.116

Chapter 9
Deep Learning in Engineering Education:
Performance Prediction Using Cuckoo–Based Hybrid Classification

Deepali R. Vora
Vidyalankar Institute of Technology, India

Kamatchi R. Iyer
Amity University, India

ABSTRACT

The goodness measure of any institute lies in minimising the dropouts and targeting good placements. So, predicting students' performance is very interesting and an important task for educational information systems. Machine learning and deep learning are the emerging areas that truly entice more research practices. This research focuses on applying the deep learning methods to educational data for classification and prediction. The educational data of students from engineering domain with cognitive and non-cognitive parameters is considered. The hybrid model with support vector machine (SVM) and deep belief network (DBN) is devised. The SVM predicts class labels from preprocessed data. These class labels and actual class labels acts as input to the DBN to perform final classification. The hybrid model is further optimised using cuckoo search with Levy flight. The results clearly show that the proposed model SVM-LCDBN gives better performance as compared to simple hybrid model and hybrid model with traditional cuckoo search.

INTRODUCTION

Nowadays, Educational Data Mining (EDM) exists as a novel trend in the Knowledge Discovery in Databases (KDD) and Data Mining (DM) field that concerns in mining valuable patterns and finding out practical knowledge from the educational systems. One important goal of the educational system among many is tracking the performance of the student. Many techniques and algorithms are used to track the

DOI: 10.4018/978-1-7998-3095-5.ch009

progress of students. However, evaluating the educational performance of students is challenging as their academic performance pivots on varied constraints. This domain has gained importance with the increase in data volume and the development of new algorithms.

Data generated from various educational sources is explored using different methods and techniques in EDM. The multidisciplinary research that deals with the development of such methods and techniques are the focus of EDM. Analysis of educational data could provide information about student's behaviours, based on which education policies could be enhanced further (Sukhija, Jindal, & Aggarwal, 2015, October). EDM discusses the techniques, tools, and research intended for automatically extracting the meaning from large repositories of educational systems' data.

According to Davies (Davis, 1998), "Education has become a commodity in which people seek to invest for their own personal gain, to ensure equality of opportunity and as a route to a better life." Because of this Higher education providers are competing mainly for students, funding, research and recognition within the wider society.

It seems important to study data of students studying professional courses as for the growth of any nation producing better professionals is the key to success. Higher education system faces two main challenges: finding placements and students dropping out. Analysis of educational data can help in answering the two major challenges satisfactorily. Predicting the performance leads to better placements and minimise the dropouts.

A statistical technique to predict future behaviour is known as Predictive modelling. Predictive analytics is used widely in the area of product management and recommendation. It is a powerful tool to understand the data at hand and get useful insights from it. Figure 1 represents Predictive analytics in education.

One of the most popular methods for predictive analytics is Machine learning (ML) to predict future behaviour. From the plethora of algorithms available, it is always interesting to discover which algorithm or technique is most suitable for analysis of data under consideration. EDM is the area of research where predictive modelling is most useful.

ML has become very popular among researchers because of the astonishing results the algorithms are giving for diverse data and applications. But when data is growing enormously simple ML are not efficient and beneficial. Meantime there are lot many advances in hardware and software. So, it was possible to have more complex and hybrid architectural models performing various DM or Big Data tasks. Big data is already posing a challenge on traditional ML models for efficiency and accuracy. Various hybrid models are proposed and tested in many domains to tackle these challenges and are proved to be useful. Thus, applying a hybrid model in the education domain will be useful.

ML is changing in a better way to tackle new age data and one of such advances is Deep Learning (DL). Nonlinear data analysis can be effectively done using deep learning. Characteristics of the data can be effectively analysed using layers in the deep learning model. DL is being applied in many domains; predominantly in image processing and natural language processing (Deng & Yu, 2014). Thus, it is interesting to apply Deep Learning in the field of education.

This chapter addresses the main objectives as:

1. Identification of areas like EDM where Deep Learning is applied and is useful
2. Applying hybrid classification method using Deep Learning on Educational Data for Classification
3. Improvising the Hybrid Model By Applying Cuckoo Search with Levy Flight optimization technique

Figure 1. Predictive Modelling

BACKGROUND

Deep Learning

Hinton and colleagues suggested the concept of Deep Learning in the year 2006. Deep Learning (DL) is capable of learning from small data sets. The learning is through a nonlinear network structure. The Deep Learning is made up of the network structure with normally more than 4 hidden layers with one input and one output layer. Such a network can transform the raw features of images into superior features thereby making classification and prediction better (Bengio, 2009) (Najafabadi, et al., 2015).

DL differs from ML in many ways. In terms of accuracy of algorithms, DL performs much better than normal ML. when data increases, DL learns fast from such ever-increasing data thereby increasing accuracy. In contrast, ML algorithms are restricted by the representation of data which hampers the response time and accuracy of the system using such algorithms. Consider an example of email spam filtering. To identify if an email is a spam or not, the ML algorithm is given various representations of a good and bad email. Using which incoming emails are categorized as good or bad. ML algorithm directly without any representations will not be able to decide on anything.

Here, DL comes to the rescue. Identification of important features and learning from them is easily performed by DL. DL algorithms can identify the features from the raw data and create representations for learning. DL has numerous algorithms of ML. These algorithms attempt to model high-level abstractions in data. They create or design architectures which are composed of many non-linear transformations.

Figure 2. A Deep Architecture

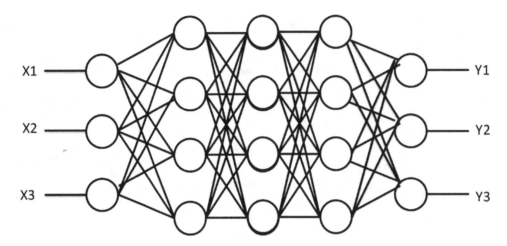

Deep architectures can be modelled using any combinations of layers of a network, but still, it has set of traditional algorithms such as Stacked AutoEncoder, Deep Boltzmann Machines, Deep Convolutional Networks and Deep Belief Networks. Figure 3 shows the set of predefined DL models.

In general, the model of deep learning technique can be classified into discriminative, generative, and hybrid models (Alwaisi & Baykan, 2017).

Figure 3. Deep Learning Models

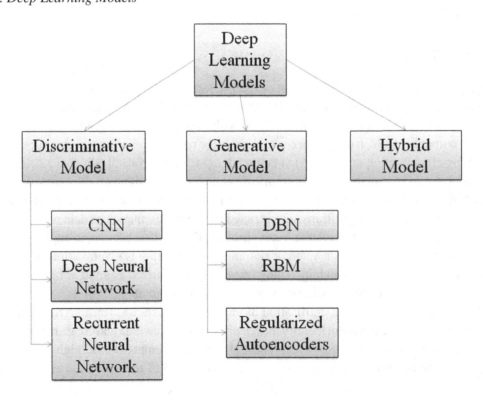

Discriminative models are used for modelling dependency of unobserved (target) variable Y on observed variables X whereas the generative models are used for learning the joint probability distribution. The generative model learns the full relationship between input X (features) and label Y giving maximum flexibility at the time of testing. Discriminative models learn from the only X to predict Y using conditional probability. By using few modelling assumptions these models can use existing data more efficiently. CNN, deep neural network and recurrent neural network are Discriminative models and DBN, restricted Boltzmann machine, and regularized autoencoders are generative models. Hybrid deep models are a combination of discriminative and generative models.

These DL models are used in various different application areas to gain better accuracy or output. Table 1 summarizes the work done in various areas:

In addition to the above mentioned, there are many applications in various domains where DL algorithms or deep networks are used very effectively.

From the study of various articles, it is evident that DL is applied widely in many areas. The improvement in hardware has also made application of DL feasible. These algorithms are proved to give better accuracy in many cases than other traditional ML algorithms. Still, there are many domains where DL may prove beneficial, one of those being Educational System. In many articles, the DL algorithms are compared with traditional machine learning algorithms and are observed to be more accurate. Many articles proved that DL algorithms improve accuracy over traditional ML algorithms.

Also, the review of articles suggests that applying Deep Learning algorithm with other generalised algorithms may give better results in classification and prediction tasks. Through the survey, it is observed that hybrid models are more popular than plain DL algorithm based models (Vora & Iyer, A Survey of Inferences from Deep Learning Algorithms, 2017). In many applications standard dimensionality reduction algorithms are used to reduce the features and then DL algorithms are applied to improve accuracy.

Educational Data Mining

EDM is a popular research area and an ample amount of research articles are available for study. These research articles indicate the experimentation and algorithms used in EDM for performing various tasks. For the performance prediction, various new techniques and ML algorithms have experimented. There are many factors or features which have a significant effect in predicting the performance of the students. These factors are classified as cognitive and non-cognitive factors. Non-cognitive factors play an important role in various EDM goals.

Wattana & Nachirat (Punlumjeak & Rachburee, 2015,October) used various techniques like K-Nearest Neighbourhood, Naïve Bays, and Neural Network to classify the students' data. The features considered were very few and majority attributes were related to marks of students.

Norlida, Usamah & Pauziah (Buniyamin, Mat, & Arshad, 2015, November) used Neuro Fuzzy algorithms to predict the performance of the engineering student. Here only 6 linguistic parameters are used for prediction.

Camilo, Elizabeth & Fabio (Guarín, Guzmán, & González, 2015) used Decision tree and Bayesian Classifier for prediction of students' performance. Students' admission test score and academic information were used for prediction. In addition, few socio-economic parameters were also used for prediction. The major stress was on the admission parameters.

Phung, Chau & Phung (Phung, Chau, & Phung, 2015,November) used Rule Extraction algorithm for classification in EDM. The algorithm is able to handle discrete and continuous data. The algorithm

Table 1. Deep Learning Application area

Application Area	Deep Learning Algorithm	Key Findings
Malware Detection	DBN (Davidt & Netanyahu, 2015,July)	• Dropout method was used while training the network. • Various layers were used to detect malware signatures. • The network was trained using a GPU to detect 30 signatures.
Intrusion Detection	DBN (GAO, GAO, Gao, & Wang, 2014,November)	• DBN has proved more accurate than SVM and Artificial Neural Network (ANN). • DBN with 4 different configurations was used. The performance of shallow DBN is same as SVM and ANN. • DBN with 2 and more hidden layers gave better output. The DBN is used for multiclass classification.
Spam Filtering	DBN (Tzortzis & Likas, 2007,October)	• DBN for Spam Filtering. • The performance was compared with SVM and DBN and was found more accurate.
Image Processing	Deep Convolutional DBN (Nguyen, Fookes, & Sridharan, 2015,September)	• Deep Convolutional DBN used for classification of images. • Accuracy is improved and training time for the deep network reduced.
Image Processing	DBN & DAE (Vincent, Larochelle, Lajoie, Bengio, & Manzagol, 2010)	• DBN and DAE (Denoising AutoEncoder) used for analysing the images. • Experimental results show that DAE was helpful for learning of higher level representations. • DBN and DAE gave better accuracy for image classification when combined with SVM.
Classification	Deep SVM (Kim, Minho, & Shen, 2015,July)	• Experimented with a new model created by combining Autoencoder, Deep SVM and GMM. • The input was fed to SVM and then to GMM forming one layer. • Thus deep layers were constructed for feature extraction and then a Naïve Bays algorithm was used for classification.
Image Processing	SVR with LRU (Kuwata & Shibasaki, 2015,July)	• Used SVR (Support Vector Regression) with Linear Rectifier Units for estimating the crop yields from remotely sensed data. • This paper described Illinois crops yield estimation using deep learning and machine learning algorithm. • Experimentation was done using Caffe tool. • SVM with Gaussian Radial Bias function was used for the same experimentation and proved that traditional SVM overfits the regression model making accuracy low.
Regression Analysis	Deep SVM (M. A. Wiering, Millea, Meijster, & Schomaker, 2016)	• Used Deep SVM for the regression analysis. The deep model was constructed by stacking two layers of SVM. • Initial layers were used for extracting the important features and final layer was used for classification.
Finance	Deep SVM with Fuzzy (Deng, Zhiquan Ren, Kong, Bao, & Dai, 2017)	• Used Fuzzy Deep Neural Network for the classification of financial trading data. • The deep network was given a high-level representation of data. This representation was generated by the fuzzy model and the neural network model.
Education	SAE (Guo, Zhang, guang, Shi, & Yang, 2015,July)	• Used sparse Autoencoders for classification and prediction. • The network was trained using a backpropagation algorithm. • The experimentation was done on data collected from 9th-grade high school children. • The experimentation was carried out on GPU and CPU. • The observed accuracy of DL algorithm was higher than SVM and Naive Bayes algorithm.
Music Classification	Deep Feed forward network and LRU (Rajanna, Aryafar, Shokoufandeh, & Ptucha, 2015)	• Rectilinear Unit (RLU) was used as an activation function in a deep neural network with 2 hidden layers. • The accuracy of the classifier is improved significantly.

has a major challenge in creating compact rules. The numerous rules formed made the system difficult to use with more parameters.

Wen and Patrick (Shiau & Chau, 2016) and Sadaf & Eydgahi (Ashtari & Eydgahi, 2017) used Statistical modelling for EDM. Statistical methods are not able to support the change in population and size. Also, it was difficult to handle lead time bias.

Fernando et al. (Koch, Assunção, Cardonha, & Netto, 2016) used Partial Least square method and proved that it was cost effective. Here the method was sensitive to the choice of parameters. The parameters used were few.

Janice et al. (Gobert, Kim, Pedro, Kennedy, & Betts, 2015) and Anjana, Smija & Kizhekkethottam (Pradeep, Das, & J, 2015) used Decision trees in EDM. Limited features were used while predicting the performance. As well tree structure was prone to sampling error. The accuracy was affected by imbalanced data.

Evandro B. Costa et al. (Costa, Fonseca, Santana, Araújo, & Rego, 2017) used Naïve Bays, Decision Tree, SVM and Neural Network to predict the performance of the students. The data used was collected from distance learning and on-campus students. Performance data per week for the four weeks was collected and analysed for the effectiveness of the algorithms.

Wanli et al. (Xing, Guo, Petakovic, & Goggins, 2015) used genetic programming for predicting Students' performance. The genetic algorithm produced an optimised prediction rate. While predicting, less consideration was given to the qualitative aspects. They monitored closed classroom learning of students and identified the factors which affect the performance. The participation of the student in various activities was majorly considered.

Xin Chen, et al. (Chen, Vorvoreanu, & Madhavan, 2013) studied social data to identify the factors which affect the behaviour or performance of students as study-life balance, lack of sleep, lack of social engagement, and lack of diversity.

Michail N. Giannakos et al. (Giannakos, et al., 2017, April) identified various cognitive factors like academic performance, attendance etc. and its effect on students' performance.

Hijazi & Naqvi (Hijazi & Naqvi, 2006) and Shoukat (Shoukat, 2013) has studied the impact of various cognitive and non-cognitive on students' performance.

Mushtaq & Khan (Mushtaq & Khan, 2012) proved that communication, learning facilities, proper guidance and family stress has a direct impact on students' performance. As well as Omar & Dennis (2015) used many factors for study and identified which factors played a vital role in students' performance.

Suryawan & Putra (Suryawan & Putra, 2016) did a detailed survey to identify the factors which affect students GPA. Also, regression tests and correlation analysis were done on various factors. It proved that the entrance exam and attendance in the class were important factors. Lecturer quality was also important and has an effect on GPA.

In an interesting article in 2016, Pooja Mondal (Mondal) identified various factors like intellect, learning, physical, mental, social and economic as factors which affected students' behaviour and performance.

Most of the research is centred on the application of Data Mining and Machine Learning techniques in the classification task for students' performance. Classification and prediction task widely uses Classification methods based on learning from examples, such as Decision Tree, Artificial Neural Networks and Support Vector Machine algorithms. Although hybrid algorithms gained popularity for solving complex problems, they are not cited as commonly as the other methods in students' performance classification and prediction (Vora & Kamatchi, EDM – Survey of Performance Factors and Algorithms Applied, 2018).

Optimization

Optimization is the selection of the best element using some criterion from some set of available alternatives. The goal of optimization is to provide near perfect, effective and all possible alternatives. Maximizing or minimizing some function related to application or features of the application is the process of optimization. For example, minimising the cost function or minimising the mean square error is the goal of optimization in typical ML algorithms. Machine learning often uses optimization algorithms to enhance their learning performance. Training optimization improves the generalization ability of any model.

Following diagram shows the taxonomy of optimization techniques.

Figure 4. Taxonomy of Optimization

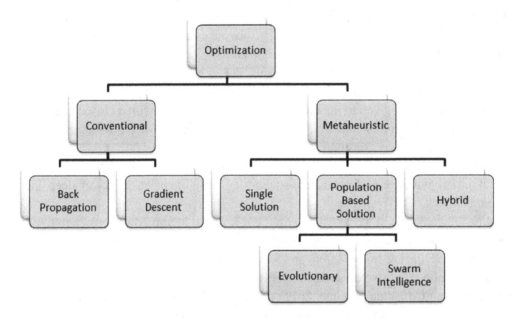

It is difficult to train the network effectively. Classification accuracy is improved with improvement in training. So, the training of deep learning algorithms can be improved using optimization techniques. There are many optimization techniques, but recent techniques indicate the use of metaheuristic algorithms for training optimization. Metaheuristic techniques are popular because they can be applied in any generalized problem domain. Among many metaheuristic nature inspired algorithms like ant and bee algorithms, particle swarm optimization, genetic algorithms, firefly algorithms, harmony search, the Cuckoo Search (CS) Algorithm (Yang & Deb, 2014) was preferred. Primary advantages of CS are as follows:

- Applied in a wide variety of problems like Face Recognition, Engineering optimization, Medical Domain etc. and proved beneficial

- Cuckoo search has better global convergence properties than other popular variants like Genetic Algorithm, Particle Swarm Optimization, Ant colony optimization etc.
- For a random walk, Cuckoo Search uses Levey Flight which helps in more exploration in search space. This guarantees early and definite global convergence.
- Hybrid model constructed with CS is proved to be beneficial.

PERFORMANCE PREDICTION USING HYBRID MODEL

Experimental Setup

The experimental setup is divided into three parts as (i) Data Collection and preparation (ii) Design and implementation of the model and finally, (iii) evaluation of the model for the problem identified. Figure 4 shows these steps clearly.

Figure 5. Experimental Setup

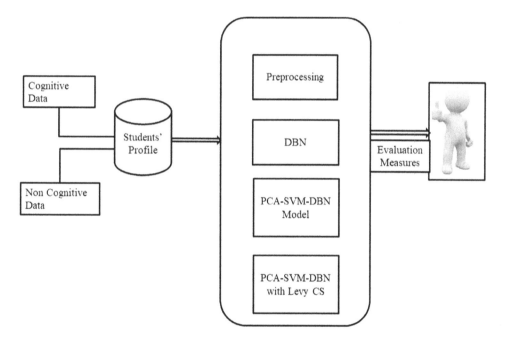

For any experimentation, input data plays a vital role. Thus one of the important steps of experimental design is the collection of relevant data. The only collection of data is not sufficient, but making it ready as per the requirement of the model is also important. Thus Data Preprocessing becomes a quintessential step in an experimental setup. Once data is prepared or preprocessed as per the requirement of the model, existing models and new suggested models are implemented. The comparative results provide new insights regarding the usefulness and accuracy of the model.

Algorithms

Dimensionality reduction using Principal Component Analysis (PCA)

In the proposed prediction model, PCA (Maćkiewicz & Ratajczak, 1993) is used for reducing the vast data. There are many reasons why one wishes to reduce the dimensionality of input data. Many times the complexity of the model depends on the number of dimensions in the data as well as the size of the data sample. When the dimensions are reduced then the cost related to extracting the not required dimensions is reduced. Many times the models are robust when the dataset is small and gives accurate results. Also, data with few dimensions can be visualized properly to reduce the outliers.

Consider a p-dimensional random variable U with the dispersion matrix $\sum$ and let $\lambda_1 .. \lambda_n$ be the eigenvalues. Consider that $P_1 ... P_n$ are the corresponding Eigenvectors of $\sum$. Then one can write:

$$\sum = \lambda_1 P_1 P_1^{'} + ... + \lambda_p P_p P_p^{'} \tag{1}$$

$$\sum = P_1 P_1^{'} + ... + P_p P_p^{'} \tag{2}$$

$$P_1^{'} £ P_i = \lambda_i , \ P_1^{'} £ P_j = 0 , \ i \neq j \tag{3}$$

The transformed random variables can be represented as:

$$Y_i = P_1^{'} U, \ i = 1, ... P \tag{4}$$

Here Y is the new random variable vector and P is the orthogonal matrix then Y can be obtained from U by the orthogonal transformation as Y=PU. Here this random variable vector Y_i is called as the ith principal component of U.

Only the basic steps of PCA are followed here. These basic steps of PCA are given in Algorithm 1.

Algorithm 1: Steps of PCA
- **Step 1:** Standardize the input data
- **Step 2:** Evaluate the covariance of the data
- **Step 3:** Deduce Eigenvectors and Eigenvalues
- **Step 4:** Re-orient data with respect to Principal Components
- **Step 5:** Plot re-oriented data
- **Step 6:** Bi-plot

Support Vector Machine (SVM)

PCA acts as dimensionality reduction techniques. The features are given as an input to the PCA and reduced extracted features are considered for further computation. If there are 12 features then PCA reduces it to 6 features and so on.

The reduced dimension and class labels are given to the SVM (Yuan, et al., 2017) for prediction of the class. The SVM here will get reduced dimensions to work on. As the model is working on reduced but important data the predictions are more accurate.

The data considered here consists of 35 features and one class label. Providing these many features directly to DBN makes it computationally intensive as well results may not be so accurate. So intermittently SVM is used to generate near accurate class labels which are fed to the DBN. SVM with a linear kernel is used to generate the class labels.

Here the tuning of SVM is obviously not so accurate with the resultant prediction (in which class the performance fall). Hence, the resultant class labels from SVM are considered as the features to DBN classifier. DBN classifier classifies the students' overall performance.

Deep Belief Network (DBN)

Generally, DBN includes multiple layers, and each and every layer has visible neurons, which establish the input layer, and hidden neurons form the output layer. Further, there presents a deep connection with hidden and input neurons; but there was no connection among hidden neurons and no connections are present in the visible neurons. The connection among visible as well as hidden neurons is symmetric and exclusive. This corresponding neuron model defines an accurate output for the input.

Since the stochastic neurons' output in Boltzmann network is probabilistic, Eq. (5) denotes the output and Eq. (6) specifies the possibility in sigmoid-shaped function, where t^P indicates the pseudo-temperature. The deterministic model of the stochastic approach is given in Eq. (7).

$$P_q(\zeta) = \frac{1}{1 + e^{\frac{-\zeta}{t^P}}} \tag{5}$$

$$PO = \begin{cases} 1, & \text{with } 1 - \overline{P_q}(\zeta) \\ 0, & \text{with } \overline{P_q}(\zeta) \end{cases} \tag{6}$$

$$\lim_{t^P \to 0^+} \overline{P}(\zeta) = \lim_{t^P \to 0^+} \frac{1}{1 + e^{\frac{-\zeta}{t^P}}} = \begin{cases} 0 & \text{for } \zeta < 0 \\ \frac{1}{2} & \text{for } \zeta = 0 \\ 1 & \text{for } \zeta > 0 \end{cases} \tag{7}$$

The diagrammatic representation of the DBN model is in Figure 10, in which the process of feature extraction takes place through a set of RBM layers and the process of classification takes place via MLP. The arithmetic model exposes the energy of Boltzmann machine for the creation of neuron or binary state b_i, and that is defined in Eq. (8), where $W_{a,l}$ indicates the weights among neurons and θ_a indicates the biases.

$$\Delta EN\left(bi_a\right) = W_{a,l} + \theta_a \tag{8}$$

The progression of energy in terms of the joint composition of visible as well as hidden neurons (x, y) is defined in Eq. (9), Eq. (10) and Eq. (11). In this, x_a indicates either the binary or neuron state of a visible unit, B_l indicates the binary state of l hidden unit, and k_a is constant.

$$EN\left(x, y\right) = \sum_{(a,l)} W_{a,l} x_a y_l - \sum_a k_a x_a - \sum_l B_l y_a \tag{9}$$

$$\Delta EN\left(x_a, \bar{y}\right) = \sum_l W_{al} y_l + k_a \tag{10}$$

$$\Delta EN\left(\vec{x}, y_a\right) = \sum_l W_{al} x_a + B_l \tag{11}$$

Figure 6. Architecture of DBN in the proposed model

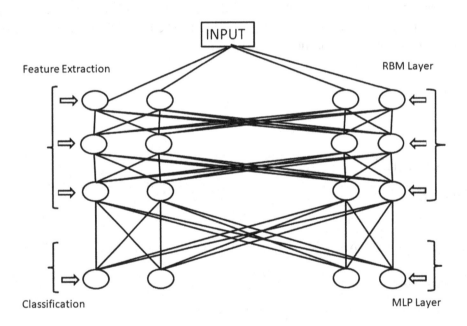

The input data's possibility dissemination is encoded into weight (parameters), which is spread as RBM's learning pattern. RBM training can attain distributed possibilities, and the consequent weight assignment is defined by Eq. (12).

$$\widehat{W}_{(\widehat{M})} = \max_{\widehat{W}} \prod_{x \in \bar{N}} C\left(\vec{x}\right) \tag{12}$$

For the visible and hidden vectors pair $\left(\vec{x}, \overrightarrow{hi}\right)$, the possibility assigned RBM approach is given in Eq. (13), where PR^F specifies the partition function as in Eq. (14).

$$c\left(\vec{x}, \overrightarrow{hi}\right) = \frac{i}{PR^F} e^{-EN(\vec{x}, \vec{y})} \tag{13}$$

$$PR^F = \sum_{\vec{x}, \vec{y}} e^{-EN(\vec{x}, \vec{y})} \tag{14}$$

The DBN is trained using CD (Contrastive Divergence) (Goodfellow, Bengio, & Courville, 2016) algorithm. The steps of the CD training are as follows:

Step 1: Choose the x training samples and brace it into visible neurons.

Step 2: Evaluate the feasibility of hidden neurons c_y by identifying the product of $\widehat{W}$ weight matrix and visible vector

Step 3: Examine the y hidden states from c_y probabilities.

Step 4: Evaluates the x exterior product of vectors and c_y that is measured as a positive gradient $\varnothing^+ = x.c_y^{t^P}$.

Step 5: Examine the reconstruction of x' visible states from y hidden states. Further, it is needed to evaluate y' hidden states from the reconstruction of x'.

Step 6: Evaluate the x' and y''s exterior product, be it as a negative gradient $\varnothing^- = x'.y'^{t^P}$.

Step 7: Define the updated weight as defined in Eq. (15), where η indicates the learning rate.

$$\Delta\widehat{W} = \eta(\varnothing^+ - \varnothing^-) \tag{15}$$

Step 8: Update the weights with new values.

The following step defines the progression of DBN training with MLP training (normal) and RBM training (pre-training)

Step 1: Initialize the DBN model with weights, biases and further associated parameters, which are randomly selected.

Step 2: Firstly, the initialization of RBM model is progressed with the input data that serves the potentials in its visible neurons and gives the unsupervised learning.

Step 3: Here, the input to the subsequent layer is subjected by potential sampling that processed in the hidden neurons of the preceding layer. Further, it follows the unsupervised learning.

Step 4: The above-specified steps are continued for the corresponding count of layers. Hence, the pre-training stage by RBM is processed till it reaches the MLP layer.

Step 5: MLP phase specifies the attained learning by supervised format and is continued till it attains the target error rate.

Finally, the classifier predicts the students' performance with increased accuracy rate. The predictions are evaluated on the basis of various evaluation measures identified.

Dataset

To predict the performance of students, the private engineering college students are decided as population. The engineering colleges under Mumbai University are selected as population.

There are more than 50+ engineering colleges under Mumbai University. Mumbai University consists of the engineering colleges from Mumbai, New Mumbai and Thane region. So at the first stage, it was decided to collect samples from Mumbai. At the second stage, it was decided to concentrate on the geographical centre part of Mumbai. The samples are collected from engineering colleges which are centrally located in Mumbai City.

Data collected here is Primary data and data collection is done using a questionnaire. Data collection through the questionnaire is the most popular method in case of big enquiries.

Various parameters are identified which have a direct or indirect effect on the performance of students. Careful selection of questions was important while keeping in mind that the questionnaire does not pose a burden on respondents. The cognitive and non-cognitive parameters are identified. The effect of cognitive and non-cognitive parameters in performance prediction is carefully understood by studying various articles. The parameters identified are shown below:

Figure 7. Cognitive Parameters

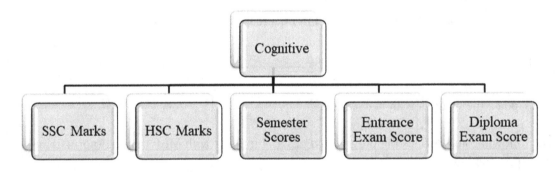

Cognitive factors are the characteristic of a person which affect the performance and learning directly. These factors are measurable. Non-cognitive factors are the parameters which are not directly linked to but may have an effect on the performance and learning. Studies have shown that non-cognitive parameters have an equivalent effect on performance and learning. Non-cognitive factors are not directly measurable. Keeping in mind the scenario of engineering students and colleges, few non-cognitive factors which may have an indirect effect on the performance of students are decided.

Based on the parameters identified the class label is decided based on CGPA (Cumulative Grade Point Average) score of 5th semester. The parameter 'class' indicates the CGPA score of the student in Semester 5. The CGPA score is calculated on the scale of 1 to 10. This parameter indicates the performance of the student in the coming semester. The implemented system predicts the performance of the student as a CGPA score range.

Figure 8. Non-cognitive Parameters

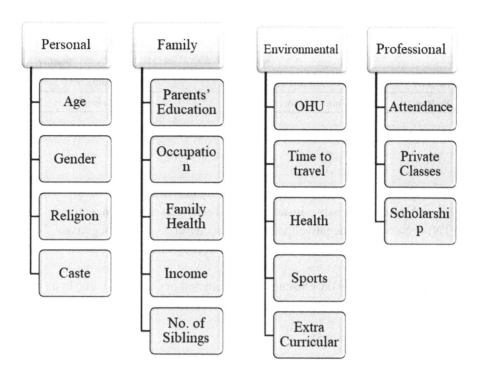

Table 2. Output class label

Class (CGPA Score)	Class Label
<5	1
Bet 5 and 7	2
Bet 7 and 9	3
More than 9	4

There are 6% and 8% samples out of total samples in class 1 and 4 respectively. There are 36% and 50% samples out of total samples in class 3 and 4 respectively.

Evaluation Measures

To evaluate the effectiveness of the Machine Learning algorithms basic measures like Accuracy, Precision, Recall and F1-Measure (Han & Kamber, 2012) were adopted. Squared error based cost functions are inconsistent for solving classification problems. Also, these measures are widely used in domains such as information retrieval, machine learning and other domains that involve classification (Olson & & Delen, 2008). A confusion matrix is a base for the determination of these measures.

- **Confusion Matrix:** The confusion matrix can be represented as follows:

		Predicted/Classified	
		Negative	Positive
Actual	**Negative**	True Negative (TN)	False Positive (FP)
	Positive	False Negative (FN)	True Positive (TP)

Where –

True Positive (TP) = Number of positive instances correctly classified as positive.

False Positive (FP) = Number of positive instances incorrectly classified as negative.

True Negative (TN) = Number of negative instances correctly classified as negative.

False Negative (FN) = Number of negative instances incorrectly classified as positive

- **Accuracy:** Accuracy indicates the closeness of a predicted or classified value to its real value. The state of being correct is called Accuracy. It can be calculated as:

Accuracy= (TP+TN)/(TP+TN+FP+FN)

- **Precision:** Precision can be defined as the number of relevant items selected out of the total number of items selected. It represents the probability that an item is relevant. It can be calculated as:

Precision = TP/(FP+TP)

Precision is the measure of exactness.

- **Recall:** The Recall can be defined as the ratio of relevant items selected to relevant items available. The recall represents a probability that a relevant item is selected. It can be calculated as:

Recall = TP/(FN+TP)

The recall is the measure of completeness.
- **F1-Measure:** F1-Measure is the harmonic mean between Precision and Recall as described below:

F1-Measure= 2 * (Precision * Recall) / (Precision +Recall)

It creates a balance between precision and recall. Accuracy may be affected by class imbalance but F1 Measure is not affected by class imbalance. So with accuracy F1-measure is also used for evaluation of classification algorithms.

- **Sensitivity:** Sensitivity is used to find out the proportion of positive samples that are correctly identified also called a true positive rate. It is calculated as:

Sensitivity=TP/P

Where,
   P = Total Number of Positive Samples
   N = Total number of Negative Samples

- **Specificity:** Specificity is used to find out the proportion of negative samples that are correctly identified and also called a true negative rate. It is calculated as:

Specificity=TN/N

- **False Positive Rate (FPR):** FPR is used to find out the proportion of negative samples that are misclassified as positive samples. It is calculated as:

FPR=FP/N

- **False Negative Rate (FNR):** FNR is used to find out the proportion of positive samples which are misclassified as negative samples. It is calculated as:

FNR=FN/P

- **Negative Predictive Value (NPV):** NPV is used to find out the number of samples which are true negative. It is calculated as:

NPV=TN/(TN+FN)

- **False Discovery Rate (FDR):** FDR is also called an error rate. It is used to find out a proportion of false positive among all the samples that are classified as positive. It is calculated as:

FDR=FP/(FP+TP)

- **Matthews's correlation coefficient (MCC):** It is calculated as:

MCC=(TP*TN)-(FP*FN) /SQRT((TP+FP)(TP+FN)(TN+FP)(TN+FN))

MCC is a balanced measure based on a confusion matrix. This measure is used even if the classes are of different sizes. It is a correlation coefficient between the actual classes and predicted classes. The value of MCC lies between -1 to 1. The value near to +1 indicates the prediction is perfect. The value 0 indicates random prediction. The value -1 indicates a total disagreement between the actual and predicted values. MCC score above zero indicates balanced classification. MCC is a good measure when the data have varying classes, unbalanced dataset and random data (Jurman, Riccadonna, & Furlanello, 2012). With F1-score the MCC guides in a better way to determine the suitable algorithm for classification.

Results

The results for various evaluation measures for the various training percentages are indicated in Figure 9, 10 and 11

The specificity of the hybrid model remains almost same to 0.85 for all training percentages. The sensitivity score is 0.80. The precision is also almost constant to 0.78 and is increased for 60% training.

The FPR is changing slightly from 0.18 to 0.20. For all training percentages, the ratio lies quite low from 0.03 to 0.06. The NPV score is good with an average value of 0.80. The FDR score is constant at 0.21 for different training percentages.

The accuracy graph shows a variation from 69% to 75% for different training percentages. The accuracy is good with 50% training. The accuracy has improved and is better than pure SVM and DBN for the considered data. The F1-score graph shows no variation in F1-score and it has a score of 0.81.

The MCC score also shows a variation with the values ranging from 0.13 to 0.18. The value of MCC score is far better than the MCC scores of SVM and DBN. The good and positive MCC score suggests that the proposed model is better suited for the data under consideration. There is a considerable improvement in MCC score indicating the suitability of the model for the educational data.

Figure 9. Results for Hybrid Model: Sensitivity, Specificity, Accuracy and F1_Score

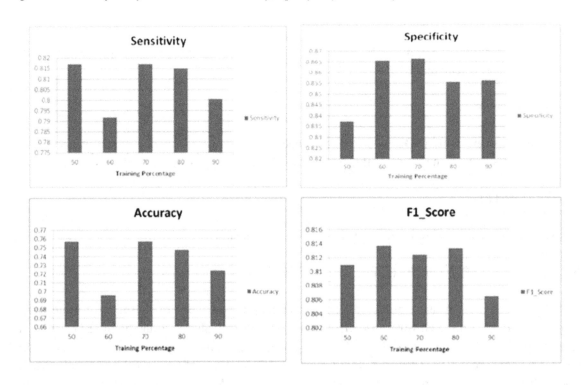

Figure 10. Results for Hybrid Model: FDR, FNR, NPV and FPR

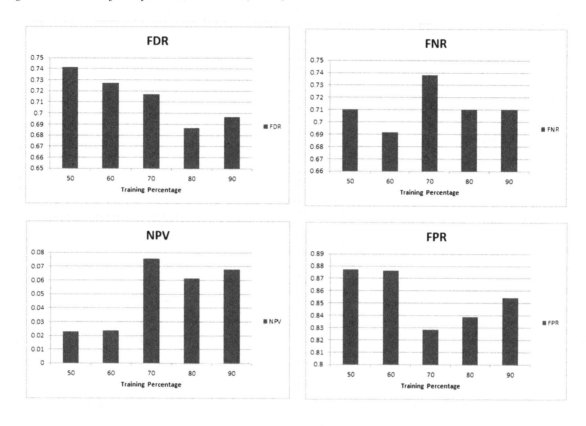

Figure 11. Results for Hybrid Model: Precision and MCC

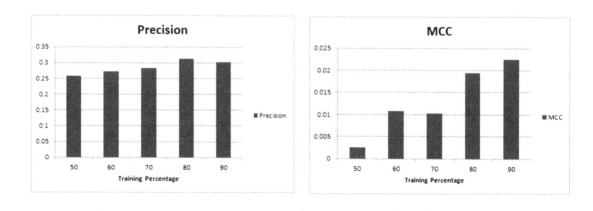

It is important to understand if the hybrid model is better than other models. It is necessary to look at evaluation measures to find the performance and suitability of the hybrid classification method for the collected educational data.

Table 3 shows the overall performance of the hybrid classification model over other models.

Table 3. Overall Performance of hybrid classification model over other methods

Algorithms→ Measures↓	SVM	DBN	SVM with DBN
Specificity	0.48	0.84	0.87
Sensitivity	0.18	0.78	0.82
Accuracy	0.65	0.7	0.76
Precision	0.36	0.38	0.79
FPR	0.83	0.23	0.19
FNR	0.53	0.17	0.04
NPV	0.18	0.78	0.82
FDR	0.65	0.63	0.22
F1- Score	0.41	0.54	0.82
MCC	0.04	0.09	0.27

From this, it is observed that the hybrid prediction model is more superior to other methods with respect to all measures. Particularly, the specificity of proposed SVM with Deep Learning model is better from DBN and SVM.

The accuracy of the hybrid model is 5.06% and 6.69% superior to DBN and SVM. The hybrid model also attained great precision over other methods. Similarly, the FPR of the hybrid model is 2.26% and 76.62% better from DBN and SVM respectively with less FPR.

The F_1-Score of the hybrid method is 49.27% and 59.64% better from DBN and SVM. From this analysis, it is proved that the hybrid prediction model is highly efficient when compared to other conventional methods.

The Graph in Figure 12 shows the overall performance of the proposed model. The hybrid model has better accuracy, F1 score and MCC indicating that the proposed hybrid model created using SVM and DBN is able to classify the educational data in a better way.

Discussion

Table 4(a), (b), (c) and (d) shows the performance score of the hybrid model for evaluation parameters Accuracy, F1 Measure, FPR and MCC for different classes. The training percentage is 60%.

Accuracy for the various classes is improved drastically for the hybrid model, mainly for the classes where data samples are less. Even F1 score and MCC score is better of the hybrid model. Low FPR indicates that prediction of classes by the hybrid model is improving through the data is imbalanced.

Figure 12. Performance of hybrid model over other algorithms

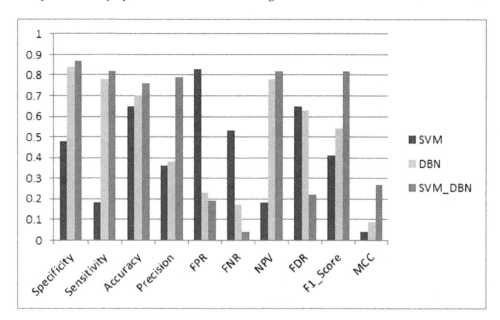

Table 4. Scores of Accuracy, FPR, F1-Score and MCC for Different Classes for Hybrid Model

Algorithm→ Class↓	SVM	DBN	SVM-DBN	Algorithm→ Class↓	SVM	DBN	SVM-DBN
1	0.47	0.77	0.77	1	0.75	0.09	0.01
2	0.36	0.76	0.8	2	0.84	0.09	0.01
3	0.37	0.79	0.79	3	0.88	0.09	0.03
4	0.15	0.37	0.43	4	0.09	0.01	0.01
Accuracy				*FPR*			
Algorithm→ Class↓	SVM	DBN	SVM-DBN	Algorithm→ Class↓	SVM	DBN	SVM-DBN
1	0.5	0.58	0.5	1	0.05	0.17	0.19
2	0.49	0.5	0.5	2	0.05	0.18	0.18
3	0.5	0.53	0.5	3	0.06	0.17	0.21
4	0.03	0.5	0	4	0.13	0.17	0.29
F1-Score				*MCC*			

The accuracy is increased to 75%. Still, there is scope for improvement in the model to achieve better accuracy. The model can be further optimised to gain better accuracy. The model can be further improved by improving training. The scores of evaluation measures for various training percentages indicated that the model can be improved with improved training experience.

SOLUTIONS AND RECOMMENDATIONS

Hybrid DL model gave better performance than the advanced ML models. In such cases, it is always interesting to investigate the combinatory models to find out the classification experience. The performance of the Combinatory models may be improved by optimizing the learning of the model.

After evaluating the performance of the Hybrid model including Deep Learning, an optimized hybrid model is implemented using Cuckoo search optimization method. The optimization is achieved in a better way when Cuckoo Search with Levy Flight is used.

Algorithms

The Optimized model - LCDBN

The input educational data is first given to the PCA for dimensionality reduction. The important features extracted are fed to the SVM for further generalized prediction. These predictions which are not so accurate are then fed to the DBN for final classification and prediction. Here in DBN, there is a change in training the DBN model. The RBM units in DBN model are trained with Cuckoo Search with Levy Flight. The training of DBN is improved using the CS with Levy Flight so the model - LCDBN.

Algorithm 2 depicts the training of the proposed LCDBN model. Here the RBM is trained using the Levy Flights of Cuckoo Search. Instead of using the simple random walk in the Cuckoo Search, Levy Flights are used to further improve the Cuckoo Search Algorithm. In traditional CS algorithm, the random walk was taken using Gaussian Processes.

A Levy Flight can be thought of as a random walk where the step size has a Levy tailed probability distribution. The weight of the DBN model has been updated as shown in Eq. (16). Here, the levy search of CSA $\left(W^{old} * t^{-\lambda} \right)$ is included in the RBM weight matrix update. From Eq. (16), W^{old} refers to Y_i^t of CSA, Er denotes the error and α indicates the scaling factor.

$$W \leftarrow W^{old} + \varepsilon * \left[Er * \alpha \right] \left(s_1 x_1^{'} - Q\left(s_2 = 1 | x_2 \right) X_2^{'} \right) + \left(W^{old} * t^{-\lambda} \right) \tag{16}$$

System Model

Figure 13 shows the optimized hybrid model.

The input parameters are split and are fed to PCA to reduce parameters. The output from each PCA is given to the individual SVM for prediction of class label. The class labels predicted by the SVM; acts as the input to the DBN. Using this input and actual class labels, the DBN predicts the classes for the data.

The DBN is constructed with 2 layers of RBM. One layer of RBM represents a hidden layer and a visible layer. The RBM layers are constructed with 3 neurons each and the activation function used is a sigmoid function. The numbers of input neurons are 3. After RBM layers an MLP layer is added for prediction of class. The MLP layer has 3 neurons and logistic regression is used as an activation function. The output layer has one neuron to predict the class label. Here the learning of DBN is optimized using Cuckoo Search with Levy Flight.

Algorithm 2. Modified RBM learning Model

RBM update ($X_1, \varepsilon, W, u, c$)

This is the RBM update process for binomial units. It is adopted to other kinds of units

X_1 denotes a sample from the training distribution for RBM

ε denotes a learning rate for stochastic gradient descent in contrastive divergence

W denotes RBM weight matrix

u denotes RBM offset vector for input units

c denotes the RBM offset vector for hidden units

$Q(s_2=1|X_2)$ indicates the vector with components $Q(s_{2i}=1|X_2)$

    for the entire hidden units, i do

$$\text{Evaluate } Q(s_{1i}=1|X_1) \text{ (for binomial units, } sigm\left(c_i + \sum_j W_{ij}s_{1i}\right)$$

        Sample $s_{1i}\epsilon\{0,1\}$ from $Q(s1_{1i}|X1)$

    end for

    for the entire hidden units, j do

$$\text{Evaluate } P(x_{2j}=1|s_1) \text{ (for binomial units, } sigm\left(u_j + \sum_i W_{ij}s_{1i}\right))$$

        Sample $x_2\epsilon\{0,1\}$ from $P(x_{2j}=1|X_1)$

    end for

$$\text{for the entire hidden units, } i \text{ do } sigm\left(c_i + \sum_j W_{ij}x_{2j}\right)$$

$$\text{Evaluate } Q(s_{2i}=1|X_2) \text{ (for binomial units, } sigm\left(c_i + \sum_j W_{ij}x_{2j}\right)$$

    end for

    Update the weight using Eq. (4)

    $u \leftarrow u+\varepsilon(x_1 - x_2)$

    $c \leftarrow c+\varepsilon(s_1 - Q(s_2=1|X_2))$

The model follows a parallel framework. If the number of features increases in future then more PCA and SVM components can be introduced. Vertical fragmentation suggests model can be easily adapted in the Map Reduce framework (Maitrey & C.K.Jha, 2015) for Big Data processing. As well as horizontal fragmentation is also done to suggest the suitability for Big Data application. Here the horizontal fragmentation may give multiple calls to single PCA block.

Figure 13. System Model

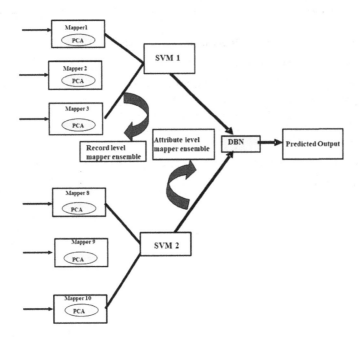

Results

The overall performance analysis regarding the students' performance prediction using proposed SVM-LCDBN model is given by Figure 14. From the analysis, better accuracy, specificity, sensitivity, precision, FPR, FNR, FDR, NPV, F1-score and MCC was determined for the adopted scheme, thus revealing its superiority when compared with other schemes.

From the simulation, the accuracy of the presented approach is 49.32% better than NN, 17.63% better than SVM, 11.32% better than DBN, 3.5% better than SVM-DBN and 2.33% better than SVM-CDBN models.

Effect of λ on results

Figure 15 shows the performance of proposed model SVM-LCDBN for the various values of CS parameter λ. The graph is plotted for training percentage 70. One can fairly see that the performance of the proposed model is best for the value λ=1. The model is tested for various values and it is observed that the proposed model gives best performance for various evaluation parameters for the value 1.

Also it is seen that the scores of various evaluation parameters is good when the training percentage is 70.

Effect of α on Prediction

The scale parameter is represented by α. The performance of the classifier depends on scaling parameter, that's why various values of α are tested for performance evaluation.

Figure 14. Performance of Optimized Model over other Algorithms

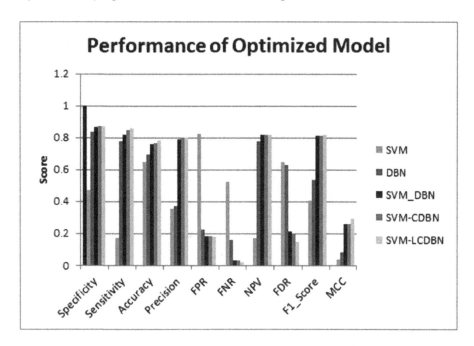

Figure 15. Effect of λ on Performance of Optimized Model

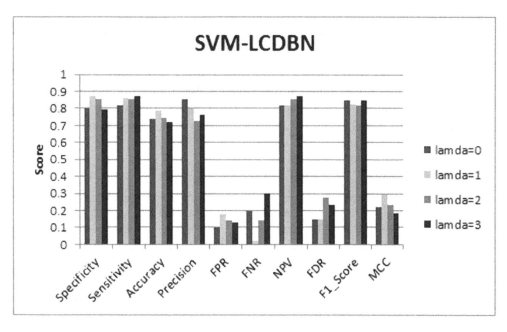

Table 5 describes the effect of scaling factor for the various performance measures on predicting the students' performance for training percentage 70. Accordingly, here the value of α is varied for $\alpha=0.2$, $\alpha=0.4$, $\alpha=0.6$ and $\alpha=0.8$ and the measures are evaluated.

Table 5. Effect of α on prediction

Parameter	α=0.2	α=0.4	α=0.6	α=0.8
	SVM-LCDBN	SVM-LCDBN	SVM-LCDBN	SVM-LCDBN
Specificity	0.88	0.86	0.8	0.8
Sensitivity	0.86	0.86	0.83	0.88
Accuracy	0.79	0.75	0.75	0.72
Precision	0.8	0.73	0.86	0.77
FPR	0.19	0.15	0.1	0.13
FNR	0.03	0.15	0.2	0.3
NPV	0.82	0.86	0.83	0.88
FDR	0.15	0.28	0.15	0.24
F1_Score	0.83	0.82	0.85	0.85
MCC	0.3	0.24	0.23	0.19

Discussion

In DBN, LC model was adopted for weight computation. Consequently, the adopted prediction model SVM-LCDBN was suggested that makes a deep connection with the hybrid classifier to obtain a more precise output. Moreover, the proposed SVM-LCDBN model was compared with traditional schemes, and the results are attained.

From the simulation, the accuracy of the presented approach was 17.63% better than SVM, 11.32% better than DBN, 3.5% better than SVM-DBN and 2.33% better than SVM-CDBN models. Thus better enhancements were obtained by the proposed SVM-LCDBN model for predicting the student's performance.

Table 6 shows the score of the evaluation measures for Accuracy, f1 Score, MCC and FPR of the optimised model. These values are calculated for $\lambda=1$ and $\alpha=0.2$. The accuracy % for any model for CGPA<5 indicates that the model is able to accurately classify % of total samples in this class.

Table 6. Evaluation Measures for the Model SVM-LCDBN

Evaluation Measure→ Class↓	Accuracy	F1-Score	MCC	FPR
CGPA Score <5	76	0.79	0.1	0.11
CGPA Score Between 5 and 7	77	0.81	0.23	0.11
CGPA Score Between 7 and 9	80	0.85	0.24	0.12
CGPA Score More than 9	78	0.74	0.13	0.11
Overall Score	79	0.83	0.28	0.13

The results show that the scores are improved for all classes. Accuracy and MCC score indicates that the optimised model is better. The model can be used to predict the class label effectively. The motivation behind the research work is to predict the performance of the student at the early stage. The implemented model is able to predict the performance of the students by identifying the appropriate class label with good accuracy. As well, improved MCC score suggests that the model is suitable for the educational data.

FUTURE RESEARCH DIRECTIONS

The chapter represents one of the ways to analyse the Educational Data using an optimised hybrid model. There are many other ways to work in the area of EDM and DL together. Some improvement in the DL model is also beneficial to improve the accuracy of prediction in Educational Domain.

The model considered here is a hybrid model for classification using SVM – DBN. The model is used for performance prediction. There are many other tasks in EDM like course recommendation where such hybrid models may be effective. SVM and DBN being generative models are applicable in many domains.

The performance of the DBN can be further improved if training is improved. There are many optimization techniques which can be combined to improve the training of the DBN. It is interesting to find out how other optimization techniques will be beneficial to improve the accuracy of the model.

CONCLUSION

A Deep Learning model for the Performance Prediction of Students in Educational Information System is implemented. The work started with the motivation to implement a hybrid model with better accuracy in Educational Domain and extended to optimised hybrid model.

ML and DL are the fields of Artificial Intelligence where algorithms learn by themselves. These algorithms can be applied in many emerging areas where they may be effective. These algorithms are found useful in many areas with an increase in data size. The main aim of using DL model is to increase accuracy.

Before devising the hybrid model, ML algorithms are applied to the data collected from the educational domain. The ML algorithms like SVM and pure DL algorithm - DBN are applied on the collected data. Additional evaluation measures are used to test the algorithms. Balanced evaluation measure like MCC particular for the ML domain is used with traditional F1-score. The results show that pure DL and advanced ML algorithms are giving similar accuracy. Hence a new hybrid model for performance prediction of students to get better accuracy is implemented

Optimization is the technique to improve the accuracy of the model by tuning learning weightsThere are many popular metaheuristic techniques but Cuckoo Search Optimization is chosen because of its many advantages.

A new students' performance prediction hybrid model is proposed and is improved by using the Cuckoo Search with Levy flight optimization technique. The proposed model uses a new hybridized classifier to predict the performance, which hybridizes the SVM and DBN classifier. The data is trained by SVM, and as the tuning is not appropriate inaccurate prediction, the resultant class labels from SVM are considered as the features to DBN, where it has classified the performance. The performance of the proposed prediction model is further improved by optimizing the training of the DBN. From the results, it was evident that the results of the optimized hybrid prediction model are better than traditional ML, advanced ML and pure DL algorithms.

REFERENCES

Alpaydin, E. (2004). *Introduction to Machine Learning*. Cambridge: MIT Press.

Alwaisi, S., & Baykan, O. K. (2017). Training Of Artificial Neural Network Using Metaheuristic Algorithm. *International Journal of Intelligent Systems and Applications in Engineering*.

Ashtari, S., & Eydgahi, A. (2017). Student perceptions of cloud applications effectiveness in higher education. *Journal of Computational Science*, *23*, 173–180. doi:10.1016/j.jocs.2016.12.007

Bengio, Y. (2009). Learning Deep Architectures for AI. *Foundations and Trends in Machine Learning*, *2*(1), 1–127. doi:10.1561/2200000006

Buniyamin, N., Mat, U. b., & Arshad, P. M. (2015, November). Educational Data Mining for Prediction and Classification of Engineering Students Achievement. In *IEEE 7th International Conference on Engineering Education (ICEED)*, (pp. 49-53). Kanazawa: IEEE.

Chen, X., Vorvoreanu, M., & Madhavan, K. (2013). Mining Social Media Data for Understanding Students' Learning Experiences. *IEEE Transactions on Learning Technologies*.

Chui, K. T., Fung, D. C., Lytras, M. D., & Lam, T. M. (2017). Predicting at-risk university students in a virtual learning environment via a machine learning algorithm. *Computers in Human Behavior*.

Costa, E., Fonseca, B., Santana, M. A., Araújo, F., & Rego, J. (2017). Evaluating the effectiveness of educational data mining techniques for early prediction of students' academic failure in introductory programming courses. *Computers in Human Behavior*, *73*, 247–256. doi:10.1016/j.chb.2017.01.047

Davidt, O. E., & Netanyahu, N. S. (2015, July). DeepSign: Deep Learning for Automatic Malware Detection. *International Joint Conference on Neural Networks (IJCNN)*, 1-8. 10.1109/IJCNN.2015.7280815

Davis, D. (1998). The virtual university: A learning university. *Journal of Workplace Learning*, *10*(4), 175–213. doi:10.1108/13665629810213935

Deng, L., & Yu, D. (2014). *Deep Learning for Signal and Information Processing*. Redmond, WA: Microsoft Research.

Deng, Y., Ren, Z., Kong, Y., Bao, F., & Dai, Q. (2017). A Hierarchical Fused Fuzzy Deep Neural Network for data classification. *IEEE Transactions on Fuzzy Systems*, *25*(4), 1006–1012. doi:10.1109/TFUZZ.2016.2574915

Gao, N., Gao, L., Gao, Q., & Wang, H. (2014, November). An Intrusion Detection Model Based on Deep Belief Networks. *Second International Conference on Advanced Cloud and Big Data*, 247-252.

Giannakos, M. N., Aalberg, T., Divitini, M., Jaccheri, L., Mikalef, P., Pappas, I. O., & Sindre, G. (2017, April). Identifying Dropout Factors in Information Technology Education: A Case Study. *IEEE Global Engineering Education Conference (EDUCON)*, 1187-1194. 10.1109/EDUCON.2017.7942999

Gobert, J. D., Kim, Y. J., Pedro, M. A., Kennedy, M., & Betts, C. G. (2015). Using educational data mining to assess students' skills at designing and conducting experiments within a complex systems microworld. *Thinking Skills and Creativity*, *18*, 81–90. doi:10.1016/j.tsc.2015.04.008

Goodfellow, I., Bengio, Y., & Courville, A. (2016). *Deep Learning*. MIT Press.

Guarín, C., Guzmán, E., & González, F. (2015). A Model to Predict Low Academic Performance at a Specific Enrollment Using Data Mining. *IEEE Journal of Latin-American Learning Technologies, 10*(3).

Guo, B., Zhang, R., Guang, X., Shi, C., & Yang, L. (2015, July). Predicting Students performance in educational data mining. *International Symposium on Educational Technology (ISET)*, 125-128. 10.1109/ISET.2015.33

Han, J., & Kamber, M. (2012). *Data Mining: Concepts and Techniques* (3rd ed.). Morgan Kaufmann.

Hijazi, S. T., & Naqvi, S. R. (2006). Factors Affecting Students' Performance. *Bangladesh e-Journal of Sociology*, 3.

Jurman, G., Riccadonna, S., & Furlanello, C. (2012). A comparison of MCC and CEN error measures in multi-class prediction. *PLoS One*, *7*(8), e41882. doi:10.1371/journal.pone.0041882 PMID:22905111

Kim, S. M. L., & Shen, J. (2015, July). A novel deep learning by combining discriminative model with generative model. *International Joint Conference on Neural Networks (IJCNN)*, 1-6. 10.1109/IJCNN.2015.7280589

Koch, F., Assunção, M. D., Cardonha, C., & Netto, M. A. (2016). Optimising resource costs of cloud computing for education. *Future Generation Computer Systems*, *55*, 473–479. doi:10.1016/j.future.2015.03.013

Kuwata, K., & Shibasaki, R. (2015, July). Estimating crop yields with deep learning and remotely sensed data. *International Geoscience and Remote Sensing Symposium (IGARSS)*, 858-861. 10.1109/IGARSS.2015.7325900

Maćkiewicz, A., & Ratajczak, W. (1993). Principal Components Analysis (PCA). *Computers & Geosciences*, *19*(3), 303–342. doi:10.1016/0098-3004(93)90090-R

Maitrey, S., & Jha, C. K. (2015). MapReduce: Simplified Data Analysis of Big Data. *Procedia Computer Science*, *57*, 563–571. doi:10.1016/j.procs.2015.07.392

Mondal, P. (n.d.). *7 Important Factors that May Affect the Learning Process*. Retrieved from http://www.yourarticlelibrary.com/learning/7-important-factors-that-may-affect-the-learning-process/6064/

Mushtaq, I., & Khan, S. N. (2012). Factors Affecting Students' Academic Performance. *Global Journal of Management and Business Research*, *12*(9).

Najafabadi, M. M., Villansutre, F., Khoshgoftaar, T. M., Seliya, N., Wald, R., & Muharemagic, E. (2015). *Deep learning applications and challenges in big data analytics*. Springer Open Journal of Big Data. doi:10.118640537-014-0007-7

Nguyen, K., Fookes, C., & Sridharan, S. (2015, September). Improving Deep Convolutional Neural Networks with Unsupervised Feature Learning. *IEEE International Conference on Image Processing (ICIP)*, 2270-2271. 10.1109/ICIP.2015.7351206

Olson, D. L., & Delen, D. (2008). *Advanced data mining techniques* (1st ed.). Springer Publishing Company.

Phung, L. T., Chau, V. T., & Phung, N. H. (2015, November). Extracting Rule RF in Educational Data Classification from a Random Forest to Interpretable Refined Rules. *International Conference on Advanced Computing and Applications (ACOMP)*, 20-27. 10.1109/ACOMP.2015.13

Pradeep, A., & Das, S., & J, J. (2015). Students Dropout Factor Prediction Using EDM Techniques. *International Conference on Soft-Computing and Network Security*. 10.1109/ICSNS.2015.7292372

Punlumjeak, W., & Rachburee, N. (2015, October). A Comparative Study of Feature Selection Techniques for Classify Student Performance. *7th International Conference on Information Technology and Electrical Engineering (ICITEE)*, 425-429. 10.1109/ICITEED.2015.7408984

Rajanna, A. R., Aryafar, K., Shokoufandeh, A., & Ptucha, R. (2015). Deep Neural Networks: A Case Study for Music Genere Classification. *14th International Conference on Machine Learning and Applications (ICMLA)*, 665-660. 10.1109/ICMLA.2015.160

Shiau, W.-L., & Chau, P. Y. (2016). Understanding behavioral intention to use a cloud computing classroom: A multiple model comparison approach. *Information & Management, 53*(3), 355–365. doi:10.1016/j.im.2015.10.004

Shoukat, A. (2013). Factors Contributing to the Students' Academic Performance: A Case Study of Islamia University Sub-Campus. *American Journal of Educational Research*, 283–289.

Sukhija, K., Jindal, D. M., & Aggarwal, D. N. (2015, October). The Recent State of Educational Data Mining: A Survey and Future Visions. *IEEE 3rd International Conference on MOOCs, Innovation and Technology in Education*, 354-359. doi: 10.1109/MITE.2015.7375344

Suryawan, A., & Putra, E. (2016). Analysis of Determining Factors for Successful Student's GPA Achievement. *11th International Conference on Knowledge, Information and Creativity Support Systems (KICSS)*, 1-7.

Tzortzis, G., & Likas, A. (2007, October). Deep Belief Networks for Spam Filtering. *IEEE International Conference on Tools with Artificial Intelligence (ICTAI 2007)*, 306-309.

Vincent, P., Larochelle, H., Lajoie, I., Bengio, Y., & Manzagol, P.-A. (2010). Stacked Denoising Autoencoders: Learning Useful Representations in a Deep Network with a Local Denoising Criterion. *Journal of Machine Learning Research, 11*, 3371–3408.

Vora, D., & Iyer, K. (2017). A Survey of Inferences from Deep Learning Algorithms. *Journal of Engineering and Applied Sciences, 12*(SI), 9467-9472.

Vora, D., & Kamatchi, R. (2018). EDM – Survey of Performance Factors and Algorithms Applied. *International Journal of Engineering & Technology, 7*(2.6), 93-97.

Wiering, M., Schutten, M., Millea, A., Meijster, A., & Schomaker, L. (2013, October). Deep Learning using Linear Support Vector Machines. *International Conference on Machine Learning: Challenges in Representation Learning Workshop.*

Wiering, M. A. M. S., Millea, A., Meijster, A., & Schomaker, L. (2016). *Deep Support Vector Machines for Regression Problems.* Retrieved from http://citeseerx.ist.psu.edu/viewdoc/download?doi=10.1.1.71 8.987&rep=rep1&type=pdf

Xing, W., Guo, R., Petakovic, E., & Goggins, S. (2015). Participation-based student final performance prediction model through interpretable Genetic Programming: Integrating learning analytics, educational data mining and theory. *Computers in Human Behavior, 47*, 168–181. doi:10.1016/j.chb.2014.09.034

Yang, X.-S., & Deb, S. (2014). Cuckoo Search: Recent Advances and Applications. *Neural Computing & Applications, 24*(1), 169–174. doi:10.100700521-013-1367-1

Yuan, Y., Zhang, M., Luo, P., Ghassemlooy, Z., Lang, L., Wang, D., ... Han, D. (2017). SVM-based detection in visible light communications. *Optik (Stuttgart), 151*, 55–64. doi:10.1016/j.ijleo.2017.08.089

ADDITIONAL READING

Asif, R., Merceron, A., Ali, S. A., & Haider, N. (2017, October). Analyzing undergraduate students' performance using educational data mining. *Computers & Education, 11*, 177–1943. doi:10.1016/j. compedu.2017.05.007

Baker, R., & Siemens, G. (2013). Educational Data Mining and Learning Analytics. Cambridge handbook of the Learning Sciences.

Echegaray-Calderon O. A., Barrios-Aranibar D. (2015, October). *Optimal selection of factors using Genetic Algorithms and Neural Networks for the prediction of students' academic performance.* IEEE Latin America Congress on Computational Intelligence (LA-CCI), Curitiba, 2015, pp. 1-6.

Fu, J., Chang, J., Huang, Y., & Chao, H. (2012). A Support Vector Regression-Based Prediction of Students' School Performance. *International Symposium on Computer, Consumer and Control.* 10.1109/ IS3C.2012.31

Guo, X., Huang, H., & Zhang, J. (2014). Comparison of Different Variants of Restricted Boltzmann Machines. *2nd International Conference on Information Technology and Electronic Commerce (ICITEC).* 10.1109/ICITEC.2014.7105610

KEY TERMS AND DEFINITIONS

Cognitive Factors: Characteristics of the student that have a direct effect on learning and performance of the student.

Educational Data Mining: Tools and techniques to extract meaningful patterns from educational data.

Non-Cognitive Factors: Characteristics of the student which do not have as such a direct effect on learning and performance but may have an indirect effect on performance and learning.

Optimization: Optimization is the technique to improve the accuracy of the model by tuning learning weights.

Predictive Analytics: Exploration of data to predict the future using various methods like statistics, machine learning etc.

Chapter 10
Malaria Detection System Using Convolutional Neural Network Algorithm

Kanika Gautam
Mody University of Science and Technology, Lakshmangarh, India

Sunil Kumar Jangir
Mody University of Science and Technology, Lakshmangarh, India

Manish Kumar
Mody Institute of Science and Technology, Lakshmangarh, India

Jay Sharma
JECRC, Jaipur, India

ABSTRACT

Malaria is a disease caused when a female Anopheles mosquito bites. There are over 200 million cases recorded per year with more than 400,000 deaths. Current methods of diagnosis are effective; however, they work on technologies that do not produce higher accuracy results. Henceforth, to improve the prediction rate of the disease, modern technologies need to be performed for obtain accurate results. Deep learning algorithms are developed to detect, learn, and determine the containing parasites from the red blood smears. This chapter shows the implementation of a deep learning algorithm to identify the malaria parasites with higher accuracy.

INTRODUCTION

Malaria is a disease which is caused by infected female Anopheles mosquitoes. The bite of the mosquito causes effects on the red blood cells of the human body. The estimations done by the world malaria report show that there are around 216 million malaria cases registered worldwide every year and around 445,000 deaths which include 75% children below 5 years of age (Widiawati, Nugroho, and Ardiyanto 2016).

DOI: 10.4018/978-1-7998-3095-5.ch010

The parasites which cause malaria in humans are *Plasmodium falciparum, plasmodium vivax, plasmodium malaria, and plasmodium ovale*. Out of the entire world population being infected with malaria, of 70%-90% approximately cases are observed in Asia, Central and South America and the Middle East.

The presence of malaria parasites in human blood cells needs to be known early so that proper diagnosis can be done and get rid of the infection. The infection in the red blood cells grows very rapidly. Various technologies are available which are used for the detection of malaria parasites in the human blood cells. However, these techniques fail to generate results with higher accuracy value and also require skills and manual labor. Hence, many automated systems are designed which resolves such problems in terms of time as well as accuracy.

In this chapter, Machine Learning technologies will be implemented and it takes the image of red blood cells as an input and applies some backend algorithm over it. Studies the image well and finally generates the output depicting the amount of infection present in the blood cells or the amount by which the taken input image is healthy. Hence, the results with higher accuracy value are generated.

LITERATURE REVIEW

The work done in the past by many authors in the field of detecting malaria parasites in the red blood smears by using modern machine learning and deep learning methodologies have given better results as compared to the traditional methods being used. In 2015, Hanung Adi Nugroho *et.al*, carried out work in the domain of feature extraction and classification for malaria detection which gave a result of 87.8% accuracy. Similarly, Yuhang Dong *et.al*, in 2017 analyzed an automated system for malaria detection which results in an accuracy of 95% (Shen et al. 2017) (Dong, Jiang, Shen, David Pan, et al. 2017). The Table 1 below shows a comparative study of the work done by different authors in different domains to obtain better results.

Analyzing various results from various systems being already designed, this CNN model is designed to get better results which gave beneficial results with the accuracy of 90% -95%.

BACKGROUND

The diagnosis is done by applying the patient's blood on a glass film and observing it under the microscope. The detection of malaria using this technology was more efficient using the thick blood cells as compared to the thin blood cells. Light microscopy methods were not very much efficient but the only option left for the diagnosis of the disease. This methodology was widely available and also less expensive and it detects the presence of malaria parasites in the blood cells but could not identify the amount of infection present in the body (Nanoti et al. 2017). Due to the absence of an *electron microscope* for malaria detection, it becomes difficult to detect the presence of parasites in red blood smears in India. People living in rural areas face a lot of problems as they could not find the presence of parasites in their bodies. If the malaria parasites enter the human body then they grow at a very higher rate if not treated timely. Since the diagnosis of this disease requires highly skilled technicians. Also, available automated machines cost huge which is difficult to install and it ultimately affects the treatment of poor people.

Above mentioned methodologies turned out to be a failure as it required great training, time taking and need highly skilled professionals for performing the detection of malaria. The use of this method-

Table 1. Comparative study of different methodologies used by different authors

S.No.	Author and Year	Approach used	Results and Discussions
1.	(Poostchi et al. 2018)	Deep learning, Image Acquisition, Feature Extraction	Enables larger test suits on the patient level. Automated microscopy turns out to be cheap, simple and reliable.
2.	(Dong, Jiang, Shen, and Pan 2017)	Deep learning, CNN, SVM, LeNet, AlexNet and GoogLeNet.	Results came out with 95% accuracy. Features of the datasets were learned automatically
3.	(Rahman et al. 2019)	Data Splitting, Stain Normalisation, Min-Max Normalisation, Data Augmentation	The results were less accurate. The layout of the original image changed.
4.	(Rahman et al. 2019)	K means clustering algorithm, classification, KNN classifier.	Separation of infected cells. Malaria parasites detected and classified.
5.	(Nugroho, Akbar, and Murhandarwati 2016)	Histogram, Feature Extraction, Classification, Backpropagation	The proposed method results in the accuracy of 87.8%, sensitivity of 81.7%, and specificity of 90.8% for detecting malaria parasites in red blood smears.
6.	(Khan et al. 2017)	Color translation, K-Means clustering.	The feature set obtained b*-color channel from the CIE L*a*b* color space provides better clustering results.
7.	(Pattanaik, Swarnkar, and Sheet 2017)	Object Detection, Kalman Filter; Kernal Based Detection, Computer vision.	The newly acquired representation enhances the detection performance of infected malaria parasites n thin blood smear images.

Figure 1. IBM Watson generated report for 3 consecutive years

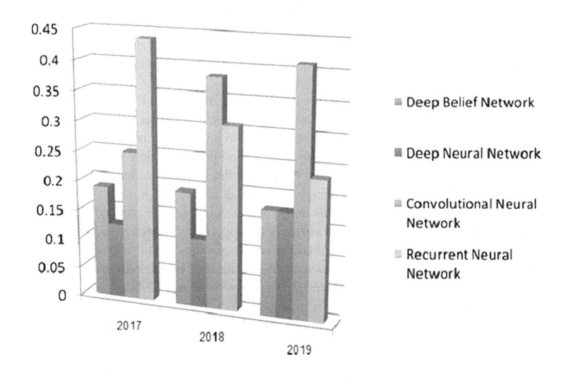

ology required a great economic effort which was indeed very difficult to maintain. Rapid diagnostic tests methodology was also used for the detection of malaria parasites in the red blood cells. This test was comparatively easy to perform as in this methodology much skills and special equipment were not required. These tests take less time as compared to the others but could not generate results with higher accuracy values.

To get the results with higher accuracy and with low costs, staining methods were used for the detection of malaria parasites. The drawback of using this method was that it is time-consuming and requires manual labor. The presence of dirt, bacterias, precipitation, etc. could not be examined by using this methodology, hence it produces false results in many cases.

Requirement Analysis

The problem with the existing system for detecting malaria and manual diagnosis needs to be rectified and hence the idea of designing an automated system came. There was a greater need to design a system that could generate better results with higher accuracies and also which are cost-effective. The automation system for detecting malaria parasites in the red blood cells became a major requirement for resource-scarce areas. Designing of the automation system does not require manual labor and is not time-consuming as well.

Automation system design enables a machine to work with greater efficiency to generate higher accuracy results with minimum or zero chances of any error being generated.

SOLUTIONS AND RECOMMENDATIONS

Considering the failures in the results obtained from the already existing outdated system, it becomes a major requirement to design a system that operates on modern deep learning methodologies to find better and more accurate results.

The automated system should be designed accurately to study the image given as input and generate the corresponding results. The working of the automated systems should take place step by step and systematically. The working of the system begins by taking an image from the dataset as an input can be infected or uninfected. Various algorithms also apply several pre-processing methods on the dataset available to arrange the images in some format. Next is the detection of the image which points out various objects (like platelets) present in the image (Poostchi et al. 2018) .

After the detection of various objects in the image, the model designed is applied which identifies various objects (whether parasite or not) and separates them as classes being created while designing the model. In the area of designing various automated systems for the detection of malaria parasites in the red blood cell images. Several Machine Learning Algorithms have been tested based on their results of predicting the best accuracies. Computer-Aided Diagnosis, SVM and CNN Algorithms have been designed to get prediction results with higher accuracy.

The binary SVM algorithm used gave the results with an accuracy of 80%-85%, which were better than the results from the existing systems.

Machine Learning Algorithms generated good results even with the datasets that contained fewer images, whereas Deep Learning Algorithms worked very efficiently with the datasets containing a large number of input images (Liang et al. 2017). Perhaps, the results obtained by both the methodologies were more or less the same. Deep CNN Algorithm with multiple layers was designed to find patches in the input image and identify them, this gave very good results with an accuracy of 94.26%.

CNN Algorithms may sometimes cause a problem of overfitting in the dataset but there are many ways to overcome this problem and hence, CNN Algorithm can be used to generate good results in detecting Malaria Parasites present in the red blood smears.

METHODOLOGIES

In this work, a CNN Model-based algorithm is used for detecting malaria parasites present in red blood smears from the American origin dataset taken as the input. The algorithm uses various Machine Learning python libraries (Keras, Tensorflow, PIL, Tkinter) and layer implementations for building model and deriving results. The working of the algorithm processes as follows:

Image Datasets

The designed CNN Algorithm requires a dataset that contains a large number of images for prediction (Red Blood Cell Images n.d.). The dataset taken is divided into two subsections one of which contains all the red blood cells images which are infected from parasites whereas the other part contains the images which are healthy and does not contain any parasites (Nanoti et al. 2017).

Figure 2. Sample Dataset containing infected and uninfected red blood smears

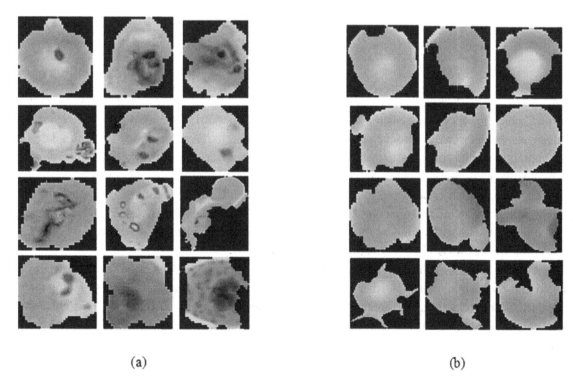

(a)   (b)

The American dataset being taken as input from kaggle is shown above in figure (2) in which both the samples of red blood cells are present. Figure 2 (a) contains all the images that contain malaria-infected red blood cells whereas figure 2 (b) contains all the uninfected red blood cells.

PROCEDURAL WORKFLOW OF THE CNN ALGORITHM

The Convolutional Neural Network is the *Feed-Forward Artificial Neural Network* specified for virtual context (Arunava 2018). The CNN Algorithm contains The Convolutional Layer, The ReLu Layer, The Pooling Layer, and The Fully Connected Layer. Figure (3) below defines the architecture of the CNN Model (CNN Workflow image n.d.).

Figure 3. Convolution Neural Networks Architecture

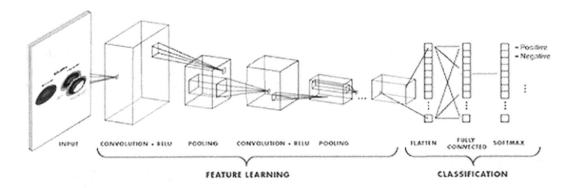

The main purpose of creating this algorithm is to identify the input images accurately even if they are deformed, which means an image is represented in the form of a matrix for classification but sometimes the image can be deformed due to the presence of noise. Hence, in the algorithm, it is specified that the image containing white color is assigned the value as -1 whereas the black portion is assigned the value as 1 for any black and white input image.

The CNN Algorithm is designed in such a way where small patches (features of the match) of an input image are considered and are compared with the actual image for classification. The classification or prediction of the image is done by the CNN Algorithm by passing the image through its layers and their specific workflow (Bibin, Nair, and Punitha 2017).

The specific features of the image are lined up in *the Convolutional Layer* and the pixel values are arranged in the form of a matrix. Further, each image pixel is multiplied with the corresponding feature pixel value. All the values obtained are then added up and the obtained sum is divided by the total number of pixels contained in the matrix. After obtaining the value, a map is created for the feature by putting the value obtained as output at the specific position.

The complete matrix obtained as the output for the particular feature is the final output generated from this layer.

$$X= (Wi-K+2P)/S +1 \ldots \tag{1}$$

$$P= (K-1)/2 = (5-1)/2 = 2 \ldots \tag{2}$$

where,
    X: output
    Wi: input
    K: the size of the filter/kernel $= 5$
    P: non-zero padding
    S: the size of stride $= 1$

The output matrix is then passed to *the ReLu Layer*; which operates the output matrix through the activation function to remove all the negative values present in the output matrix of the convolutional layer. In this layer, the node values of the matrix are activated if the input is above a certain threshold value and remains zero if the input value is zero. The activation function is applied in such a way so that there is a linear relationship between the dependent variables.

After the activation function is applied to the matrix, the output matrix is passed to *the pooling layer*. The main objective of using this image is to shrink the size of the feature matrix. Here, window size is considered that is applied to the entire matrix. From that window the maximum pixel value is taken and put into the final matrix. Hence, a shrinked matrix is formed containing the maximum values from each section of the window applied to the matrix obtained after the relu layer (Rahman et al. 2019).

$$X= (Wi-K)/S + 1 \ldots \tag{3}$$

where,
    Wi: input
    X: output
    K: the size of filter $= 2$
    S: the size of the stride $=$ the size of filter given

All the layers applied in the model are now stacked up wherein the layers are applied again in the same sequence over the shrinked matrix to obtain further shrinked matrix. This shrinking of the matrix for specific features helps for generating strong models and easy classifications.

After the model is being generated the final classification of the image is done using *the fully connected layer*. The shrinked matrix obtained from the pooling layer is now converted into a single list or vector form in which the matrix is arranged row-wise. In the original image, some vector values are reserved for the specific features, they are then compared with the vector created from the shrink matrix. The values at the specific vectors are added up and divided by the sum of the vectors of the original image to represent the specific features, and the higher value is classified as the particular feature in the image. Hence, the detection is done based on the higher vector addition values. Figure 4 represents the fully connected layer in the CNN Model.

Figure 4. A fully connected network

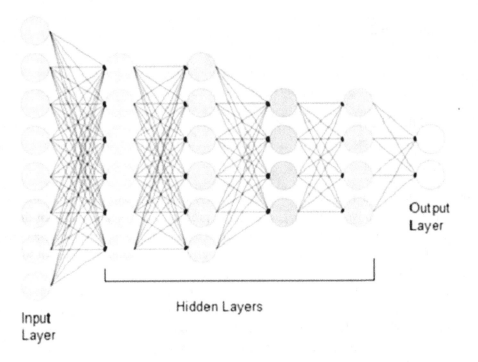

Experimental Implementation

Initially, the work begins with data collection in which a relevant dataset is selected which contains a large number of images that can be processed further. Hence, American data is considered to be recorded for predictions as the outputs are machine-generated and are more accurate. Once the relevant data is selected, it is then pre-processed further to be converted to a model which can be processed by the algorithm.

Figure 5. Image dataset being converted to a model using keras library of python

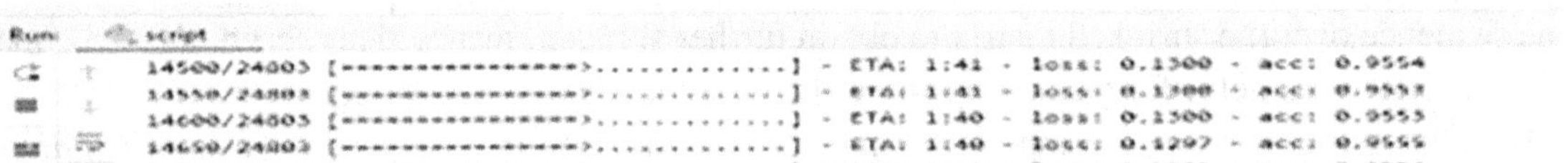

To drive out better results using specified Machine Learning Algorithms datasets need to be pre-processed into a relevant format. Hence, softwares supporting the ML Algorithms are used for designing which includes pyCharm (for coding in python) and Anaconda (for setting up the interpreter configuration). The dataset contains some redundant data as well which makes the dataset bulky which is hence to be removed.

Using Keras and Tensorflow libraries form the Anaconda environment in the backend the dataset taken is converted into a model that can be easily processed with the CNN Algorithm as shown in Figure 5. The need for the project is to deal with the dataset containing the samples of red blood cells only. Hence, white blood cells and platelets sample contained in the dataset are removed for the process. The process takes place using the code procedures contained in the scikit library. Once the model is evaluated by the Machine Learning Algorithm, the images of the red blood smear are to be detected for the presence of malaria parasites. Using the ML Algorithms, input blood cell image is compared with the sample of training data present and then the input cells are examined to be parasitic or uninfected.

RESULTS AND DISCUSSIONS

In this chapter, a CNN Model is examined on PyCharm that configures with Anaconda as an interpreter. The image dataset being taken from kaggle contains a total of around 12000 images out of which 10000 are infected and 2000 are uninfected. This dataset is being processed using astype() function which converts the dataset into an appropriate model by dividing the data into training and testing data separately. Using Keras library the input dataset is converted and stored as the warehouse of the input images wherein, keras. models is used to arrange the dataset in the sequential order, keras.layers is used to build up the several layers of the CNN model and also keras.utils is used to store the various images of the dataset in the form of an array.

Images from the dataset are considered and recognized using the cv2 library. Using the hidden layers, the entire dataset is converted into two subsets of cells and labels. The input images are being normalized and stored in the model. Finally, a sequential CNN model is developed using various layers. Conv2D and MaxPooling2D layers are used with the relu activation function on which the dataset is treated to be generated and finally converted into a model. The dense() function is used to define the number of neurons in the output layer as 2. Dropout function is used with a value 0.2 in which 20% of images are discarded which may be redundant or not useful for the model. Finally, the model is evaluated and generated with accuracy as 1, i.e., dataset converted to a working model accurately and also compiled using optimizer, loss and verbose. Figure (6) below depicts the 12 input test images are taken as input to the model designed to check how accurate is the model created to predict malaria parasites in the red blood cells (Infected and Uninfected Image datasets n.d.). The images are passed as random to the model as the input and the corresponding output is generated which depicts the accuracy of the designed CNN model. As per the amount of malaria parasites present in the red blood smear, the corresponding accuracy results are evaluated and can be seen in the Table 2 below.

INPUT IMAGES

Since these images are taken from the already generated model, they are directly passed as an input without any processing being done on the individual input image. Using score() function the accuracy of each input image is calculated depending upon its verbose count.Images 1 to 12 are considered as input passed to the created model. Table 2 above generates the output of the individual input image by detecting the accuracy level of the malaria parasite present in the red blood smear which is operated by the CNN Algorithm. The Table 2 also broadly classifies the content/accuracy of the malaria parasite in the red blood smear taken as input and identifies whether the input red blood cell image is infected or uninfected with its specific accuracy value.

Table 2. The output generated by the CNN model using python code shows the accuracy of the malaria infection in the red blood cells taken as input

S.No.	Input Images	% infected visually	Result accuracy
1	Img 1	98-100%	0.97
2	Img 2	90-92%	0.91
3	Img 3	85-87%	0.88
4	Img 4	70-75%	0.73
5	Img 5	60-62%	0.66
6	Img 6	50-55%	0.53
7	Img 7	40-42%	0.41
8	Img 8	30-35%	0.33
9	Img 9	22-25%	0.24
10	Img 10	10-12%	0.11
11	1mg 11	5-7%	0.67
12	Img 12	0%	0.03

CONCLUSION AND FUTURE DIRECTIONS

A medical system is investigated in this work that is capable of taking its own decisions based on the working of the CNN Algorithm. Several experiments are conducted on various images of red blood cells to detect the presence of malaria parasites. It is seen that the implemented system yields the higher classification accuracies of 90% -95% for the detection of malaria infection in the human body. Considering the results for different input images, the CNN-based model we have stimulated in the above work gives us promising results in detecting malaria in the red blood cells. The developed model works more accurately in the arena of medical science in making decisions.

The work done also focuses on some of the crucial areas for future research. The key points that can be considered for future research include the following:

(i)   Malaria detection is being performed using various other state-of-the-art machine learning methodologies so that more accurate results can be obtained.

(ii)   Since the dataset used for this work is the pre-designed one for the American origin and does not allow the result detection for the Indian origin. Hence, a local dataset for the Indian origin can be created to detect the disease locally.

REFERENCES

Arunava. (2018). *Convolutional Neural Networks-Brief Study.* https://towardsdatascience.com/convolutional-neural-network-17fb77e76c05

Bibin, D., Nair, M. S., & Punitha, P. (2017). Malaria Parasite Detection from Peripheral Blood Smear Images Using Deep Belief Networks. *IEEE Access: Practical Innovations, Open Solutions, 5,* 9099–9108. doi:10.1109/ACCESS.2017.2705642

CNN Workflow Image. (2020). *Deep learning wizard.* https://www.deeplearningwizard.com/deep_learning/practical_pytorch/pytorch_convolutional_neuralnetwork/

Dong, Y., Jiang, Z., Shen, H., & David Pan, W. (2017). Classification Accuracies of Malaria Infected Cells Using Deep Convolutional Neural Networks Based on Decompressed Images."*Conference Proceedings - IEEE SOUTHEASTCON,* 1–6. 10.1109/SECON.2017.7925268

Dong, Y., Jiang, Z., Shen, H., & Pan, W. D. (2017). Evaluations of Deep Convolutional Neural Networks for Automatic Identification of Malaria Infected Cells. *2017 IEEE EMBS International Conference on Biomedical and Health Informatics, BHI 2017,* 101–4. 10.1109/BHI.2017.7897215

Infected and Uninfected Image Datasets. (n.d.). https://storage.googleapis.com/kaggle-datasets/87153/200743/cell-images-for-detecting-malaria.zip

Khan, N. A., Pervaz, H., Latif, A., & Musharaff, A. (2017). Unsupervised Identification of Malaria Parasites Using Computer Vision. *Pakistan Journal of Pharmaceutical Sciences, 30*(1), 223–228. PMID:28603136

Liang, Z. (2017). CNN-Based Image Analysis for Malaria Diagnosis. *Proceedings - 2016 IEEE International Conference on Bioinformatics and Biomedicine, BIBM 2016,* 493–96.

Nanoti, A., Jain, S., Gupta, C., & Vyas, G. (2017). Detection of Malaria Parasite Species and Life Cycle Stages Using Microscopic Images of Thin Blood Smear. *Proceedings of the International Conference on Inventive Computation Technologies, ICICT 2016, 1,* 1–6.

Nugroho, H. A., Akbar, S. A., & Herdiana Murhandarwati, E. (2016). Feature Extraction and Classification for Detection Malaria Parasites in Thin Blood Smear. *ICITACEE 2015 - 2nd International Conference on Information Technology, Computer, and Electrical Engineering: Green Technology Strengthening in Information Technology, Electrical and Computer Engineering Implementation Proceedings, 1*(c), 197–201.

Pattanaik, Swarnkar, & Sheet. (2017). Object Detection Technique for Malaria Parasite in Thin Blood Smear Images. *Proceedings - 2017 IEEE International Conference on Bioinformatics and Biomedicine, BIBM 2017*, 2120–23.

Poostchi, M., Silamut, K., Maude, R. J., Jaeger, S., & Thoma, G. (2018). Image Analysis and Machine Learning for Detecting Malaria. *Translational Research; the Journal of Laboratory and Clinical Medicine, 194*, 36–55. doi:10.1016/j.trsl.2017.12.004 PMID:29360430

Rahman, A. (2019). *Improving Malaria Parasite Detection from Red Blood Cell Using Deep Convolutional Neural Networks.* Https://Arxiv.Org/Ftp/Arxiv/Papers/1907/1907.10418.Pdf

Red Blood Cell Images. (2019). https://me.me//normal-malaria-red-blood-cell-infected-with-malaria-red-blood-a017e8a3cd7447b499beb75a51129868

Shen, H., Pan, W. D., Dong, Y., & Alim, M. (2017). Lossless Compression of Curated Erythrocyte Images Using Deep Autoencoders for Malaria Infection Diagnosis. *2016 Picture Coding Symposium, PCS 2016*, 1–5.

Widiawati, C. R. A., Nugroho, H. A., & Ardiyanto, I. (2016). Plasmodium Detection Methods in Thick Blood Smear Images for Diagnosing Malaria: A Review. *Proceedings - 2016 1st International Conference on Information Technology, Information Systems and Electrical Engineering, ICITISEE 2016*, 142–47. 10.1109/ICITISEE.2016.7803063

Chapter 11
An Introduction to Deep Convolutional Neural Networks With Keras

Wazir Muhammad

Electrical Engineering Department, BUET, Khuzdar, Pakistan

Irfan Ullah

Department of Electrical Engineering, Chulalongkorn University, Bangkok, Thailand

Mohammad Ashfaq

School of Life Sciences, B. S. Abdur Rahman Crescent Institute of Science and Technology, Chennai, India

ABSTRACT

Deep learning (DL) is the new buzzword for researchers in the research area of computer vision that unlocked the doors to solving complex problems. With the assistance of Keras library, machine learning (ML)-based DL and various complicated or unresolved issues such as face recognition and voice recognition might be resolved easily. This chapter focuses on the basic concept of Keras-based framework DL library to handle the different real-life problems. The authors discuss the codes of previous libraries and same code run on Keras library and assess the performance on Google Colab Cloud Graphics Processing Units (GPUs). The goal of this chapter is to provide you with the newer concept, algorithm, and technology to solve the real-life problems with the help of Keras framework. Moreover, they discuss how to write the code of standard convolutional neural network (CNN) architectures using Keras libraries. Finally, the codes of validation and training data set to start the training procedure are explored.

DOI: 10.4018/978-1-7998-3095-5.ch011

INTRODUCTION

Artificial Intelligence (AI) or machine intelligence, is mainly the simulation of the natural intelligence of humans with the help of machines. AI systems are able to learn and recognized the configurations to reach any decisions as well as conclusions on the basis of different analytical situations, thereby the utmost chance of successfully accomplishing the goals (Dreyfus, 1979). Usually, machines have the ability to complete any task in a given time interval for completion of task required intelligence, which is referred to as the AI-effect (McCorduck, 2004). According to Tesler'shypothesis states, "whatever has not been completed yet, with the help of AI is possible (Maloof, 2006). For example, recognition of optical character is possible by using an AI system (Levin & Pieraccini, 1992). With the advancement in AI technology, machines are able to understand human speech (Underwood, 1977) that competes for the utmost level in the strategic system including different computer games including chess, etc., operational cars and militant simulations.

Advancement in the research of AI into various sub-areas that frequently nosedive to connect with each other in a specific domain (Linn & Clancy, 1992). These various sub-fields are established on scientific concerns including specific objectives like modern robotics (Struijk, 2012), with the help of specific tools i.e is as logic, Artificial Neural Networks (ANN), deep theoretical changes. These various sub-areas have also been established on social aspects, mainly research institutions or particular researchers state of the artwork. However, various new different challenges associated with AI research with the passage of time such as reasoning, representation of information, preparation, planning, learning ability, language processing, observation and capability to relocate and control the objects (Kellman & Spelke, 1983). In this context, General Intelligence (GI) have the potential ability to resolve such issue and suitable alternative for the field's long-term goals (Voss, 2007).

Numerous methodologies mainly statistical approach and computational intelligence technique were extensively applied in the AI field. Various different tools are utilized in their field, including different types of exploration and numerical optimization, ANNs, and approaches established on statistical values, probability, and economics fields. The AI field attracts by computer science, information technology, fields of different branches of math, psychology, semantics, philosophy, and various different area of science. AI area was initiated on the hypothesis on human intelligence can accurate that suggested that machines might be finished to simulate it (Moravec, 1988). The advancement leads to logical opinions about the nature of the human mind and beliefs of making artificial things that offer human identical intelligence to the real world. Such associated problems have been identified by using fiction, myth, and philosophy (Morgan, 2000). Some of the researchers also suggested that AI might be dangerous to the human community, thereby need to be restricted progress or development (Woolgar, 1985). On the other hand, some researchers also believe that AI-based technologies might be producing mass-unemployment like previous technologies (Boyd & Holton, 2018). Moreover, AI technologies have experienced are surrection subsequent innovations in computer power, a huge amount of data processing, and theoretical interpretation. AI technologies have developed an indispensable portion of the industrial technologies that unravel various challenges in the area of computer science and operations research. The development of newer AI-based technologies has been one of the acute approaches of various sectors throughout the world. Several studies have been performed, however, the results of these approaches still need to be organized. In this context, ML with AI technologies is an essential tool for social development in various aspects.

ML is mainly studying algorithms and statistical modeling in computer science, which are used to achieve a precise assignment without using unambiguous instructions, mainly depend on the patterns and inference. Usually, ML develops a theoretical model on the basis data (training-data), thereby easily reach any prediction or decision. ML algorithms are extensively used in several applications mainly filtering of email, computer vision, where the conventional algorithm was failing or infeasible to perform the task. The ML and cybersecurity (Thomas, Vijayaraghavan, & Emmanuel, 2020) are strictly related to the statistics that focus to achieve any predictions with the help of a computer. The data mining is an area of study in ML and emphasis examining data using unsupervised learning in various applications mainly the business problem. Therefore, ML is a very valuable tool for the study of data mining, and mathematical optimization delivers process, theory and application domains. On the other hand, deep learning (DL) is required to make accurate predictions and decisions.

Deep learning is a branch of machine learning that aims to automatically learn the relationship between input and output directly from the data. The deep learning algorithms have shown promising results in the fields of Artificial Intelligence (Khan, Rahmani, Shah, & Bennamoun, 2018) such as object classification (He, Zhang, Ren, & Sun, 2016) and detection(Ren, He, Girshick, & Sun, 2015), natural language processing (Collobert et al., 2011; Kumar et al., 2016), image processing (Anwar, Huynh, & Porikli, 2017; Li et al., 2016) especially in the area image super-resolution (Dong, Loy, He, & Tang, 2015; Dong, Loy, & Tang, 2016; Kim, Kwon Lee, & Mu Lee, 2016; Muhammad & Aramvith, 2019), audio and video signal processing (Dahl, Yu, Deng, & Acero, 2011; Tekalp & Tekalp, 1995).

In other words, deep structured learning is one of the parts of the ML process based on ANN (Bui, Nguyen, Ngo, & Nguyen-Xuan, 2020). The learning process can be divided into three categories i.e. supervised, semi-supervised, and unsupervised learning. The DL structural design such as neural network, belief network, recurrent neural network, and convolutional neural network have been applied in various fields mainly computer vision, speech recognition, language processing, audio/ video recognition, social network filtering, machine translation, bioinformatics, drug modeling, medical image investigation, drug delivery, types of material identification and programming of high games. The produce results are comparable or superior with the help of the DL process. ANNs were inspired by the neurons in biological systems, as neuron processes and distributed the information. Indeed, ANNs have numerous differences from the biological system, especially neural networks tend to be stagnant and representative, whereas, the biological brain of the majority of the living organism is dynamic and analog. ANNs might be able to resolve a very complicated problem with the help of a neural-network library like Keras.

Keras is an open-source code for a neural-network library that was written in Python programming language. Keras library has the ability to run on top of TensorFlow, Microsoft Cognitive Toolkit, or Theano. The relatively faster experimental time, user-friendly, modular, and extensible with the use of Keras library with deep neural networks. The book chapter discusses the novel concept, algorithm, and technologies to resolve the real-life associated issues with the help of Keras library.

Artificial Intelligence (AI)

The AI system is mainly the branch of the computer science field, which focuses on developing intelligence and provides a similar response as a human being. For example, computers with AI systems are specially designed for various activities such as reorganization of speech, learning, planning, and solving the problems (Ertel, 2018). Moreover, novel AI-based technologies have been one of the critical approaches to resolving various real-life associated problems around the world.

AI system might be classified into mainly three systems; (1) analytical AI, has features dependable with cognitive intelligence (learning on the basis of past experience to reach any decisions for generating a cognitive representation), (2) Human-inspired AI, has elements from emotional and cognitive intelligence for understanding emotions of the human as well as cognitive elements that help to make any decisions, and (3) Humanized AI, has characteristics of all capabilities such as intellectual, emotional, and social intelligence that are capable to be self-conscious and self-aware in communications.

Machine Learning (ML)

ML is an application of AI-based technologies that have the ability to learn and improve from experience without using programming. The ML mainly focuses on the development of newer computer programming, which is able to access data and self-learn. Usually, the learning process begins with observations or previous data like direct experience or instruction for analyzing the pattern in data to achieved accurate decisions. The main aim of ML is to allow the computers that automatically learn without human intervention and also modified accordingly (Bishop, 2006; Samuel, 1988).In other words, ML is a theoretical construct a suit of the process that enhances prediction or decision compare with another conventional statistical modeling. Moreover, ML approaches might be provided newer pathways to learn brain activation patterns to behavior at an individual level. ML producing in the development of predictive models to diagnose different disease conditions, thereby frequently used in medical diagnostics. ML is basically categorized into two types on the basis of learning behavior. (1) Supervised learning, learning-task as a function, which maps input to output on the basis of an example (input-output pairs) (Russell & Norvig, 2016), and (2) unsupervised learning, an ML algorithm that used to draw extrapolations from the data-set (input-data). The cluster analysis is one of the most common examples of the unsupervised learning process used for experimental data analysis to find unknown patterns. The cluster model analysis is used to measure similarity that defined upon metrics mainly probabilistic distance or Euclidean (Hinton, Sejnowski, & Poggio, 1999). The following describes the difference between supervised and unsupervised learning.

- **Supervised Learning**
    a. Regression (linear, polynomial)
    b. Decision Trees, Random Forests
    c. Classification (KNN, trees, logistic regression, naïve bayes, and SVM)
    d. Learning with a labeled training set
    e. Data has known labels or output
- **Unsupervised Learning**
    a. Clustering and dimensionality reduction
    b. SVD, PCA, and K-means
    c. Hidden Markov Model
    d. Discovering a pattern in unlabeled data
    e. Labels or output unknown

Deep Learning (DL)

DL is a subset of ML in AI-based technologies that are able to learn without any supervision from the unlabeled or unstructured data. DL process is recognized as deep neural-network or deep neural-learning. DL is the newer member of the data science algorithm. The DL is an emerging area of knowledge, thereby gaining the attention of scientists, business leaders, and nonprofessional peoples. Figure. 1 shows the schematically representation of the interrelation of AI, ML, and DL.

Figure 1. A schematically representation of the interrelation of AI, ML, and DL

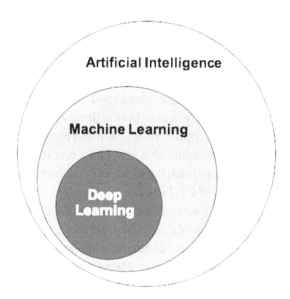

Python

Python is a programming language developed by Guido Van Rossum (1991). The Python language mainly organized an object-oriented process with the goal to help the programmers in various aspects such as clear writing, logical code for mini and big projects. Usually, Python supports various programming paradigms at the same time mainly technical, object-oriented, and efficient programming. Python was considered as a replacement to the ABC language in 1980. Python 2.0, contains new features such as the list of understandings and a trash collection system that is able to collect reference cycles and released in 2000, whereas Python 3.0, is not completely backward-compatible and released in 2008.

Open CV

Open CV is developed by Intel, primarily attentive on the real-time data with computer vision. The open CV is an open-source code for a computer vision library that provides free uses and cross-platform with an open-source license.

TensorFlow

TensorFlow is also a library (open-source) for various computer programming with a range of variety of tasks. TensorFlow is the free representative mathematical library, which was used for ML functions mainly neural networks (Abadi, Barham, et al., 2016). Google Brain team developed the TensorFlow library for core uses like mainly for research and production (Abadi, Agarwal, et al., 2016). TensorFlow was distributed under the Apache License 2.0 on 9th November 2015.

KERAS

Keras is a neural network library (open-source) and coding in Python programming language that able to run on most of the high levels of TensorFlow, Theano, or Microsoft Cognitive Toolkit. Usually, Keras developed to facilitate rapid experimentation using deep neural-networks with user-approachable, modular, and extensible. The Keras was established by François Chollet, a Google engineer in the research project of ONEIROS (Open-ended Neuro-Electronic Intelligent Robot Operating System). Chollet is also one of the authors of the XCeption deep neural network model (Chollet, 2017). Interestingly, Google's TensorFlow supporting Keras in TensorFlow's core public library in back 2017. Cholletsuggested that the Keraswas considered being an edge rather than a self-governing ML-framework. Keras library provides a higher-level approach, an extra impulsive set of concepts that create it simple to develop DL based models irrespective use of computational backend. In this context, Microsoft incorporatesCNTK backend to Keras, which is available as of CNTK v2.0.

Keras library comprises various neural-network-based operations including types of layers, objectives, activation functions, optimizers, and host tools that make suitable for working with image and text data mining. The code is introduced on GitHub, and community support forums that contain GitHub issues, and slack-channel. Keras support for convolutional, persistent neural-networks, and supplementary general utility layers (dropout, batch normalization, and pooling). Furthermore, Kerasgive consents to his users for the development of deep models on smartphones like iOS and Android, on the web, and Java Virtual Machine. Additionally, Keras permit the use of circulated training of DL models on clusters of GPUs and Tensor processing units (TPUs). In recent times, Keras claims more than 200,000 users as 2017 and 10[th]utmost cited tools in the KD Nuggets (2018) software poll and also approximately 22% usage. Therefore, DL neural-networks with Keras library is an essential tool for AI-based technologies.

Whywefocus on Keras Library

There are various reason for using Keras library compare with that of other existing alternatives: (1) Keras is an application program interface (API), mainly designed for human not for machines that monitors superlative practices for reducing intellectual load, (2) Keras library provides reliable and simple APIs that reduces required number of user actions and also offers clear and unlawful feedback upon error, thereby more productive, (3) Keras combined with the lower-level DL languages mainly TensorFlow that enables to implement anything like tf.keras, the Keras API impeccably with your TensorFlow workflows. Therefore, Keras library is used research and industry. Figure. 2 shows the ranking of different DL frameworks. Approximately more than 250,000 individual users of Keras registered as 2018 due to stronger approval in the industry and research compare with that of other DL framework except for TensorFlow. Keras is also a favorite choice among DL researchers like CERN, and NASA due to its advantages over other DL frameworks.

Figure 2. Ranking of different deep learning frameworks

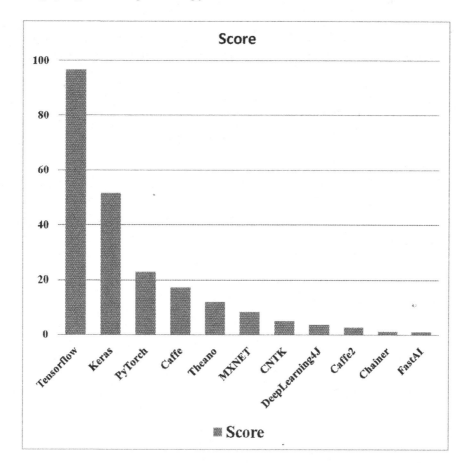

Keras Model

Keras models might be developing with a range of various DL backends. Interestingly, Keras model influences built-in layers will be moveable across all backends. Therefore, train a model with one backend and load with another like used for arrangement. The utmost popular available Keras model with backbends are given below:

(1). The TensorFlow backend (developed by Google)
(2). The CNTK backend (developed by Microsoft)
(3). The Theano backend

The Keras model can be trained on various hardware programs beyond CPUs like (1) NVIDIA GPUs, (2) Google TPUs using TensorFlow backend and Google Cloud, and (3) OpenCL-enabled GPUs, such as that these are from AMD, via the PlaidMLKeras backend.

How to Install Keras

Keras is comparatively simple to install if you have already installed Python, SciPy and TensorFlow environment. Keras installed on two operating systems (1) Microsoft Windows operating system (OS) and (2) Linux OS.

```
#In Microsoft Windows Operating System
pip install Keras
```

```
#In Linux Operating System
sudo pip install Keras
```

After installation, you can check the installed Keras version on the command line (in Windows OS) and on the terminal (in Ubuntu OS)

```
python -c "import Keras; print(Keras.__version__)"
```

```
python
import Keras
print(Keras.__version__)"
```

Upgrade the Keras library with pip command

```
sudo pip install --upgrade Keras
```

Procedure to Build aDL Model Using Keras Library

Initially, you define the model architecture using a Sequential model linear stacked as many as possible layers. Once your model is defined completely and then you start to compile Keras model with predefined function as compile (). After compiling the procedure, you start the training of the model with the help of fit () function. Finally, test the model or predict the quality of the model using predict () or evaluate () function. Figure 3 shows the basic building diagram to develop a complete DL Model.

Figure 3. Basic building diagram to develop a complete DL Model

Develop Your First Basic Model with Keras

AND gate is logical gate, which implements logical combination and performs on the basis off act table to right. A HIGH output (1) data obtained when all inputs to the AND gate are HIGH (1), whereas, LOW input data obtained when not all inputs to the AND gate are HIGH. The function may be an increase to a number of inputs even some extent. The schematic diagram of AND as well as the truth table of AND gate as shown in Figure 4.

Figure 4. Circuit symbol diagram of AND gate

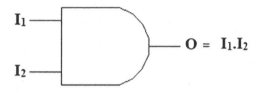

I_1	I_2	$O = I_1.I_2$
0	0	0
0	1	0
1	0	0
1	1	1

```
#DESIGN A TRAINING AND TESTING MODEL FOR AND GATE SIMULATION PURPOSE
import Keras # import means call any function or library.
import numpy as np
input = np.array([[0,0],[0,1],[1,0],[1,1]])
print(input) # This command shows input values of AND gate truth table
```

[[0 0] [0 1] [1 0] [1 1]]

```
output = np.array([[0], [0], [0], [1]]) #Here define the output of AND gate
print(output)
```

[[0] [0] [0] [1]]

```
model = keras.models.Sequential(layers=[ keras.layers.Dense(input_dim =2, units = 1),
keras.layers.Activation(keras.activations.sigmoid)])
model.summary() # shows the summary of model in terms of total parameters and trainable parameters
```

Layer (type)	Output Shape	Param #
dense_1 (Dense)	(None, 1)	3
activation_1 (Activation)	(None, 1)	0

Total params: 3
Trainable params: 3
Non-trainable params: 0

#We want show the model designed by Keras, so we used Scalable Vector Graphics (SVG) format
SVG(model_to_dot(model, show_shapes=True).create(prog='dot', format='svg'))

Figure 5. AND gate Model design through Keras API, AND gate network with 2 input and 1 output

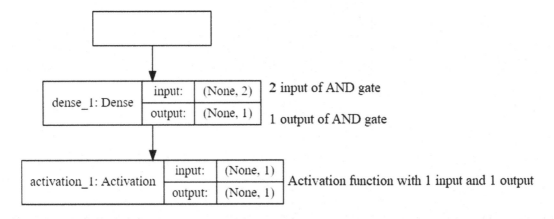

\# now we want to compile AND gate model using SGD optimizer, with mean squared error loss
model.compile(optimizer=keras.optimizers.SGD(lr=.5),loss='mse')
model.fit(input, output, epochs = 1000) # model.fit function we start training of the model, epoch =1000

Epoch 1/1000
4/4 [==============================] - 0s - loss: 0.2655
Epoch 2/1000
4/4 [==============================] - 0s - loss: 0.2614
Epoch 3/1000
4/4 [==============================] - 0s - loss: 0.2575
Epoch 4/1000
4/4 [==============================] - 0s - loss: 0.2538
Epoch 5/1000
4/4 [==============================] - 0s - loss: 0.2503

Epoch 6/1000

4/4 [==============================] - 0s - loss: 0.2469

Epoch 7/1000

model.predict(np.array([[0,1]])) # now used predict function and we ask if input of AND gate is 0 and 1
What is the output, so model give response, and shows 0.1, means less than 0.5 it means result is 0, if
    response greater than 0 it means output is 1

array([[0.12101924]], dtype=float32)

#Similarly we apply input all inputs equal to 1 and 1, the output shows 0.8, it means model declare
    output is 1

model.predict(np.array([[1,1]]))

array([[0.8546715]], dtype=float32)

Build an OR Gate Model Using Keras

Figure 6. shows the OR gate diagram. The OR gate is a digital logic gate, which implements logical
disconnection and performs according to the fact table to the right. A HIGH output (1) results if one or
both the inputs to the gate are HIGH (1). If neither input is high, a LOW output (0) results. In another
aspect, the function of OR effectually finds the maximum between two binary digits as complementary
AND function finds minimum (Bloomfield, 2001). Figure 7 OR gate Model design through Keras API,
OR gate network with 2 input and 1 output.

Figure 6. OR gate circuit symbol

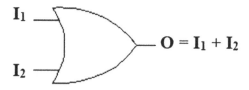

I_1	I_2	$O = I_1 + I_2$
0	0	0
0	1	1
1	0	1
1	1	1

Now we write the program on two-input OR gate.

```
#TRAIN AND TEST MODEL ON OR GATE
import Keras
import numpy as np
from IPython.display import SVG
from keras.utils.vis_utils import model_to_dot

input = np.array([[0,0], [0,1],1,0], [1,1]])
print(input)
```

  [[0 0] [0 1] [1 0] [1 1]]

```
output = np.array([[0], [1],[1], [1]])
print(output)
```

  [[0] [1] [1] [1]]

```
model=keras.models.Sequential(layers=[keras.layers.Dense(input_dim =2, units = 1), keras.layers.
    Activation (keras.activations.sigmoid)])
model.compile(optimizer=keras.optimizers.SGD(lr=.5),loss='mse')
model.summary()
```

Layer (type)	Output Shape	Param #
dense_2 (Dense)	(None, 1)	3
activation_2 (Activation)	(None, 1)	0

Total params: 3
Trainable params: 3
Non-trainable params:

```
SVG(model_to_dot(model, show_shapes=True).create(prog='dot', format='svg'))

model.fit(input, output, epochs = 1000)
```

```
Epoch 1/1000
4/4 [==============================] - 0s - loss: 0.2879
Epoch 2/1000
4/4 [==============================] - 0s - loss: 0.2681
Epoch 3/1000
```

Figure 7. OR gate Model design through Keras API, OR gate network with 2 input and 1 output

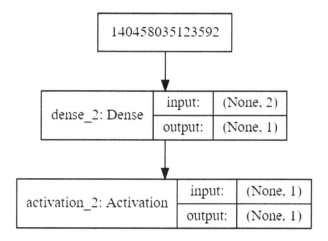

```
4/4 [==============================] - 0s - loss: 0.2506
Epoch 4/1000
4/4 [==============================] - 0s - loss: 0.2354
Epoch 5/1000
4/4 [==============================] - 0s - loss: 0.2223
Epoch 6/1000
4/4 [==============================] - 0s - loss: 0.2110
```

model.predict(np.array([[0,0]]))

array([[0.12083659]], dtype=float32)

Dense Layer

A dense layer is a regular layer of neurons in a neural-network and each neurons receives input from all neurons (previous layer), thereby densely connected. Figure 8 Build a model with dense Layer through Keras API.The layer has a weight matrix W, a bias vector b, and the activations of previous layer a.

```
from keras.models import Model
from keras.layers import Input, Dense
from IPython.display import SVG
from keras.utils.vis_utils import model_to_dot
inputsD = Input(shape=(684,))
D = Dense(32, activation='relu')(inputsD)
D = Dense(16, activation='relu')(D)
D = Dense(8, activation='relu')(D)
response = Dense(4, activation='softmax')(D)
model = Model(inputs=inputsD, outputs=response)
```

model.compile(optimizer='adam', loss='categorical_crossentropy', metrics=['accuracy'])
model.summary()

Layer (type)	Output Shape	Param #
input_2 (InputLayer)	(None, 684)	0
dense_4 (Dense)	(None, 32)	21920
dense_5 (Dense)	(None, 16)	528
dense_6 (Dense)	(None, 8)	136
dense_7 (Dense)	(None, 4)	36

SVG(model_to_dot(model, show_shapes=True).create(prog='dot', format='svg'))

Figure 8. Build a model with dense Layer through Keras API

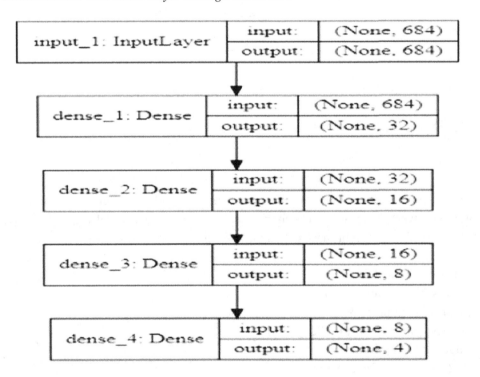

Flatten Layer

The flattening layer is used to change a multi-dimensional tensor to a single 1-D tensor. Figure 9 shows the flatten Layer. For example, if the output of the previous layer is shaped (15, 3, 3, 4), flatten unstacks all the tensor values into a 1-D tensor of shape (15*3*3*4,) so that it can be used as input for the dense layer. Also, 64 by 64 grayscale image passed through Flatten Layer, the output is 64*64*1 is equal to 4096. Figure. 10. Build a model with Flatten Layer through Keras API.

Figure 9. Apply the Grayscale Image on Flatten Layer

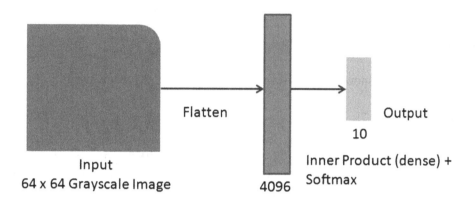

Figure 10. Build a model with Flatten Layer through Keras API

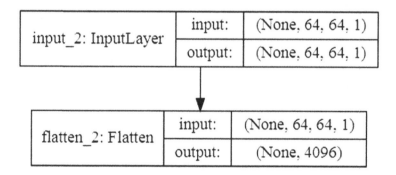

```
from keras.layers import Convolution2D, Conv2D, Flatten, Input
from keras import optimizers
from keras.models import Model
from IPython.display import SVG
from keras.utils.vis_utils import model_to_dot

img_shape = (64,64,1)
inputimg = Input(shape=(img_shape))
```

```
Fl = Flatten()(inputimg)
model = Model(inputimg, Fl)
opt = optimizers.Adam(lr=0.0003)
model.compile(optimizer='adam',loss='mean_squared_error')
model.summary()
```

Layer (type)	Output Shape	Param #
input_2 (InputLayer)	(None, 64, 64, 1)	0
flatten_2 (Flatten)	(None, 4096)	0

```
SVG(model_to_dot(model, show_shapes=True).create(prog='dot', format='svg'))
```

Convolution 2D-layer

The 2-D convolutional layer applied as sliding convolutional filters to the input. The layer convolves the input by moving the filters along the input vertically and horizontally and computing the dot product of the weights and the input and then adding a bias term. Figure 11 build a model with Convolution 2D Layer through Keras API.

```
from Keras.layers import Conv2D, Convolution2D, Activation, Input
from keras.models import Model

img_shape = (32,32,1)
inputimg = Input(shape=(img_shape))
C1 = Conv2D(64,(9,9),padding='SAME',name='CONVOL1')(inputimg)
A1 = Activation('relu', name='act1')(C1)
C2 = Conv2D(32,(1,1),padding='SAME',name='CONVOL2')(A1)
A2 = Activation('relu', name='act2')(C2)
model = Model(inputimg, A2)
opt = optimizers.Adam(lr=0.0003)
model.compile(optimizer=opt,loss='mean_squared_error')
model.summary()
```

Layer (type)	Output Shape	Param #
input_4 (InputLayer)	(None, 32, 32, 1)	0
CONVOL1 (Conv2D)	(None, 32, 32, 64)	5248

act1 (Activation)	(None, 32, 32, 64)	0
CONVOL2 (Conv2D)	(None, 32, 32, 32)	2080
act2 (Activation)	(None, 32, 32, 32)	0

Figure 11. Build a model with Convolution 2D Layer through Keras API

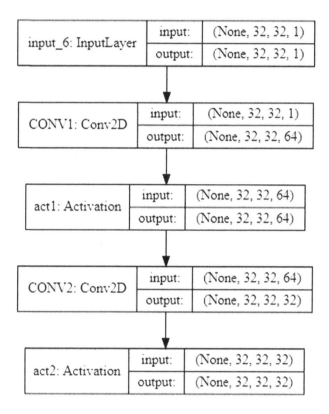

==

Depth Wise Separable 2D Convolution

Separable convolutions contain mainly performance a depth-wise spatial convolution that acts on every input channel in the model, individually followed by a pointwise convolution, which combines together the resulting output channels. The depth-multiplier argument operates, how many output channels are produced per input channel in the depth-wise step. Figure. 12. Shows the regular convolution vs depth-wise separable convolution.

Intuitively, separable convolutions can be understood as a way to factorize a convolution kernel into two smaller kernels factors, or as an extreme version of an Inception block. Figure 13 build a model with Regular vs Depth-wise Convolution through Keras API.

Figure 12. Regular convolution vs depth-wise separable convolution

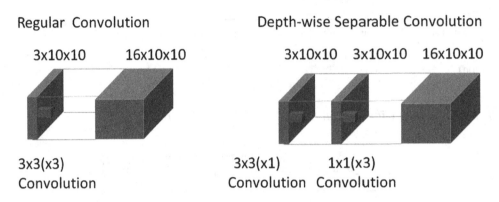

```
from keras.layers import Input, Conv2D, SeparableConv2D, Activation
from keras.models import Model
from keras import optimizers
from IPython.display import SVG
from keras.utils.vis_utils import model_to_dot
imageshape = (32,32,1)
inputimage = Input(shape=(imageshape))
C1 = SeparableConv2D(64,(9,9),padding='SAME')(inputimage)
A1 = Activation('relu', name='act1')(C1)
C2 = SeparableConv2D(32,(1,1),padding='SAME')(A1)
A2 = Activation('relu', name='act2')(C2)
model = Model(inputimage, A2)
opt = optimizers.Adam(lr=0.0003)
model.compile(optimizer=opt,loss='mean_squared_error')
model.summary()
```

===

input_2 (InputLayer)	(None, 32, 32, 1)	0
separable_conv2d_3 (Separabl	(None, 32, 32, 64)	209
act1 (Activation)	(None, 32, 32, 64)	0
separable_conv2d_4 (Separabl	(None, 32, 32, 32)	2144
act2 (Activation)	(None, 32, 32, 32)	0

===

Figure 13. Build a model with regular vs depth-wise convolution through Keras API

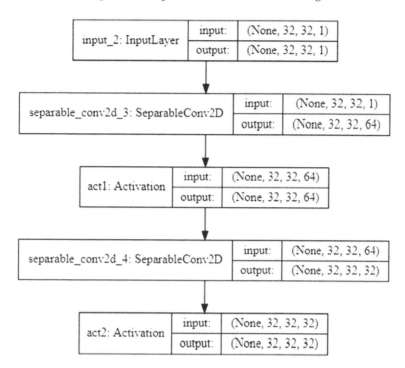

Transposed Convolution Layer or Deconvolution Layer

The transposed convolutions usually generated from the aspiration to use a transformation going in the opposite direction of a standard convolution, i.e., from anything that has the shape of the output of some convolution to something that has the shape of its input while preserving a connectivity model that is compatible with said convolution. Figure 14 shows the 2D transpose convolution. Figure 15 shows the various step of building a model with transpose convolution through Keras API.

Figure 14. 2D Transpose Convolution

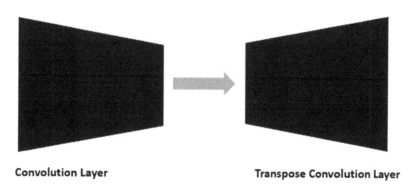

```
from keras.layers import Input, Conv2DTranspose, Conv2D
from keras.models import Model
img_shape = (32,32,1)
inputimage = Input(shape=(img_shape))
D1 = Conv2DTranspose(32,(3,3),strides=(2,2),padding='same',name='TRANS_CONV1')(inputimage)
C1 = Conv2D(32,(1,1),padding='SAME',name='CONV1')(D1)
model = Model(inputimage, C1)
model.summary()
```

Layer (type)	Output Shape	Param #
input_2 (InputLayer)	(None, 32, 32, 1)	0
TRANS_CONV1 (Conv2DTranspose	(None, 64, 64, 32)	320
CONV1 (Conv2D)	(None, 64, 64, 32)	1056

```
from IPython.display import SVG
from keras.utils.vis_utils import model_to_dot
SVG(model_to_dot(model, show_shapes=True).create(prog='dot', format='svg'))
```

Figure 15. Build a model with transpose convolution through Keras API

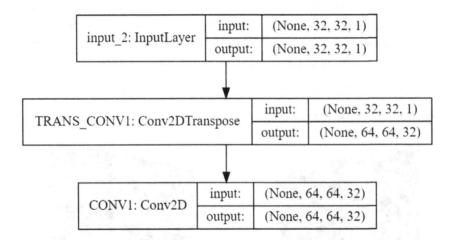

Max Pooling and Average Pooling Layers

A max-pooling layer operates down-sampling by splitting the input into specific rectangular pooling zones and computing the maximized of each zone. An average pooling layer operates down-sampling by dividing the input into rectangular pooling regions and computing the average values of each area. Figure 16 shows a comparison between max-pooling vs, Average pooling. Figure 17 shows the various step involving to build a model using max-pooling through Keras.

Figure 16. Max pooling vs Average pooling

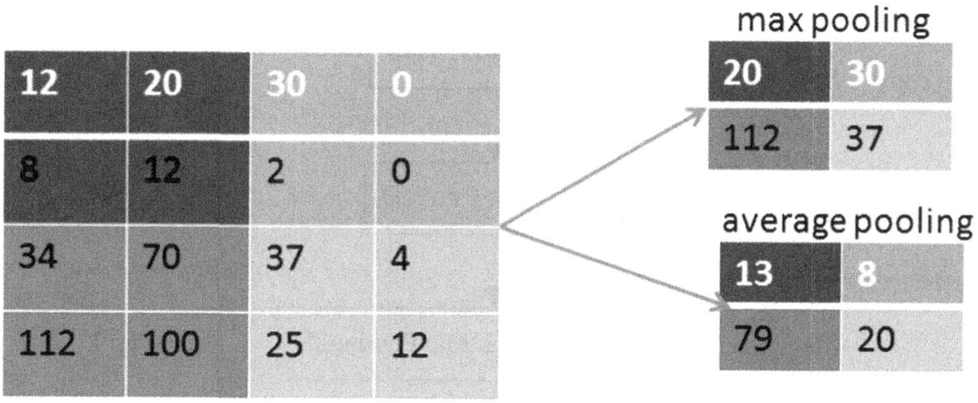

```
from keras import layers, models
model = models.Sequential()
model.add(layers.Conv2D(32,(5,5),activation= 'relu',input_shape=(28,28,1)))
model.add(layers.MaxPooling2D((2, 2)))
model.add(layers.Conv2D(64, (5, 5), activation='relu'))
model.add(layers.MaxPooling2D((2, 2)))
model.summary()
```

Layer (type)	Output Shape	Param #
conv2d_5 (Conv2D)	(None, 24, 24, 32)	832
max_pooling2d_5 (MaxPooling2	(None, 12, 12, 32)	0
conv2d_6 (Conv2D)	(None, 8, 8, 64)	51264
max_pooling2d_6 (MaxPooling2	(None, 4, 4, 64)	0

Total params: 52,096

Trainable params: 52,096

Non-trainable params: 0

```
from IPython.display import SVG
from keras.utils.vis_utils import model_to_dot
SVG(model_to_dot(model, show_shapes=True).create(prog='dot', format='svg'))
```

Figure 17. Build a model using max-pooling through Keras

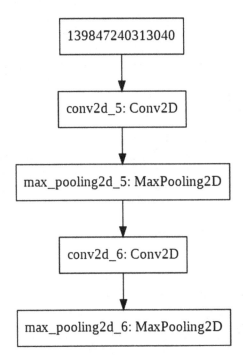

15. Create a Single Layer Keras Model

Figure 18 shows the block diagram of a Single Layer Keras Model. Figure 19 shows the various step involving to build a single-layer model using convolution with the activation layer using Keras.

Figure 18. Block diagram of a Single Layer Keras Model

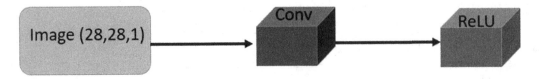

```
import keras.backend as K
from keras.models import Sequential, Model
from keras.layers import Conv2D, Activation
from IPython.display import SVG
from keras.utils.vis_utils import model_to_dot
img_shape = (28,28,1)
input_img = Input(shape=(img_shape))
C1 = Conv2D(32,(3,3),name='CONV1')(input_img)
A1 = Activation('relu', name='act1')(C1)
model = Model(input_img, A1)
model.summary()
```

Layer (type)	Output Shape	Param #
==		
input_8 (InputLayer)	(None, 28, 28, 1)	0
CONV1 (Conv2D)	(None, 26, 26, 32)	320
act1 (Activation)	(None, 26, 26, 32)	0
==		

Total params: 320
Trainable params: 320
Non-trainable params: 0

```
SVG(model_to_dot(model, show_shapes=True).create(prog='dot', format='svg'))
```

Figure 19. Build a single layer model using convolution with an activation layer using Keras

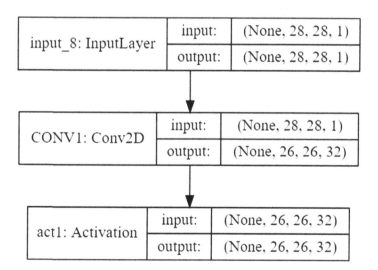

Create a Five Layer Keras Model

Figure 20 shows the general diagram of five convolution layers followed by ReLU activation layer. Figure 21 shows the five-layer CNN model using convolution followed by an activation layer.

Figure 20. General diagram of five convolution layers followed by ReLU activation layer

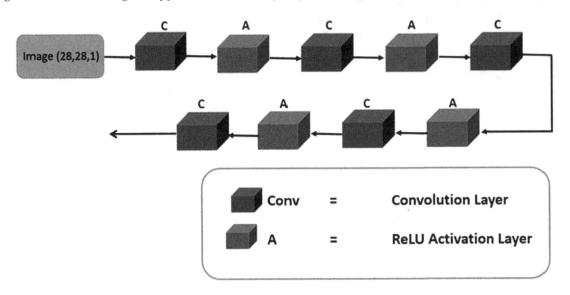

```
import keras.backend as K
from keras.models import Sequential, Model
from keras.layers import Conv2D, Activation
from IPython.display import SVG
from keras.utils.vis_utils import model_to_dot
img_shape = (28,28,1)
input_img = Input(shape=(img_shape))
C1 = Conv2D(32,(3,3),name='CONV1')(input_img)
A1 = Activation('relu', name='act1')(C1)
C2 = Conv2D(32,(3,3),name='CONV2')(A1)
A2 = Activation('relu', name='act2')(C2)
C3 = Conv2D(32,(3,3),name='CONV3')(A2)
A3 = Activation('relu', name='act3')(C3)
C4 = Conv2D(32,(3,3),name='CONV4')(A3)
```

```
A4 = Activation('relu', name='act4')(C4)
C5 = Conv2D(32,(3,3),name='CONV5')(A4)
A5 = Activation('relu', name='act5')(C5)
model = Model(input_img, A5)
model.summary()
```

Layer (type)	Output Shape	Param #
input_10 (InputLayer)	(None, 28, 28, 1)	0
CONV1 (Conv2D)	(None, 26, 26, 32)	320
act1 (Activation)	(None, 26, 26, 32)	0
CONV2 (Conv2D)	(None, 24, 24, 32)	9248
act2 (Activation)	(None, 24, 24, 32)	0
CONV3 (Conv2D)	(None, 22, 22, 32)	9248
act3 (Activation)	(None, 22, 22, 32)	0
CONV4 (Conv2D)	(None, 20, 20, 32)	9248
act4 (Activation)	(None, 20, 20, 32)	0
CONV5 (Conv2D)	(None, 18, 18, 32)	9248
act5 (Activation)	(None, 18, 18, 32)	0

Total params: 37,312
Trainable params: 37,312
Non-trainable params: 0

```
SVG(model_to_dot(model, show_shapes=True).create(prog='dot', format='svg'))
```

Figure 21. Five layer CNN model using convolution followed by activation layer

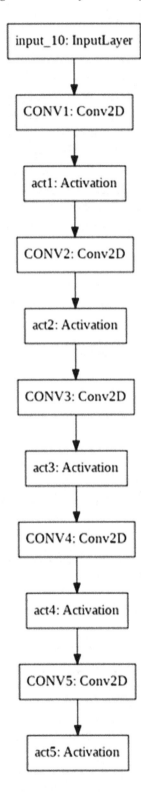

DownloadKerasmodel on a Local Machine

```
import keras.backend as K
from keras.models import Sequential, Model
from keras.layers import Conv2D, Activation
from IPython.display import SVG
from keras.utils.vis_utils import model_to_dot
img_shape = (28,28,1)
input_img = Input(shape=(img_shape))
C1 = Conv2D(32,(3,3),name='CONV1')(input_img)
A1 = Activation('relu', name='act1')(C1)
C2 = Conv2D(32,(3,3),name='CONV2')(A1)
A2 = Activation('relu', name='act2')(C2)
C3 = Conv2D(32,(3,3),name='CONV3')(A2)
A3 = Activation('relu', name='act3')(C3)
C4 = Conv2D(32,(3,3),name='CONV4')(A3)
A4 = Activation('relu', name='act4')(C4)
C5 = Conv2D(32,(3,3),name='CONV5')(A4)
A5 = Activation('relu', name='act5')(C5)
model = Model(input_img, A5)
model.summary()

#NOW DOWNLOAD THIS DIAGRAM
from keras.utils import plot_model

#GIVE THE NAME OF MODEL
plot_model(model, to_file='FIVE_LAYER_KERAS_MODEL.png')

#CHECK THIS MODEL IS AVAILABLE ON COLAB WITH THIS NAME
!ls

FIVE_LAYER_KERAS_MODEL.png sample_data

from google.colab import files
files.download('FIVE_LAYER_KERAS_MODEL.png')
```

Finally, your model is download on the local machine.

Addition of Three Keras Layers

The addition of Keras Layers takes as an input value of tensors, and values of all tensors have the same shape and size and return a single value tensor. Figure 22 shows the schematically representation of the addition of three dense layers. Figure 23 shows the addition of three layers builds by Keras API.

Figure 22. Addition of three dense layers

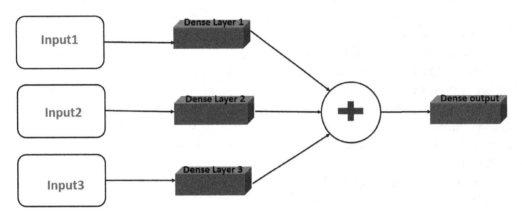

```
import keras
input1 = keras.layers.Input(shape=(32,))
z1 = keras.layers.Dense(8, activation='relu')(input1)
input2 = keras.layers.Input(shape=(32,))
z2 = keras.layers.Dense(8, activation='relu')(input2)
input3 = keras.layers.Input(shape=(32,))
z3 = keras.layers.Dense(8, activation='relu')(input3)
added = keras.layers.Add()([z1, z2, z3])
out = keras.layers.Dense(4)(added)
model = keras.models.Model(inputs=[input1, input2,input3,], outputs=out)
model.summary()
```

Layer (type)	Output Shape	Param #	Connected to
input_25 (InputLayer)	(None, 32)	0	
input_26 (InputLayer)	(None, 32)	0	
input_27 (InputLayer)	(None, 32)	0	
dense_18 (Dense)	(None, 8)	264	input_25[0][0]
dense_19 (Dense)	(None, 8)	264	input_26[0][0]
dense_20 (Dense)	(None, 8)	264	input_27[0][0]
add_6 (Add)	(None, 8)	0	dense_18[0][0]
			dense_19[0][0]
			dense_20[0][0]

| dense_21 (Dense) | (None, 4) | 36 | add_6[0][0] |

===

Total params: 828
Trainable params: 828
Non-trainable params: 0

Figure 23. Addition of three layers build by Keras API

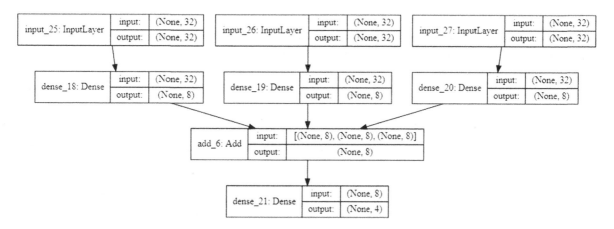

Subtraction of Two Keras Layers

The subtraction function of Keras layer takes as an input a list of tensors with size 2 and has both the same shape and provides a single tensor output with the same shape. The command is used for this purpose is keras.layers.Subtract(). Figure 24 shows the subtraction of two layers. Figure 25 shows the subtraction of two layers builds by Keras API.

Figure 24. Subtraction of two layers

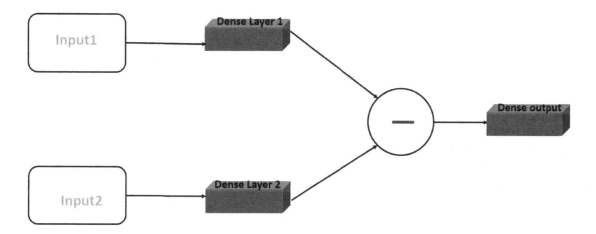

```
_____ import keras
input1 = keras.layers.Input(shape=(16,))
l1 = keras.layers.Dense(8, activation='relu')(input1)
input2 = keras.layers.Input(shape=(32,))
l2 = keras.layers.Dense(8, activation='relu')(input2)
subtracted = keras.layers.Subtract()([l1, l2])
out = keras.layers.Dense(4)(subtracted)
model = keras.models.Model(inputs=[input1, input2], outputs=out)
model.summary()
```

Layer (type)	Output Shape	Param #	Connected to
input_35 (InputLayer)	(None, 16)	0	
input_36 (InputLayer)	(None, 32)	0	
dense_31 (Dense)	(None, 8)	136	input_35[0][0]
dense_32 (Dense)	(None, 8)	264	input_36[0][0]
subtract_4 (Subtract)	(None, 8)	0	dense_31[0][0] dense_32[0][0]
dense_33 (Dense)	(None, 4)	36	subtract_4[0][0]

Total params: 436
Trainable params: 436
Non-trainable params: 0

```
SVG(model_to_dot(model, show_shapes=True).create(prog='dot', format='svg'))
```

Multiplication of Two Keras Layers

The multiplication operation performs the element-wise multiplication and takes as an input of a list of tensors having all of them have the same shape and returns a single tensor output with the same shape. Figure 26 shows the multiplication of two layers. Figure 27 shows the multiplication of two layers builds by Keras API.

```
import keras
input1 = keras.layers.Input(shape=(16,))
x1 = keras.layers.Dense(8, activation='relu')(input1)
input2 = keras.layers.Input(shape=(32,))
x2 = keras.layers.Dense(8, activation='relu')(input2)
subtracted = keras.layers.multiply([x1, x2])
```

Figure 25. Subtraction of two layers builds by Keras API

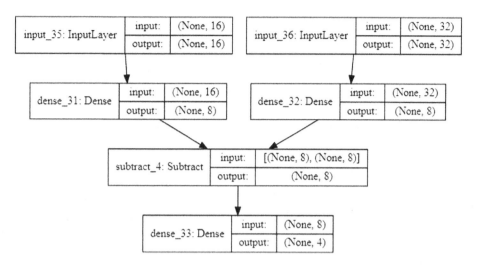

Figure 26. Multiplication of two layers

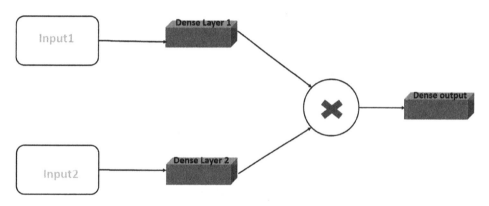

out = keras.layers.Dense(4)(subtracted)
model = keras.models.Model(inputs=[input1, input2], outputs=out)
model.summary()

Layer (type)	Output Shape	Param #	Connected to
input_39 (InputLayer)	(None, 16)	0	
input_40 (InputLayer)	(None, 32)	0	
dense_37 (Dense)	(None, 8)	136	input_39[0][0]
dense_38 (Dense)	(None, 8)	264	input_40[0][0]

| multiply_2 (Multiply) | (None, 8) | 0 | dense_37[0][0] |
| | | | dense_38[0][0] |

| dense_39 (Dense) | (None, 4) | 36 | multiply_2[0][0] |

==

SVG(model_to_dot(model, show_shapes=True).create(prog='dot', format='svg'))

Figure 27. Multiplication of two layers build by Keras API

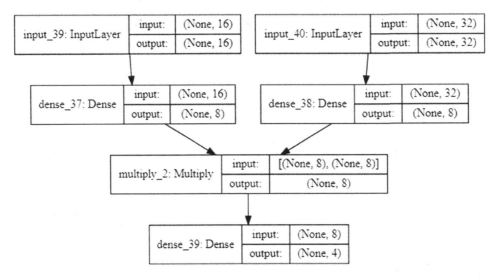

Build a Skip or Short Cut Connection Model Using Keras Library

Traditional convolutional neural networks feed the output into the next layer. In a residual network with residual blocks, each layer feeds the output to the next layer and directly 2-3 hops away into the layers. Figure 28 shows the skip connection diagram. Figure 29 skip Connection build by Keras API.

Figure 28. Skip Connection Diagram

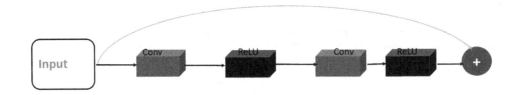

import keras

```
from keras.layers import Conv2D,Input, Activation
from keras.models import Model, load_model
from IPython.display import SVG
from keras.utils.vis_utils import model_to_dot
img_shape = (41, 41, 1)
input_img = Input(shape=(img_shape))
#01 LAYER
model1 = Conv2D(64, (3, 3), padding='same', name='conv1')(input_img)
model1 = Activation('relu', name='act1')(model1)
#02 LAYER
model2 = Conv2D(1, (3, 3), padding='same', name='conv2')(model1)
model2 = Activation('relu', name='act2')(model2)
res_img = model2
output_img = keras.layers.add([res_img, input_img])
model = Model(input_img, output_img)
model.summary()
```

Layer (type)	Output Shape	Param #	Connected to
input_3 (InputLayer)	(None, 41, 41, 1)	0	
conv1 (Conv2D)	(None, 41, 41, 64)	640	input_3[0][0]
act1 (Activation)	(None, 41, 41, 64)	0	conv1[0][0]
conv2 (Conv2D)	(None, 41, 41, 1)	577	act1[0][0]
act2 (Activation)	(None, 41, 41, 1)	0	conv2[0][0]
add_2 (Add)	(None, 41, 41, 1)	0	act2[0][0] input_3[0][0]

Total params: 1,217

Build a Residual or Skip Connection Model Using Keras Library

Usually, neural networks contain layers and each layer feeds into the next layer, whereas neural network with residual blocks each layer feeds into the next layer and then directly into layers about 3-2 hopes away, as shown in Figure 30.

$R(X) = Output - Input = H(X) - X.$

$H(X) = R(X) + X$

Figure 29. Skip Connection build by Keras API

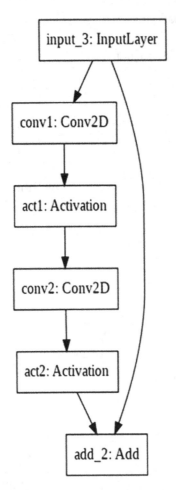

Figure 30. Single residual block

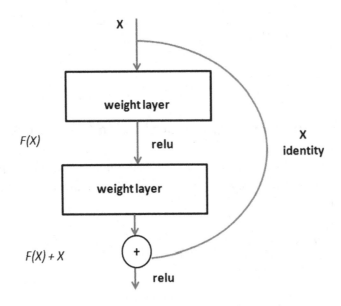

Write the Keras Code of the Residual Block Convolution, Batch Normalization, and ReLu Activation Layers

Figure 31 shows the skip/shortcut connection of the convolution and batch normalization layer. Figure 32 Skip/shortcut connection of convolution and batch normalization layer using KerasAPI. Figure 33 Multipath skip/shortcut connection of convolution and batch normalization layer using Keras API.

Figure 31. Skip/shortcut connection of convolution and batch normalization layer

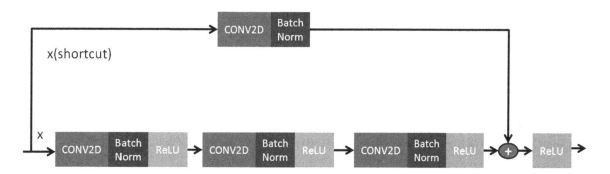

```
import keras
from keras.layers import Input
from keras.layers import Conv2D
from keras.layers import BatchNormalization
from keras.layers import Activation
from keras.models import Model
from IPython.display import SVG
from keras.utils.vis_utils import model_to_dot
img_shape = (41, 41, 1)
input_img = Input(shape=(img_shape),name = 'X')
#SKIP LAYER LAYER CONNECTION
#01 LAYER
C1 = Conv2D(64, (3, 3), padding='same', name='CONV2D1')(input_img)
BN1 = BatchNormalization(axis = 3, name = 'BatchNorm1')(C1)
#STRAIGHT PATH CONNECTION
#02 LAYER
C2 = Conv2D(64, (3, 3), padding='same', name='CONV2D2')(input_img)
BN2 = BatchNormalization(axis = 3, name = 'BatchNorm2')(C2)
A2 = Activation('relu', name='ReLU1')(BN2)
#03 LAYER
C3 = Conv2D(64, (3, 3), padding='same', name='CONV2D3')(A2)
BN3 = BatchNormalization(axis = 3, name = 'BatchNorm3')(C3)
A3 = Activation('relu', name='ReLU2')(BN3)
```

#04 LAYER
C4 = Conv2D(1, (3, 3), padding='same', name='CONV2D4')(A3)
BN4 = BatchNormalization(axis = 3, name = 'BatchNorm4')(C4)
#05 SUM LAYER
output_img = keras.layers.add([BN4, BN1])
A4 = Activation('relu', name='ReLU4')(output_img)
model = Model(input_img, A4)
model.summary()

Layer (type)	Output Shape	Param #	Connected to
X (InputLayer)	(None, 41, 41, 1)	0	
CONV2D2 (Conv2D)	(None, 41, 41, 64)	640	X[0][0]
BatchNorm2 (BatchNormalization)	(None, 41, 41, 64)	256	CONV2D2[0][0]
ReLU1 (Activation)	(None, 41, 41, 64)	0	BatchNorm2[0][0]
CONV2D3 (Conv2D)	(None, 41, 41, 64)	36928	ReLU1[0][0]
BatchNorm3 (BatchNormalization)	(None, 41, 41, 64)	256	CONV2D3[0][0]
ReLU2 (Activation)	(None, 41, 41, 64)	0	BatchNorm3[0][0]
CONV2D4 (Conv2D)	(None, 41, 41, 1)	577	ReLU2[0][0]
CONV2D1 (Conv2D)	(None, 41, 41, 64)	640	X[0][0]
BatchNorm4 (BatchNormalization)	(None, 41, 41, 1)	4	CONV2D4[0][0]
BatchNorm1 (BatchNormalization)	(None, 41, 41, 64)	256	CONV2D1[0][0]
add_3 (Add)	(None, 41, 41, 64)	0	BatchNorm4[0][0]
			BatchNorm1[0][0]
ReLU4 (Activation)	(None, 41, 41, 64)	0	add_3[0][0]

Figure 32. Skip/shortcut connection of convolution and batch normalization layer using Keras API

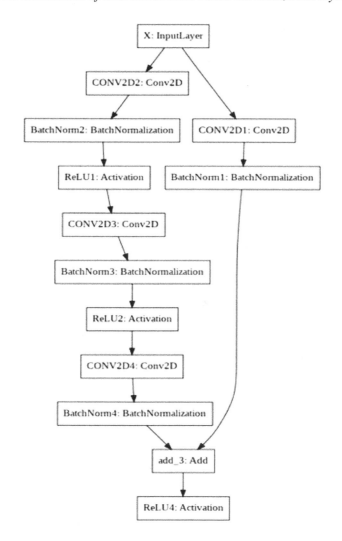

Multiple Path Skip Connection

Multiple path Skip Connection is an alternative way to reduce the model complexity and avoid the overfitting problem during the training of the model. In this techniques, we use more than two skip connections with the same shape and take the different skip connections from the input as well as from the different stages of the layers. Here we show the Keras code of Multiple path Skip Connection and uses the Convolution Layer, Batch Normalization Layer and ReLU Activation Layer. The Multipath connection of convolution and batch normalization layer using Keras API as shown in Figure 3.

Figure 33. Multipath skip/shortcut connection of convolution and batch normalization layer using Keras API

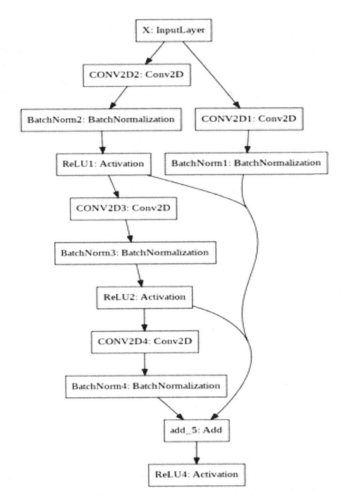

```
import keras
from keras.layers import Input, Conv2D, Model, Activation, BatchNormalization
from IPython.display import SVG
from keras.utils.vis_utils import model_to_dot
imageshape = (41, 41, 1)
inputimage = Input(shape=(imageshape),name = 'X')
#SKIP LAYER LAYER CONNECTION
#01 LAYER
C1 = Conv2D(64, (3, 3), padding='same', name='CONV2D1')(inputimage)
BN1 = BatchNormalization(axis = 3, name = 'BatchNorm1')(C1)
#STRAIGHT PATH CONNECTION
#02 LAYER
C2 = Conv2D(64, (3, 3), padding='same', name='CONV2D2')(inputimage)
BN2 = BatchNormalization(axis = 3, name = 'BatchNorm2')(C2)
```

A2 = Activation('relu', name='ReLU1')(BN2)
#03 LAYER
C3 = Conv2D(64, (3, 3), padding='same', name='CONV2D3')(A2)
BN3 = BatchNormalization(axis = 3, name = 'BatchNorm3')(C3)
A3 = Activation('relu', name='ReLU2')(BN3)
#04 LAYER
C4 = Conv2D(1, (3, 3), padding='same', name='CONV2D4')(A3)
BN4 = BatchNormalization(axis = 3, name = 'BatchNorm4')(C4)
#05 SUM LAYER
outputimage = keras.layers.add([BN4, BN1,A2,A3])
A4 = Activation('relu', name='ReLU4')(outputimage)
model = Model(inputimage, A4)
model.summary()

X (InputLayer)	(None, 41, 41, 1)	0	
CONV2D2 (Conv2D)	(None, 41, 41, 64)	640	X[0][0]
BatchNorm2 (BatchNormalization)	(None, 41, 41, 64)	256	CONV2D2[0][0]
ReLU1 (Activation)	(None, 41, 41, 64)	0	BatchNorm2[0][0]
CONV2D3 (Conv2D)	(None, 41, 41, 64)	36928	ReLU1[0][0]
BatchNorm3 (BatchNormalization)	(None, 41, 41, 64)	256	CONV2D3[0][0]
ReLU2 (Activation)	(None, 41, 41, 64)	0	BatchNorm3[0][0]
CONV2D4 (Conv2D)	(None, 41, 41, 1)	577	ReLU2[0][0]
CONV2D1 (Conv2D)	(None, 41, 41, 64)	640	X[0][0]
BatchNorm4 (BatchNormalization)	(None, 41, 41, 1)	4	CONV2D4[0][0]
BatchNorm1 (BatchNormalization)	(None, 41, 41, 64)	256	CONV2D1[0][0]
add_5 (Add)	(None, 41, 41, 64)	0	BatchNorm4[0][0]
			BatchNorm1[0][0]
			ReLU1[0][0]
			ReLU2[0][0]
ReLU4 (Activation)	(None, 41, 41, 64)	0	add_5[0][0]

==

REFERENCES

Abadi, M., Agarwal, A., Barham, P., Brevdo, E., Chen, Z., Citro, C., . . . Devin, M. (2016). *Tensorflow: Large-scale machine learning on heterogeneous distributed systems.* arXiv preprint arXiv:1603.04467

Abadi, M., Barham, P., Chen, J., Chen, Z., Davis, A., Dean, J., . . . Isard, M. (2016). *Tensorflow: A system for large-scale machine learning.* Paper presented at the 12th {USENIX} Symposium on Operating Systems Design and Implementation.

Anwar, S., Huynh, C. P., & Porikli, F. (2017). *Chaining identity mapping modules for image denoising.* arXiv preprint arXiv:1712.02933

Bishop, C. M. (2006). *Pattern recognition and machine learning.* Springer.

Bloomfield, L. A. (2001). *How things work.* Louis A. Bloomfield.

Boyd, R., & Holton, R. J. (2018). Technology, innovation, employment and power: Does robotics and artificial intelligence really mean social transformation? *Journal of Sociology (Melbourne, Vic.), 54*(3), 331–345. doi:10.1177/1440783317726591

Bui, D.-K., Nguyen, T. N., Ngo, T. D., & Nguyen-Xuan, H. (2020). An artificial neural network (ANN) expert system enhanced with the electromagnetism-based firefly algorithm (EFA) for predicting the energy consumption in buildings. *Energy, 190*, 116370. doi:10.1016/j.energy.2019.116370

Chollet, F. (2017). *Xception: Deep learning with depthwise separable convolutions.* arXiv preprint, 1610.02357.

Collobert, R., Weston, J., Bottou, L., Karlen, M., Kavukcuoglu, K., & Kuksa, P. (2011). Natural language processing (almost) from scratch. *Journal of Machine Learning Research, 12*(Aug), 2493–2537.

Dahl, G. E., Yu, D., Deng, L., & Acero, A. (2011). Context-dependent pre-trained deep neural networks for large-vocabulary speech recognition. *IEEE Transactions on Audio, Speech, and Language Processing, 20*(1), 30–42. doi:10.1109/TASL.2011.2134090

Dong, C., Loy, C. C., He, K., & Tang, X. (2015). Image super-resolution using deep convolutional networks. *IEEE Transactions on Pattern Analysis and Machine Intelligence, 38*(2), 295–307. doi:10.1109/TPAMI.2015.2439281 PMID:26761735

Dong, C., Loy, C. C., & Tang, X. (2016). *Accelerating the super-resolution convolutional neural network.* Paper presented at the European conference on computer vision.

Dreyfus, H. L. (1979). *What computers can't do: The limits of artificial intelligence* (Vol. 1972). Harper & Row.

Ertel, W. (2018). *Introduction to artificial intelligence.* Springer.

He, K., Zhang, X., Ren, S., & Sun, J. (2016). Deep residual learning for image recognition. *Proceedings of the IEEE conference on computer vision and pattern recognition.*

Hinton, G. E., Sejnowski, T. J., & Poggio, T. A. (1999). *Unsupervised learning: foundations of neural computation.* MIT Press. doi:10.7551/mitpress/7011.001.0001

Kellman, P. J., & Spelke, E. S. (1983). Perception of partly occluded objects in infancy. *Cognitive Psychology, 15*(4), 483–524. doi:10.1016/0010-0285(83)90017-8 PMID:6641127

Khan, S., Rahmani, H., Shah, S. A. A., & Bennamoun, M. (2018). A guide to convolutional neural networks for computer vision. *Synthesis Lectures on Computer Vision, 8*(1), 1–207. doi:10.2200/S00822ED1V01Y201712COV015

Kim, J., Kwon Lee, J., & Lee, M., K. (2016). Accurate image super-resolution using very deep convolutional networks. *Proceedings of the IEEE conference on computer vision and pattern recognition.* 10.1109/CVPR.2016.182

Kumar, A., Irsoy, O., Ondruska, P., Iyyer, M., Bradbury, J., Gulrajani, I., . . . Socher, R. (2016). *Ask me anything: Dynamic memory networks for natural language processing.* Paper presented at the International conference on machine learning.

Levin, E., & Pieraccini, R. (1992). *Dynamic planar warping for optical character recognition.* Paper presented at the ICASSP-92: 1992 IEEE International Conference on Acoustics, Speech, and Signal Processing. 10.1109/ICASSP.1992.226254

Li, Y., Lu, H., Li, J., Li, X., Li, Y., & Serikawa, S. (2016). Underwater image de-scattering and classification by deep neural network. *Computers & Electrical Engineering, 54*, 68–77. doi:10.1016/j.compeleceng.2016.08.008

Linn, M. C., & Clancy, M. J. (1992). The case for case studies of programming problems. *Communications of the ACM, 35*(3), 121–133. doi:10.1145/131295.131301

Maloof, M. A. (2006). *Machine learning and data mining for computer security: methods and applications.* Springer. doi:10.1007/1-84628-253-5

McCorduck, P. (2004). *Machines who think.* Academic Press.

Moravec, H. (1988). *Mind children: The future of robot and human intelligence.* Harvard University Press.

Morgan, K. A. (2000). *Myth and Philosophy from the Presocratics to Plato.* Cambridge University Press. doi:10.1017/CBO9780511482540

Muhammad, W., & Aramvith, S. (2019). Multi-Scale Inception Based Super-Resolution Using Deep Learning Approach. *Electronics (Basel), 8*(8), 892. doi:10.3390/electronics8080892

Ren, S., He, K., Girshick, R., & Sun, J. (2015). *Faster r-cnn: Towards real-time object detection with region proposal networks.* Paper presented at the Advances in neural information processing systems.

Russell, S. J., & Norvig, P. (2016). *Artificial intelligence: a modern approach.* Pearson Education Limited.

Samuel, A. L. (1988). *Some studies in machine learning using the game of checkers. II—recent progress. In Computer Games I* (pp. 366–400). Springer.

Struijk, B. (2012). A new understanding of modern robotics. *Hadmérnök, 7*(2).

Tekalp, A. M., & Tekalp, A. M. (1995). Digital video processing (Vol. 1). Prentice Hall.

Thomas, T., Vijayaraghavan, A. P., & Emmanuel, S. (2020). *Machine Learning and Cybersecurity. In Machine Learning Approaches in Cyber Security Analytics* (pp. 37–47). Springer.

Underwood, M. (1977). Machines that understand speech. *Radio and Electronic Engineer, 47*(8), 368–376. doi:10.1049/ree.1977.0055

Voss, P. (2007). *Essentials of general intelligence: The direct path to artificial general intelligence. In Artificial general intelligence* (pp. 131–157). Springer. doi:10.1007/978-3-540-68677-4_4

Woolgar, S. (1985). Why not a sociology of machines? The case of sociology and artificial intelligence. *Sociology, 19*(4), 557–572. doi:10.1177/0038038585019004005

Chapter 12
Emotion Recognition With Facial Expression Using Machine Learning for Social Network and Healthcare

Anju Yadav

ⓘD https://orcid.org/0000-0001-7725-1025
Manipal University Jaipur, India

Venkatesh Gauri Shankar
Manipal University Jaipur, India

Vivek Kumar Verma
Manipal University Jaipur, India

ABSTRACT

In this chapter, machine learning application on facial expression recognition (FER) is studied for seven emotional states (disgust, joy, surprise, anger, sadness, contempt, and fear) based on FER describing coefficient. FER has many practical importance in various area like social network, robotics, healthcare, etc. Further, a literature review of existing machine learning approaches for FER is discussed, and a novel approach for FER is given for static and dynamic images. Then the results are compared with the other existing approaches. The chapter also covers additional related issues of applications, various challenges, and opportunities in future FER. For security-based face detection systems that can identify an individual, in any form of expression he introduces himself. Doctors will use this system to find the intensity of illness or pain of a deaf and dumb patient. The proposed model is based on machine learning application with three types of prototypes, which are pre-trained model, single layer augmented model, and multi-layered augmented model, having a combined accuracy of approx. 99%.

DOI: 10.4018/978-1-7998-3095-5.ch012

INTRODUCTION

Facial expression recognition have various applications in different areas of social networks and in other fields as well (Tian et.al., 2001; Mao et.al., 2015). The prime objective of the model is to be able to identify the emotions of the subjects based on facial expressions with a good accuracy. The models that exist today give lower accuracies when it comes to identifying angry and fearful expressions (Li et.al., 2013b). This chapter will be focusing on improving the accuracies of all the scheduled emotions including anger and fear from users facial expression and thus we aim to identify whether to patient is satisfied with the assigned doctor or not.

There are a total of 7 defined classes for the expressions which are shown as follows:

Class 0: Angry,   Class 1: Disgust,   Class 2: Fear,   Class 3: Happy,   Class 4: Sad,   Class 5: Surprise
        Class 6: Neutral (Ratliff &Patterson, 2008b).

Figure 1. defined classes for the expressions

Motivation and Problem Statement:

Emotion recognition using facial detection has got valuable attention because of its many applications in marketing, call center systems, employee satisfaction management system etc (Ogiela & Tadeusiewicz, 2008a). Despite significant progress, state of the art emotion detection systems only yield suitable enactment under measured circumstances and significantly degrade when faced with real-world applications (Koelstra & Patras, 2013a). That's why AI and machine learning are rising and in demand these days, we wanted to do a project in this area. Also, as far as PSMS is concerned patients usually hesitate to tell whether they are satisfied with their doctor or not. So this will help to correct the problem.

Objectives

Facial expressions having a vital role in emotional perception and are imported in the nonverbal interaction system as well as in the identification of individuals. In everyday emotional interaction, they are very necessary, just next to the tone of voice. Therefore, our research aims to read the emotion of the user from his/her facial expression. PSMS is patient management satisfaction system in which we aim to identify whether the patient is happy from his/her assigned doctor.

BACKGROUND

Conceptual Overview

A convolutional neural network (CNN or ConvNet) is a type of neural networks, usually used for analysis of visual images.

CNNs are multilayer perceptron's regularized models. Multilayer perceptron usually refers to networks that are entirely connected, i.e. each neuron in one layer is linked to all neurons in the next layer. These networks "full connectivity" makes them predisposed to over-fitting data. Many types of regularization adding to the loss function some form of weight measurement of magnitude (Sankar et.al., 2018a). However, CNNs take a different approach to regularization: using smaller and simpler patterns, they take advantage of the data hierarchy arrangement and accumulate more complex patterns (Devi et.al., 2020a).

Therefore, CNNs are at the lower extreme on the scale of connectivity and complexity. These are also known as Artificial Neural Networks (SIANN) shift invariant or space invariant, based on the characteristics of their mutual invariance in design and translation. CNNs were encouraged by natural processes in that the pattern of connectivity between neurons is similar to the visual cortex of the animal. Many restricted region of the pictorial field known as the receptive field, different cortical neurons respond to incitements. Different neurons ' receptive fields partially overlap to concealment the whole field of vision.

Comparison with the other algorithms for object identification, CNNs use very little pre-processing. This ensures that the network knows about the filters in conventional algorithms that were hand-crafted. An important advantage in feature development is this freedom from previous knowledge and human effort.

Multi-Layered CNN

For better and efficient accuracy, we have added two more layers of max pooling to our CNN model Max pooling- Max pooling is an efficient sample based discretization process with the aim of sampling an input illustration (output matrix, image, hidden-layer etc.), decreasing its dimensional and allowing conventions to be created about features in binned sub-regions. This is done partly by providing the representation with an abstract form to help over fit. It also minimizes the cost of computing by reducing the number of parameters to be learned and provides basic invariance of translation for the internal representation (Goel et.al., 2020b). Dropout-Dropout is a Google patented regularization technique to reduce over fitting in neural networks by preventing complex co-adjustments to training data. It is a very efficient way to use neural networks to perform model average. The term "dropout" refers to the removal of units in a neural network (both hidden and visible) (Soni et.al., 2019b).

Technologies Used

Jupyter Notebook

Jupyter Notebook is a collaborative web based programming background aimed to generate Jupyter notebook structure. The term "notebook" may refer colloquially to a number of different units, primarily the Jupyter web based presentation, Jupyter based Python client servers, or Jupyter file format depending on background. A Jupyter Notebook file is a JSON database which follows a typed schema and includes a well-ordered list of input and output cells that may have code, text (by Markdown), maths, graphs, and documents file, mainly ending with ".ipynb" file extension. A Jupyter file will be convert with the "Download As" interface, the nbconvert library or the "jupyter nbconvert" shell CMD interface to a number of standard open output formats (PDF, ReStructuredText, Markdown, Python, HTML, presentation slides). NbViewer provides the nbconvert library as a tool that will take an URL to any public JN file, convert it to HTML on the NB file, and show it to the user, to simplify the visualization of Jupyter notebook documents on the internet.

Python

Python is a language of comprehension programming, high level, general purpose, and developed by Guido Rossum and first available in 1991, Python has a design library that based on code visibility, utilizing considerable white space in specific (Devi et.al., 2019a). It delivers that it can enable both small based and large scaled based programming language. Until July 2018, Van Rossum headed this programming family (Shankar et.al., 2018b). This provisions several programming standards, including programming methods, object oriented, and functions. Python has a widespread robust standard library and is graded as "excluding batteries."

EXPERIMENTAL SETUP

Face recognition have lots of application in various different areas. Some of the application are listed as follows:

1. Payments: Online shopping and various different payment mode are based on selfie app. Recently Master Card is launched that app to do the payment in UK.
2. Security and access: In mobile phone or in home for security we will consider password based on face. So there are lots of applications where we can use this concept to improve the security.
3. Criminal Detection: The recognition of face is also important in identification of criminal or detect their face from the crowd of peoples.
4. Advertising: By seeing the faces of the customer whether it is female or male companies will send the advertisements of related products, these are called as targeted oriented advertisements.
5. Healthcare: Doctor can identify illness of their patients by looking of their expression. How the patient is feeling and seriousness of the disease. This will work mostly for the Telemedicine or in virtual consultancy.

Some of the applications we have already discussed for face recognition but there are lot of challenges as well which are discussed as follows:

1.   Pose variations:

In changing the point of views of camera lead to rotation of the angle of face. Such type of variation will may change the facial expression as well and sometime recognize wrong faces. For such type of case it is difficult to design the algorithm.

Figure 2. Pose Variations

2.   Presence or absence of structuring elements:

In some cases if the person wear glasses or cap the face will change or have beard or moustache. Such type of cases face recognition is difficult.

3.   Facial expression changes:

In some cases facial expression will totally changes or as we know we will consider seven case to recognize the expression. But some time peoples will make an expression that will give wrong result.

4.   Ageing of the face:

In some cases, if the aged people is considered the expressions of the faces will concludes wrong result. Even if we identify the face it is very difficult to conclude.

5.   Poor resolution of an image: If resolution is not clear, face recognition is not possible or if done will not give right results?

Detailed Methodology That Will be Adopted

- Image Acquisition: Images used for facial expression recognition will be of static nature. The webcam will be used to capture the images.
- Feature Extraction: This is the most important part of Facial Emotion Recognition. The image will be converted into grayscale matrix. The matrix will be used to identify the emotion of the subject.
    - Classification: a classifier conducts the categorization of language. The six prototypical expressions refer to joy, sorrow, surprise, rage, fear, and disgust emotional states.
    - Post-processing: The aim of post-processing is to improve accuracy of recognition by using domain knowledge to correct errors in classification.

- Statistical analysis: A monthly based analysis will be done on the patients to know about their overall emotions.

In figure 3, The block diagram is given which is divided in two steps training data and test data. In step 1, initially data sampling is done, on that data emotion test and feature extraction is performed. Further their results is transferred to next step in which discriminant analysis id done. Finally, discriminant classification function is applied. The output of step 1 process is passed to step 2 where feature are extracted from the new data sampling that is performed on test data. After feature extraction discriminant classification function is applied from which emotions are recognized.

Figure 3. Circuit Layouts / Block Diagrams

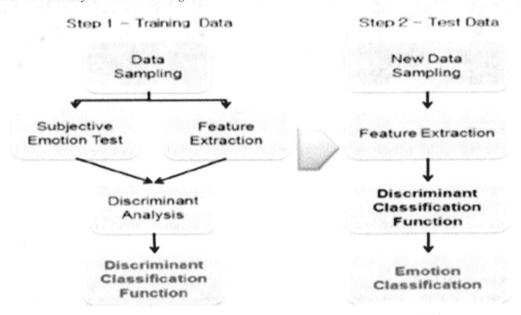

IMPLEMENTATION AND RESULT

Accuracy and Loss Curves

We had created 2 models. One, a normal CNN model and the other with data augmentation and multiple layers. Data augmentation is a methodology that empowers professionals to essentially expand the assorted variety of information accessible for preparing models, without really gathering new information. Information enlargement systems, for example, trimming, cushioning, and even flipping are regularly used to prepare enormous neural systems. Expectations to learn and adapt are a broadly utilized demonstrative device in AI for calculations that gain from a preparation dataset steadily. The model can be assessed on the preparation dataset and on a hold out approval dataset after each update during preparing and plots of the deliberate exhibition can made to show expectations to absorb data as well as information.

Model 1

Training accuracy for our first model comes out to be around 75% while the validation accuracy is around 60%. Right now model has a precision of ~75% on the preparation set and ~60% on the approval set. This implies you can anticipate that your model should perform with ~60% precision on new information. We notice that accuracy metric increments, while validation accuracy metric declines.

The model fails to decrease the validation loss. Training loss is around 0.6 and the validation loss is around 1.4.

Figure 4. Model-1 Processing

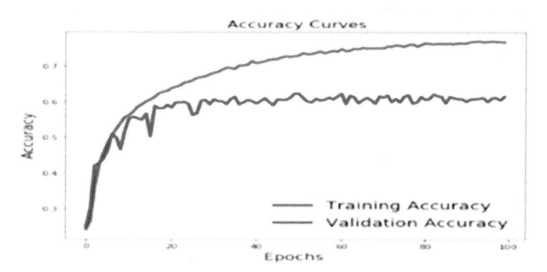

Figure 5. Model-1 Accuracy

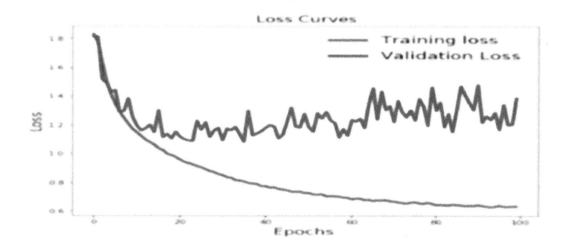

The difference between test and train accuracy is a clear case of over fitting. Overfitting is a demonstrating mistake that happens when a capacity is excessively firmly fit to a restricted arrangement of information focuses. Overfitting the model for the most part appears as making an excessively mind boggling model to clarify eccentricities in the information under examination. To overcome that we used data augmentation and the results are as follows:

Model 2

Training accuracy as well as validation accuracy for our second augmented model comes out to be around 60%. Clearly, we have eliminated over fitting.

It is clearly visible that the validation loss has decreased drastically. Training loss is at 1.1 and validation loss is 1.2 which is better than the earlier loss of 1.4.

Figure 6. Model-2 Processing

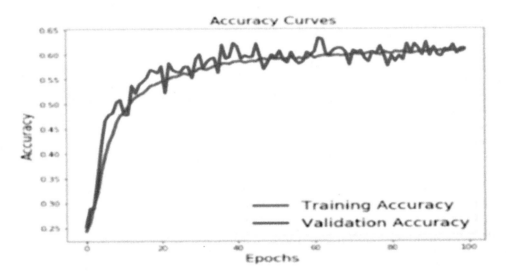

Figure 7. Model-2 Accuracy

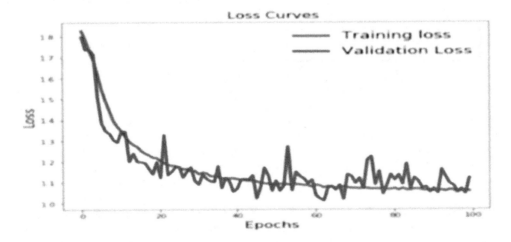

Prototype

The complete comparison of 2 of our models and the reference model that we took from the internet naming 'fer2013_mini_XCEPTION.99-0.65' are as follows:

Figure 8. Proposed Work Prototype

Images	Pre trained model (fer2013_mini_XCEPTION.99-0.65)	Single layered non-augmented model	Multi layered model with augmentation
 (Happy)	99.91%	85.94%	99.99%
 (Surprise)	75.55%	60.33%	99.88%
 (Angry)	72.55%	Wrong emotion shown(happy)	99.32%

FUTURE WORK AND CONCLUSION

In many security applications, that will identify a person, in any usage of expression he expresses himself, this work can also be done using our analysis. Rooms in homes, once they enter the room, may set the lights, TV to the taste of a person. Doctors will be use this system to find the intensity of illness or pain of a deaf and dumb patient. Proposed model is based on Machine Learning Application with three type of prototype, which are pre trained model, single layer augmented model and multi layered augmented model. All models has given an accuracy as approx. 99%. In the end our research with the help of traditional pen and paper feedback system can really know about how a patient feels about the services of the doctor.

REFERENCES

Devi, B., Kumar, S., & Anuradha, S. V. G. (2019a). AnaData: A novel approach for data analytics using random forest tree and SVM. *Computing, communication and signal processing. Advances in intelligent systems and computing, 810.*

Devi, B., Shankar, V. G., Srivastava, S., & Srivastava, D. K. (2020a). *AnaBus: A Proposed Sampling Retrieval Model for Business and Historical Data Analytics* (Vol. 1016). Data Management, Analytics and Innovation. Advances in Intelligent Systems and Computing.

Goel, V., Jangir, V., & Shankar, V. G. (2020b). *DataCan: Robust Approach for Genome Cancer Data Analysis* (Vol. 1016). Data Management, Analytics and Innovation. Advances in Intelligent Systems and Computing.

Koelstra, S., & Patras, I. (2013a). Fusion of facial expressions and EEG for implicit affective tagging. *Image and Vision Computing, 31*(2), 164–174. doi:10.1016/j.imavis.2012.10.002

Li, B. Y. L., Mian, A. S., Liu, W., & Krishna, A. (2013b). Using Kinect for face recognition under varying poses, expressions, illumination and disguise. *IEEE Workshop on Applications of Computer Vision (WACV)*, 186–192. 10.1109/WACV.2013.6475017

Mao, Q., Pan, X., Zhan, Y., & Shen, X. (2015). Using Kinect for real-time emotion recognition via facial expressions. *Frontiers Inf Technol Electronic Eng, 16*(4), 272–282. doi:10.1631/FITEE.1400209

Ogiela, M. R., & Tadeusiewicz, R. (2008a). Pattern recognition, clustering and classification applied to selected medical images. *Studies in Computational Intelligence, 84*, 117–151. doi:10.1007/978-3-540-75402-2_6

Ratliff, M. S., & Patterson, E. (2008b). Emotion recognition using facial expressions with active appearance models. *Proceedings of the Third IASTED International Conference on Human Computer Interaction*, 138–143.

Shankar, V. G., Devi, B., & Srivastava, S. (2018a). DataSpeak: Data extraction, aggregation, and classification using big data novel algorithm. *Computing, communication and signal processing. Advances in intelligent systems and computing, 810.*

Shankar, V. G., Jangid, M., Devi, B., & Kabra, S. (2018b). Mobile big data: Malware and its analysis. *Proceedings of First International Conference on Smart System, Innovations and Computing. Smart Innovation, Systems and Technologies, 79*, 831–842.

Soni, S., Shankar, V. G., & Chaurasia, S. (2019b). Route-The Safe: A Robust Model for Safest Route Prediction Using Crime and Accidental Data. International Journal of Advanced Science and Technology, 28(16).

Tian, Y. I., Kanade, T., & Cohn, J. F. (2001). Recognizing action units for facial expression analysis. *IEEE Transactions on Pattern Analysis and Machine Intelligence, 23*(2), 97–115. doi:10.1109/34.908962 PMID:25210210

Chapter 13
Text Separation From Document Images:
A Deep Learning Approach

Priti P. Rege
ⓘ https://orcid.org/0000-0003-0584-5208
Government College of Engineering, Pune, India

Shaheera Akhter
ⓘ https://orcid.org/0000-0001-6313-3933
Government College of Engineering, Pune, India

ABSTRACT

Text separation in document image analysis is an important preprocessing step before executing an optical character recognition (OCR) task. It is necessary to improve the accuracy of an OCR system. Traditionally, for separating text from a document, different feature extraction processes have been used that require handcrafting of the features. However, deep learning-based methods are excellent feature extractors that learn features from the training data automatically. Deep learning gives state-of-the-art results on various computer vision, image classification, segmentation, image captioning, object detection, and recognition tasks. This chapter compares various traditional as well as deep-learning techniques and uses a semantic segmentation method for separating text from Devanagari document images using U-Net and ResU-Net models. These models are further fine-tuned for transfer learning to get more precise results. The final results show that deep learning methods give more accurate results compared with conventional methods of image processing for Devanagari text extraction.

INTRODUCTION

Development in advanced computers and scanners has increased interest in document image analysis. Fax machines are used to send and receive many documents digitally. Large available memory is used to store document databases. Thus, the thrust is to do more with document images than merely view and

DOI: 10.4018/978-1-7998-3095-5.ch013

print them. OCR is a technique to make a document readable by a machine. OCR is utilized extensively in industries such as finance, banking, healthcare as well as in governmental agencies, and education. Physical books or files stored for long periods can get degraded, destroyed, or damaged. Converting these documents/books into digital copies helps preserve the heritage value associated with them. For example, a large number of old papers/books/documents present in libraries will be replaced digitally by computer files of page images. These digital files then can be searched content-wise and accessed by many people at the same time. Therefore, it is necessary to develop a complete Document Image Analysis System. Before OCR can process a document, the system needs to identify or segment the text present in a document image from the non-text part of the image like tables, figures, graphs, etc. (K. C. Santosh, et. al., 2012; Viet Phuong Le, et al., 2015; Oyebade K. Oyedotun, et. al., 2016). The text separation is essential as the OCR system does not process non-text components. The text part is the central informative part of many applications. Segmenting the text region from the non-text areas of the document image helps in recognition of the extracted text. Researchers have found many solutions to text separation from document images to date (Tran, T., et. al, 2015; Oyebade K. Oyedotun, et. al., 2016).

The main goal of the chapter is to compare methods used to separate or segment text regions from printed Devanagari document images using traditional image processing techniques and different models of deep learning. Conventional methods of image processing discussed in the chapter include preprocessing, features extraction, and text separation methods. On the other hand, deep learning methods involve the use of different models/architecture (U-Net and ResU-Net model) required for semantic segmentation by making use of transfer learning. Deep learning methods learn the features automatically. The segmentation results obtained from deep learning models give better results without handcrafting the features when compared with the conventional methods which require various steps for feature extraction

BACKGROUND

Document text segmentation uses three approaches: top-down, bottom-up, and a hybrid approach. Each of the three approaches, top-down, bottom-up, and hybrid, in turn, consists of three steps: pre-processing, segmentation, and classification or feature extraction. The deep learning approach does not require pre-processing and feature extraction steps. Some work has been carried out using the deep learning approach by making use of Semantic Segmentation. Literature reviewed explains text segmentation using top-down, bottom-up, hybrid, and deep learning approaches.

Top-Down Approach

This approach first detects large-scale features also called the highest level of the structure (like images, columns, etc.) in the input data. Further, it splits the highest-level structure into small segments until it reaches the small-scale features (like individual characters). Thus, top-down methods require prior knowledge of the input image (i.e., document image).

Jean Duong and Hubert Emptoz (2002) sed printed documents to extract features for text separation. They introduced entropic discrimination, which is a simple separation using one feature. Entropy heuristics are used to separate text and non-text areas. The non-text region gives random histograms while the text region gives regular horizontal projection histograms.

R. M. K. Sinha and Veena Bansal (1995) first segmented the text zone of a document image into lines, lines into words and then the words are split into characters. As Devanagari text is composed of complex characters, various algorithms are used to segment the characters/symbols based on their shapes. These segmented symbols are then recognized using multiple features.

T. Perroud and K. Sobottka (2002) ,proposed a color clustering algorithm using a two-method based histogram. The first method considers the RGB color space. The second method finds spatial information along with colors. This approach shows that spatial information has a positive effect on the clustering algorithm. It helps to improve text retrieval in document images.

Sindhuri, M. S., & Anusha, N. (2016) extracted text from document images using Otsu's method. The method is used to segment the lowest intensity object, and the method continues until the darkest part of the image is cleared.

Nandedkar, A. V., Mukhopadhyay, J.,and Sural, S. (2015) detected graphics such as stamps and logos from the scanned document images using spectral filtering-based text-graphics separation. The high spatial frequency component of the text is used to identify the text. Thus, a high-frequency filtering technique is used to separate the text. Further, a segmentation process is applied for portraying the remaining text and graphics. The graphics content is then further divided into two classes i.e. logos and stamps. The proposed method does not require any supervised learning. The overall performance achieved by Nandedkar, A. V., Mukhopadhyay, J., & Sural, S. (2015) is 89.1% for recall and 96.6% precision for their proposed algorithm.

Duan, L., Yuan, B., Wu, C., Li, J., & Guo, Q. (2015) applied Kernel Extreme Learning Machine (kernel-ELM) method for separating text from images to retrieve historic patent documents. The technique has a good optimization constraint and generalization at fast speed. The input document image is first segmented into blocks of images by using segmentation based on 8-connectivity criteria. Each block is used for training the classifier. Training is carried out using a four-class kernel ELM classifier.

Kuo-Chin Fan, Chi-Hwa Liu and Yuan-Kai Wang (1994) utilize domain knowledge to segment text and non-text regions in an image. A run-length smearing operation is performed on the image first, and then a stripe merging procedure segments the text/non-text blocks in the document.

Hung-Ming Sun (2006) proposed a well-known method for document segmentation called Constrained Run-Length Algorithm (CRLA). The algorithm works well on Manhattan layouts but does not perform well on complex layout pages. Its uses only local information during smearing, which is its main drawback and leads to erroneous linkage of text and graphics.

Kuo-Chin Fan, Liang-Shen Wang and Yuan-Kai Wang (1995) proposed a system which does document segmentation and then performed identification of the segmented block. They used novel recursive segmentation to segment a document into several blocks. The blocks are non-overlapping. Later, they extracted the features of the segmented block using a connectivity histogram and multiresolution analysis.

Bottom-Up Approach

Bottom-up methods start with the smallest elements (pixels) and then merge these elements recursively in connected components or regions (characters and words). This approach requires prior knowledge of the input image. It depends on techniques like Region-growing, Connected Component Analysis, Run-Length smoothing methods, and Neighborhood-Line density.

Tran, T. A., Na, I. S., & Kim, S. H. (2015) classified text and non-text parts of the document image using a recursive filter, which is a combination of whitespace analysis and multi-layer homogeneous regions. The binarized input document image is processed through connected component analysis followed by whitespace extraction. Further, a heuristic filter is used to identify the non-text part in the input image. The recursive filter is then applied on the multi-layer homogeneous part of the image to separate the text and non-text regions of the image.

Yuan, Tan (2001) extracted the edges of text in a gray-scaled document image. The edge detector extracts the textual regions from newspaper images which are affected by noise and separates them from the non-text areas. This algorithm further groups the edge points of the text regions using line approximation and layout categorization. Finally, feature-based connected component merging is used to group similar textual areas. Dimitrios Drivas and Adnan Amin (1995) analyzed the use of connected components after extraction from the binarized document image. It proves to be useful in skew correction, classification, and segmentation in document images. Antonacopoulos and Ritchings (1995) proposed a White Tiles approach for page segmentation and classification. Pre-processing is applied to the document image first. Next complete background information of the input image is recorded in terms of a series of tiles called white tiles of varying sizes.

Nikoluos G. Bourbakis (1996) uses the OCR approach to segment text. The document methodology separates text from images by keeping their relationships for a possible reconstruction of the original page. The segmentation and extraction of text depend on a hierarchical framing process. The process starts with recognition of a single character, and continues with framing a word, and ends with a text line. This method can use printed and handwritten document images (suitable for skewed text). The entire image is binarized first. Secondly, a pyramidal form of the input image is generated. As soon as the region in the image detects text/non-text region, the algorithm defines it as the first pyramidal level. Later, it focuses on the upper left corner of the region for identifying text character. Mitchell and Hong Yan (2001) proposed an algorithm for segmenting newspaper documents. The algorithm can detect lines which connect to other components. They use a bottom-up approach. These classified patterns form an entire region, which has loosely connected black pixels. This rectangle has at least one black pixel in every 9 pixels. The locating of boxes involves scanning these 9 pixels - the pattern formed by merging these adjacent rectangles. It generally has a single character or word, depending on style and font, while patterns of non-text regions have various kinds of shapes and sizes.

Hybrid Approach

Top-down and bottom-up methods require high computation; there are many methods which do not even fit into either of these categories and thus, come under hybrid methods. Among such methods are Texture-based, Gabor Filter, etc.

George and Krishnamoorthy (1984) characterized the spatial structure of document images by using two complementary methods. They labeled various logical components without making use of optical character recognition using both top-down and bottom-up methods. Segmentation of a document into rectangles of the contained individual connected component is performed using a bottom-up approach using the knowledge of the generic layout of objects. Both methods use an X-Y tree representation of a document image. An X-Y tree for a document page is generated using recursive segmenting of the horizontal and vertical profile of each block. It has a horizontal projection (on the vertical axis) and a vertical projection (on the horizontal axis) of the array. A block then can be divided into grey and white sub-blocks by segmenting it between the columns or rows using the given profile.

Kyong-Ho Lee et al. (2000) proposed a knowledge-based method that takes the hybrid of top-down and bottom-up techniques. The algorithm consists of two phases: region segmentation and identification. The method splits the segmented region into layout components and identifies the text and non-text regions in the document.

Deep Learning Approach

Deep learning is an end-to-end system that does not require pre-processing or prior knowledge of the input. For segmenting images, deep learning uses semantic segmentation and instance segmentation. Semantic segmentation labels each pixel of the input image with a respective class label while instance segmentation assigns boundaries to the detected object obtained by semantic segmentation. This section explains the text segmentation using semantic segmentation. Deep learning methods have given state-of-the-art results on various applications like image classification, image captioning, segmentation, speech analysis, etc. which are described by B. Zhou et al., (2014) and S. Renet al., (2017). Krizhevsky et al. (2012) explain various reasons for better performance of deep learning. The presence of an activation layer helps to resolve multiple training problems; regularization and different optimization techniques used in training a deep architecture help to avoid overfitting problems. Most of the deep learning models are affected by the vanishing gradient problem due to the intense deep architecture. To avoid this problem, He et al., (2016) introduced a deep residual learning method that added identity mapping. Deep learning provides different models for semantic segmentation. Shelhamer, E., Long, and J. Darrell (2016) proposed Fully Convolutional Neural Network (FCN), which has given a better result on various segmentation tasks. FCN is the basic model for image segmentation.

A deep learning model used for classification consists of an encoding part and maps the outputs of the classification model to class probabilities. The architecture consists of a set of repeated convolution and max-pooling layer (or average pooling layer) followed by the fully connected layer and the output layer. When input traverses the model path, the feature maps of the model increase with a decrease in the number of dimensions. The number of parameters of the model increases as the number of feature maps increases. The encoding is the same as the classification model, while the decoding part has an up-sampling layer followed by a deconvolution layer and finally the segmented output. The parameters in the segmentation model are double when compared to a classification model. Ronneberger et al. (2015) proposed U-Net (a deep learning-based segmentation model) mainly designed for medical image segmentation. This U-Net architecture improves the accuracy of the output by concatenating feature maps from various levels. This concatenation reduces the vanishing gradient problem as it takes features from a higher level. SegNet, proposed by Badrinarayanan et al. (2015) another variant of FCN, is also used for semantic-based segmentation. There are different variants of FCN, depending upon the various applications of image segmentation. ResU-Net, proposed by Zhengxin et al., (2017), was designed to extract the roads from the remote sensing images. U-Net architecture and residual learning inspire the design of ResU-Net. It has residual connections, and the architecture resembles the architecture of U-Net.

Stewart, S., & Barrett, B. (2017) applied the idea of a convolutional neural network (CNN) in document processing to English text. A fully supervised Deep CNN is used to separate the content of document images. The network designed by Stewart, S., & Barrett, B. (2017) consists of downsampling and upsampling layers, which are then used for document segmentation, segmenting the text, figures, and tables in the input image.

Oliveira, S. A., Seguin, B., & Kaplan, F. (2018) addressed the issue of extracting text, baseline, layout and photographs in the document image. They proposed a CNN based model for predicting the output image after segmentation.

Chen, K., Seuret, M., Liwicki, M., Hennebert, J., & Ingold, R. (2015) used an unsupervised approach for feature learning in page segmentation of historical handwritten color document images. Page segmentation is considered as the pixel labeling problem i.e., semantic segmentation that labels each pixel of the input image as background, text, figures, tables, etc. Chen, K. et al. applied a convolutional autoencoder that learns the features automatically. These features are then used to train SVM to get high-quality results.

Belabiod, A., & Belaïd, A. (2018) suggested that extracting lines and words is the most important step before any recognition task. The proposed segmentation of Arabic document images using the deep learning approach. The line is segmented using the RU-net structure, and further, the words are segmented using BLSTM from CNN applied on the segmented line image. Belabiod, A., & Belaïd, A. (2018) tested their results on the KHATT Arabic database. The deep learning model that was designed was able to achieve 96.7% correct lines and 80.1% correct words

Summary

There has not been much work done in OCR research of the Indic script, and even the accuracy level has not been improved compared to the Latin script. Text separation is one of the pre-processing steps of an OCR system. Literature review shows that text separation from the document images can be classified as a top-down approach, bottom-up approach, hybrid technique, and deep learning methods. The first three approaches (i.e., top-down approach, bottom-up approach, and hybrid technology) come under traditional methods for text separation. Literature shows that conventional methods require many steps for hand-coding features and then performing text and non-text segmentation.

On the other hand, deep learning is an end-to-end system. It does not require any pre-processing or hand-coded feature extraction steps and learns features automatically while training. Deep learning has different models for classification, segmentation, object detection, and various other applications. Deep learning gives state-of-the-art results on these applications compared to traditional methods. Text separation with deep learning methods improves accuracy. The literature survey shows that not much work has been done in the field of text separation using image processing and deep learning methods.

METHODS FOR TEXT SEGMENTATION/EXTRACTION

Dataset

The authors have created a dataset for the chapter from different Marathi books. Color images are scanned and cropped to the size of 256x256 in Microsoft Office 2010. There are 1300 images in total in the dataset. The whole dataset of 1300 images is used to train the deep learning models, while the traditional image processing methods require each image to be processed separately.

TRADITIONAL IMAGE PROCESSING METHODS

This section discusses text separation from a Devanagari printed document image using one of the traditional image processing methods proposed by Priti P. Rege and Chanchal A. Chandrakant (2013) (using a top-down approach) on Devanagari document images.

Pre-Processing

1. Key Features of the Implemented Method
   a. It mainly performs two tasks:
      i. To convert the input color image (document image) to a gray-scale image.
      ii. To convert the gray-scale image to a binary image.
   b. Use of Otsu's method for automatically setting the threshold value for binarization.
2. Description of the Method

The methodology used to pre-process the input Devanagari document image is given by Algorithm 1. The first step in the algorithm is the conversion of the input color image to a gray-scale image. The methodology converts three-channel input to a single channel (gray-scale image) with each pixel ranging in value from 0-255. If the input image is not a color image and is a gray-scale image, then it is directly given to the next step. The second step is to convert the gray-scale image obtained in the first step to a binary image. Each pixel in the binary image has a value of either 0 or 1 by applying a specific threshold value. Algorithm 1 uses Otsu's method to get a binary image.

Algorithm 1. Pre-Processing of Document Images

```
Input: Printed Devanagari text document image.
Output: Pre-processed image.
Begin
1. Read the input image.
2. If the image is a color image, convert to a gray-scale image else go to the
next step.
3. Binarize the gray-scale image using Otsu's method of thresholding.
End
```

Results and Discussion

The input color image of size 256x256 is first converted to a gray-scale image. The image is further binarized to separate the foreground pixels in the image from the background pixels by selecting a suitable threshold value. Instead of using a trial and error approach for threshold selection, a well-known method of binarization called Otsu's method is implemented. Otsu's method selects the threshold automatically using an image histogram and separates foreground and background pixels by maximizing the discriminate measure. Thus, an optimum threshold is obtained. Figures 1(a)and (b) show the original document image with Devanagari text and, Figure 1(b) is the binary image for the given input. The binary image has sharp characters compared to the original text. Different images are used for the various results in the chapter.

Figure 1. (a) Original Image (b)Binary image

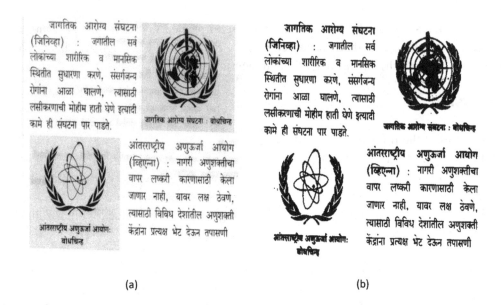

(a)   (b)

BLOCK EXTRACTION

Key Features of the Implemented Method

Essential features of the method are:

a.   Extraction of meaningful blocks; either a text word or a figure in the image which can be easily recognized by human beings.
b.   Grouping the pixels belonging to the same block using a smearing method (Run-length Smearing Algorithm (RLSA))
c.   Combination of horizontal and vertical smearing operations using RLSA and a logical AND operation to produce meaningful blocks.

Description of the Method

RLSA is used to extract blocks of text and non-text part of the document image. This method is specially used for document analysis and is divided into two parts. First, segmentation is applied, which divides the area of the image into blocks or regions. These regions will contain either text or an image. Secondly, the features of each block are used to classify the content of the block (i.e., text or non-text). RLSA is applied only on the binary input sequence. '0' represents the background pixels, and '1' represents the foreground part. The algorithm converts the binary sequence of the input to output by the following rule:

a.   0's in the data are changed to 1's in the production when the count of adjacent 0's is not more than the defined limit C.
b.   1's in the input remain unchanged in the output.

The value of C helps to link the region belonging to the same data type. Thus, RLSA can tie together neighboring pixels separated by less than C pixels. The RLSA algorithm applies vertical and horizontal smearing operations on the document image. It creates two distinct bit-maps; these bitmaps, combined with a logical AND operation result in the final segmentation. Sometimes additional smoothing using RLSA is applied to get more accurately segmented results.

Algorithm 2. Pre-processing of Document Images

```
Input: Pre-processed image.
Output: Block extracted image.
Begin
1. Initialize the pre-processed binary image and the threshold value for hori-
zontal and vertical smearing operations as CHer and CVer to 4 and 2 respec-
tively.
2. Compute horizontal smearing operation on the binarized image.
3. Start with the first row in the image and count the number of 0's and 1's
in the first row sequentially.
a) If (count number of 0's in input image <CHer = 4)
change the 0's to 1's in the output
else
keep as the sequence unchanged
b) 1's in the input remain unchanged in the output.
For example, for the following binary input sequence, the output sequence will
be as shown below (for C = 4):
Input: 0 0 0 1 0 0 0 0 0 1 0 1 0 0 0 0 1 0 0 0 0 0 0 0 1 1 0 0 0
Output: 1 1 1 1 0 0 0 0 0 1 1 1 1 1 1 1 1 0 0 0 0 0 0 0 1 1 1 1 1
4. Continue step 3 for every row in the image to create a horizontal bitmapped
image.
5. Compute the vertical smearing operation on the pre-processed binary image
with the same method defined in step 3 and continue the action for every col-
umn.
6. Create another bitmapped image using a vertical smearing operation.
7. Combine the bitmapped images obtained in step 4 and 6 by a logical AND op-
eration to produce meaningful blocks.
8. Set the threshold value (CHersm and CVersm) to 5, for both, the additional
horizontal and vertical smearing operations.
9. Compute horizontal and vertical smearing operations on the resulting image
obtained by the logical AND operation.
10. Combine the two images to obtain the resultant block extracted image.
End
```

Results and Discussion

The binarized image obtained after the pre-processing step has either 1 (white) or 0 (black) as the pixel values. Horizontal and vertical RLSA groups the pixels of the binarized image, belonging to the same block. During the horizontal smearing operation, the threshold value is set as 4 (Cher = 4). If the number of 0's between 1's in the binarized image is less than or equal to 4, then the 0 is replaced by 1. A similar operation is carried out during the vertical smearing operation with the threshold value of 2 (CVer = 2). The horizontal and vertical run smearing is performed row-by-row and column-by-column respectively. The results of both the operation are ANDed to get the final extracted blocks. The processes are repeated if the blocks are not properly extracted. Figures 2 (a) and (b) illustrate the image after additional application of horizontal and vertical RLSA. The final result of this task is obtained after a logical AND operation on the horizontal and vertical RLSA results. This results in meaningful blocks of either the text or the non-text part of the document image, as shown in Figure. 3. The text and the non-text part are separated successfully.

Figure 2. (a) Bitmapped image after final horizontal smearing operation (b)Bitmapped image after final vertical smearing operation

(a)　　　　　　　　　　(b)

BOUNDARY/PERIMETER DETECTION

Key Features of the Implemented Method

Essential features of the method are:

a.　Detect the boundary of the extracted block.
b.　Denote the boundary by black pixels and the content of the block by white pixels

Figure 3. Block extraction image

1. Description of the Method

The 4-connectivity method helps to detect the boundary of the extracted blocks. The pixels surrounding the extracted block form the boundary of the respective block. Thus, the white pixels that are surrounding the extracted block are the outside boundary. Edge detection techniques are unable to obtain boundary detection as it results in an open contour if applied on a one-pixel width line block. The perimeter of the border may contain some pixels which are not present on the edge. Connectivity helps to join those pixels and detect the proper boundary of the blocks extracted.

Algorithm 3. Boundary/Perimeter Extraction

```
Input: Block extracted document image.
Output: Perimeter/Boundary detected output.
Begin
1. Initialize the block extracted image.
2. Calculate and find the mean length of horizontal black runs in the block
```

```
extracted image, which represents the text/non-text regions in the image.
3. Find the perimeter of pixels of the objects in the image which gives the
boundary of the input image.
End
```

Results and Discussion

The extracted blocks of the image have grouped pixels. Each group represents a region in the image, which can be text or non-text. A group of black pixels represents the content of the image, and the white group represents background. While moving horizontally across the image, it is easy to find the presence of the text/non-text regions in the image. The boundaries of the block are the white pixel values that surround the black extracted area. 4 connectivity connects the boundary of the area, and the perimeter of the boundary is calculated. Figure 4 shows the boundary separated image from the block extracted input image.

Figure 4. Boundary/Perimeter detection on block extracted image

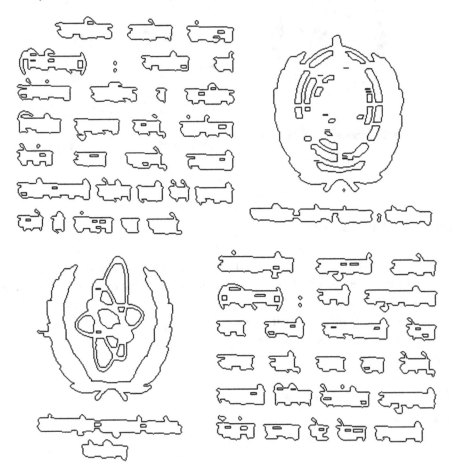

CONNECTED COMPONENT, AREA COMPUTATION, AND TEXT SEPARATION

Key Features of the Implemented Method

Essential features of this method are:

a.   To find the connected components of the boundary extracted part of the image.
b.   To calculate the area of the close-loop after boundary/perimeter detection.
c.   To separate/segment the text after finding the closed area.

Description of the Method

The connected component method helps to find the boxes around the distinct regions of connected black pixels in the document image and computes the area of the box. This area is uniform and helps to fill the zeros in a smaller space. ORing the original image and the image filled by zeros results in the image with the entire text separated from the original image.

Algorithm 4. Text Separation

```
Input: Perimeter/boundary detected of blocks in a document image.
Output: Text extracted image.
Begin
1. Initialize the perimeter detected image for text separation.
2. Find the connected component in the image as:
a) Scan the image pixels and assign a label to the pixels which are non-zero
and record these label equivalences in a union-find table.
b) Use the union-find algorithm to resolve the equivalence classes.
c) Based on resolved equivalence classes, relabel the pixels.
3. Compare the area of the closed-loop which has the uniform stripes formed by
run-length smearing, with the open-loop area
4. Fill zeros in a smaller space.
5. OR the image from step 4 with the original image to get text separated out-
put image.
End
```

Results and Discussion

The area inside the boundary of the extracted block is not uniform, as there can be some white (1's) pixel values. The area within the boundary is made uniform by connecting the components and filling the zeros. Figure 5 (a) illustrates the connected component algorithm, and Figure 5 (b) shows an image filled with zeros in the extracted CC blocks. If the zero-filled area is ORed with the Original binary image, then all the text in the image is separated from the original document images. Figure 6 gives the text extracted document image. The final result shows that the text has been extracted successfully from the input document image.

Figure 5. (a)Image obtained after connected components. (b) Image after filling the corresponding area with zeros

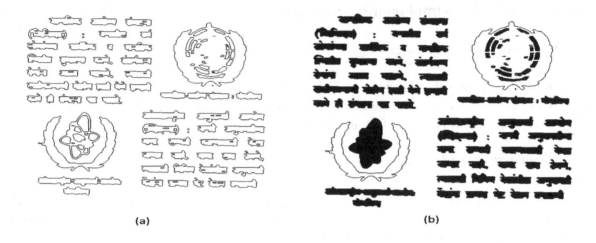

(a)   (b)

Figure 6. Text extracted image

जागतिक आरोग्य संघटना
(जिनिव्हा) : जगातील सर्व
लोकांच्या शारीरिक व मानसिक
स्थितीत सुधारणा करणे, संसर्गजन्य
रोगांना आळा घालणे, त्यासाठी
लसीकरणाची मोहीम हाती घेणे इत्यादी
कामे ही संघटना पार पाडते.

जागतिक आरोग्य संघटना : बोधचिन्ह

आंतरराष्ट्रीय अणुऊर्जा आयोग:
बोधचिन्ह

आंतरराष्ट्रीय अणुऊर्जा आयोग
(व्हिएन्ना) : नागरी अणुशक्तीचा
वापर लष्करी कारणासाठी केला
जाणार नाही, यावर लक्ष ठेवणे,
त्यासाठी विविध देशांतील अणुशक्ती
केंद्रांना प्रत्यक्ष भेट देऊन तपासणी

DEEP LEARNING METHODS

This section discusses text separation from a Devanagari printed document image using deep learning methods. Deep learning methods for text extraction help improve the accuracy of the Devanagari document recognition.

Deep Learning Architectures

Deep learning originated from the concept of artificial neural network (ANN). An excellent example of the models with deep architectures is the multilayer perceptron with many hidden layers. An example of deep learning architecture is shown in Figure 7 (Afshine Amidi and Shervine Amidi, 2018). The input layer varies depending on applications. It can be a speech signal, an array of features, an image, a sequence of text, etc. The output layer also varies with the application to be performed. The number of hidden layers can be one or more depending on how deep the model should be. Various factors including calculations of complicated theoretical results, machine learning experiments and inspiration from the human brain and its cognition led to the use of deep learning architectures. Deep learning finds applications in various types of problems in vision, language, real-time systems, and other Machine Learning (ML) tasks.

Figure 7. An example of deep learning architecture (Afshine Amidi and Shervine Amidi, 2018)

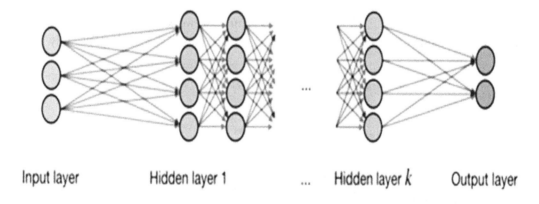

Input layer   Hidden layer 1   ...   Hidden layer k Output layer

Each neuron in the hidden layer of the deep architecture is associated with a non-linear operation and a weight which results in millions of parameters in the entire deep network. Each stage in the architecture extracts features, i.e., the model has an abstract/latent representation of the input at each level of the architecture. The starting stage in the architecture has low-level features, and the ending stage has high-level features of the data. This abstract/latent representation of the input is independent of the type of input considered (either speech, image, structured data, etc.).

The framework to train deep architecture depends on the six elements: Data, tasks, models, loss functions, learning algorithm, and evaluation. For any deep architecture, the necessary and most important part is the dataset preparation. Deep models are data-hungry, and the datasets are application-specific. The more the data there is, the more accurate the model is. After dataset preparation, next comes the 'task' to apply on the dataset (like activity recognition, image classification, segmentation, speech recognition, etc.). The task application on the model depends on the type of dataset (i.e., unsupervised, supervised, regression, and generation). A good model is needed for the task to be successful. An appropriate loss function then trains the model. Every model requires a learning algorithm to optimize the training of the model. Various learning algorithms available for optimization are Back Propagation (BP), Back Propagation Through Time (BPTT), Adagard, Adam, RMSProp, AdaDelta, etc. After training the model, it is necessary to evaluate the model on the test data. This step completes the training and testing of a deep architecture.

Selection of the Network for Segmentation

There are various deep models like classification model, regression model, and an encoder-decoder model and their implementation is available for different applications and tasks. The classification model predicts the class of the input data like image, speech, text, and non-text. The regression model helps to predict the continuous value for the given input features. And an encoder-decoder model generally encodes the input sequence to an abstract/latent representation called 'context' at the encoder side, which is then used by the decoder to generate the output sequence. The first consideration in the selection of these models is to identify if the dataset is supervised, unsupervised, or semi-supervised. The next thing to do is to decide which model to use for the specific task/application. Feed Feedforward Neural Network (FFNN) can be used to solve a regression problem, for example, for estimating the duration of a taxi for a trip. The model can also be used for a classification task, for example, to find out whether a person has cancer or not depending on the features given as input to FFNN. Figure 7 (*Afshine Amidi and Shervine Amidi, 2018*) is a basic architecture of FFNN. Convolutional Neural Network (CNN) is used for classification of the image input (whether the given image is of a dog or cat) (see Figure 8 Katy W., July 2019).

Figure 8. A typical CNN architecture (Katy W., July 2019)

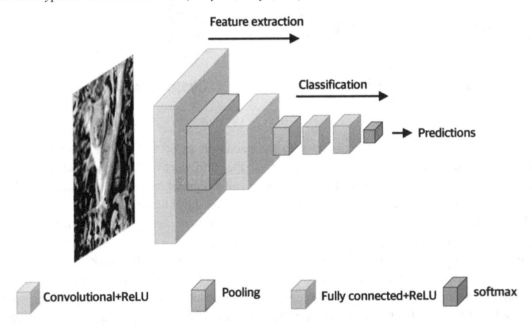

Recurrent Neural Network (RNN) model is the most suitable model to handle sequential data like the text used in Natural Language Processing. FFNN, CNN, and RNN are encoder models, i.e. they do not have the decoder part. For the application of segmentation, it is necessary to use the encoder-decoder type of model so that the output image has the same size as the input with segmented results. Thus, depending on the application, one can choose which model is best suited to the task. For segmentation, an encoder-decoder model using a combination of CNN, FFNN, and RNN model is desirable.

Semantic Segmentation

Image segmentation is defined as dividing or partitioning an image into meaningful regions/segments. These segments are sets of pixels related to some objects, also called super-pixels. The method defines a boundary around objects present in the image by assigning a label to each pixel in the image to be segmented. Tags that have the same features are connected and grouped to define an object. Figure 9 (Saurabh Pal, 2019) shows a segmented image.

Figure 9. (a) Input image (b) Semantic Segmentation (c) Instance Segmentation (Saurabh Pal, 2019)

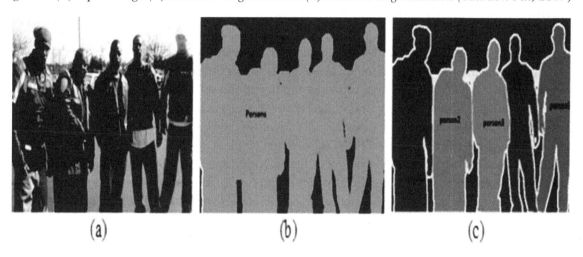

Semantic segmentation and instance segmentation are two classes of Image Segmentation. Semantic segmentation is the most classic version (2017) in which each pixel of the input image assigns a class label (supervised task). .Instance segmentation, on the other hand, detects objects in the segmented result. This chapter uses semantic segmentation for text separation from document images.

Semantic segmentation progresses from fine to coarse inference and then again from coarse to fine inference. This progression map is in the form of an encoder-decoder model. The encoder part generates coarse output from the fine input given to the model for segmentation. This part is similar to the classification model used in deep learning. It helps in predicting the content in the image. The next step comprises localization/detection. It helps to provide the information of the labeled classes and also helps to detect the spatial location of the classes in the image for segmentation. The final part is the semantic segmentation, which generates dense prediction defining the labels for every pixel, resulting in a segmented output. The decoder part constitutes of localization and semantic segmentation of the model. Figure 10 (Mathworks, 2018) shows the basic model for segmentation.

Figure 10. A Deep network architecture for Semantic Segmentation (image taken from MathWorks, 2018)

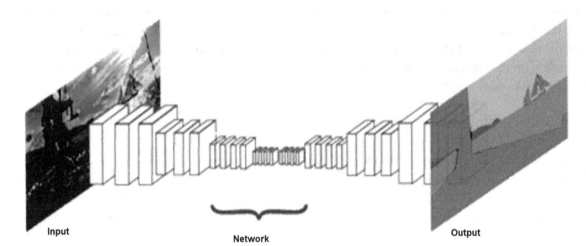

Existing Networks for Semantic Segmentation

A large and growing body of literature has investigated various semantic segmentation deep models applied to multiple applications. Some of them are discussed here. Shelhamer and Long (2015) demonstrated a segmentation task on numerous applications using one of the semantic segmentation models called Fully Convolutional Neural Network (FCN). The network uses a skip connection to avoid the vanishing gradient problem. Other segmentation models are variants of the FCN model. Ronneberger et al. (2015) found U-Net architecture (a variant of FCN) to solve the problem of medical image segmentation. The architecture does not use the skip-connection of the FCN; instead, it has the concatenation of different feature maps from the encoder to the decoder part to improve segmentation accuracy. Another variant of the FCN is SegNet designed by Badrinarayanan et al., (2017) that has a modified network with 13 convolutional layers of VGG16. It also includes the usage of pooling indices in the decoder part of the model for deconvolution. ResU-Net proposed by Zhengxinet al., (2018) is designed for extracting roads from the satellite images and has residual connections.

Transfer Learning Scenarios and Selection in Deep Learning

Humans can transfer knowledge which they learn from one task to some other related job. For example, once a person learns to ride a bike, he/she can learn to ride motorcycle. This task is done by transferring the knowledge acquired/learned from riding a bicycle to learning the motorcycle. Things learned in the past are made use of to learn new things.

The same idea of transferring knowledge is used in Deep Learning. It is called Transfer Learning (TL). Most of the deep learning models are specially designed for specific or particular tasks and domains. These models can give state-of-the-art results with high accuracy on the test data of the assigned task. But it can result in the worst outcome when applied on a new task which has a similar type of dataset. The same model is then rebuilt for the second task. The models also require a lot of data to solve complex problems. The dataset requires considerable effort and time for preparation. For example, ImageNet dataset is a labeled dataset which has millions of images in it. To collect such a dataset for a particular domain is a very tough job. Transfer learning helps to leverage the knowledge of the previously trained model, i.e., pre-trained model on the new problems with either a similar dataset or tasks instead of building an isolated model. The transferred experience/knowledge can either be weights, features, standard models, or pre-trained models and can tackle the problem of creating a large dataset. It speeds up the training of the second task and also improves the performance. Transfer learning is also beneficial when the number of datasets is less. There are various ways which explain the modes to transfer the knowledge of the previously learned task to the new task in deep learning. These modes help to decide the best method for using a transfer learning approach in the respective applications.

MODES IN TRANSFER LEARNING

Pre-Trained Model as a Feature Extractor

A pre-trained model is a network already trained and saved using a large dataset. It is used directly on a new dataset, but the accuracy will not be as good as with the dataset with which it was trained earlier. Thus, a pre-trained model can be used as a feature extractor, and further used by another dataset with higher accuracy. Deep learning architecture is a layered model made of many hidden layers (like CNN, max-pooling, fully connected layer, etc.). The output at each layer represents either a low-level feature or a high-level feature. The deep model already trained on some dataset for a specific task has learned parameters (i.e., weights). A pre-trained network (such as Inception V3 or VGG) used with another dataset for particular tasks is formed by removing the classification layer of the base model. The classification layer usually is the FC layer or some last hidden layer of the model. The output of the final segment of the pre-trained model is given as input to other classifiers (like SVM, etc.). The dataset used with the pre-trained network is similar to the one with which the model was trained.

Figure 11. Pre-trained model as a feature extractor. (a) The network trained on earlier (b) Network as a feature extractor (Shreya Ghelani, 2019).

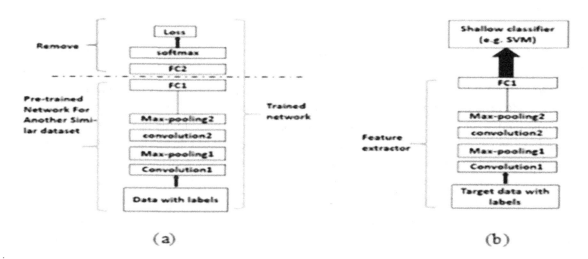

(a) (b)

The model in Figure 11 (a) (Shreya Ghelani, 2019) is already trained on the earlier dataset and the last three layers are removed. The pre-trained model now acts as a feature extractor with trained weights and is connected to another shallow classifier (e.g. SVM). The input from a new dataset is applied to the network as shown in Figure 11 (b) (Shreya Ghelani, 2019) which extracts meaningful features from the samples from a pre-trained network and passes it on to the classifier. The base layers already contain the features that are useful for classifying purpose for another dataset. The model with another dataset is trained using this feature and weights provided from the base model.

Fine Tuning

The input required when training with a pre-trained model should be similar to the dataset input with which the model was trained earlier. In some cases, the input data to the pre-trained network is not what is usable by the network. In such cases, the pre-trained network needs to be fine-tuned. For fine-tuning, the weights of the initial layer of the base model are frozen, and the fine-tuning is performed on the last layers attached to the pre-trained model. Or, fine-tuning uses the entire model, which is initialized with pre-trained weights, and the whole model is fine-tuned. The whole model is tuned when the dataset is different from the dataset used to train the pre-trained network.

METHODOLOGY TO SEPARATE DEVANAGARI TEXT FROM IMAGES USING TRANSFER LEARNING

Key Features of the Implemented Method

Important features of the method are:

a.   To prepare a dataset for text segmentation of Devanagari document images.
b.   To segment the text from the document image using a deep learning and transfer learning approach (semantic segmentation).

Description of the Method

The methodology to separate Devanagari text from document images is given in Algorithm 5 using two base deep learning models called U-Net and ResU-Net. U-Net is used for biomedical image segmentation, and ResU-Net is used to extract roads from satellite images. The task of Devanagari text segmentation is quite different from the task used for training U-Net and ResU-Net. Therefore, fine-tuning of the whole model, which is a mode of transfer learning, is best suited to the task of text segmentation. Figure 12 (Ronneberger, O., Fischer, P., & Brox, T., 2015) shows the architecture of U-Net. It consists of contractive (encoder) and expansive (decoder) paths. The contractive path architecture is similar to that designed for the classification path. The contractive path extracts important features of the input image, which are then given as input to the expansive path. The expansive path has upsampling of the feature maps received from the encoder and deconvolution. It helps to localize and segment the input image. The U-Net model has the concatenation of feature maps from the encoder to the decoder to increase the resolution of the output image. ResU-Net has a similar architecture as that of U-Net with an extra residual connection in the model (Figure13 (Zhang, Z., Liu, Q., & Wang, Y., 2018)).

The residual connections help to train the model fast and avoid the vanishing gradient problem, which occurs in most of the deep learning networks. The following equation gives the residual connection:

$$y_l = h(x_l) + F(x_l, W_l) . x_{l+1} = f(y_l).$$

x_l, x_{l+1} .re the input, $f(y_l)$ .s the activation function, and output to the residual layer at the l-*th* position. $F(.)$ is the residual function of the section and $h(x_l$. is the identity mapping.

Figure 12. U-Net architecture

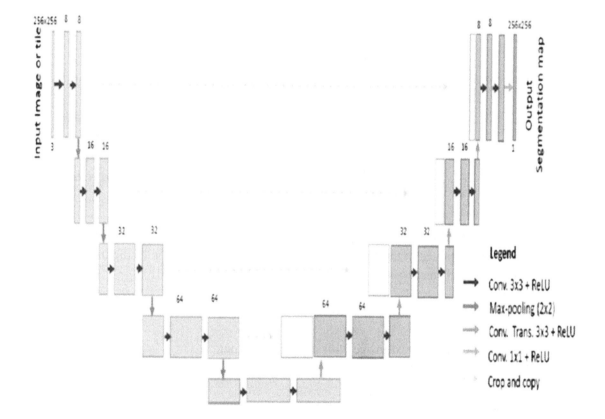

The Number below the box defines the no. of channels (input has three and output has 1). Numbers above the boxes indicate the no. of filters of the convolution layer (or feature maps). The dotted arrow and empty boxes indicate concatenation of the feature map of the encoder with the up-convolution operation of the decoder. Green colored boxes are convolution + BN + ReLU while blue boxes are up-convolution + BN + Relu. And arrows have their meanings mentioned in the figure above. 256x256 is the dimension of input image and mask (Ronneberger, O., Fischer, P., & Brox, T., 2015).

Figure 13. ResU-Net Model architecture

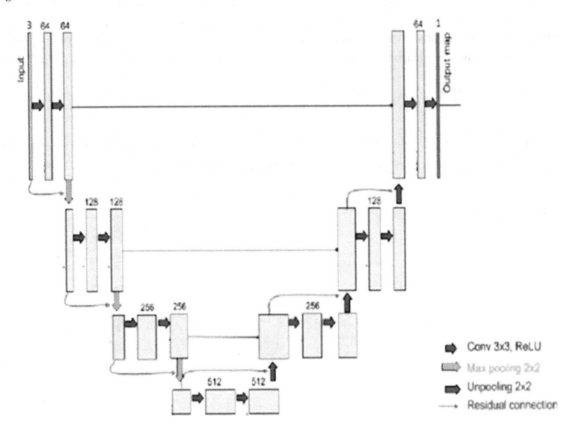

Numbers above the boxes indicate no. of filters of the convolution layer (or feature maps). Arrows have their meanings mentioned in the figure above. 256x256 is the dimension of the input image and mask with 3 and 1 channels respectively (Zhang, Z., Liu, Q., & Wang, Y., 2018)

Algorithm 5. Text Separation using Deep learning base model
    Training
    Input: Dataset of Devanagari text image with segmented output.
    Output: Minimized loss function.

Testing/Validation

Input: Test images of Devanagari text document images.
    Output: Segmented text image.

```
Begin
1. Prepare a dataset for segmentation of text from Devanagari document images.
The dataset requires an input image with the respective segmented output to
train the model.
2. Initialize the weights of the base deep learning model (U-Net and ResU-Net)
```

for transfer learning. As the architecture of both the models is standard, it is pre-designed with different layers.

3. Use loss function as Binary Cross-entropy.

$$binaryCE\left(p,\widehat{p}\right)=-\left(plog\left(\widehat{p}\right)+\left(1-p\right)\log\left(1-\widehat{p}\right)\right)$$

4. Set the hyperparameters:
* Minimum learning rate as 1e-4
* Patience parameter as 3
* Epochs equal to 100
* Batch size is 32
* Dropout as regularization

5. Retrain and compile both the models by using Adam as optimizer (learning rate = 0.001) and metrics using accuracy, precision, recall, and F1 measure.

6. Save the model.

7. Monitor the validation loss, the training loss, and the accuracy of the models.

8. Evaluate the model using the test dataset

9. Plot the training and test accuracies with loss.

End

Results and Discussions

The results on the test dataset obtained after training both the base deep learning models (i.e. U-Net and ResU-Net) are discussed in this section. Semantic segmentation of Devanagari text document images using the second mode of transfer learning (i.e., fine-tuning) is performed and discussed. Fine-tuning of the whole base model is required as the dataset for both models is different from the Devanagari text dataset. Fine-tuning the models, which is a mode of transfer learning, takes less time than learning the network from scratch. U-Net and ResU-Net networks are trained using the training dataset and tested on images other than the training dataset. The result shown in the chapter is on the test dataset. Training any deep learning model requires a lot of time, while testing is completed in a very short amount of time. The encoder part of the model learns the features and parameters of the network, and localizes the features learned by the encoder to generate the output as required. The lower layer of the encoder learns the low-level features like edge detection, etc. As we go deeper into the network, the layers learn the high-level features like localization, etc.

a. U-Net Results

Figures 14 and 15 demonstrate the results of the U-Net after fine-tuning the model to segment text from the Devanagari document images. Figure 1 (a) is the test input image and Figure 15 (b) shows text segmented output image. And Figures 14 (a), (b) and Figure 15 (a) show the U-Net model's feature map visualization at the intermediate layers of the model. Figure 14 (a) is the output of the feature map of the model at the starting layer which indicates the low-level features of the input image. Figure 14 (b) and Figure 15 (a) represent the mid-level and high-level features of the input image respectively.

Figure 14. (a) Low-level feature map of the model, (b) Mid-level feature map of the model

(a)   (b)

Figure 15. (a) Low-level feature map of the model, and (b) Segmented output

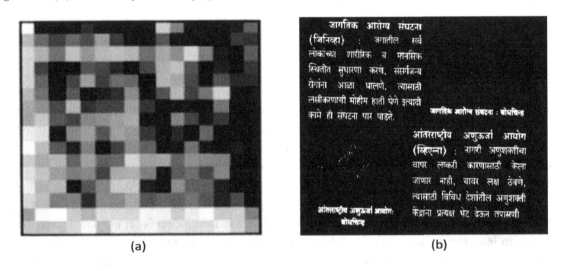

(a)   (b)

Figures 16 (a) and (b) show the graph for accuracy and loss while training and validating the U-Net model on the training and validation datasets respectively

b. ResU-Net Results

Figure 1 (a) and Figure 18 (b) are the input and segmented text output of the input test data on the ResU-Net model after fine-tuning the base model. The segmented output of ResU-Net demonstrates that segmentation is better than the U-Net model due to the presence of the residual connections present in the network. Figures 17 (a), (b), and Figure 18 (a) are the low-level, mid-level and high-level features of the model respectively. This helps to visualize the intermediate layers of the model.

Figures 19 (a) and (b) give quantitative analysis and loss on training and validation datasets respectively.

Figure 16. (a) Quantitative Analysis and (b) Training and Validation Loss of U-Net

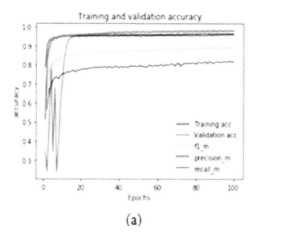

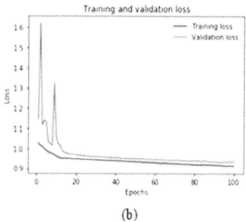

(a)

(b)

Figure 17. (a) Low-level feature map of the model, (b) Mid-level feature map

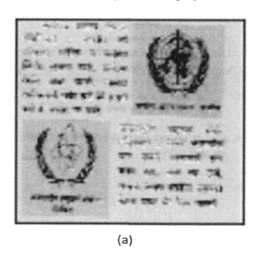

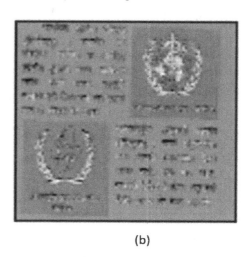

(a)

(b)

Figure 18. (a) High-level feature map of the model, (b) Segmented output

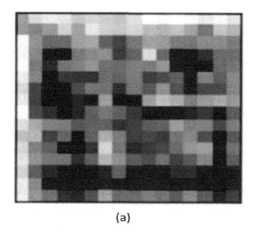

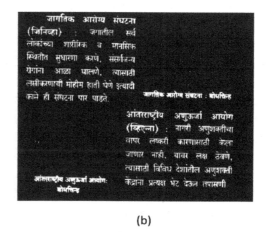

(a)

(b)

Figure 19. (a) Quantitative Analysis and (b) Training and Validation Loss of ResU-Net

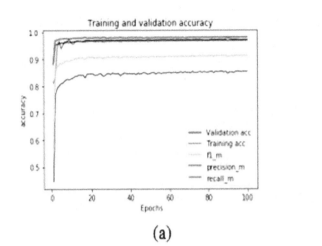
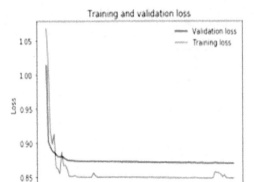

(a)   (b)

c. Results of U-Net and ResU-Net Results on test data

Table 1 shows the quantitative analysis on both deep models (U-Net and ResU-Net) which were fine-tuned on the document text dataset. The results of ResU-Net are better than U-Net due to the presence of the residual connections in it.

Table 1. Comparative results of text segmentation of Devnagari scanned images on U-Net and ResU-Net model

Parameters	U-Net	ResU-Net
Loss	0.9763	0.8479
Accuracy	95.031%	98.802%
Precision	94.729%	98.480%
Recall	80.4912%	83.220%
F1-Score	86.106%	90.032%

SUMMARY (COMPARISON OF TRADITIONAL TECHNIQUES WITH THE DEEP LEARNING APPROACH)

Conventional or traditional image processing methods require the features that need to be classified to be hand-coded. The image needs to be analysed at every step in traditional methods of image processing. Pre-processing, transformations, and identification of filters are some necessary steps to apply to the input to find the features. As discussed in the chapter, text extraction using traditional image processing methods includes pre-processing, block extraction, perimeter detection, and text extraction. On the other hand, deep learning learns the features while training the models. The network is very deep and is made up of a large number of layers of neurons. Each layer has features extracted at the output of the layers. Different deep learning models have proven to give state-of-the-art results. The collection of the dataset for training the model is extensive and requires more powerful machines to train the model. It provides excellent results when the dataset is large. Conventional image processing is still used when the dataset is not vast. Transfer learning transfers knowledge from one model to another, similar to what a human does when learning some task. Thus, it makes deep learning give accurate results and solve the more complex tasks.

Despite various advantages of deep learning, it suffers from disadvantages too. Deep learning is data-hungry. The dataset used in the chapters are created by the author, which requires human efforts. Again, the deep networks are costly during training, as they require expensive GPUs for implementation. The selection of the network is also a cumbersome task. There is no standard theory available to select the appropriate network. Deep learning requires knowledge of topology, parameters and training methods for designing and selecting any network.

CONCLUSION

Research in the field of text extraction from document images is explored in this chapter. Traditional image processing and deep learning methods using transfer learning (fine-tuning the base model) for Devanagari text separation are explained. From the literature survey, it is evident that there are four types of approaches for segmenting text: top-down, bottom-up, hybrid, and deep learning.

For conventional methods, the features need to be hand-coded which is required for text extraction, while in the deep learning approach, the features are automatically learned. The deep learning methods give better accuracy compared to conventional methods. A transfer learning method of fine-tuning the base model (U-Net and ResU-Net) again improves the result. U-Net network gives 95% text segmentation accuracy on test data while ResU-Net gives 98% accuracy. The higher efficiency of the ResU-Net is due to the presence of residual connections present in the network. Further, word and line segmentation can be added to the proposed method for Optical Character Recognition. The accuracy of the proposed model for Devanagari text segmentation can be further improved by designing new deep network models.

REFERENCES

Afshine Amidi and Shervine Amidi. (2018). *Deep Learning cheatsheet* [CS 229 - Machine Learning]. Retrieved from https://stanford.edu/~shervine/teaching/cs-229/cheatsheet-deep-learning

Amin, A., & Shiu, R. (2001). Page segmentation and classification utilizing bottom-up approach. *International Journal of Image and Graphics*, *1*(02), 345–361. doi:10.1142/S0219467801000219

Antonacopoulos, A., & Ritchings, R. T. (1995). *Segmentation and classification of document images*. Academic Press.

Badrinarayanan, V., Kendall, A., & Cipolla, R. (2017). Segnet: A deep convolutional encoder-decoder architecture for image segmentation. *IEEE Transactions on Pattern Analysis and Machine Intelligence*, *39*(12), 2481–2495. doi:10.1109/TPAMI.2016.2644615 PMID:28060704

Belabiod, A., & Belaïd, A. (2018). Line and Word Segmentation of Arabic handwritten documents using. *Neural Networks*.

Boulid, Y., Souhar, A., & Elkettani, M. Y. (2015, December). Arabic handwritten text line extraction using connected component analysis from a multi agent perspective. In *2015 15th International Conference on Intelligent Systems Design and Applications (ISDA)* (pp. 80-87). IEEE. 10.1109/ISDA.2015.7489204

Bourbakis, N. G. (1996, November). A methodology of separating images from text using an OCR approach. In *Proceedings IEEE International Joint Symposia on Intelligence and Systems* (pp. 311-317). IEEE. 10.1109/IJSIS.1996.565084

Chen, K., Seuret, M., Liwicki, M., Hennebert, J., & Ingold, R. (2015, August). Page segmentation of historical document images with convolutional autoencoders. In *2015 13th International Conference on Document Analysis and Recognition (ICDAR)* (pp. 1011-1015). IEEE.

Dai, J., He, K., & Sun, J. (2016). Instance-aware semantic segmentation via multi-task network cascades. In *Proceedings of the IEEE Conference on Computer Vision and Pattern Recognition* (pp. 3150-3158). IEEE. 10.1109/CVPR.2016.343

Duan, L., Yuan, B., Wu, C., Li, J., & Guo, Q. (2015). Text-image separation and indexing in historic patent document image based on extreme learning machine. In *Proceedings of ELM-2014* (vol. 2, pp. 299-307). Springer. 10.1007/978-3-319-14066-7_29

Fan, K. C., Liu, C. H., & Wang, Y. K. (1994). Segmentation and classification of mixed text/graphics/image documents. *Pattern Recognition Letters*, *15*(12), 1201–1209. doi:10.1016/0167-8655(94)90110-4

Fan, K. C., Wang, L. S., & Wang, Y. K. (1995). Page segmentation and identification for intelligent signal processing. *Signal Processing*, *45*(3), 329–346. doi:10.1016/0165-1684(95)00061-H

Garcia-Garcia, A., Orts-Escolano, S., Oprea, S., Villena-Martinez, V., & Garcia-Rodriguez, J. (2017). *A review on deep learning techniques applied to semantic segmentation*. arXiv preprint arXiv:1704.06857

He, K., Zhang, X., Ren, S., & Sun, J. (2016, October). Identity mappings in deep residual networks. In *European conference on computer vision* (pp. 630-645). Springer.

Katy, W. (2019). DNN Processing for Image, Audio, and Video In Strengthening Deep Neural Networks. O'Reilly Media, Inc.

Krizhevsky, A., Sutskever, I., & Hinton, G. E. (2012). Imagenet classification with deep convolutional neural networks. In Advances in neural information processing systems (pp. 1097-1105). Academic Press.

Le, V. P., Nayef, N., Visani, M., Ogier, J. M., & De Tran, C. (2015, August). Text and non-text segmentation based on connected component features. In *2015 13th International Conference on Document Analysis and Recognition (ICDAR)* (pp. 1096-1100). IEEE. 10.1109/ICDAR.2015.7333930

Lee, K. H., Choy, Y. C., & Cho, S. B. (2000). Geometric structure analysis of document images: A knowledge-based approach. *IEEE Transactions on Pattern Analysis and Machine Intelligence*, *22*(11), 1224–1240. doi:10.1109/34.888708

Long, J., Shelhamer, E., & Darrell, T. (2015). Fully convolutional networks for semantic segmentation. In *Proceedings of the IEEE conference on computer vision and pattern recognition* (pp. 3431-3440). IEEE.

MATLAB and Statistics Toolbox Release. (2018b). Natick, MA: The MathWorks, Inc.

Mitchell, P. E., & Yan, H. (2001, September). Newspaper document analysis featuring connected line segmentation. In *Proceedings of Sixth International Conference on Document Analysis and Recognition* (pp. 1181-1185). IEEE. 10.1109/ICDAR.2001.953971

Nagy, G., & Seth, S. C. (1984). *Hierarchical representation of optically scanned documents.* Academic Press.

Nandedkar, A. V., Mukhopadhyay, J., & Sural, S. (2015, August). Text-graphics separation to detect logo and stamp from color document images: A spectral approach. In *2015 13th International Conference on Document Analysis and Recognition (ICDAR)* (pp. 571-575). IEEE.

Oliveira, S. A., Seguin, B., & Kaplan, F. (2018, August). dhSegment: A generic deep-learning approach for document segmentation. In *2018 16th International Conference on Frontiers in Handwriting Recognition (ICFHR)* (pp. 7-12). IEEE.

Oyedotun, O. K., & Khashman, A. (2016). Document segmentation using textural features summarization and feedforward neural network. *Applied Intelligence, 45*(1), 198–212. doi:10.100710489-015-0753-z

Perroud, T., Sobottka, K., & Bunke, H. (2001, September). Text extraction from color documents-clustering approaches in three and four dimensions. In *Proceedings of Sixth International Conference on Document Analysis and Recognition* (pp. 937-941). IEEE. 10.1109/ICDAR.2001.953923

Rege, P. P., & Chandrakar, C. A. (2012). Text-image separation in document images using boundary/perimeter detection. *ACEEE International Journal on Signal and Image Processing, 3*(1), 10–14.

Ren, S., He, K., Girshick, R., & Sun, J. (2015). Faster r-cnn: Towards real-time object detection with region proposal networks. In Advances in neural information processing systems (pp. 91-99). Academic Press.

Ronneberger, O., Fischer, P., & Brox, T. (2015, October). U-net: Convolutional networks for biomedical image segmentation. In *International Conference on Medical image computing and computer-assisted intervention* (pp. 234-241). Springer. 10.1007/978-3-319-24574-4_28

Santosh, K. C., & Iwata, E. (2012). Stroke-Based Cursive Character Recognition. *Advances in Character Recognition*, 175.

Santosh, K. C., Nattee, C., & Lamiroy, B. (2012). Relative positioning of stroke-based clustering: A new approach to online handwritten devanagari character recognition. *International Journal of Image and Graphics, 12*(02), 1250016. doi:10.1142/S0219467812500167

Santosh, K. C., & Wendling, L. (2015). Character recognition based on non-linear multi-projection profiles measure. *Frontiers of Computer Science, 9*(5), 678–690. doi:10.100711704-015-3400-2

Saurabh Pal. (2019, February 26). Semantic Segmentation: Introduction to the Deep Learning Technique Behind Google Pixel's Camera! [Blog post]. Retrieved from https://www.analyticsvidhya.com/blog/2019/02/tutorial-semantic-segmentation-google-deeplab/

Shreya Ghelani. (2019, May 16). From Word Embeddings to Pretrained Language Models — A New Age in NLP — Part 2 [Blog Post]. Retrieved from https://towardsdatascience.com/from-word-embeddings-to-pretrained-language-models-a-new-age-in-nlp-part-2-e9af9a0bdcd9

Sindhuri, M. S., & Anusha, N. (2016, March). Text separation in document images through Otsu's method. In *2016 International Conference on Wireless Communications, Signal Processing and Networking (WiSPNET)*, (pp. 2395-2399). IEEE. 10.1109/WiSPNET.2016.7566571

Sinha, R. M. K., & Bansal, V. (1995, October). On Devanagari document processing. In *1995 IEEE International Conference on Systems, Man and Cybernetics. Intelligent Systems for the 21st Century* (Vol. 2, pp. 1621-1626). IEEE. 10.1109/ICSMC.1995.538004

Stewart, S., & Barrett, B. (2017, November). Document image page segmentation and character recognition as semantic segmentation. In *Proceedings of the 4th International Workshop on Historical Document Imaging and Processing* (pp. 101-106). ACM. 10.1145/3151509.3151518

Sun, H. M. (2006). Enhanced constrained run-length algorithm for complex layout document processing. *International Journal of Applied Science and Engineering*, *4*(3), 297–309.

Tran, T. A., Na, I. S., & Kim, S. H. (2015). Separation of Text and Non-text in Document Layout Analysis using a Recursive Filter. *Transactions on Internet and Information Systems (Seoul)*, *9*(10).

Yuan, Q., & Tan, C. L. (2001, September). Text extraction from gray scale document images using edge information. In *Proceedings of sixth international conference on document analysis and recognition* (pp. 302-306). IEEE. 10.1109/ICDAR.2001.953803

Zhang, Z., Liu, Q., & Wang, Y. (2018). Road extraction by deep residual u-net. *IEEE Geoscience and Remote Sensing Letters*, *15*(5), 749–753. doi:10.1109/LGRS.2018.2802944

Zhou, B., Lapedriza, A., Xiao, J., Torralba, A., & Oliva, A. (2014). Learning deep features for scene recognition using places database. In Advances in neural information processing systems (pp. 487-495). Academic Press.

KEY TERMS AND DEFINITIONS

Accuracy: Accuracy is a percentage of correctly classified normal as well as abnormal samples out of total samples. It is given by the ratio of the addition of True Positive and True Negative samples to the total number of samples under test. Accuracy = TP+TN/TP+FP+FN+TN.

F1 Score: F1 score is the weighted average of precision and recall. Therefore, this score takes both false positives and false negatives into account. Intuitively it is not as easy to understand as accuracy, but F1 is usually more useful than accuracy, especially if you have an uneven class distribution. Accuracy works best if false positives and false negatives have similar cost. If the value of false positives and false negatives are very different, it's better to look at both Precision and Recall. F1 Score = 2*(Recall * Precision) / (Recall + Precision).

False Negative (FN): It is the number of abnormal samples detected as normal samples by the classifier algorithm.

False Positive (FP): It is the number of normal samples detected as abnormal samples by the classifier algorithm.

Precision: Precision is the ratio of correctly predicted positive observations of the total predicted positive observations. Precision = TP/TP+FP.

Recall (Sensitivity): Recall is the ratio of correctly predicted positive observations to all observations in actual class - yes. Recall = TP/TP+FN.

Sensitivity: Sensitivity is a percentage of correctly classified abnormal samples, and it is given by the ratio of true positive to the addition of true positive and false negative samples.

Specificity: Specificity is a percentage of correctly classified normal samples, and it is given by the ratio of true negative to the addition of true negative and false positive samples.

True Negative (TN): It is the number of normal samples detected as normal samples by the classifier algorithm.

True Positive (TP): It is the number of abnormal samples detected as abnormal samples by the classifier algorithm.

314

Compilation of References

Abadi, M., Agarwal, A., Barham, P., Brevdo, E., Chen, Z., Citro, C., . . . Devin, M. (2016). *Tensorflow: Large-scale machine learning on heterogeneous distributed systems.* arXiv preprint arXiv:1603.04467

Abadi, M., Agarwal, A., Barham, P., Brevdo, E., Chen, Z., Citro, C., . . . Ghemawat, S. (2016). *Tensorflow: Large-scale machine learning on heterogeneous distributed systems.* arXiv preprint arXiv:1603.04467

Abadi, M., Barham, P., Chen, J., Chen, Z., Davis, A., Dean, J., . . . Isard, M. (2016). *Tensorflow: A system for large-scale machine learning.* Paper presented at the 12th {USENIX} Symposium on Operating Systems Design and Implementation.

Abhigoku. (2018). *Activation functions and its Types in Artificial Neural network.* Retrieved January 11, 2020, from https://medium.com/@abhigoku10/activation-functions-and-its-types-in-artifical-neural-network-14511f3080a8

Adabor, Acquaah-Mensah, & Oduro. (2015). SAGA: A hybrid search algorithm for Bayesian Network structure learning of transcriptional regulatory networks. *Journal of Biomedical Informatics, Elsevier, 53,* 27–35. doi:10.1016/j.jbi.2014.08.010

Adeshina, S. A., Adedigba, A. P., Adeniyi, A. A., & Aibinu, A. M. (2018). Breast Cancer Histopathology Image Classification with Deep Convolutional Neural Networks. *Proceedings of 14th International Conference on Electronics Computer and Computation (ICECCO),* 206-212. 10.1109/ICECCO.2018.8634690

Afshine Amidi and Shervine Amidi. (2018). *Deep Learning cheatsheet* [CS 229 - Machine Learning]. Retrieved from https://stanford.edu/~shervine/teaching/cs-229/cheatsheet-deep-learning

Agaian, S., Madhukar, M., & Chronopoulos, A. (2014). Automated Screening System for Acute Myelogenous Leukemia Detection in Blood Microscopic Images. *IEEE Systems Journal, 8*(3), 995–1004. doi:10.1109/JSYST.2014.2308452

Ajit, P. (2016). Prediction of employee turnover in organizations using machine learning algorithms. *Algorithms, 4*(5), C5.

Alao, D., & Adeyemo, A. B. (2013). Analyzing employee attrition using decision tree algorithms. *Computing, Information Systems, Development Informatics and Allied Research Journal, 4.*

Alduayj, S. S., & Rajpoot, K. (2018). Predicting Employee Attrition using Machine Learning. *2018 International Conference on Innovations in Information Technology (IIT),* 93–98. 10.1109/INNOVATIONS.2018.8605976

Alférez, S., Merino, A., Bigorra, L., & Rodellar, J. (2016). Characterization and automatic screening of reactive and abnormal neoplastic B lymphoid cells from peripheral blood. *International Journal of Laboratory Hematology, 38*(2), 209–219. doi:10.1111/ijlh.12473 PMID:26995648

Alpaydin, E. (2004). *Introduction to Machine Learning.* Cambridge: MIT Press.

Al-Radaideh, Q. A., & Al Nagi, E. (2012). Using data mining techniques to build a classification model for predicting employees performance. *International Journal of Advanced Computer Science and Applications, 3*(2).

Alwaisi, S., & Baykan, O. K. (2017). Training Of Artificial Neural Network Using Metaheuristic Algorithm. *International Journal of Intelligent Systems and Applications in Engineering*.

American Cancer Society. (2019). *Cancer Facts & Figures 2019*. Atlanta: American Cancer Society.

Amin, A., & Shiu, R. (2001). Page segmentation and classification utilizing bottom-up approach. *International Journal of Image and Graphics*, *1*(02), 345–361. doi:10.1142/S0219467801000219

Androulakis, I. P., Yang, E., & Almon, R. R. (2007). Analysis of time-series gene expression data: Methods, challenges, and opportunities. *Annual Review of Biomedical Engineering*, *9*(1), 205–228. doi:10.1146/annurev.bioeng.9.060906.151904 PMID:17341157

Angelini & Riccardo. (2016). Deep Learning Approach to DNA Sequence Classifification',Springer International Publishing Switzerland 2016,C. CIBB 2015. *LNBI*, *9874*, 129–140.

Antonacopoulos, A., & Ritchings, R. T. (1995). *Segmentation and classification of document images*. Academic Press.

Anwar, S., Huynh, C. P., & Porikli, F. (2017). *Chaining identity mapping modules for image denoising.* arXiv preprint arXiv:1712.02933

Araújo, T., Aresta, G., Castro, E., Rouco, J., Aguiar, P., Eloy, C., ... Campilho, A. (2017). Classification of breast cancer histology images using Convolutional Neural Networks. *PLoS One*, *12*(6), e0177544. doi:10.1371/journal.pone.0177544 PMID:28570557

Arunava. (2018). *Convolutional Neural Networks-Brief Study.* https://towardsdatascience.com/convolutional-neural-network-17fb77e76c05

Aryan, M. (2018). *How to Use TensorBorad?* Retrieved 12 September 2019, from https://itnext.io/how-to-use-tensorboard-5d82f8654496

Ashtari, S., & Eydgahi, A. (2017). Student perceptions of cloud applications effectiveness in higher education. *Journal of Computational Science*, *23*, 173–180. doi:10.1016/j.jocs.2016.12.007

Ayadi, W., Elloumi, M., & Hao, J. K. (2012). Pattern-Driven Neighborhood Search for Biclustering of Microarray Data. *BMC Bioinformatics*, *13*(7), 1–15. doi:10.1186/1471-2105-13-S7-S11 PMID:22594997

Ayadi, W., & Hao, J. K. (2014). A Memetic Algorithm for Discovering Negative Correlation Biclusters of DNA Microarray Data. *Neurocomputing*, *145*(7), 14–22. doi:10.1016/j.neucom.2014.05.074

Badrinarayanan, V., Kendall, A., & Cipolla, R. (2017). Segnet: A deep convolutional encoder-decoder architecture for image segmentation. *IEEE Transactions on Pattern Analysis and Machine Intelligence*, *39*(12), 2481–2495. doi:10.1109/TPAMI.2016.2644615 PMID:28060704

Balamurugan. (2016). ' modified harmony search method for biclustering microarray gene expression data. *International Journal of Data Mining and Bioinformatics, 16*(4), 269 – 289.

Bándi, P., Geessink, O., Manson, Q., Van Dijk, M., Balkenhol, M., Hermsen, M., ... Litjens, G. (2019). From Detection of Individual Metastases to Classification of Lymph Node Status at the Patient Level: The CAMELYON17 Challenge. *IEEE Transactions on Medical Imaging*, *38*(2), 550–560. doi:10.1109/TMI.2018.2867350 PMID:30716025

Bardou, D., Zhang, K., & Ahmad, S. (2018). Classification of Breast Cancer Based on Histology Images Using Convolutional Neural Networks. *IEEE Access*.

Belabiod, A., & Belaïd, A. (2018). Line and Word Segmentation of Arabic handwritten documents using. *Neural Networks*.

Bengio, Y. (2009). Learning Deep Architectures for AI. *Foundations and Trends in Machine Learning*, *2*(1), 1–127. doi:10.1561/2200000006

Bhadauria, H. S., Devgun, J. S., Virmani, J., & Rawat, J. (2018, January). Application of ensemble artificial neural network for the classification of white blood cells using microscopic blood images. *International Journal of Computational Systems Engineering*, 202–216.

Bhangale, T., & Patole, R. (2019). Tampering Detection in Digital Audio Recording Based on Statistical Reverberation Features. In *Soft Computing and Signal Processing* (pp. 583–591). Singapore: Springer. doi:10.1007/978-981-13-3600-3_55

Bhat, H. F. (2017). Evaluating SVM Algorithms for Bioinformatics Gene Expression Analysis. *International Journal on Computer Science and Engineering*, *6*(02), 42–52.

Bibin, D., Nair, M. S., & Punitha, P. (2017). Malaria Parasite Detection from Peripheral Blood Smear Images Using Deep Belief Networks. *IEEE Access: Practical Innovations, Open Solutions*, *5*, 9099–9108. doi:10.1109/ACCESS.2017.2705642

Bingham, E., Chen, J. P., Jankowiak, M., Obermeyer, F., Pradhan, N., Karaletsos, T., ... Goodman, N. D. (2019). Pyro: Deep universal probabilistic programming. *Journal of Machine Learning Research*, *20*(1), 973–978.

Bishop, C. M. (2006). *Pattern recognition and machine learning*. Springer.

Bloomfield, L. A. (2001). *How things work*. Louis A. Bloomfield.

Bojarski, M., Del Testa, D., Dworakowski, D., Firner, B., Flepp, B., Goyal, P., . . . Zhang, X. (2016). *End to end learning for self-driving cars.* arXiv preprint arXiv:1604.07316

Boulid, Y., Souhar, A., & Elkettani, M. Y. (2015, December). Arabic handwritten text line extraction using connected component analysis from a multi agent perspective. In *2015 15th International Conference on Intelligent Systems Design and Applications (ISDA)* (pp. 80-87). IEEE. 10.1109/ISDA.2015.7489204

Bourbakis, N. G. (1996, November). A methodology of separating images from text using an OCR approach. In *Proceedings IEEE International Joint Symposia on Intelligence and Systems* (pp. 311-317). IEEE. 10.1109/IJSIS.1996.565084

Boureau, Y., Ponce, J., & LeCun, Y. (2010). A theoretical analysis of feature pooling in visual recognition. *Proceedings of the 27th international conference on machine learning (ICML-10)*, 111-118.

Boyd, R., & Holton, R. J. (2018). Technology, innovation, employment and power: Does robotics and artificial intelligence really mean social transformation? *Journal of Sociology (Melbourne, Vic.)*, *54*(3), 331–345. doi:10.1177/1440783317726591

Bui, D.-K., Nguyen, T. N., Ngo, T. D., & Nguyen-Xuan, H. (2020). An artificial neural network (ANN) expert system enhanced with the electromagnetism-based firefly algorithm (EFA) for predicting the energy consumption in buildings. *Energy*, *190*, 116370. doi:10.1016/j.energy.2019.116370

Buniyamin, N., Mat, U. b., & Arshad, P. M. (2015, November). Educational Data Mining for Prediction and Classification of Engineering Students Achievement. In *IEEE 7th International Conference on Engineering Education (ICEED)*, (pp. 49-53). Kanazawa: IEEE.

Bush, P., & Sejnowski, T. (1996). Inhibition synchronizes sparsely connected cortical neurons within and between columns in realistic network models. *Journal of Computational Neuroscience*, *3*(2), 91–110. doi:10.1007/BF00160806 PMID:8840227

Chaira, T. (2014). Accurate segmentation of leukocyte in blood cell images using Atanassov's intuitionistic fuzzy and interval Type II fuzzy set theory. *Micron (Oxford, England)*, *61*, 1–8. doi:10.1016/j.micron.2014.01.004 PMID:24792441

Chansung, P. (2018). *CIFAR-10 Image Classification in TensorFlow*. Retrieved September 7, 2019, from https://towards-datascience.com/cifar-10-image-classification-in-tensorflow-5b501f7dc77c

Chaudhary, U. A., & Malik, H. (2010, November). Automatic recording environment identification using acoustic features. In *Audio Engineering Society Convention 129*. Audio Engineering Society.

Chen, K., Seuret, M., Liwicki, M., Hennebert, J., & Ingold, R. (2015, August). Page segmentation of historical document images with convolutional autoencoders. In *2015 13th International Conference on Document Analysis and Recognition (ICDAR)* (pp. 1011-1015). IEEE.

Cheng, Y., & Church, G. M. (2000). Biclustering of Expression Data. *Proceedings of the Eighth International Conference on Intelligent Systems for Molecular Biology*, 93-103.

Chen, K. M., Cofer, E. M., Zhou, J., & Troyanskaya, O. G. (2019). Selene: A PyTorch-based deep learning library for sequence data. *Nature Methods*, *16*(4), 315–318. doi:10.103841592-019-0360-8 PMID:30923381

Chen, K.-H. (2014). Gene selection for cancer identification: A decision tree model empowered by particle swarm optimization algorithm. *BMC Bioinformatics*, *15*(49), 1–10.

Chen, X., Vorvoreanu, M., & Madhavan, K. (2013). Mining Social Media Data for Understanding Students' Learning Experiences. *IEEE Transactions on Learning Technologies*.

Chen, Y., Li, Y., Narayan, R., Subramanian, A., & Xie, X. (2016). Gene expression inference with deep learning. *Bioinformatics (Oxford, England)*, *32*(12), 1832–1839. doi:10.1093/bioinformatics/btw074 PMID:26873929

Chetlur, S., Woolley, C., Vandermersch, P., Cohen, J., Tran, J., Catanzaro, B., & Shelhamer, E. (2014). *cudnn: Efficient primitives for deep learning*. arXiv preprint arXiv:1410.0759

Choi, J., Ku, Y., Yoo, B., Kim, J., Lee, D., Chai, Y., ... Kim, H. C. (2017). White blood cell differential count of maturation stages in bone marrow smear using dual-stage convolutional neural networks. *PLoS One*, *12*(12), e0189259. doi:10.1371/journal.pone.0189259 PMID:29228051

Chollet, F. (2005). *Keras: Deep learning library for theano and tensorflow*. https://keras. io/k

Chollet, F. (2015). Keras documentation. *keras.io*.

Chollet, F. (2015). *Keras documentation*. Retrieved August 28, 2019, from https://keras.io/why-use-keras/

Chollet, F. (2017). *Xception: Deep learning with depthwise separable convolutions*. arXiv preprint, 1610.02357.

Chollet, F. (2016, October 7). Xception: Deep Learning with Depthwise Separable Convolutions. *CVPR*, *2017*, 5–6.

Christian, S., Sergey, I., Vincent, V., & Alexander, A.A. (2016). *Inception-v4, inception-resnet and the impact of residual connections on learning*, ArXiv:1602.07261v2

Chui, K. T., Fung, D. C., Lytras, M. D., & Lam, T. M. (2017). Predicting at-risk university students in a virtual learning environment via a machine learning algorithm. *Computers in Human Behavior*.

Cireşan, D. C., Giusti, A., Gambardella, L. M., & Schmidhuber, J. (2013). Mitosis Detection in Breast Cancer Histology Images with Deep Neural Networks. In K. Mori, I. Sakuma, Y. Sato, C. Barillot, & N. Navab (Eds.), Lecture Notes in Computer Science: Vol. 8150. *Proceedings of Medical Image Computing and Computer-Assisted Intervention – MICCAI 2013*. Berlin: Springer. doi:10.1007/978-3-642-40763-5_51

CNN Workflow Image. (2020). *Deep learning wizard*. https://www.deeplearningwizard.com/deep_learning/practical_pytorch/pytorch_convolutional_neuralnetwork/

Colah. (2015). *Understanding LSTM*. Retrieved 2019, from http://colah.github.io/posts/2015-08-Understanding-LSTMs/

Collobert, R., Weston, J., Bottou, L., Karlen, M., Kavukcuoglu, K., & Kuksa, P. (2011). Natural language processing (almost) from scratch. *Journal of Machine Learning Research*, *12*(Aug), 2493–2537.

Cortes, C., & Vapnik, V. (1995). Support-vector networks. *Machine Learning*, *20*(3), 273–297. doi:10.1007/BF00994018

Costa, E., Fonseca, B., Santana, M. A., Araújo, F., & Rego, J. (2017). Evaluating the effectiveness of educational data mining techniques for early prediction of students' academic failure in introductory programming courses. *Computers in Human Behavior*, *73*, 247–256. doi:10.1016/j.chb.2017.01.047

Cruz-Roa, A. (2014). Automatic detection of invasive ductal carcinoma in whole slide images with convolutional neural networks. *SPIE Medical Imaging. International Society for Optics and Photonics*, *9041*, 904103.

CS224n, Stanford. (n.d.). Retrieved 2019, from http://web.stanford.edu/class/cs224n/slides/cs224n-2019-lecture04-backprop.pdf

CS231n, Stanford. (n.d.). Retrieved 2019, from http://cs231n.github.io/neural-networks-1/

Cuccovillo, L., Mann, S., Tagliasacchi, M., & Aichroth, P. (2013, September). Audio tampering detection via microphone classification. In *2013 IEEE 15th International Workshop on Multimedia Signal Processing (MMSP)* (pp. 177-182). IEEE. 10.1109/MMSP.2013.6659284

Cuccovillo, L., & Aichroth, P. (2016, March). Open-set microphone classification via blind channel analysis. In *2016 IEEE International Conference on Acoustics, Speech and Signal Processing (ICASSP)* (pp. 2074-2078). IEEE. 10.1109/ICASSP.2016.7472042

Cuiru. (2019). Breast cancer classification in pathological images based on hybrid features. *Multimedia Tools and Applications*, *78*. doi:10.100711042-019-7468-9

Dahl, G. E., Yu, D., Deng, L., & Acero, A. (2011). Context-dependent pre-trained deep neural networks for large-vocabulary speech recognition. *IEEE Transactions on Audio, Speech, and Language Processing*, *20*(1), 30–42. doi:10.1109/TASL.2011.2134090

Dai, J., He, K., & Sun, J. (2016). Instance-aware semantic segmentation via multi-task network cascades. In *Proceedings of the IEEE Conference on Computer Vision and Pattern Recognition* (pp. 3150-3158). IEEE. 10.1109/CVPR.2016.343

Das, S. (2018, July 23). *CNN Architectures: LeNet, AlexNet, VGG, GoogLeNet, ResNet and more....* Retrieved from Medium: https://medium.com/@sidereal/cnns-architectures-lenet-alexnet-vgg-googlenet-resnet-and-more-666091488df5

Das, K., Karri, S. P. K., Roy, A. G., Chatterjee, J., & Sheet, D. (2017). Classifying histopathology whole-slides using fusion of decisions from deep convolutional network on a collection of random multi-views at multi-magnification. *Proceedings of IEEE 14th International Symposium on Biomedical Imaging (ISBI 2017)*, 1024–1027. 10.1109/ISBI.2017.7950690

Davidt, O. E., & Netanyahu, N. S. (2015, July). DeepSign: Deep Learning for Automatic Malware Detection. *International Joint Conference on Neural Networks (IJCNN)*, 1-8. 10.1109/IJCNN.2015.7280815

Davis, D. (1998). The virtual university: A learning university. *Journal of Workplace Learning*, *10*(4), 175–213. doi:10.1108/13665629810213935

Deng, L., & Yu, D. (2014). *Deep Learning for Signal and Information Processing*. Redmond, WA: Microsoft Research.

Deng, Y., Ren, Z., Kong, Y., Bao, F., & Dai, Q. (2017). A Hierarchical Fused Fuzzy Deep Neural Network for data classification. *IEEE Transactions on Fuzzy Systems*, *25*(4), 1006–1012. doi:10.1109/TFUZZ.2016.2574915

Deshpande, A. (2016). *A Beginner's Guide To Understanding Convolutional Neural Networks*. Retrieved from A Beginner's Guide To Understanding Convolutional Neural Networks: https://adeshpande3.github.io/A-Beginner%27s-Guide-To-Understanding-Convolutional-Neural-Networks/

Devi, B., Kumar, S., & Anuradha, S. V. G. (2019a). AnaData: A novel approach for data analytics using random forest tree and SVM. *Computing, communication and signal processing. Advances in intelligent systems and computing, 810.*

Devi, B., Shankar, V. G., Srivastava, S., & Srivastava, D. K. (2020a). *AnaBus: A Proposed Sampling Retrieval Model for Business and Historical Data Analytics* (Vol. 1016). Data Management, Analytics and Innovation. Advances in Intelligent Systems and Computing.

Doi, K. (2007). Computer-aided diagnosis in medical imaging: historical review, current status and future potential. *Computerized Medical Imaging and Graphics: The Official Journal of the Computerized Medical Imaging Society, 31*(4-5), 198–211.

Dong, C., Loy, C. C., & Tang, X. (2016). *Accelerating the super-resolution convolutional neural network*. Paper presented at the European conference on computer vision.

Dong, C., Loy, C. C., He, K., & Tang, X. (2015). Image super-resolution using deep convolutional networks. *IEEE Transactions on Pattern Analysis and Machine Intelligence, 38*(2), 295–307. doi:10.1109/TPAMI.2015.2439281 PMID:26761735

Dong, Y., Jiang, Z., Shen, H., & David Pan, W. (2017). Classification Accuracies of Malaria Infected Cells Using Deep Convolutional Neural Networks Based on Decompressed Images."*Conference Proceedings - IEEE SOUTHEASTCON,* 1–6. 10.1109/SECON.2017.7925268

Dong, Y., Jiang, Z., Shen, H., & Pan, W. D. (2017). Evaluations of Deep Convolutional Neural Networks for Automatic Identification of Malaria Infected Cells. *2017 IEEE EMBS International Conference on Biomedical and Health Informatics, BHI 2017,* 101–4. 10.1109/BHI.2017.7897215

Dreyfus, H. L. (1979). *What computers can't do: The limits of artificial intelligence* (Vol. 1972). Harper & Row.

Duan, L., Yuan, B., Wu, C., Li, J., & Guo, Q. (2015). Text-image separation and indexing in historic patent document image based on extreme learning machine. In *Proceedings of ELM-2014* (vol. 2, pp. 299-307). Springer. 10.1007/978-3-319-14066-7_29

Ehteshami Bejnordi, B., Veta, M., Johannes van Diest, P., van Ginneken, B., Karssemeijer, N., Litjens, G., ... Venâncio, R. (2017). Diagnostic Assessment of Deep Learning Algorithms for Detection of Lymph Node Metastases in Women with Breast Cancer. *Journal of the American Medical Association, 318*(22), 2199–2210. doi:10.1001/jama.2017.14585 PMID:29234806

Ertel, W. (2018). *Introduction to artificial intelligence*. Springer.

Fadja, A. N., Lamma, E., & Riguzzi, F. (2018). Vision Inspection with Neural Networks. RiCeRcA@ AI* IA.

Fan, K. C., Liu, C. H., & Wang, Y. K. (1994). Segmentation and classification of mixed text/graphics/image documents. *Pattern Recognition Letters, 15*(12), 1201–1209. doi:10.1016/0167-8655(94)90110-4

Fan, K. C., Wang, L. S., & Wang, Y. K. (1995). Page segmentation and identification for intelligent signal processing. *Signal Processing, 45*(3), 329–346. doi:10.1016/0165-1684(95)00061-H

Fatimaezzahra, Loubna, Mohamed, & Abdelaziz. (2017). A Combined Cuckoo Search Algorithm and Genetic Algorithm for Parameter Optimization in Computer Vision. *International Journal of Applied Engineering Research, 12*(22), 12940-12954.

Free Spoken Digit Database. (n.d.). Retrieved from https://github.com/Jakobovski/freespoken-digit-dataset

Gao, N., Gao, L., Gao, Q., & Wang, H. (2014, November). An Intrusion Detection Model Based on Deep Belief Networks. *Second International Conference on Advanced Cloud and Big Data*, 247-252.

Garcia-Garcia, A., Orts-Escolano, S., Oprea, S., Villena-Martinez, V., & Garcia-Rodriguez, J. (2017). *A review on deep learning techniques applied to semantic segmentation.* arXiv preprint arXiv:1704.06857

Gärtner, D., Dittmar, C., Aichroth, P., Cuccovillo, L., Mann, S., & Schuller, G. (2014, April). Efficient cross-codec framing grid analysis for audio tampering detection. In *Audio Engineering Society Convention 136*. Audio Engineering Society.

George, Y. M., Zayed, H. H., Roushdy, M. I., & Elbagoury, B. M. (2014). Remote computer aided breast cancer detection and diagnosis system based on cytological images. *IEEE Systems Journal, 8*(3), 949–964. doi:10.1109/JSYST.2013.2279415

Giannakos, M. N., Aalberg, T., Divitini, M., Jaccheri, L., Mikalef, P., Pappas, I. O., & Sindre, G. (2017, April). Identifying Dropout Factors in Information Technology Education: A Case Study. *IEEE Global Engineering Education Conference (EDUCON)*, 1187-1194. 10.1109/EDUCON.2017.7942999

Girshick, R., Donahue, J., Darrell, T., & Malik, J. (2020). *Rich feature hierarchies for accurate object detection and semantic segmentation.* ArXiv.

Glorot, X., Bordes, A., & Bengio, Y. (2011). Deep Sparse Rectifier Neural Networks. *Proceedings of the Fourteenth International Conference on Artificial Intelligence and Statistics*, 315-323.

Gobert, J. D., Kim, Y. J., Pedro, M. A., Kennedy, M., & Betts, C. G. (2015). Using educational data mining to assess students' skills at designing and conducting experiments within a complex systems microworld. *Thinking Skills and Creativity, 18*, 81–90. doi:10.1016/j.tsc.2015.04.008

Goel, V., Jangir, V., & Shankar, V. G. (2020b). *DataCan: Robust Approach for Genome Cancer Data Analysis* (Vol. 1016). Data Management, Analytics and Innovation. Advances in Intelligent Systems and Computing.

Golatkar, A., Anand, D., & Sethi, A. (2018). Classification of Breast Cancer Histology using Deep Learning. In A. Campilho, F. Karray, & B. ter Haar Romeny (Eds.), Lecture Notes in Computer Science: Vol. 10882. *Proceedings of Image Analysis and Recognition (ICIAR 2018)*. Cham: Springer. doi:10.1007/978-3-319-93000-8_95

Goodfellow, I., Bengio, Y., & Courville, A. (2016). *Deep learning*. MIT Press.

Goodfellow, I., Bengio, Y., & Courville, A. (2016). *Deep Learning*. MIT Press.

Gradient Descent. (n.d.). Retrieved 2019, from https://saugatbhattarai.com.np/what-is-gradient-descent-in-machine-learning/

Grigoras, C., Rappaport, D., & Smith, J. M. (2012, June). Analytical framework for digital audio authentication. In *Audio Engineering Society Conference: 46th International Conference: Audio Forensics*. Audio Engineering Society.

Grigoras, C., & Smith, J. (2017, June). Large scale test of digital audio file structure and format for forensic analysis. In *Audio Engineering Society Conference: 2017 AES International Conference on Audio Forensics*. Audio Engineering Society.

Grigoras, C., & Smith, J. M. (2012, June). Advances in ENF analysis for digital media authentication. In *Audio Engineering Society Conference: 46th International Conference: Audio Forensics*. Audio Engineering Society.

Guarín, C., Guzmán, E., & González, F. (2015). A Model to Predict Low Academic Performance at a Specific Enrollment Using Data Mining. *IEEE Journal of Latin-American Learning Technologies, 10*(3).

Guo, B., Zhang, R., Guang, X., Shi, C., & Yang, L. (2015, July). Predicting Students performance in educational data mining. *International Symposium on Educational Technology (ISET)*, 125-128. 10.1109/ISET.2015.33

Guolin, K. (2017). LightGBM: A highly efficient gradient boosting decision tree. *Advances in Neural Information Processing Systems*, 3149–3157.

Habibzadeh, M., Jannesari, M., Rezaei, Z., & Totonchi, M. (2018, April). Automatic white blood cell classification using pre-trained deep learning models. *Tenth International Conference on Machine Vision (ICMV 2017)*. 10.1117/12.2311282

Han, J., & Kamber, M. (2012). *Data Mining: Concepts and Techniques* (3rd ed.). Morgan Kaufmann.

Han, Z., Wei, B., Zheng, Y., Yin, Y., Li, K., & Li, S. (2017). Breast cancer multi-classification from histopathological images with structured deep learning model. *Scientific Reports*, 7(1), 4172. doi:10.103841598-017-04075-z PMID:28646155

He, K., Zhang, X., Ren, S., & Sun, J. (2016, March 16). Identity Mappings in Deep Residual Networks. *CVPR*.

He, K., Zhang, X., Ren, S., & Sun, J. (2015, December). 2015). Deep Residual Learning for Image Recognition. *CVPR*, *2015*, 6–8.

He, K., Zhang, X., Ren, S., & Sun, J. (2016). Deep residual learning for image recognition. *Proceedings of the IEEE conference on computer vision and pattern recognition*.

He, K., Zhang, X., Ren, S., & Sun, J. (2016, October). Identity mappings in deep residual networks. In *European conference on computer vision* (pp. 630-645). Springer.

Hijazi, S. T., & Naqvi, S. R. (2006). Factors Affecting Students' Performance. *Bangladesh e-Journal of Sociology*, 3.

Hinton, G. E., Sejnowski, T. J., & Poggio, T. A. (1999). *Unsupervised learning: foundations of neural computation*. MIT Press. doi:10.7551/mitpress/7011.001.0001

Hochreiter, S., & Schmidhuber, J. (1997). Long short-term memory. *Neural Computation*, 9(8), 1735–1780. doi:10.1162/neco.1997.9.8.1735 PMID:9377276

Ho, T. K. (1995). Random decision forests. *Proceedings of 3rd International Conference on Document Analysis and Recognition*, *1*, 278–282.

Houari, A., Ayadi, W., & Yahia, S. B. (2017). Mining Negative Correlation Biclusters from Gene Expression Data using Generic Association Rules. *Procedia Computer Science*, *112*, 278–287. doi:10.1016/j.procs.2017.08.262

Hou, L. (2016). Patch-based convolutional neural network for whole slide tissue image classification. *Proceedings of the IEEE Conference on Computer Vision and Pattern Recognition*, 2424–2433. 10.1109/CVPR.2016.266

Hua, G., Zhang, Y., Goh, J., & Thing, V. L. (2016). Audio authentication by exploring the absolute-error-map of ENF signals. *IEEE Transactions on Information Forensics and Security*, *11*(5), 1003–1016. doi:10.1109/TIFS.2016.2516824

Huang, G., Liu, Z., Maaten, L. v., & Weinberger, K. Q. (2016, August 25). Densely Connected Convolutional Networks. *CVPR*, 4.

Huang, G., Sun, Y., Liu, Z., Sedra, D., & Weinberger, K. (2016, July). Deep Networks with Stochastic Depth. *Machine Learning*.

Huang, Q., Tao, D., Li, X., & Liew. (2012). Parallelized evolutionary learning for detection of biclusters in gene expression data. *IEEE/ACM Transaction Computational Biology and Bioinformatics, 9*(1), 560-570.

Huang, C. H., & ... . (2018). Automated Breast Cancer Image Classification Based on Integration of Noisy-And Model and Fully Connected Network. In A. Campilho, F. Karray, & B. ter Haar Romeny (Eds.), Lecture Notes in Computer Science: Vol. 10882. *Proceedings of Image Analysis and Recognition (ICIAR 2018).* Cham: Springer. doi:10.1007/978-3-319-93000-8_105

Huang, Z., Duan, H., & Li, H. (2015, Sept.). Identification of Gene Expression Pattern Related to Breast Cancer Survival Using Integrated TCGA Datasets and Genomic Tools. *BioMed Research International*, 1–10.

Iandola, F. N., Han, S., Moskewicz, M. W., Ashraf, K., Dally, W. J., & Keutzer, K. (2016, November 4). SqueezeNet: AlexNet-level accuracy with 50x fewer parameters and <0.5MB model size. *CVPR*.

ICIAR. (2018). *Grand Challenge on Breast Cancer Histology Images*. Retrieved from https://iciar2018-challenge. grand-challenge.org/

Ierusalimschy, R., De Figueiredo, L. H., & Filho, W. C. (1996). Lua—An extensible extension language. *Software, Practice & Experience*, 26(6), 635–652. doi:10.1002/(SICI)1097-024X(199606)26:6<635::AID-SPE26>3.0.CO;2-P

Infected and Uninfected Image Datasets. (n.d.). https://storage.googleapis.com/kaggle-datasets/87153/200743/cell-images-for-detecting-malaria.zip

Introducing TensorFlow Datasets. (2019). Retrieved 8 September 2019, from https://medium.com/tensorflow/introducing-tensorflow-datasets-c7f01f7e19f3

ISO. (2009). *Measurement of room acoustic parameters part 1*. ISO Std.

Jantan, H., Hamdan, A. R., & Othman, Z. A. (2010). Human talent prediction in HRM using C4. 5 classification algorithm. *International Journal on Computer Science and Engineering*, 2(8), 2526–2534.

Jason, B. (2019). *What is Deep Learning?* Retrieved 10 January 2020, from https://machinelearningmastery.com/what-is-deep-learning/

Jauhari, S., & Rizvi, S. A. M. (2014). Mining Gene Expression Data Focusing Cancer Therapeutics: A Digest. *IEEE/ACM Transactions on Computational Biology and Bioinformatics*, 11(3), 53. doi:10.1109/TCBB.2014.2312002 PMID:26356021

Jiang, M., Cheng, L., Qin, F., Du, L., & Zhang, M. (2018). White Blood Cells Classification with Deep Convolutional Neural Networks. *International Journal of Pattern Recognition and Artificial Intelligence*, 32(09), 1857006. doi:10.1142/S0218001418570069

Jiang, Y., Chen, L., Zhang, H., & Xiao, X. (2019). Breast cancer histopathological image classification using convolutional neural networks with small SE-ResNet module. *PLoS One*, 14(3), e0214587. doi:10.1371/journal.pone.0214587 PMID:30925170

Jia, Y., Shelhamer, E., Donahue, J., Karayev, S., Long, J., Girshick, R., ... Darrell, T. (2014, November). Caffe: Convolutional architecture for fast feature embedding. In *Proceedings of the 22nd ACM international conference on Multimedia* (pp. 675-678). ACM.

JonesE.OliphantT.PetersonP. (2001). https://www.scipy. Org

Jurafsky, D. (2000). *Speech & language processing*. Pearson Education India.

Jurman, G., Riccadonna, S., & Furlanello, C. (2012). A comparison of MCC and CEN error measures in multi-class prediction. *PLoS One*, 7(8), e41882. doi:10.1371/journal.pone.0041882 PMID:22905111

Kaggle. (n.d.). Retrieved September 10, 2019, from https://www.kaggle.com/c/cifar-10

Katy, W. (2019). DNN Processing for Image, Audio, and Video In Strengthening Deep Neural Networks. O'Reilly Media, Inc.

Kaur, S., & Vijay, M. R. (2016). Job satisfaction-A major factor behind attrition of retention in retail industry. *Imperial Journal of Interdisciplinary Research*, 2(8), 993–996.

Kellman, P. J., & Spelke, E. S. (1983). Perception of partly occluded objects in infancy. *Cognitive Psychology*, 15(4), 483–524. doi:10.1016/0010-0285(83)90017-8 PMID:6641127

Keng, W. L., & Graesser, L. (2017). *"SLM Lab", kengz/SLM-Lab*. GitHub.

Kensert, A., Harrison, P. J., & Spjuth, P. (2018, June 14). Transfer learning with deep convolutional neural network for classifying cellular morphological changes. *SLAS Discovery: Advancing Life Sciences R&D*, 8.

Ketkar, N. (2017). Introduction to PyTorch. In *Deep learning with python* (pp. 195–208). Berkeley, CA: Apress. doi:10.1007/978-1-4842-2766-4_12

Khan, N. A., Pervaz, H., Latif, A., & Musharaff, A. (2017). Unsupervised Identification of Malaria Parasites Using Computer Vision. *Pakistan Journal of Pharmaceutical Sciences*, 30(1), 223–228. PMID:28603136

Khan, S., Rahmani, H., Shah, S. A. A., & Bennamoun, M. (2018). A guide to convolutional neural networks for computer vision. *Synthesis Lectures on Computer Vision*, 8(1), 1–207. doi:10.2200/S00822ED1V01Y201712COV015

Khedidja. (2015). Using Multiobjective optimization for biclustering microarray data. *Applied Soft Computing, 33*, 239-249.

Kim, J., Kwon Lee, J., & Lee, M., K. (2016). Accurate image super-resolution using very deep convolutional networks. *Proceedings of the IEEE conference on computer vision and pattern recognition.* 10.1109/CVPR.2016.182

Kim, S. M. L., & Shen, J. (2015, July). A novel deep learning by combining discriminative model with generative model. *International Joint Conference on Neural Networks (IJCNN)*, 1-6. 10.1109/IJCNN.2015.7280589

Kloss, A. (2015). *Object Detection Using Deep Learning - Learning where to search using visual attention.* Tübingen: Eberhard Karls Universitat Tubingen.

Koch, F., Assunção, M. D., Cardonha, C., & Netto, M. A. (2016). Optimising resource costs of cloud computing for education. *Future Generation Computer Systems*, 55, 473–479. doi:10.1016/j.future.2015.03.013

Koelstra, S., & Patras, I. (2013a). Fusion of facial expressions and EEG for implicit affective tagging. *Image and Vision Computing*, 31(2), 164–174. doi:10.1016/j.imavis.2012.10.002

Kourou, K., Exarchos, T. P., Exarchos, K. P., Karamouzisc, M. V., & Fotiadis, D. I. (2015). Machine learning applications in cancer prognosis and prediction. *Computational and Structural Biotechnology Journal, Elsevier*, 13, 8–17. doi:10.1016/j.csbj.2014.11.005 PMID:25750696

Kowal, M., Filipczuk, P., Obuchowicz, A., Korbicz, J., & Monczak, R. (2013). Computer aided diagnosis of breast cancer based on fine needle biopsy microscopic images. *Computers in Biology and Medicine*, 43(10), 1563–1572. doi:10.1016/j.compbiomed.2013.08.003 PMID:24034748

Krizhevsky, A., Nair, V., & Hinton, G. (2014). *The cifar-10 dataset.* http://www.cs.toronto.edu/kriz/cifar.html

Krizhevsky, A., Sutskever, I., & Hinton, G. E. (2012). Imagenet classification with deep convolutional neural networks. In Advances in neural information processing systems (pp. 1097-1105). Academic Press.

Krizhevsky, A., Sutskever, I., & Hinton, G. E. (2012). ImageNet classification with deep convolutional neural networks. *Proceedings of the 25th International Conference on Neural Information Processing Systems*, 1.

Kumar, A., Irsoy, O., Ondruska, P., Iyyer, M., Bradbury, J., Gulrajani, I., . . . Socher, R. (2016). *Ask me anything: Dynamic memory networks for natural language processing.* Paper presented at the International conference on machine learning.

Kuwata, K., & Shibasaki, R. (2015, July). Estimating crop yields with deep learning and remotely sensed data. *International Geoscience and Remote Sensing Symposium (IGARSS)*, 858-861. 10.1109/IGARSS.2015.7325900

Larsson, G., Maire, M., & Shakhnarovich, G. (2017, May 24). FractalNet: Ultra-Deep Neural Networks without Residuals. *CVPR*.

Le, V. P., Nayef, N., Visani, M., Ogier, J. M., & De Tran, C. (2015, August). Text and non-text segmentation based on connected component features. In *2015 13th International Conference on Document Analysis and Recognition (ICDAR)* (pp. 1096-1100). IEEE. 10.1109/ICDAR.2015.7333930

LeCun, Y., Cortes, C., & Burges, C. J. (1998). *The MNIST database of handwritten digits, 1998.* http://yann. lecun. com/exdb/mnist

LeCun, Y., Bottou, L., Bengio, Y., & Haffner, P. (1998). Gradient-based learning applied to document recognition. *Proceedings of the IEEE, 86*(11), 2278–2324. doi:10.1109/5.726791

Lee, K. H., Choy, Y. C., & Cho, S. B. (2000). Geometric structure analysis of document images: A knowledge-based approach. *IEEE Transactions on Pattern Analysis and Machine Intelligence, 22*(11), 1224–1240. doi:10.1109/34.888708

Levin, E., & Pieraccini, R. (1992). *Dynamic planar warping for optical character recognition.* Paper presented at the ICASSP-92: 1992 IEEE International Conference on Acoustics, Speech, and Signal Processing. 10.1109/ICASSP.1992.226254

Liang, Z. (2017). CNN-Based Image Analysis for Malaria Diagnosis. *Proceedings - 2016 IEEE International Conference on Bioinformatics and Biomedicine, BIBM 2016*, 493–96.

Li, B. Y. L., Mian, A. S., Liu, W., & Krishna, A. (2013b). Using Kinect for face recognition under varying poses, expressions, illumination and disguise. *IEEE Workshop on Applications of Computer Vision (WACV)*, 186–192. 10.1109/WACV.2013.6475017

Linn, M. C., & Clancy, M. J. (1992). The case for case studies of programming problems. *Communications of the ACM, 35*(3), 121–133. doi:10.1145/131295.131301

Litjens, G., Kooi, T., Bejnordi, B. E., Setio, A. A. A., Ciompi, F., Ghafoorian, M., ... Sánchez, C. I. (2017). A survey on deep learning in medical image analysis. *Medical Image Analysis, 42*, 60–88. doi:10.1016/j.media.2017.07.005 PMID:28778026

Liu, W., Anguelov, D., Erhan, D., Szegedy, C., Reed, S., Fu, C., & Berg, A. (2020). *SSD: Single Shot MultiBox Detector.* arXiv.

Liu, Y. (2017). *Detecting Cancer Metastases on Gigapixel Pathology Images.* ArXiv, abs/1703.02442

Li, Y., Liu, W., Jia, Y., & Dong, H. (2016). A Weighted Mutual Information Biclustering Algorithm for Gene Expression Data. *Computer Science and Information Systems, 14*(3), 643–660. doi:10.2298/CSIS170301021Y

Li, Y., Lu, H., Li, J., Li, X., Li, Y., & Serikawa, S. (2016). Underwater image de-scattering and classification by deep neural network. *Computers & Electrical Engineering, 54*, 68–77. doi:10.1016/j.compeleceng.2016.08.008

Long, J., Shelhamer, E., & Darrell, T. (2015). Fully convolutional networks for semantic segmentation. In *Proceedings of the IEEE conference on computer vision and pattern recognition* (pp. 3431-3440). IEEE.

López-Puigdollers, D., Javier Traver, V., & Pla, F. (2020). Recognizing white blood cells with local image descriptors. *Expert Systems with Applications, 115*, 695–708. doi:10.1016/j.eswa.2018.08.029

Lowe, D. (2004). Distinctive Image Features from Scale-Invariant Keypoints. *International Journal of Computer Vision, 60*(2), 91–110. doi:10.1023/B:VISI.0000029664.99615.94

Lv, Y., Duan, Y., Kang, W., Li, Z., & Wang, F. Y. (2014). Traffic flow prediction with big data: A deep learning approach. *IEEE Transactions on Intelligent Transportation Systems, 16*(2), 865–873. doi:10.1109/TITS.2014.2345663

Maatouk, O., Ayadi, W., Bouziri, H., & Duval, B. (2014). Evolutionary Algorithm Based on New Crossover for the Biclustering of Gene Expression Data. Proceedings of the Pattern Recognition in Bioinformatics, 48-59. doi:10.1007/978-3-319-09192-1_5

Macenko, M. (2009). A method for normalizing histology slides for quantitative analysis. *IEEE International Symposium on Biomedical Imaging: From Nano to Macro*, 1107-1110. 10.1109/ISBI.2009.5193250

Maćkiewicz, A., & Ratajczak, W. (1993). Principal Components Analysis (PCA). *Computers & Geosciences, 19*(3), 303–342. doi:10.1016/0098-3004(93)90090-R

Maitrey, S., & Jha, C. K. (2015). MapReduce: Simplified Data Analysis of Big Data. *Procedia Computer Science, 57*, 563–571. doi:10.1016/j.procs.2015.07.392

Maksimovic, M., Cuccovillo, L., & Aichroth, P. (2019, June). Copy-Move Forgery Detection and Localization via Partial Audio Matching. In *Audio Engineering Society Conference: 2019 AES International Conference On Audio Forensics*. Audio Engineering Society.

Malik, H. (2013). Acoustic environment identification and its applications to audio forensics. *IEEE Transactions on Information Forensics and Security, 8*(11), 1827–1837. doi:10.1109/TIFS.2013.2280888

Malik, H., & Farid, H. (2010, March). Audio forensics from acoustic reverberation. In *2010 IEEE International Conference on Acoustics, Speech and Signal Processing* (pp. 1710-1713). IEEE. 10.1109/ICASSP.2010.5495479

Maloof, M. A. (2006). *Machine learning and data mining for computer security: methods and applications*. Springer. doi:10.1007/1-84628-253-5

Mamoshina, P., Vieira, A., Putin, E., & Zhavoronkov, A. (2016). Applications of deep learning in biomedicine. *Molecular Pharmaceutics, 13*(5), 1445–1454. doi:10.1021/acs.molpharmaceut.5b00982 PMID:27007977

Mao, Q., Pan, X., Zhan, Y., & Shen, X. (2015). Using Kinect for real-time emotion recognition via facial expressions. *Frontiers Inf Technol Electronic Eng, 16*(4), 272–282. doi:10.1631/FITEE.1400209

Mardy (multichannel acoustic reverberation database at york) database a Speech and audio processing laboratory. (n.d.). Retrieved from http://commsp.ee.ic.ac.uk/~sap/resources/mardy-multichannel-acoustic-reverberation-database-at-york-database/

MATLAB and Statistics Toolbox Release. (2018b). Natick, MA: The MathWorks, Inc.

McCorduck, P. (2004). *Machines who think.* Academic Press.

McKinley Stacker, I. V. (2015). IBM waston analytics. Sample data: HR employee attrition and performance [Data file]. McKinley Stacker.

Mikolov, T., Karafiát, M., Burget, L., Černocký, J., & Khudanpur, S. (2010). Recurrent neural network based language model. *Eleventh annual conference of the international speech communication association.*

Mishra, P. (2019). Introduction to PyTorch, Tensors, and Tensor Operations. In PyTorch Recipes (pp. 1-27). Apress.

Mitchell, P. E., & Yan, H. (2001, September). Newspaper document analysis featuring connected line segmentation. In *Proceedings of Sixth International Conference on Document Analysis and Recognition* (pp. 1181-1185). IEEE. 10.1109/ICDAR.2001.953971

Mohamad, M. S., Omatu, S., Deris, S., & Yoshioka, M. (2011). A Modified Binary Particle Swarm Optimization for Selecting the Small Subset of Informative Genes From Gene Expression Data. *IEEE Transactions on Information Technology in Biomedicine*, *15*(6), 813–822. doi:10.1109/TITB.2011.2167756 PMID:21914573

Mohammadi, M., Al-Fuqaha, A., Sorour, S., & Guizani, M. (2018). Deep learning for IoT big data and streaming analytics: A survey. *IEEE Communications Surveys and Tutorials*, *20*(4), 2923–2960. doi:10.1109/COMST.2018.2844341

Moncarz, E., Zhao, J., & Kay, C. (2009). An exploratory study of US lodging properties' organizational practices on employee turnover and retention. *International Journal of Contemporary Hospitality Management*, *21*(4), 437–458. doi:10.1108/09596110910955695

Mondal, P. (n.d.). *7 Important Factors that May Affect the Learning Process*. Retrieved from http://www.yourarticlelibrary.com/learning/7-important-factors-that-may-affect-the-learning-process/6064/

MoradiAmin, M., Memari, A., Samadzadehaghdam, N., Kermani, S., & Talebi, A.MoradiAmin. (2016). Computer aided detection and classification of acute lymphoblastic leukemia cell subtypes based on microscopic image analysis. *Microscopy Research and Technique*, *79*(10), 908–916. doi:10.1002/jemt.22718 PMID:27406956

Moravec, H. (1988). *Mind children: The future of robot and human intelligence*. Harvard University Press.

Morgan, J. N., & Sonquist, J. A. (1963). Problems in the analysis of survey data, and a proposal. *Journal of the American Statistical Association*, *58*(302), 415–434. doi:10.1080/01621459.1963.10500855

Morgan, K. A. (2000). *Myth and Philosophy from the Presocratics to Plato*. Cambridge University Press. doi:10.1017/CBO9780511482540

Muhammad, W., & Aramvith, S. (2019). Multi-Scale Inception Based Super-Resolution Using Deep Learning Approach. *Electronics (Basel)*, *8*(8), 892. doi:10.3390/electronics8080892

Mushtaq, I., & Khan, S. N. (2012). Factors Affecting Students' Academic Performance. *Global Journal of Management and Business Research*, *12*(9).

MXNet. (2017). *A flexible and efficient library for deep learning*. Author.

Nagy, G., & Seth, S. C. (1984). *Hierarchical representation of optically scanned documents*. Academic Press.

Nahid, A.-A., Mehrabi, M. A., & Kong, Y. (2018). Histopathological Breast Cancer Image Classification by Deep Neural Network Techniques Guided by Local Clustering. *BioMed Research International*, *2018*, 1–20. doi:10.1155/2018/2362108 PMID:29707566

Najafabadi, M. M., Villansutre, F., Khoshgoftaar, T. M., Seliya, N., Wald, R., & Muharemagic, E. (2015). *Deep learning applications and challenges in big data analytics*. Springer Open Journal of Big Data. doi:10.118640537-014-0007-7

Nandedkar, A. V., Mukhopadhyay, J., & Sural, S. (2015, August). Text-graphics separation to detect logo and stamp from color document images: A spectral approach. In *2015 13th International Conference on Document Analysis and Recognition (ICDAR)* (pp. 571-575). IEEE.

Nanoti, A., Jain, S., Gupta, C., & Vyas, G. (2017). Detection of Malaria Parasite Species and Life Cycle Stages Using Microscopic Images of Thin Blood Smear. *Proceedings of the International Conference on Inventive Computation Technologies, ICICT 2016, 1*, 1–6.

Narkhede, M., & Patole, R. (2019). Acoustic Scene Identification for Audio Authentication. In *Soft Computing and Signal Processing* (pp. 593–602). Singapore: Springer. doi:10.1007/978-981-13-3600-3_56

Nascimento, P. P. (2016). *Applications of Deep Learning Techniques on NILM*. Rio de Janeiro: Academic Press.

Nazeri, K., Aminpour, A., & Ebrahimi, M. (2018). Two-Stage Convolutional Neural Network for Breast Cancer Histology Image Classification. In A. Campilho, F. Karray, & B. ter Haar Romeny (Eds.), Lecture Notes in Computer Science: Vol. 10882. *Proceedings of Image Analysis and Recognition (ICIAR 2018)*. Cham: Springer. doi:10.1007/978-3-319-93000-8_81

Nazlibilek, S., Karacor, D., Ercan, T., Sazli, M., Kalender, O., & Ege, Y. (2014). Automatic segmentation, counting, size determination and classification of white blood cells. *Measurement, 55*, 58–65. doi:10.1016/j.measurement.2014.04.008

Nesrine, A., Asma, M., & Sahbi, M. (2019). A comparative study of nonlinear Bayesian filtering algorithms for estimation of gene expression time series data. *Turkish Journal of Electrical Engineering and Computer Sciences, 27*(4), 2648–2665. doi:10.3906/elk-1809-187

Nguyen, G., Dlugolinsky, S., Bobák, M., Tran, V., García, Á. L., Heredia, I., ... Hluchý, L. (2019). Machine Learning and Deep Learning frameworks and libraries for large-scale data mining: A survey. *Artificial Intelligence Review, 52*(1), 77–124. doi:10.100710462-018-09679-z

Nguyen, K., Fookes, C., & Sridharan, S. (2015, September). Improving Deep Convolutional Neural Networks with Unsupervised Feature Learning. *IEEE International Conference on Image Processing (ICIP)*, 2270-2271. 10.1109/ICIP.2015.7351206

Nguyen, T., Khosravi, A., Creighton, D., & Nahavandi, S. (2015). Hidden Markov models for cancer classification using gene expression profiles. *Information Sciences, Elsevier, 316*, 293–307. doi:10.1016/j.ins.2015.04.012

Nielsen, M. (2017). *Neural Networks and Deep Learning*. Retrieved from neuralnetworksanddeeplearning.com: http://neuralnetworksanddeeplearning.com/

NobleR. (2019). *Leucocytes*. Retrieved from Pinterest: https://www.pinterest.pt/pin/83457399321177163

Nugroho, H. A., Akbar, S. A., & Herdiana Murhandarwati, E. (2016). Feature Extraction and Classification for Detection Malaria Parasites in Thin Blood Smear. *ICITACEE 2015 - 2nd International Conference on Information Technology, Computer, and Electrical Engineering: Green Technology Strengthening in Information Technology, Electrical and Computer Engineering Implementation Proceedings, 1*(c), 197–201.

NumPy. (2018). *NumPy—the fundamental package for scientific computing with Python*. Retrieved 2019, from http://www.numpy. org/

Nvidia CUDA. (2007). *Compute unified device architecture programming guide*. Author.

NVIDIA. (2017). *NVIDIA Collective Communications Library (NCCL)*. Author.

Ogiela, M. R., & Tadeusiewicz, R. (2008a). Pattern recognition, clustering and classification applied to selected medical images. *Studies in Computational Intelligence, 84*, 117–151. doi:10.1007/978-3-540-75402-2_6

Oliveira, S. A., Seguin, B., & Kaplan, F. (2018, August). dhSegment: A generic deep-learning approach for document segmentation. In *2018 16th International Conference on Frontiers in Handwriting Recognition (ICFHR)* (pp. 7-12). IEEE.

Olson, D. L., & Delen, D. (2008). *Advanced data mining techniques* (1st ed.). Springer Publishing Company.

Oyedotun, O. K., & Khashman, A. (2016). Document segmentation using textural features summarization and feedforward neural network. *Applied Intelligence*, *45*(1), 198–212. doi:10.100710489-015-0753-z

Padideh. (2017). A Deep Learning Approach For Cancer Detection And Relevant Gene Identification. *Pacific Symposium on Biocomputing*, 219-229.

Pan, S. J., & Yang, Q. (2009). A survey on transfer learning. *IEEE Transactions on Knowledge and Data Engineering*, *22*(10), 1345–1359. doi:10.1109/TKDE.2009.191

Pascanu, R., Stokes, J. W., Sanossian, H., Marinescu, M., & Thomas, A. (2015, April). Malware classification with recurrent networks. In *2015 IEEE International Conference on Acoustics, Speech and Signal Processing (ICASSP)* (pp. 1916-1920). IEEE. 10.1109/ICASSP.2015.7178304

Paszke, A., Gross, S., Massa, F., Lerer, A., Bradbury, J., Chanan, G., . . . Desmaison, A. (2019). PyTorch: An imperative style, high-performance deep learning library. In Advances in Neural Information Processing Systems (pp. 8024-8035). Academic Press.

Paszke, A., Gross, S., Chintala, S., Chanan, G., Yang, E., DeVito, Z., & Lerer, A. (2017). *Automatic differentiation in PyTorch*. Academic Press.

Patole, R., Kore, G., & Rege, P. (2017, June). Reverberation based tampering detection in audio recordings. In *Audio Engineering Society Conference: 2017 AES International Conference on Audio Forensics*. Audio Engineering Society.

Pattanaik, Swarnkar, & Sheet. (2017). Object Detection Technique for Malaria Parasite in Thin Blood Smear Images. *Proceedings - 2017 IEEE International Conference on Bioinformatics and Biomedicine, BIBM 2017*, 2120–23.

Pedregosa, F., Varoquaux, G., Gramfort, A., Michel, V., Thirion, B., Grisel, O., & ... . (2011). Scikit-learn: Machine learning in Python. *Journal of Machine Learning Research*, *12*(Oct), 2825–2830.

Perez, L., & Wang, J. (2017, December). *The Effectiveness of Data Augmentation in Image Classification using Deep Learning*. ArXiv.

Perone, C.S., Saravia, E., Ballester, P., & Tare, M. (2018, November 24). *perone/medicaltorch: Release v0.2* (Version v0.2). Zenodo. doi:10.5281/zenodo.1495335

Perroud, T., Sobottka, K., & Bunke, H. (2001, September). Text extraction from color documents-clustering approaches in three and four dimensions. In *Proceedings of Sixth International Conference on Document Analysis and Recognition* (pp. 937-941). IEEE. 10.1109/ICDAR.2001.953923

Phung, L. T., Chau, V. T., & Phung, N. H. (2015, November). Extracting Rule RF in Educational Data Classification from a Random Forest to Interpretable Refined Rules. *International Conference on Advanced Computing and Applications (ACOMP)*, 20-27. 10.1109/ACOMP.2015.13

Pokharna, H. (2016). *The best explanation of Convolutional Neural Networks on the Internet!* Retrieved August 12, 2019, from https://medium.com/technologymadeeasy/the-best-explanation-of-convolutional-neural-networks-on-the-internet-fbb8b1ad5df8

Poostchi, M., Silamut, K., Maude, R. J., Jaeger, S., & Thoma, G. (2018). Image Analysis and Machine Learning for Detecting Malaria. *Translational Research; the Journal of Laboratory and Clinical Medicine*, *194*, 36–55. doi:10.1016/j.trsl.2017.12.004 PMID:29360430

Powers, D. M. (2011). *Evaluation: from precision, recall and F-measure to ROC, informedness, markedness and correlation*. Academic Press.

Pradeep, A., & Das, S., & J, J. (2015). Students Dropout Factor Prediction Using EDM Techniques. *International Conference on Soft-Computing and Network Security*. 10.1109/ICSNS.2015.7292372

Prinyakupt, J., & Pluempitiwiriyawej, C. (2015). Segmentation of white blood cells and comparison of cell morphology by linear and naïve Bayes classifiers. *Biomedical Engineering Online*, *14*(1), 63. doi:10.118612938-015-0037-1 PMID:26123131

Punlumjeak, W., & Rachburee, N. (2015, October). A Comparative Study of Feature Selection Techniques for Classify Student Performance. *7th International Conference on Information Technology and Electrical Engineering (ICITEE)*, 425-429. 10.1109/ICITEED.2015.7408984

Putzu, L., Caocci, G., & Di Ruberto, C. (2014). Leucocyte classification for leukaemia detection using image processing techniques. *Artificial Intelligence in Medicine*, *62*(3), 179–191. doi:10.1016/j.artmed.2014.09.002 PMID:25241903

Pyingkodi, M., & Thangarajan, R. (2017, February). Meta-Analysis in Autism Gene Expression Dataset with Biclustering Methods using Random Cuckoo Search Algorithm. *Asian Journal of Research in Social Sciences and Humanities*, *7*(2), 186–194. doi:10.5958/2249-7315.2017.00082.X

Qin, F., Gao, N., Peng, Y., Wu, Z., Shen, S., & Grudtsin, A. (2018). Fine-grained leukocyte classification with deep residual learning for microscopic images. *Computer Methods and Programs in Biomedicine*, *162*, 243–252. doi:10.1016/j.cmpb.2018.05.024 PMID:29903491

Rahman, A. (2019). *Improving Malaria Parasite Detection from Red Blood Cell Using Deep Convolutional Neural Networks*. Https://Arxiv.Org/Ftp/Arxiv/Papers/1907/1907.10418.Pdf

Rajanna, A. R., Aryafar, K., Shokoufandeh, A., & Ptucha, R. (2015). Deep Neural Networks: A Case Study for Music Genere Classification. *14th International Conference on Machine Learning and Applications (ICMLA)*, 665-660. 10.1109/ICMLA.2015.160

Ramsundar, B., & Zadeh, R. B. (2018). *TensorFlow for deep learning: from linear regression to reinforcement learning*. O'Reilly Media, Inc.

Rane, A., & Kumar, A. (2018, July). Sentiment Classification System of Twitter Data for {US} Airline Service Analysis. In *2018 {IEEE} 42nd Annual Computer Software and Applications Conference ({COMPSAC})*. IEEE. 10.1109/compsac.2018.00114

Raschka, S. (2015). *Python machine learning*. Packt Publishing Ltd.

Rathore, S., Hussain, M., & Khan, A. (2014). GECC: Gene Expression Based Ensemble Classification of Colon Samples. *IEEE/ACM Transactions on Computational Biology and Bioinformatics*, *11*(6), 1131–1145. doi:10.1109/TCBB.2014.2344655 PMID:26357050

Ratliff, M. S., & Patterson, E. (2008b). Emotion recognition using facial expressions with active appearance models. *Proceedings of the Third IASTED International Conference on Human Computer Interaction*, 138–143.

Ravanelli, M., Parcollet, T., & Bengio, Y. (2019, May). The pytorch-kaldi speech recognition toolkit. In *ICASSP 2019-2019 IEEE International Conference on Acoustics, Speech and Signal Processing (ICASSP)* (pp. 6465-6469). IEEE. 10.1109/ICASSP.2019.8683713

Red Blood Cell Images. (2019). https://me.me//normal-malaria-red-blood-cell-infected-with-malaria-red-blood-a017e8a3cd7447b499beb75a51129868

Redmon, J., & Farhadi, A. (2020). *YOLO9000: Better, Faster, Stronger*. arXiv.

Redmon, J., & Farhadi, A. (2020). *YOLOv3: An Incremental Improvement.* arXiv

Redmon, J., Divvala, S., Girshick, R., & Farhadi, A. (2020). *You Only Look Once: Unified, Real-Time Object Detection.* arXiv.

Rege, P. P., & Chandrakar, C. A. (2012). Text-image separation in document images using boundary/perimeter detection. *ACEEE International Journal on Signal and Image Processing, 3*(1), 10–14.

Rehman, A., Abbas, N., Saba, T., Rahman, S., Mehmood, Z., & Kolivand, H. (2018). Classification of acute lymphoblastic leukemia using deep learning. *Microscopy Research and Technique, 81*(11), 1310–1317. doi:10.1002/jemt.23139 PMID:30351463

Ren, S., He, K., Girshick, R., & Sun, J. (2015). Faster r-cnn: Towards real-time object detection with region proposal networks. In Advances in neural information processing systems (pp. 91-99). Academic Press.

Ren, S., He, K., Girshick, R., & Sun, J. (2015). *Faster r-cnn: Towards real-time object detection with region proposal networks.* Paper presented at the Advances in neural information processing systems.

Rengeswaran, B., Mathaiyan, N., & Kandasamy, P. (2017, May). Cuckoo Search with Mutation for Biclustering of Microarray Gene Expression Data. *The International Arab Journal of Information Technology, 14*(3).

Ren, S., He, K., Girshick, R., & Sun, J. (2017). Faster R-CNN: Towards Real-Time Object Detection with Region Proposal Networks. *IEEE Transactions on Pattern Analysis and Machine Intelligence, 39*(6), 1137–1149. doi:10.1109/TPAMI.2016.2577031 PMID:27295650

Reyes, A. K., J. C., & Camargo1, J. E. (2015). Fine-tuning Deep Convolutional Networks for plant recognition. *CLEF 2015.*

Rezatofighi, S., & Soltanian-Zadeh, H. (2011). Automatic recognition of five types of white blood cells in peripheral blood. *Computerized Medical Imaging and Graphics, 35*(4), 333–343. doi:10.1016/j.compmedimag.2011.01.003 PMID:21300521

Ronneberger, O., Fischer, P., & Brox, T. (2015, October). U-net: Convolutional networks for biomedical image segmentation. In *International Conference on Medical image computing and computer-assisted intervention* (pp. 234-241). Springer. 10.1007/978-3-319-24574-4_28

Rosebrock, A. (2017, March 20). *ImageNet: VGGNet, ResNet, Inception, and Xception with Keras.* Retrieved from pyimagesearch: https://www.pyimagesearch.com/2017/03/20/imagenet-vggnet-resnet-inception-xception-keras/

Rosenblatt, F. (1958). The perceptron: A probabilistic model for information storage and organization in the brain. *Psychological Review, 65*(6), 386–408. doi:10.1037/h0042519 PMID:13602029

Rubio-Largo, A., Vega-Rodriguez, M. A., & Gonzalez-Alvarez, D. L. (2016). Miguel A. Vega-Rodríguez, David L. González-Álvarez, 'A Hybrid Multiobjective Memetic Metaheuristic for Multiple Sequence Alignment'. *IEEE Transactions on Evolutionary Computation, 20*(4), 499–514. doi:10.1109/TEVC.2015.2469546

Ruifrok, A., & Johnston, D. (2001). Quantification of histochemical staining by color deconvolution. *Analytical and Quantitative Cytology and Histology, 23.* PMID:11531144

Ruiz, P. (2018, October 10). *Understanding and visualizing DenseNets.* Retrieved from Medium: https://towardsdatascience.com/understanding-and-visualizing-densenets-7f688092391a

Rumelhart, D. E., Hinton, G. E., & Williams, R. J. (1986). Learning representations by back-propagating errors. *Nature, 323*(6088), 533-536.

Rumelhart, D. E., Hinton, G. E., & Williams, R. J. (1988). Learning representations by back-propagating errors. *Cognitive Modeling, 5*(3), 1.

Russakovsky, O., Jia Deng, H. S., Krause, J., Satheesh, S., Ma, S., Huang, Z., ... Fei-Fei, L. (2015). ImageNet Large Scale Visual Recognition Challenge. *International Journal of Computer Vision, 115*(3), 211–252. doi:10.100711263-015-0816-y

Russell, S. J., & Norvig, P. (2016). *Artificial intelligence: a modern approach*. Malaysia: Pearson Education Limited.

Saber, H. B., & Elloumi, M. (2015). Efficiently Mining Gene Expression Data via Novel Binary Biclustering Algorithms. *Journal of Proteomics & Bioinformatics, S9*(8).

Sajjad, M., Khan, S., & Jan, Z. (2016, December). Leukocytes Classification and Segmentation in Microscopic Blood Smear: A Resource-Aware Healthcare Service in Smart Cities. *IEEE Access: Practical Innovations, Open Solutions*, 3475–3489.

Samuel, A. L. (1988). *Some studies in machine learning using the game of checkers. II—recent progress. In Computer Games I* (pp. 366–400). Springer.

Santosh, K. C., & Iwata, E. (2012). Stroke-Based Cursive Character Recognition. *Advances in Character Recognition*, 175.

Santosh, K. C., Nattee, C., & Lamiroy, B. (2012). Relative positioning of stroke-based clustering: A new approach to online handwritten devanagari character recognition. *International Journal of Image and Graphics, 12*(02), 1250016. doi:10.1142/S0219467812500167

Santosh, K. C., & Wendling, L. (2015). Character recognition based on non-linear multi-projection profiles measure. *Frontiers of Computer Science, 9*(5), 678–690. doi:10.100711704-015-3400-2

Saradhi, V. V., & Palshikar, G. K. (2011). Employee churn prediction. *Expert Systems with Applications, 38*(3), 1999–2006. doi:10.1016/j.eswa.2010.07.134

Sarmiento, A., & Fondón, I. (2018). Automatic Breast Cancer Grading of Histological Images Based on Colour and Texture Descriptors. In A. Campilho, F. Karray, & B. ter Haar Romeny (Eds.), Lecture Notes in Computer Science: Vol. 10882. *Proceedings of Image Analysis and Recognition (ICIAR 2018)*. Cham: Springer. doi:10.1007/978-3-319-93000-8_101

Saurabh Pal. (2019, February 26). Semantic Segmentation: Introduction to the Deep Learning Technique Behind Google Pixel's Camera! [Blog post]. Retrieved from https://www.analyticsvidhya.com/blog/2019/02/tutorial-semantic-segmentation-google-deeplab/

Scherer, D., Muller, A., & Behnke, S. (2010, September). Evaluation of Pooling Operations. *20th International Conference on Artificial Neural Networks (ICANN)*, 4.

Schnitt, S. (2010). Classification and prognosis of invasive breast cancer: From morphology to molecular taxonomy. *Modern Pathology, 23*(S2), S60–S64. doi:10.1038/modpathol.2010.33 PMID:20436504

Scientific Working Group on Digital Evidence. (2008, Jan.). *SWGDE Best Practices for Forensic Audio, Version 1.0*. Retrieved from https://www.swgde.org/documents

Seichter, D., Cuccovillo, L., & Aichroth, P. (2016, March). AAC encoding detection and bitrate estimation using a convolutional neural network. In *2016 IEEE International Conference on Acoustics, Speech and Signal Processing (ICASSP)* (pp. 2069-2073). IEEE. 10.1109/ICASSP.2016.7472041

Seide, F., & Agarwal, A. (2016, August). CNTK: Microsoft's open-source deep-learning toolkit. In *Proceedings of the 22nd ACM SIGKDD International Conference on Knowledge Discovery and Data Mining* (pp. 2135-2135). ACM. 10.1145/2939672.2945397

Sexton, R. S., McMurtrey, S., Michalopoulos, J. O., & Smith, A. M. (2005). Employee turnover: A neural network solution. *Computers & Operations Research, 32*(10), 2635–2651. doi:10.1016/j.cor.2004.06.022

Shahin, A., Guo, Y., Amin, K., & Sharawi, A. (2019). White blood cells identification system based on convolutional deep neural learning networks. *Computer Methods and Programs in Biomedicine, 168,* 69–80. doi:10.1016/j.cmpb.2017.11.015 PMID:29173802

Shankar, V. G., Devi, B., & Srivastava, S. (2018a). DataSpeak: Data extraction, aggregation, and classification using big data novel algorithm. *Computing, communication and signal processing. Advances in intelligent systems and computing, 810.*

Shankar, V. G., Jangid, M., Devi, B., & Kabra, S. (2018b). Mobile big data: Malware and its analysis. *Proceedings of First International Conference on Smart System, Innovations and Computing. Smart Innovation, Systems and Technologies, 79,* 831–842.

Shen, H., Pan, W. D., Dong, Y., & Alim, M. (2017). Lossless Compression of Curated Erythrocyte Images Using Deep Autoencoders for Malaria Infection Diagnosis. *2016 Picture Coding Symposium, PCS 2016,* 1–5.

Shiau, W.-L., & Chau, P. Y. (2016). Understanding behavioral intention to use a cloud computing classroom: A multiple model comparison approach. *Information & Management, 53*(3), 355–365. doi:10.1016/j.im.2015.10.004

Shoham, Y. (2018). The AI Index 2018 Annual Report. *AI Index Steering Committee, Human-Centered AI Initiative, Stanford University.* Available at http://cdn.aiindex.org/2018/AI%20Index%202018%20Annual%20Report.pdf

Shoukat, A. (2013). Factors Contributing to the Students' Academic Performance: A Case Study of Islamia University Sub-Campus. *American Journal of Educational Research,* 283–289.

Shouno, H., Suzuki, S., & Kido, S. (2015, November). A transfer learning method with deep convolutional neural network for diffuse lung disease classification. In *International Conference on Neural Information Processing* (pp. 199-207). Springer. 10.1007/978-3-319-26532-2_22

Shreya Ghelani. (2019, May 16). From Word Embeddings to Pretrained Language Models — A New Age in NLP — Part 2 [Blog Post]. Retrieved from https://towardsdatascience.com/from-word-embeddings-to-pretrained-language-models-a-new-age-in-nlp-part-2-e9af9a0bdcd9

Sikaroudi, E., Mohammad, A., Ghousi, R., & Sikaroudi, A. (2015). A data mining approach to employee turnover prediction (case study: Arak automotive parts manufacturing). *Journal of Industrial and Systems Engineering, 8*(4), 106–121.

Simonyan, K., & Zisserman, A. (2014, September 4). Very Deep Convolutional Networks for Large-Scale Image Recognition. *ILCR, 2015,* 2–4.

Sindhuri, M. S., & Anusha, N. (2016, March). Text separation in document images through Otsu's method. In *2016 International Conference on Wireless Communications, Signal Processing and Networking (WiSPNET),* (pp. 2395-2399). IEEE. 10.1109/WiSPNET.2016.7566571

Sinha, R. M. K., & Bansal, V. (1995, October). On Devanagari document processing. In *1995 IEEE International Conference on Systems, Man and Cybernetics. Intelligent Systems for the 21st Century* (Vol. 2, pp. 1621-1626). IEEE. 10.1109/ICSMC.1995.538004

Slaoui, M., & Fiette, L. (2011). Histopathology Procedures: From Tissue Sampling to Histopathological Evaluation. In J. C. Gautier (Ed.), *Drug Safety Evaluation. Methods in Molecular Biology (Methods and Protocols)* (Vol. 691). Humana Press. doi:10.1007/978-1-60761-849-2_4

Soni, S., Shankar, V. G., & Chaurasia, S. (2019b). Route-The Safe: A Robust Model for Safest Route Prediction Using Crime and Accidental Data. International Journal of Advanced Science and Technology, 28(16).

Sree, S. V., Ng, E. Y., Acharya, R. U., & Faust, O. (2011). Breast imaging: A survey. *World Journal of Clinical Oncology, 2*(4), 171–178. doi:10.5306/wjco.v2.i4.171 PMID:21611093

Stan, G. B., Embrechts, J. J., & Archambeau, D. (2002). Comparison of different impulse response measurement techniques. *Journal of the Audio Engineering Society, 50*(4), 249–262.

Stathonikos, N., Veta, M., Huisman, A., & van Diest, P. (2013). Going fully digital: Perspective of a Dutch academic pathology lab. *Journal of Pathology Informatics, 4*(1), 15. doi:10.4103/2153-3539.114206 PMID:23858390

Stewart, S., & Barrett, B. (2017, November). Document image page segmentation and character recognition as semantic segmentation. In *Proceedings of the 4th International Workshop on Historical Document Imaging and Processing* (pp. 101-106). ACM. 10.1145/3151509.3151518

Struijk, B. (2012). A new understanding of modern robotics. *Hadmérnök, 7*(2).

Subramanian, J., & Simon, R. (2010). Gene expression-based prognostic signatures in lung cancer: Ready for clinical use? *Journal of the National Cancer Institute, 102*(7), 464–474. doi:10.1093/jnci/djq025 PMID:20233996

Sudheer Kumar, E., & Shoba Bindu, C. (2019). Medical Image Analysis Using Deep Learning: A Systematic Literature Review. In Proceedings of Emerging Technologies in Computer Engineering: Microservices in Big Data Analytics (ICETCE 2019). Communications in Computer and Information Science (vol. 985, pp. 81-97). Springer. doi:10.1007/978-981-13-8300-7_8

Sukhija, K., Jindal, D. M., & Aggarwal, D. N. (2015, October). The Recent State of Educational Data Mining: A Survey and Future Visions. *IEEE 3rd International Conference on MOOCs, Innovation and Technology in Education*, 354-359. doi: 10.1109/MITE.2015.7375344

Sun, H. M. (2006). Enhanced constrained run-length algorithm for complex layout document processing. *International Journal of Applied Science and Engineering, 4*(3), 297–309.

Suryawan, A., & Putra, E. (2016). Analysis of Determining Factors for Successful Student's GPA Achievement. *11th International Conference on Knowledge, Information and Creativity Support Systems (KICSS)*, 1-7.

Sutskever, I., Vinyals, O., & Le, Q. V. (2014). Sequence to sequence learning with neural networks. In Advances in neural information processing systems (pp. 3104-3112). Academic Press.

Szegedy, C., Liu, W., Jia, Y., Sermanet, P., Reed, S., Anguelov, D., ... Rabinovich, A. (2014, September 17). Going Deeper with Convolutions. *CVPR, 2015*, 4.

Tan. (2015). Unsupervised feature construction and knowledge extraction from genome-wide assays of breast cancer with denoising autoencoders. *Pacific Symposium on Biocomputing, 20*, 132–143. PMID:25592575

Tanya, A., Sharan, R., & Shamir, R. (2002). Discovering Statistically Significant Biclusters in Gene Expression Data. *BMC Bioinformatics, 18*(Suppl 1), 136–144. doi:10.1093/bioinformatics/18.suppl_1.S136

Tekalp, A. M., & Tekalp, A. M. (1995). Digital video processing (Vol. 1). Prentice Hall.

TensorFlow. (2016). Retrieved 4 September 2019, from https://www.tensorflow.org/guide/graphs

Thomas, T., Vijayaraghavan, A. P., & Emmanuel, S. (2020). *Machine Learning and Cybersecurity. In Machine Learning Approaches in Cyber Security Analytics* (pp. 37–47). Springer.

Tian, Y. I., Kanade, T., & Cohn, J. F. (2001). Recognizing action units for facial expression analysis. *IEEE Transactions on Pattern Analysis and Machine Intelligence, 23*(2), 97–115. doi:10.1109/34.908962 PMID:25210210

Tiwari, M. (2012). An gene expression pattern. *Journal of Natural Science, Biology, and Medicine, 3*(1), 12–18. doi:10.4103/0976-9668.95935 PMID:22690045

Tiwari, P., Qian, J., Li, Q., Wang, B., Gupta, D., Khanna, A., ... de Albuquerque, V. H. C. (2018). Detection of subtype blood cells using deep learning. *Cognitive Systems Research, 52*, 1036–1044. doi:10.1016/j.cogsys.2018.08.022

Tran, T. A., Na, I. S., & Kim, S. H. (2015). Separation of Text and Non-text in Document Layout Analysis using a Recursive Filter. *Transactions on Internet and Information Systems (Seoul), 9*(10).

Turing awards press note. (2018). Retrieved from https://awards.acm.org/binaries/content/assets/press-releases/2019/march/turing-award-2018.pdf

Tzeng, H.-M., Hsieh, J.-G., & Lin, Y.-L. (2004). Predicting Nurses' Intention to Quit with a Support Vector Machine: A New Approach to Set up an Early Warning Mechanism in Human Resource Management. *CIN: Computers, Informatics, Nursing, 22*(4), 232–242. PMID:15494654

Tzortzis, G., & Likas, A. (2007, October). Deep Belief Networks for Spam Filtering. *IEEE International Conference on Tools with Artificial Intelligence (ICTAI 2007)*, 306-309.

Underwood, M. (1977). Machines that understand speech. *Radio and Electronic Engineer, 47*(8), 368–376. doi:10.1049/ree.1977.0055

van de Leemput, S. C., Teuwen, J., & Manniesing, R. (2018). *MemCNN: a Framework for Developing Memory Efficient Deep Invertible Networks*. Academic Press.

Vang, Y. S., Chen, Z., & Xie, X. (2018). Deep Learning Framework for Multi-class Breast Cancer Histology Image Classification. In A. Campilho, F. Karray, & B. ter Haar Romeny (Eds.), Lecture Notes in Computer Science: Vol. 10882. *Proceedings of Image Analysis and Recognition (ICIAR 2018)*. Cham: Springer. doi:10.1007/978-3-319-93000-8_104

Vincent, P., Larochelle, H., Lajoie, I., Bengio, Y., & Manzagol, P.-A. (2010). Stacked Denoising Autoencoders: Learning Useful Representations in a Deep Network with a Local Denoising Criterion. *Journal of Machine Learning Research, 11*, 3371–3408.

Vitor. (2017). Learning inflfluential genes on cancer geneexpression data with stacked denoising autoencoders. *IEEE International Conference on Bioinformatics and Biomedicine*.

Vora, D., & Iyer, K. (2017). A Survey of Inferences from Deep Learning Algorithms. *Journal of Engineering and Applied Sciences, 12*(SI), 9467-9472.

Vora, D., & Kamatchi, R. (2018). EDM – Survey of Performance Factors and Algorithms Applied. *International Journal of Engineering & Technology, 7*(2.6), 93-97.

Voss, P. (2007). *Essentials of general intelligence: The direct path to artificial general intelligence. In Artificial general intelligence* (pp. 131–157). Springer. doi:10.1007/978-3-540-68677-4_4

Wang, Q., Bi, S., Sun, M., Wang, Y., Wang, D., & Yang, S. (2019). Deep learning approach to peripheral leukocyte recognition. *PLoS One, 14*(6), e0218808. doi:10.1371/journal.pone.0218808 PMID:31237896

Werbos, P. J. (1990). Backpropagation through time: What it does and how to do it. *Proceedings of the IEEE, 78*(10), 1550–1560. doi:10.1109/5.58337

Widiawati, C. R. A., Nugroho, H. A., & Ardiyanto, I. (2016). Plasmodium Detection Methods in Thick Blood Smear Images for Diagnosing Malaria: A Review. *Proceedings - 2016 1st International Conference on Information Technology, Information Systems and Electrical Engineering, ICITISEE 2016*, 142–47. 10.1109/ICITISEE.2016.7803063

Wiering, M. A. M. S., Millea, A., Meijster, A., & Schomaker, L. (2016). *Deep Support Vector Machines for Regression Problems*. Retrieved from http://citeseerx.ist.psu.edu/viewdoc/download?doi=10.1.1.718.987&rep=rep1&type=pdf

Wiering, M., Schutten, M., Millea, A., Meijster, A., & Schomaker, L. (2013, October). Deep Learning using Linear Support Vector Machines. *International Conference on Machine Learning: Challenges in Representation Learning Workshop.*

Woolgar, S. (1985). Why not a sociology of machines? The case of sociology and artificial intelligence. *Sociology, 19*(4), 557–572. doi:10.1177/0038038585019004005

World Health Organization breast cancer statistics. (2018). Retrieved from https://www.who.int/cancer/prevention/diagnosis-screening/breast-cancer/en/

Wu, J. (2017, May 1). Introduction to Convolutional Neural Networks. *National Key Lab for Novel Software Technology,* 5-8.

Xiaoshu. (2017). A multi-objective biclustering algorithm based on fuzzy mathematics. *Neurocomputing, 253,* 177–182.

Xie, S., Girshick, R., Dollár, P., Tu, Z., & He, K. (2017, April 11). Aggregated Residual Transformations for Deep Neural Networks. *CVPR.*

Xing, W., Guo, R., Petakovic, E., & Goggins, S. (2015). Participation-based student final performance prediction model through interpretable Genetic Programming: Integrating learning analytics, educational data mining and theory. *Computers in Human Behavior, 47,* 168–181. doi:10.1016/j.chb.2014.09.034

Yang, X.-S., & Deb, S. (2014). Cuckoo Search: Recent Advances and Applications. *Neural Computing & Applications, 24*(1), 169–174. doi:10.100700521-013-1367-1

Yanming, G. (2016). Deep learning for visual understanding: A review. *Neurocomputing, 187,* 27–48. doi:10.1016/j.neucom.2015.09.116

Yan, Q., Yang, R., & Huang, J. (2015, April). Copy-move detection of audio recording with pitch similarity. In *2015 IEEE International Conference on Acoustics, Speech and Signal Processing (ICASSP)* (pp. 1782-1786). IEEE. 10.1109/ICASSP.2015.7178277

Yes you should understand backprop. (n.d.). *Karpathy.* retrieved 2019, from https://medium.com/@karpathy/yes-you-should-understand-backprop-e2f06eab496b

Yuan, Q., & Tan, C. L. (2001, September). Text extraction from gray scale document images using edge information. In *Proceedings of sixth international conference on document analysis and recognition* (pp. 302-306). IEEE. 10.1109/ICDAR.2001.953803

Yuan, Y., Zhang, M., Luo, P., Ghassemlooy, Z., Lang, L., Wang, D., ... Han, D. (2017). SVM-based detection in visible light communications. *Optik (Stuttgart), 151,* 55–64. doi:10.1016/j.ijleo.2017.08.089

Yuan, Z., Lu, Y., Wang, Z., & Xue, Y. (2014, August). Droid-sec: Deep learning in android malware detection. *Computer Communication Review, 44*(4), 371–372. doi:10.1145/2740070.2631434

Zaccone, G., Karim, M. R., & Menshawy, A. (2017). *Deep Learning with TensorFlow.* Packt Publishing Ltd.

Zeiler, M. D., & Fergus, R. (2014, September). Visualizing and understanding convolutional networks. In *European conference on computer vision* (pp. 818-833). Springer.

Zhang, Q.-J., & Devabhaktuni, V. K. (2003, APRIL). *Artificial Neural Networks for RF and Microwave.* IEEE.

Zhang, Z., Liu, Q., & Wang, Y. (2018). Road extraction by deep residual u-net. *IEEE Geoscience and Remote Sensing Letters, 15*(5), 749–753. doi:10.1109/LGRS.2018.2802944

Zhao, H., & Malik, H. (2012, August). Audio forensics using acoustic environment traces. In 2012 IEEE Statistical Signal Processing Workshop (SSP) (pp. 373-376). IEEE. doi:10.1109/SSP.2012.6319707

Zhao, H., Chen, Y., Wang, R., & Malik, H. (2017). Audio splicing detection and localization using environmental signature. *Multimedia Tools and Applications*, 76(12), 13897–13927. doi:10.100711042-016-3758-7

Zhao, J., Zhang, M., Zhou, Z., Chu, J., & Cao, F. (2016). Automatic detection and classification of leukocytes using convolutional neural networks. *Medical & Biological Engineering & Computing*, 55(8), 1287–1301. doi:10.100711517-016-1590-x PMID:27822698

Zhao, Y., Hryniewicki, M. K., Cheng, F., Fu, B., & Zhu, X. (2018). Employee turnover prediction with machine learning: A reliable approach. *Proceedings of SAI Intelligent Systems Conference*, 737–758.

Zhou, B., Lapedriza, A., Xiao, J., Torralba, A., & Oliva, A. (2014). Learning deep features for scene recognition using places database. In Advances in neural information processing systems (pp. 487-495). Academic Press.

Zhu, H., Zheng, M. A., Pelegris, A., Jayarajan, A., Phanishayee, A., Shroeder, B., & Pekhimenko, G. (2016, April 14). Benchmarking and Analyzing Deep Neural Network. In *2018 IEEE International Symposium on Workload Characterization (IISWC)*, (pp. 13-15). IEEE.

About the Contributors

Mehul Mahrishi is currently working as an Associate Professor in the faculty of computer Science & Engineering at the Swami Keshvanand Institute of Technology, Management and Gramothan, Jaipur – India. He is a Professional Member of IEEE Delhi Section, Life Member of Institution of Engineers, India (L-IEI) and Life member of International Association of Engineers (IAENG). He was a member of an Indian contingent of BRICS International Forum that travelled to Moscow, Russia to attend Russian Energy Week-2018 and BRICS Youth Energy Summit. He has published more than 20 research papers in national and international Journals/conferences including 19th ISDA, 4th SoCTA, 3rd International Conference on Machine Learning and Computing (ICMLC 2011), 3rd IACC 2013 and chapters in books. He has also participated in a range of forums by Infosys, TCS, and WIPRO-Mission 10 X, IBM etc. His research activities are currently twofold: while the first research activity is set to explore the developmental enhancements in applications in computer vision; the second major research theme focused on the emerging capabilities of parallel and cloud computing. Mr. Mahrishi is rewarded at number of occasions in various domains including Recognition as an active reviewer by Journal of Parallel and Distributed Computing (JPDC, Elsevier, and SCI & Scopus Indexed), IEEE continuing education certification for "Cloud Computing Enable Technologies and Recognition for outstanding performance in Campus Connect Program by Infosys, India.

Kamal Hiran is an Innovative and Enthusiastic Academic Professional having more than 14 years of experience in Academic Administration, Teaching and Research experience in India, Europe, and Africa. The editor has worked on various academic positions such as Lecturer, Sr. Lecturer, Asst. Professor, Associate Professor, Head IT, Head Academics, Founder, IEEE Liberia, IEEE Ghana Technical & Professional Activity Chair, IEEE SB Coordinator. The editor has done the tie-up with Academic-Industry collaboration as part of jobs such as Turnitin (Plagiarism Checker), Founder IEEE Student Branch, Ghana, and Oracle WDP. The editor has published and presented research papers in peer-reviewed journals as well as international conferences in India, Denmark, USA, Germany, Jordan, Ghana, and Ethiopia. Working as a Reviewer and Member in the International Program Committee in the International Journals: Journal of Medical and Biological Engineering (JMBE), Springer, Germany, IJCA USA, IGI-Global USA, and IJERT, India.

* * *

Shaheera Akhter received the B.E. degree from Government Engineering College, Aurangabad (2013) and M.E. degree from College of Engineering, Pune India (2017). She is currently working as a research fellow at College of Engineering, Her research interests include Signal and Image Processing, Pattern Recognition, Machine learning and Deep learning.

Shahina Anwarul received the B. Tech degree in Computer Science & Engineering from UPTU and M. tech degree in Information Security from MNNIT Allahabad, in 2013 and 2016, respectively. She is pursuing her PhD from University of Petroleum & Energy Studies. Since 2016, she has been with the University of Petroleum & Energy Studies, where she is currently working as an Assistant Professor. Her main areas of research interest are Image Processing, Information Security and Deep Learning.

Mohammad Ashfaq is currently working as Assistant Professor, School of Life Sciences, BS Abdur Rahman Institute of Science and Technology, Chennai, India. He has completed Ph.D. in Biotechnology from joint collaboration of Indian Institute of Technology, Kanpur, India and Banasthali University, Banasthali, India. He is a researcher in Multidisciplinary Research Institute for Science and Technology, IIMCT, University of La Serena, Benavente 980, La Serena, Chile. He worked as a Visiting Professor in the Department of mechanical engineering, Faculty of engineering at Chulalongkorn University, Bangkok, Thailand (August 2018 - May 2019). In addition, He worked as a Post-Doctoral-Researcher in Polymer Microneedle Lab, School of Materials Science and Engineering, Beijing University of Chemical Technology, Beijing, China. Dr. Ashfaq research mainly focuses on interdisciplinary research involving nanomaterials, polymeric composite, biological sciences, artificial intelligence and energy such as synthesis, characterization and their various applications of nanomaterials/carbon nanofibers, polymeric composite based bio-materials, and solar cells (dye-sensitized and perovskite solar cells). The leading field of science that are relevant to his area of interest consist of nanotechnology, energy, nano-bioscience, biomedical applications of polymeric composite/nanotechnology (newer antibiotics and novel wound dressing materials), nano-cytotoxicity, biosensor, controlled release drug delivery system (polymeric microneedles), nanoparticle systems of metals and metal oxides and its interaction of plants and animal cells.

Shoba Bindu C., Ph.D. in CSE from JNTUA, Anantapuramu, Andhra Pradesh. She is currently working as Professor in the department of CSE, JNTUA. Her research areas include Network Security, Data Mining, Data Analytics, and Cloud Computing.

Hemalatha D. completed Master of Computer applications on 2008 and joined as lecturer in bannari Amman institute of technology. Joined as assistant professor in Kongu Engineering College in 2010. Eleven years of teaching experience. Area of interest include web technologies and cloud computing.

Venkatesh Gauri Shankar is working as Assistant Professor in Department of Information Technology at Manipal University Jaipur.

Kanika Gautam has received her Bachelor's degree from Mody University of Science and Technology, lakshmangarh in Computer Science and technology (Big Data Specialization). She is currently working in core areas of Machine Learning, Deep Learning, Predictive Analysis and Big Data Analytics.

Getúlio Paulo Peixoto Igrejas has a PhD in Electronic and Computer Engineering. Is a teacher in High Education Institutions since 1997. Since 2001 is a teacher at Instituto Politécnico de Bragança, where he teaches electronics, instrumentation and control. Author and co-author of several scientific publications in the field of instrumentation and computational intelligence. Participated in several funded applied research projects and supervised several Master Thesis.

Sunil Kumar Jangir received Ph.D. degree in Computer Science and Engineering. He is currently an Assistant Professor with the Department of Computer Science and Engineering, Mody University of Science and Technology, Sikar, Rajasthan, India. His area of interest are algorithm design and Machine Learning.

Deepa Joshi received the B. Tech degree in Computer Science & Engineering from UTU and M. tech degree in Computer Engineering from GBPUAT, in 2012 and 2014 respectively. She is pursuing her Ph.D. from University of Petroleum & Energy Studies. Since 2016, she has been with the University of Petroleum & Energy Studies, where she is currently working as an Assistant Professor. Her main areas of research interest are Computer Vision, Machine Learning and Deep Learning.

Thenmozhi K. is working as an Assistant Professor in the Department of MCA, Selvam College of Technology, Namakkal, Tamil Nadu, and India. She is pursuing her Ph.D degree in Anna University, Chennai, TamilNadu, India. She received her MCA degree in 2010 from Anna University, Chennai, TamilNadu, India. She completed her B.Sc., Degree in Physics in 2007 from Bharathidasan University, Trichy, TamilNadu, India. She has 7 years of Teaching Experience and published research papers in various National and International Journals. She received Best Faculty Award at Selvam College of Technology, Namakkal during the academic year 2017-18. Her area of interest includes Data Mining, Clustering, Distributed Clustering, Bio informatics, Soft Computing.

R. Kamatchi is a Professor, Head of Computer Science department, Amity University, Mumbai. She completed her Ph.D with Mother Teresa Women's University, Kodaikanal under the guidance of Dr. Atanu Rakshit, Director, IIM, Rohtak. She has 16 years of teaching experience with various premier institutes in Mumbai. She has co-authored 5 books and presented more than 35 papers in National and International conferences. She has conducted various sessions on the topics of Service modeling, CRM, Internet Security, Current IT trends in various students and faculty forums. She was appointed as a Syllabus Revision Committee member with Mumbai University and developed the course content for B.Sc., and M.Sc.,(Information Technology) courses. She is IRCA certified Lead auditor. She authored a course material for the subjects of CRM, Internet Security, Data communication for the M.C.A., Distance education Programme with Mumbai University. She is the approved guide for M.phil. and Ph.d., programmes with Madurai Kamaraj, Barathiyar & Amity University. 7 students completed their M.Phil., dissertation under her guidance and Seven students are pursuing their doctoral research . She is in the editorial board of various peer reviewed journals and books. She is also an invited member of various Science & Technology forums.

E. Sudheer Kumar is pursuing a Ph.D. from JNTUA University, Anantapur, received B.Tech and M.Tech in Information Technology from JNTUA, Ananthapuramu, India. His research interests include Data Science, Software Engineering, Software Architecture, and other latest trends in technology.

Manish Kumar received the B.Tech. degree in Applied Electronics and Instrumentation Engineering from Biju Patnaik University, Rourkela, India, in 2010 and the M.Tech. Degree in Biomedical Engineering from the Manipal University, Udupi, India, in 2013. He recieved Ph.D. degree in Electrical and Electronics Engineering, Birla Institute of Technology, Ranchi, India. He is currently an Assistant Professor with the Department of Biomedical Engineering, Mody University of Science and Technology, Sikar, Rajasthan, India His area of interests are Medical Image Processing and Computational Intelligence.

Wazir Muhammad Laghari was born in 1971 in small village Palyo Khan Laghari, Taluka Sinjhoro, District Sanghar, Sindh, Pakistan. He was received the B.E. degree in Electrical Engineering from Mehran University of Engineering & Technology, Jamshoro, Sindh, Pakistan, in 1998, M.E. degree in Communication Systems & Networks from Mehran University of Engineering & Technology, Jamshoro, Sindh, Pakistan, in 2008. He obtained a Ph.D. degree in Electrical Engineering Department from Chulalongkorn University Bangkok, Thailand in 2019. He is currently a Postdoc Researcher at the Electrical Engineering Department, Chulalongkorn University, Bangkok, Thailand. He is currently a Lecturer Electrical Engineering Department, Balochistan University of Engineering and Technology Khuzdar, Balochistan, Pakistan. His current research interests are machine learning specially in Deep Convolutional Neural Networks, Digital Image Processing and Face Recognition.

S. Madhu completed his MCA from JNTUA University. His Interests include Data Science, Image Processing. Qualified UGC-NET Computer Science.

Pyingkodi Maran is pursuing her PhD degree in Computer Applications at Anna University, Chennai, India . She is presently working as an Assistant Professor in the Department of Computer Applications, Kongu Engineering College, Tamil Nadu, India. Her area of interest includes, Bioinformatics, Data Mining, Image Processing, Pattern Recognition, Soft Computing, Big data Analytics, Healthcare Informatics and IoT. She organised various programmes such as seminar/ workshop/ International Conference, etc.

Vidyanand Mishra received the B. Tech degree in Computer Science & Engineering from RGPV Bhopal and M. tech degree in Information Security from MNNIT Allahabad, in 2011 and 2016, respectively. He is pursuing his Ph.D. from University of Petroleum & Energy Studies. Since 2016, he has been with the University of Petroleum & Energy Studies, where he is currently working as an Assistant Professor. His main areas of research interest are Computer Vision, Machine Learning and Deep Learning.

Krishna Kumar Mohbey is an Assistant Professor of Computer Science at Central University of Rajasthan, India. He received his Bachelor's degree in Computer Application from MCRPV Bhopal (2006), Master's in Computer Application from Rajiv Gandhi Technological University Bhopal (2009) and PhD from Department of Mathematics and Computer Applications from National Institute of Technology Bhopal, India (2015). His areas of interest are data mining, mobile web services, big data analysis and user behaviour analysis.

Rashmika Patole received the B.Tech degree in Electronics and Telecommunication Engineering from College of Engineering Pune, India, in 2010 and M.Tech degree in Signal Processing from the same institute. She is currently pursuing the Ph.D degree from Savitribai Phule Pune University, Pune, India. She has been working with Department of Telecommunication Engineering, College of Engineering,

Pune, India as Assistant Professor since 2013. Her research interests include speech processing, audio authentication, audio forensics and Machine Learning.

Priti Rege received the B.E and M.E(Gold Medal) degrees from Devi Ahilya University of Indore, India, and Ph.D degree from the University of Pune, India in 2002. Since 1989, she has been with the College of College of Engineering Pune, where she is currently working as Professor in the Department of Electronics and Telecommunications. Her research interests include Signal Processing and Pattern Recognition. Several of her papers have appeared in leading journals and conferences. Dr. Rege was the recipient of Nagarkar Fellowship for carrying out research in sub-band coding of images, Best Faculty Award by Cognizant for the year 2012-13, IETE"s Prof. SVC Aiya award for Excellence in Telecom Education for the year 2016-17 and Prof. Indira Parekh 50 Women in Education Leaders" award at 7th World Education Congress in July 2018. She has 31 years of teaching experience and has published more than 100 papers in reputed national and international conferences/refereed journals. She is senior member of IEEE and Fellow of IETE.

Pedro João Soares Rodrigues is graduated in Electronics and Informatics Engineering (1996), he has a MSc in Electronics and Telecommunications (2000) and he has a PhD in Industrial Electronics (2008). Currently, he is an Adjunct Professor at the School of Technology and Management of the Polytechnic Institute of Bragança. He is author of several chapters in international books; he is author/co-author of papers in national and international conferences/journals; he is co-author of one patent. He has been supervisor/co-supervisor of graduate projects and MSc thesis.

Shanthi S. received her PhD degree in Computer Science and Engineering at Anna University, Chennai, India in 2015. She is presently working as an Assistant Professor (SLG) in the Department of Computer Applications, Kongu Engineering College, Tamil Nadu, India. Her area of interest includes, Data Mining, Image Processing, Pattern Recognition, Soft Computing, Big data Analytics, Healthcare Informatics and IoT. She received grants from AICTE, CSIR, ICMR, and DBT to organize various programmes such as seminar/ workshop/ SDP/ International Conference, etc. She published more than 25 papers in international journals.

Bhavna Sharma is working at the Institute of Technology, Jaipur as Associate Professor. Completed M.Tech from Banasthali University and PHD from MLSU, Udaipur. Experience of 16 years in Teaching and Research specialization is in Machine and Deep learning.

Jay Sharma has completed his M.Tech degree from Rajasthan Technical University and is currently an Assistant Professor in the Department of Information Technology at JECRC, Jaipur. His main working domain includes Image Processing.

Irfan Ullah graduated from the Sarhad University of Science and Information Technology Peshawar, with a BSc. Degree (Electrical Engineering) in 2012 and MSc (Electrical Engineering) in 2015. He obtained a Ph.D. degree (Electrical Engineering) in 2019 from the Chongqing University, China. He is currently a Postdoc Researcher at the Electrical Engineering Department, Chulalongkorn University, Bangkok, Thailand. His current research interests include deep learning, machine learning, and recognition and Thermal Imaging.

Vivek Kumar Verma is working as Assistant Professor in Department of Information Technology at Manipal University Jaipur.

Deepali R. Vora is a Professor in Vidyalankar Institute of Technology, Mumbai and has completed her PhD in Computer Science and Engineering from Amity University, Mumbai. She has more than 18 years of experience in total in teaching, research and Industry. She has published more than 40 research papers in reputed national, international conferences and journals. She has co-authored two books and delivered various talks in Data Science and Machine learning. She has conducted hands-on session in Data Science using Python for students and faculties. She was appointed as a Syllabus Revision Committee member with Mumbai University and developed the course content for B.E. (Information Technology) course. She has received grants for conducting research and organising training courses for faculties. She is acting as a reviewer for many International Conferences and Journals. She has organised many value added courses for the benefit of the students. More than 15 students have completed and currently, 6 students are pursuing their post-graduate studies under her guidance.

Index

Ensure Quality Research is Introduced to the Academic Community

Become an IGI Global Reviewer for Authored Book Projects

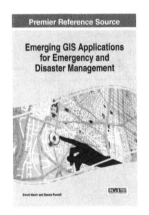
Premier Reference Source
Emerging GIS Applications for Emergency and Disaster Management

Premier Reference Source
Managerial Strategies and Green Solutions for Project Sustainability

Premier Reference Source
Comparative Approaches to Using R and Python for Statistical Data Analysis

Premier Reference Source
Solutions for High-Touch Communications in a High-Tech World

The overall success of an authored book project is dependent on quality and timely reviews.

In this competitive age of scholarly publishing, constructive and timely feedback significantly expedites the turnaround time of manuscripts from submission to acceptance, allowing the publication and discovery of forward-thinking research at a much more expeditious rate. Several IGI Global authored book projects are currently seeking highly-qualified experts in the field to fill vacancies on their respective editorial review boards:

Applications and Inquiries may be sent to:
development@igi-global.com

Applicants must have a doctorate (or an equivalent degree) as well as publishing and reviewing experience. Reviewers are asked to complete the open-ended evaluation questions with as much detail as possible in a timely, collegial, and constructive manner. All reviewers' tenures run for one-year terms on the editorial review boards and are expected to complete at least three reviews per term. Upon successful completion of this term, reviewers can be considered for an additional term.

If you have a colleague that may be interested in this opportunity, we encourage you to share this information with them.

IGI Global's Transformative Open Access (OA) Model:
How to Turn Your University Library's Database Acquisitions Into a Source of OA Funding

In response to the OA movement and well in advance of Plan S, IGI Global, early last year, unveiled their OA Fee Waiver (Offset Model) Initiative.

Under this initiative, librarians who invest in IGI Global's InfoSci-Books (5,300+ reference books) and/or InfoSci-Journals (185+ scholarly journals) databases will be able to subsidize their patron's OA article processing charges (APC) when their work is submitted and accepted (after the peer review process) into an IGI Global journal.*

How Does it Work?

1. When a library subscribes or perpetually purchases IGI Global's InfoSci-Databases including InfoSci-Books (5,300+ e-books), InfoSci-Journals (185+ e-journals), and/or their discipline/subject-focused subsets, IGI Global will match the library's investment with a fund of equal value to go toward subsidizing the OA article processing charges (APCs) for their patrons.

   Researchers: Be sure to recommend the InfoSci-Books and InfoSci-Journals to take advantage of this initiative.

2. When a student, faculty, or staff member submits a paper and it is accepted (following the peer review) into one of IGI Global's 185+ scholarly journals, the author will have the option to have their paper published under a traditional publishing model or as OA.

3. When the author chooses to have their paper published under OA, IGI Global will notify them of the OA Fee Waiver (Offset Model) Initiative. If the author decides they would like to take advantage of this initiative, IGI Global will deduct the US$ 1,500 APC from the created fund.

4. This fund will be offered on an annual basis and will renew as the subscription is renewed for each year thereafter. IGI Global will manage the fund and award the APC waivers unless the librarian has a preference as to how the funds should be managed.

Hear From the Experts on This Initiative:

"I'm very happy to have been able to make one of my recent research contributions, 'Visualizing the Social Media Conversations of a National Information Technology Professional Association' featured in the *International Journal of Human Capital and Information Technology Professionals*, freely available along with having access to the valuable resources found within IGI Global's InfoSci-Journals database."

– **Prof. Stuart Palmer**,
Deakin University, Australia

For More Information, Visit: www.igi-global.com/publish/contributor-resources/open-access or contact IGI Global's Database Team at eresources@igi-global.com.

Are You Ready to Publish Your Research?

IGI Global offers book authorship and editorship opportunities across 11 subject areas, including business, computer science, education, science and engineering, social sciences, and more!

Benefits of Publishing with IGI Global:

- Free one-on-one editorial and promotional support.

- Expedited publishing timelines that can take your book from start to finish in less than one (1) year.

- Choose from a variety of formats including: Edited and Authored References, Handbooks of Research, Encyclopedias, and Research Insights.

- Utilize IGI Global's eEditorial Discovery® submission system in support of conducting the submission and blind review process.

- IGI Global maintains a strict adherence to ethical practices due in part to our full membership with the Committee on Publication Ethics (COPE).

- Indexing potential in prestigious indices such as Scopus®, Web of Science™, PsycINFO®, and ERIC – Education Resources Information Center.

- Ability to connect your ORCID iD to your IGI Global publications.

- Earn royalties on your publication as well as receive complimentary copies and exclusive discounts.

Get Started Today by Contacting the Acquisitions Department at:

acquisition@igi-global.com

Printed in the United States
By Bookmasters